TRANSITION PROGRAMS FOR CHILDREN AND YOUTH WITH DIVERSE NEEDS

INTERNATIONAL PERSPECTIVES ON INCLUSIVE EDUCATION

Series Editor: Chris Forlin

Recent volumes:

INTERNATIONAL PERSPECTIVES ON INCLUSIVE
EDUCATION   VOLUME 18

TRANSITION PROGRAMS FOR CHILDREN AND YOUTH WITH DIVERSE NEEDS

EDITED BY

KATE SCORGIE

Azusa Pacific University (retired), USA

And

CHRIS FORLIN

University of Notre Dame, Australia

United Kingdom – North America – Japan
India – Malaysia – China

Emerald Publishing Limited
Howard House, Wagon Lane, Bingley BD16 1WA, UK

First edition 2022

Reprints and permissions service
Contact: permissions@emeraldinsight.com

British Library Cataloguing in Publication Data
A catalogue record for this book is available from the British Library

ISBN: 978-1-80117-102-1 (Print)
ISBN: 978-1-80117-101-4 (Online)
ISBN: 978-1-80117-103-8 (Epub)

ISSN: 1479-3636 (Series)

Printed and bound by CPI Group (UK) Ltd, Croydon, CR0 4YY

ISOQAR certified
Management System,
awarded to Emerald
for adherence to
Environmental
standard
ISO 14001:2004.

ISOQAR
REGISTERED
Certificate Number 1985
ISO 14001

INVESTOR IN PEOPLE

CONTENTS

SECTION 4: COLLABORATIVE PROGRAMS, PARTNERSHIPS, AND RESOURCES FOR TRANSITION

LIST OF FIGURES

ABOUT THE EDITORS

Kate Scorgie is retired Professor, School of Education, Azusa Pacific University. Her research interests have included families of children with disabilities, and disclosure and equity accommodation for persons with disability transitioning to postsecondary settings. She has also served as an adjunct professor at Alliant International University and a doctoral research advisor for Bethel University.

Chris Forlin is an International Education Consultant, Adjunct Professor at the University of Notre Dame Australia, Series Editor for Emerald Publishing for *International Perspectives on Inclusive Education*, Researcher and Independent Nongovernment School Reviewer, based in Perth, Western Australia.

ABOUT THE CONTRIBUTORS

Rawhi Abdat holds a PhD in Special and Inclusive Education and works at the Ministry of Community Development in Dubai, UAE. His research focuses on children with SEND in early childhood and their transition to inclusive environments and the importance of families' roles in early childhood intervention.

Des Aston is the National & Schools Coordinator at the Trinity Centre for People with Intellectual Disabilities [TCPID], School of Education, Trinity College Dublin. His research interests are inclusive education, postschool education, and employment opportunities for students with intellectual disabilities. Des is the current Chairperson of the Inclusive National Higher Education Forum (INHEF).

Dr Nur Azizah currently teaches at the Special Education Department Universitas Negeri Yogyakarta (UNY). Prior to UNY, she was a special education teacher in a primary school and worked with students with disabilities from different backgrounds. Her research includes inclusive education and transition education.

Dr Joanne Banks is a Lecturer and Researcher in inclusive education at the School of Education, Trinity College Dublin. Joanne's research interests are in the field of inclusive education and educational inequality. She has published widely on the social and academic experiences of students who encounter barriers to learning in mainstream education. She is creator/presenter of the Inclusion Dialogue podcast series.

Emma Barrett is a mother of four boys, with three identified as needing support for autism. Emma is a qualified special education teacher who is currently on leave to look after her boys.

Dr Wendi Beamish is an Adjunct Senior Lecturer in Special Needs Education at Griffith University, Australia. Her research interests focus on teacher practice in the areas of educational transitions, autism, inclusive education, behavioral support, and early childhood intervention.

Patricia Bowman is the Chief Executive Officer of Inclusion Alberta and began her career in the first inclusive postsecondary education initiative in Alberta. Trish has worked for over 30 years supporting individuals and families to live inclusive lives and advocates at the individual and systemic level to ensure children and adults with developmental disabilities and their families' voices are heard and inform public policy and practice.

Dr Brent Bradford is an Associate Professor (Faculty of Education) and Chair (Department of Physical Education & Wellness) at Concordia University of Edmonton (CUE). Brent's research interests include physical and health education, teacher education, and campus wellness. In 2019, Brent was the recipient of CUE's Gerald S. Krispin Research Award.

Robert Tubb Carstens is an Educator as well as a PhD student in Educational Psychology at the University of the Western Cape, South Africa, and his research focuses on the promotion of health and holistic well-being within school communities.

Therese M. Cumming is a Professor of Special Education at the School of Education at UNSW Sydney and the Academic Lead Education at UNSW Disability Innovation Institute. Her research is focused on students with emotional and behavioral disabilities, transitions, mobile technology, and Universal Design for Learning.

Dr Kerry Dally is a Senior Lecturer at the University of Newcastle, Australia. Current research interests include school improvement initiatives aimed at increasing student engagement and well-being, as well as investigation of the links between writing and reading acquisition in the early years of schooling.

Joanne Danker is a Lecturer in Special Education in the School of Education at the University of New South Wales. Her research interests include the well-being of students with developmental disabilities, inclusive and special education, and engaging individuals with disabilities in research using participatory research approaches.

Joanne Deppeler is Professor in the Faculty of Education, Monash University, based in Victoria, Australia. For the past decade, she has worked to support countries in the Asia-Pacific region, Europe, and Canada to further develop and advance inclusive education.

Ilaria Di Maggio is a Post-doc Fellow in the Department of Philosophy, Sociology, Education and Applied Psychology, University of Padova. Her research focuses on career guidance and vocational guidance in an inclusive perspective.

Petra Engelbrecht is an Extraordinary Professor at North-West University, South Africa, and her research focuses on equity in education with specific reference to the implementation of inclusive education in diverse cultural–historical contexts.

Eman Gaad is a Professor of Special and Inclusive Education at the British University in Dubai, UAE. Her research focuses on inclusivity and diversity in education and impact of social construction of learners with disability on their inclusive education in mainstream schooling.

Annetta Galer is a Primary and Middle School Trained Teacher and is currently completing a Master of Inclusive Education at the Queensland University of

Technology (QUT). She is also a mother of four, including a child on the autism spectrum.

M. Cristina Ginevra is an Assistant Professor in the Department of Philosophy, Sociology, Education and Applied Psychology, University of Padova. Her research focuses on career guidance and vocational guidance in an inclusive perspective.

Heather Griller Clark is a Principal Research Specialist in the Teachers College at Arizona State University. Her research is driven by her desire to ensure that system involved youth, especially those with disabilities, are provided relevant, effective, research-based instruction, and transition services that promote productive engagement upon release.

Dr Tamai A. Johnson is an Assistant Principal with the Los Angeles Unified School District, an Adjunct Instructor for University of Phoenix, and an Alumna of Azusa Pacific University. Her research focuses on special education, transition to adulthood, and college and career readiness.

Ansie Elizabeth Kitching is an Associate Professor in Educational Psychology at the University of the Western Cape, South Africa, and her research focuses on the coconstruction of schools into enabling environments through the implementation of a holistic well-being process to develop capacity for the promotion of mental health and well-being.

Dr Stephen M. Kwiatek is a Postdoctoral Research Associate at the University of Illinois Urbana-Champaign. Stephen's research interests focus on three strands: (1) general education teacher involvement in college and career readiness efforts; (2) secondary transition best practices (i.e., evidence-based practices, predictors of postschool success); and (3) interagency collaboration.

Ratika Malkani is Postdoctoral Researcher at the University of Northampton. Her current research includes a study to evaluate the impact of introducing critical reflexivity into teaching, especially on Black and Asian students, and a study of provision for children with special educational needs and their families in rural Telangana, India.

Dr Sarup R. Mathur is a Professor of Special Education in the Division of Educational Leadership and Innovation at Arizona State University. Her research has focused on issues related to emotional and behavioral disorders, effective classroom behavior management, professional development of teachers, and transition and reentry of juvenile offenders.

Dr Valerie L. Mazzotti is a Professor of Special Education at the University of North Carolina at Charlotte. Her research interests include self-determination, secondary transition evidence-based practices and predictors of postschool success, and interagency collaboration for students with disabilities.

Msenga Anyelwisye Mulungu is currently working with Parents of Disabled Children Association of Malawi (PODCAM). His role is to advocate for the Rights of Children with Disability. He is a member of the National Inclusive Education Technical Working Group. He also lectures in History at Catholic University of Malawi on adjunct basis.

Laura Nota is a Full Professor in the Department of Philosophy, Sociology, Education and Applied Psychology, University of Padova. Her research focuses on career guidance and vocational guidance in an inclusive perspective.

Sue O'Neill is a Senior Lecturer in Special Education with the School of Education. Her research focuses on transitions in the lives of youth with special or complex needs, managing challenging behaviors, and evidence-based classroom and behavior management practices.

Maria A. Pacino is Interim Director of the Azusa Pacific University Libraries, Chair of the Department of Library and Information Studies, and Director of the Teacher Librarian Program. She is the author of several articles on social justice education and a book, *Reflections on Equity, Diversity and Schooling*.

Sarah Pereira finished her studies at CUE in 2019. Sarah is now an employee of CUE, and works part-time in the Student Life and Learning Office as a General Assistant. One of her favorite parts of her job is her coworkers. Sarah is an aunt to eight nieces and nephews and loves every minute she is with them.

Michelle Ralston is a Lecturer at the University of Newcastle, Australia. Current research interests include the role of legislation, policy, and school leadership in guiding and supporting inclusive education.

Simon Reid has extensive experience as an educational leader and education consultant for student disadvantage. He has been a principal in remote, isolated, rural, low, and high socioeconomic areas in both primary and large secondary schools, school reviewer, and an executive network principal. He has a highly regarded reputation for his ability to understand the complexities of leadership and shape and manage strategy to provide the highest level of service and raise the quality of outcomes for all students.

Richard Rose is Professor Emeritus in Inclusive Education at the University of Northampton UK. His current research includes a study of provision for children with special educational needs and their families in rural Telangana, India, and the development of family support in rural communities in Cambodia.

Sara Santilli is a Post-doc Fellow in the Department of Philosophy, Sociology, Education, and Applied Psychology, University of Padova. Her research focuses on career guidance and vocational guidance in an inclusive perspective.

Michael Shevlin is Professor of Inclusive Education and is the Director of the Trinity Centre for People with Intellectual Disabilities, School of Education,

Trinity College Dublin. He has researched widely in the area of inclusive education and contributed to policy making in establishing inclusive learning environments in Ireland.

Jaime Skidmore is a Regional Coordinator of Inclusive Post-Secondary Education at Inclusion Alberta. Supporting university students with developmental disabilities to have rich and authentic experiences has been her passion for the past 4 years. In addition to supporting students and team members across the province, Jaime supports families to dream of and advocate for an inclusive life after postsecondary.

Dr Jared Stewart-Ginsburg is Graduate Research Assistant at the University of North Carolina at Charlotte. His research focuses on increasing community supports for students with disabilities.

Iva Strnadová is a Professor of Special Education and Disability Studies at the School of Education at UNSW Sydney and the Academic Lead Research at UNSW Disability Innovation Institute. Her research aims to contribute to better understanding and the improvement of the life experiences of people with intellectual disabilities. Combining research with advocacy is essential in her research program, which builds on supporting the self-determination (including self-advocacy) of people with intellectual disabilities, and is grounded in an innovative inclusive research approach, in which people with intellectual disabilities are included in the role of researcher.

Dr Annalise Taylor is a Registered Special Education Teacher who completed her doctorate with the Cooperative Research Centre for Living with Autism and Griffith University. Her PhD research focused on bridging the research-to-practice gap in relation to the effective and inclusive education of students on the autism spectrum in the first year of school.

Bruce Uditsky, MEd, is the CEO Emeritus of Inclusion Alberta, an advisor to Inclusion Canada, Inclusive Education Canada (IEC) Associate, author, and international consultant on inclusion and social justice. Bruce is credited with establishing the first inclusive postsecondary university initiative and has been recognized provincially, nationally, and internationally for his innovative approaches to inclusion.

Dr Barbara van Ingen is the Vice President, Student Life and Learning at Concordia University of Edmonton, with over 20 years' experience in postsecondary education. Her research focuses on university student wellness, cyberbullying, and posttraumatic stress disorder.

Janie N. Vicchio is a doctoral student and Graduate Research Assistant at the University of North Carolina at Charlotte. Her research interests include career technical education and postschool employment.

Susan R. Warren, Professor Emeritus of Azusa Pacific University, is Assistant Director of the RLC and a Research and Evaluation Associate at Claremont Graduate University's Evaluation Center. Her research areas include Diversity, Equity, and Inclusion in PK-12 schools and universities; Family/Community/School Collaboration; Urban Leadership; Teacher Education, Action Research; and College Attainment.

Timothy C. Wells is a Faculty Associate at Arizona State University. His research explores issues of accessibility at the intersection of culture, disability, and curriculum.

Nazanin Zargarpour, Associate Professor of Evaluation Practice and Core Faculty of the Claremont Evaluation Center at Claremont Graduate University, is Founding Executive Director of the Regional Learning Collaborative (www.rlcollab.com/). She is Founding President of Capacity To Impact consulting (www.capacitytoimpact.org/). Her research includes Education Reform, College Attainment, Developmental Evaluation, Collaboratives, Organizational Capacity-Building.

SERIES INTRODUCTION

The adoption internationally of inclusive practice as the most equitable and all-encompassing approach to education and its relation to compliance with various international Declarations and Conventions underpins the importance of this series for people working at all levels of education and schooling in both developed and less developed countries. There is little doubt that inclusive education is complex and diverse and that there are enormous disparities in understanding and application at both inter- and intracountry levels. A broad perspective on inclusive education throughout this series is taken, encompassing a wide range of contemporary viewpoints, ideas, and research for enabling the development of more inclusive schools, education systems, and communities.

Volumes in this series on *International Perspectives on Inclusive Education* contribute to the academic and professional discourse by providing a collection of philosophies and practices that can be reviewed by considering local, contextual, and cultural situations to assist governments, educators, peripatetic staffs, and other professionals to provide the best education for all children. Each volume in the series focuses on a key aspect of inclusive education and provides critical chapters by contributing leaders in the field who discuss theoretical positions, quality research, and impacts on school and classroom practice. Different volumes address issues relating to the diversity of student need within heterogeneous classrooms and the preparation of teachers and other staff to work in inclusive schools. Systemic changes and practice in schools encompass a wide perspective of learners to provide ideas on reframing education to ensure that it is inclusive of all. Evidence-based research practices underpin a plethora of suggestions for decision-makers and practitioners, incorporating current ways of thinking about and implementing inclusive education.

While many barriers have been identified that may potentially constrain the implementation of effective inclusive practices, this series aims to identify such key concerns and offer practical and best practice approaches to overcoming them. Adopting a thematic approach for each volume, readers will be able to quickly locate a collection of research and practice related to a topic of interest. By transforming schools into inclusive communities of practice all children can have the opportunity to access and participate in quality and equitable education to enable them to obtain the skills to become contributory global citizens. This series, therefore, is highly recommended to support education decision-makers, practitioners, researchers, and academics, who have a professional interest in the inclusion of children and youth who are marginalizing in inclusive schools and classrooms.

This volume on *Transition Programs for Children and Youth with Diverse Needs* was unintentionally impacted in many ways by the international COVID-19 pandemic that occurred throughout 2020 and continued into 2021. Authors of this volume grafted ideas in supporting learners with disabilities, marginalized, vulnerable, or underrepresented populations, with transitions during extended amounts of lockdown time, and while grappling with new models of online teaching. In the midst of these new challenges, they dedicated themselves to writing chapters for this book as they were keen to have their information available to help support others. The result is testament to their dedication to become involved in this important volume and I applaud them on their efforts.

During these days of extreme public health issues, transitions are affecting all who are involved in educational systems, with education as a whole needing to be engaged in a newly emerging transition process. Like a liminal space which continues with an uncertain ending, unknowing what will happen to traditional models of schooling as systems emerge from the pandemic provides little guidance for teachers when planning to reengage their students. In many instances transitions are likely to be even more demanding than previously, especially for those with diverse learning needs. The future of schooling as we know it will need to adapt to unstable certainties as countries plan how to contend with this pandemic and are cognizant of potential future instabilities. Planners will need to be better equipped to identify and support the educational and emotional needs of children and youth during such uncertainties, who may be even more marginalized than previously. Prolonged absences from attending an actual school environment have the capacity to destabilize those who have previously found inclusion in education challenging. Transitioning back into a school environment after extended periods of working from home may raise anxiety levels and pose the need for additional support to ensure the needs of all children and youth are met. In addition to normal school transitions, transition back into schooling for the most vulnerable children and youth may require the implementation of models that offer interim placements in more supportive environments, so that they can become reacquainted with the expectations of schooling before being reintegrated into a large regular class.

This volume contains a plethora of excellent ideas and practical approaches for supporting a range of transitions that children and youth with diverse needs encounter across their life span. Many of these approaches will be of particular benefit to those involved in providing support during these unprecedented times. Although the book has grouped these into different levels of schooling for easy access by readers, the strategies employed at one level with minimal adaptation may well be utilized at other stages of a child's life. I encourage readers to access sections that are most useful to them depending upon their level of teaching, but also invite them strongly to review other sections that may provide further extremely helpful ideas.

Although this volume focuses mainly on transition support for learners, it must be acknowledged that parents are also in a liminal space, and they too may need support in decision-making for their children. As children and youth go through a range of emotions when being expected to return to school, parents also may find this transition psychologically demanding as they let go of their children and hand them back to new teachers who will not have the under-standings of exactly how extended absences have or may have impacted on their children's lives. This volume includes two chapters with parent reflections on transitions and in addition, several chapters highlight the role of partnerships by giving considerable thought to how parents and schools can better collaborate for a more stable and less difficult transition.

Volume 18 builds considerably and highly effectively on previous books in this series by tackling the far-reaching aspects of establishing and supporting effective transitions throughout a child's life. This could not be timelier with the uncer-tainties that currently surround education for learners with diverse needs. Like the model of inclusion, schools need to transform themselves to ensure that they meet the needs of their students who constantly have to cope with an enormous range of different transitions. From the research identified in this volume it is evident that this will not happen unless schools reform and become considerably more proactive in their approaches to better enabling transitions. Where authors have reported that this has occurred, through implementation of a range of different models, the outcome for children and youth with diverse needs has been positive and stabilizing, giving them confidence in their ability to achieve and emotional support to know that they are welcomed and valued members of society. This book is essential reading for all involved in working with learners with challenging needs throughout their schooling and into postschool options. I recommend this to you as an exceptional addition to the *International Perspectives on Inclusive Education* series.

Chris Forlin
Series Editor

PREFACE

INTRODUCTION

Life consists of change. Change of seasons. Change of locations. Change of roles and responsibilities. Change can be minimal or significant; predictable and expected, or unpredictable and surprising. Life changes often involve a shift from one status, position, or identity to another. Changes associated with developmental or chronological markers, such as entering and leaving formal schooling, and entry into or exit from the workplace, have often been referred to as transitions (Strnadová & Cumming, 2016). According to Baker and Irwin (2019), "... the word 'transition' is commonly used to signify movements made—which are often ritualized—as people 'transfer' into and out of different stages and domains in their life courses" (p. 4). Typically, transitions are envisioned as linear sequences that incorporate a socially and culturally constructed conceptualization of both the process, that is how one should navigate the transition, and the acceptable or prescribed outcomes, or what is expected to be achieved. When a person develops and demonstrates the skills or assumes the roles and responsibilities that are expected by society, the transition is considered to be successful.

THE TRANSITION PROCESS

The process of transition is often depicted as consisting of three phases that incorporate the concepts of before, during, and after; that is, leaving something behind and passing through an in-between phase with the objective of emerging with a new or revised orientation or position. During a child's school life, they must go through many transitions, ranging from major changes to minor ones. The most challenging times usually occur when transitioning between different types of schooling. Such transitions commence in the early years when starting kindergarten and then moving into formal schooling. Following five to seven years in a primary school children transition into either a middle school or directly into a high school. At the end of compulsory schooling many students will also need to move to a senior college before transitioning into either further study at a university or undertaking tertiary and further education. Transition from education into the workforce can occur at two different stages, at the end of compulsory schooling or following any further study.

While major life transitions can and often do incorporate challenges, Strnadová and Cumming (2016) suggest that "... these challenges may be greatly exacerbated for those with disabilities" (p. 2). In addition, children and youth representing marginalized, vulnerable, or underrepresented groups, students from culturally and linguistically diverse backgrounds, and refugee and immigrant populations, may experience transitions that are less linear and more complex as they navigate unfamiliar or disparate educational structures and systems (Baker & Irwin, 2019; Osgood et al., 2010).

Transition Considerations for Students with Disabilities and Diverse or Marginalized Groups

During transitions, a range of aspects need to be considered and addressed by all stakeholders. These tend to fall into three major categories of physical, educational, and social-emotional needs.

Physical aspects can involve consideration of access to facilities, the provision of assistive technologies and physical aids, classroom facilities and layout structures, transportation to and from school, system level supports, and for some children and youth at certain times during their schooling the provision of appropriate onsite accommodation.

Educational considerations relate more directly to forms of instructional collaboration, curriculum and pedagogical modifications, the use of education assistants, and the involvement of peripatetic staff. There may also be a need for alternative assessments that must be planned to provide an appropriate way for students to demonstrate learning. The development and ongoing review of a child's individual education plan will also have to be scheduled with parental involvement organized to maximize the educational opportunities provided. Adopting a universal design for learning where whole school change occurs to meet the needs of all children and youth is seen as being the optimal approach to enabling educational inclusion (Semon et al., 2021).

Emotional support is a key aspect of any transition planning as individuals with additional needs are more likely to experience anxiety, worry, concerns, and fear, when their regulated, stable, and structured environment alters. Promoting social inclusion is of the utmost importance as placing children and youth into new environments without effective emotional support can lead to ineffective and unsustainable inclusion (Scorgie & Forlin, 2019). Having a positive sense of belonging through acceptance, strong interpersonal relationships with teachers and peers, and school values of evidence-based culturally responsive practices (Hagiwara et al., 2019) will all assist in helping students through the process of transition.

TRANSITION AND LIMINAL SPACES

Originating from the work of van Gennep in the early 1900s and Turner in the 1960s that examined ritual rites of passage, the term *liminality* has emerged to represent the in-between period occurring during a transition (Baker & Irwin, 2019; Brown et al., 2017). Baker and Irwin (2019) describe liminality as "... the ambiguous, unstable middle ground of a ritual where the individual has moved from one state but is yet to navigate the changes to move into the next state" (p. 5). The liminal phase is often viewed as a period of identity construction. According to Conroy and O'Leary-Kelly (2014), it incorporates a "… dynamic process of self-construal, a time in which the sense of 'who I was' gives way to a sense of 'who I am becoming'" (pp. 67–68), and finally culminates in "who I have become." This involves the crafting or revisioning of an individual's personal narrative with a focus on both self-perception, that is how one views or desires to view oneself, and the responses that are received or hoped to be received from others (Conroy & O'Leary-Kelly, 2014; Vincent, 2019).

Effective transitions, therefore, require components that incorporate both internal and external confirmation or acceptance. For example, Brown et al. (2017), who examined the experiences of 16 people who attested recovery from Myalgic Encephalomyelitis (ME) or chronic fatigue syndrome (CFS), suggested that when personal accounts of recovery were not validated or affirmed by others, a new experience of liminality was introduced which placed the individuals "… 'betwixt and between' health and illness" (p. 706). Similarly, Reid-Cunningham (2009) cited the work of Murray and colleagues to suggest that persons with disability "… may experience an extended or even perpetual state of liminality because of role confusion and a lack of acceptance by others" (p. 106).

While liminal spaces involve anticipation and hope, they can also incorporate a sense of apprehension and loss, which is particularly noticeable for those with diverse needs. Vincent (2019), for example, explored transition from higher education into postuniversity options for young adults with autism and found that several mentioned loss associated with the predictable and familiar educational environment and the friendships formed, and anxiety regarding the unknowns and potential loss of control associated with the transition. Individuals who had some introduction to and experience with the posttransition environment prior to the period of transition demonstrated more positive and optimistic perspectives during transition. Vincent suggested the need for transition planning to begin prior to the final year of university.

Liminal spaces provide opportunities for learning and change to occur within a person, organization, or community, as individuals and stakeholders reflect on how integrating new perspectives, information, and actions might enhance the ability to achieve a desired outcome or result in personal or organizational transformation (Land et al., 2014). Navigating transitions for persons with disability or unique life experiences often requires the input of others who can envision possibilities and facilitate the acquisition of skills and attributes to promote optimal outcomes. What this might involve is the willingness of others to enter a liminal space, such as teachers who demonstrate willingness to acquire and utilize inclusive pedagogy; employers who recognize and value the unique strengths, abilities, and perspectives an individual brings to a work environment; policy makers who affirm the right of individuals to access accommodations, and environments that promote inclusion and equity. It may also involve community leaders who collaborate with members to provide resources to assure quality of life for all, and parents who act as facilitators, supporters, mediators, and often catalysts throughout the process. Therefore, successful transition through liminal spaces may require collaboration from multiple stakeholders willing to consider new perspectives, processes, and potential opportunities.

FAMILY, COMMUNITY, AND LIMINAL SPACES

Liminality impacts on more than just the person in transition, with many uncertainties and emotional challenges also experienced by the parent, the child's siblings, the extended family, and other stakeholders such as teachers. Most importantly throughout these periods is the role that parents play regarding supporting their child's transition through their schooling and into postschool options (Leonard et al., 2016). For many parents, their greatest concerns occur during the liminal space periods that happen between the major transitions in their child's life. The parent frequently finds themselves embedded in their child's liminal space and acting as a facilitator between their child and the school to enable an effective transition. This role appears to be ongoing, especially when the child has a disability. This is clearly illustrated in this small clip from a parent of Rose who is now in Year 11 in high school.

Rose is 16. She's in Year 11. She had quite a bit of bullying in primary school. So she was quite traumatized when she was in school. She just wasn't really happy. I think the most challenging transition was going from primary school to high school. I just think that was the most difficult thing. It was a very difficult transition for her. So now she's got anxiety from the early years of problems. I think what if she had told me? I could approach the principal and I could've said something. I can't do anything because she didn't let me know. In high school she was basically getting straight E's in the class. So I took her to a tutor to try and help her. I've taken her to a psychologist to help with her confidence. She was not diagnosed until she was 14 with Asperger's Syndrome. She now gets some support.

As a parent I think you need to stay on top of what your child is doing and stay on top of what the school is doing. And if there's any different changes in her, speak to her, then if you aren't happy about something, you need to go back to school. So I'm sort of the go-between with Rose and the school. I don't think parents should just leave things up to the school's wishes especially if the child's got a disability or they're getting behind. I think parents need to step up and be involved more. I'm very much involved in what Rose does a lot and I know exactly where she is in the school.

I don't really know what sort of career she will do when she leaves school; and that's what kind of worries me, 'cos I know she wants to take a year off. I don't know what she's going to do. I've no idea. I will just gauge how she goes, what she does in the first year. Otherwise, I may look at putting her into a TAFE course. I will just gauge it for the first couple of months and see what she's doing.

Lourdes, mother (extracted from a Zoom interview)

EFFECTIVE TRANSITIONING

The purpose of this volume in the series, *International Perspectives on Inclusive Education*, is to invite readers to navigate the liminal space of transition through exploring innovative perspectives and practices regarding transition programs that incorporate effective interventions and strategies for potentially marginalized individuals from multiple frameworks. In addition to knowledge and skill training, programs, and strategies explored throughout the volume address attitudes, expectations, and perceptions about what it means to be accorded acceptance and to achieve a sense of belonging through cocrafting of identity, with sensitivity to cultural, family and individual perspectives, values, and aspirations. With this in mind, the volume investigates ways in which systems and structures influence transition options. It examines both barriers to and innovative, evidence-based practices that facilitate a range of educational transitions with an emphasis on children and youth with diverse needs.

OVERVIEW OF VOLUME 18

Section One of the volume, *Transitions to and Through Schooling for ECE Primary and Elementary*, begins with a moving account by Emma Barrett describing her experience navigating inclusive school systems for three children with autism. She emphasizes the critical role parents play in negotiating optimal schooling for their children incorporating occupational therapy, classroom supports and assistance, curriculum modifications, effective learning strategies and pedagogy, and social inclusion. As she transitions two sons into early schooling Barrett invites readers into the feelings of stress, anxiety, frustration, fatigue, and yet hope, that many parents experience during transition. Parent perspectives of transition are further explored by Abdat and Gaad, who conducted research with parents in the United Arab Emirates whose children were transitioning from early care to primary education. Parents described transitions as oscillating between smooth, stressful, and blurring categories based on the challenges faced during various stages of transition and the type of settings to which the children were transitioning. The authors propose a transition framework based on three main pillars of enablers, stakeholders, and inclusive educational settings.

In order to facilitate effective early elementary transition for children with diverse needs, Beamish and Taylor introduce the Early Years-Model of Practice (EY-MoP) framework, a collection of 23 evidence-based practices to guide teachers in program planning and delivery for students on the autism spectrum, situated in three categories: *belonging, being,* and *becoming.* Each strategy utilizes a teacher-what-how format, supported by a range of easily accessible online resources. In the next chapter, Malkani and Rose explore transition from children's perspectives through a study that examined the experiences of first-generation learners who transitioned from a government school to an inclusive privately funded school in a tribal community in Maharashtra, India. Students described how the experience increased their self-confidence as learners and broadened their perceptions of future opportunities.

Section Two, Transitions to and Through Schooling for Secondary, begins with a parent perspective on transitioning from primary school into secondary school for a child with autism, provided by Galer who reflects on both the challenges and use of effective practices respective to the transition, with recommendations regarding the importance of obtaining an early diagnosis so that intervention strategies can be implemented at the outset of schooling and professional development provided regarding innovative and inclusive practices.

The issue of well-being is a key focus of the next chapter by Kitching and colleagues. They describe how understanding children's concerns regarding transition from primary to secondary education and the importance of well-being in educational outcomes resulted in the implementation of a successful peer mentoring program to provide opportunities for children to voice concerns regarding academic and social issues; prepare them with information, strategies, and support relationship networks for transition; and build collaborative partnerships between schools. Given the movement toward more inclusive educational placements, Forlin and Deppeler then explore a number of international programs and student support models to facilitate transition from special schools to inclusive schools for children with complex needs.

The final chapters in this section utilize case studies to describe how schools transformed teaching and learning practices. Ralston and Dally highlight that transitions don't just happen but require collaboration and commitment across an educational team to acquire knowledge and skills, and implement practices that are individualized for diverse learners. Reid continues the discussion on leadership for transition from a principal's perspective through use of several case studies that highlight teacher practices in primary and secondary schools to facilitate academic and social inclusion for students with special needs.

Section Three of the volume, *Transition to Post-Secondary Education and Vocational Opportunities*, explores various programs and interventions to foster transition into young adulthood, incorporating further education and employment. Highlighting the need to integrate career intervention across the educational system, Ginevra and colleagues describe the creation of a number of innovative of career education programs designed for children, adolescents, and young adults, with the objective of assisting students to propose a self-determined inclusive and sustainable future and acquire the skills needed for goal achievement.

Acknowledging the role of guidance counseling in preparing youth for post-secondary transitions, Banks, Aston and Shevlin examine the school guidance and transition program for students with intellectual disabilities in the Republic of Ireland through exploring the perceptions of special education needs coordinators, guidance counselors, and principals. Lack of clarity regarding role responsibility for guiding students through postsecondary transition, perceived obstacles within the transition process, and the importance of incorporating an inclusive school ethos emphasizing shared responsibility for transition planning were shared by study participants.

The California WorkAbility 1 Program is designed to equip youth with disabilities with knowledge and skills needed in the workplace through providing paid employment opportunities to high school students. Perceptions of teachers representing various roles in the WA1 program describing the benefits and challenges of the program, as well as strategies suggested for implementing effective work transition programs are presented by Johnson. Zargarpour and Warren describe further how an intersegmental collaborative solution-building partnership, the *Regional Learning Collaboration*, was formed to facilitate transition to and through postsecondary education for vulnerable and low-income student populations in Southern California, based on the willingness to assume shared responsibility to facilitate student pathways and outcomes. Through use of a case study, van Ingen and colleagues describe how the partnership between a university and an organization that provides advocacy to persons with disabilities and their families has resulted in effective transitions to postsecondary educational settings that highlight authentic student experiences, meaningful relationships, identity formation and self-confidence, and employment prospects to the benefit of all members of the community.

Section Four of this volume proposes a number of *Collaborative Programs, Partnerships and Resources for Transition.* Underscoring the need for interagency collaborative partnerships to facilitate transition from school to adult services, Kwiatek and colleagues present the CIRCLES model, a three-team approach consisting of a community-level team, a school-level team, and a student's individualized education program team, with examples of how the model has been effectively implemented. The chapter by Azizah also proposes a collaborative interagency model designed to advance school to work transition for youth with disabilities in an Indonesian special school incorporating input from government agencies, districts, schools, students, and families. Strnadová and colleagues review stakeholders' perspectives of barriers that impact community reentry for youth transitioning from juvenile justice facilities, comparing findings of studies conducted in Australia and the United States. Pacino describes a range of programs and services developed by a library in Southern California, in partnership with various community services, to serve the transitional needs of children, youth, and adults who represent diverse populations. Finally, Mulungo discusses ways in which parent groups work in partnership with school personnel and community members to facilitate educational opportunities for children with disabilities in Malawi.

Kate Scorgie & Chris Forlin

ACKNOWLEDGMENTS AND GRATITUDE

Putting together a volume during the pandemic has been truly challenging, and we are beyond grateful to chapter authors and peer reviewers who have come together, committed to the value of their work and to the volume, to submit innovative and informative programs and share strategies and insights on how to achieve effective transitions for children and youth with diverse needs. Sincere appreciation to all who have committed to the successful launch of this volume. We are deeply indebted to each.

REFERENCES

Azizah, N. (2016). *School to work transition programs for students with physical disabilities in Indonesian special schools.* Doctoral Dissertation, The Flinders University. https://flex.flinders.edu.au/file/3165517e-5f70-4c3b-94dc-1054f2d35fb0/1/ThesisAzizah2016.pdf

Baker, S., & Irwin, E. (2019). Disrupting the dominance of 'linear pathways': How institutional assumptions create 'stuck places' for refugee students' transitions into higher education. *Research Papers in Education.* https://doi.org/10.1080/02671522.2019.1633561

Brown, B., Huszar, K., & Chapman, R. (2017). "Betwixt and between": Liminality in recovery stories from people with myalgic encephalomyelitis (ME) or chronic fatigue syndrome (CFS). *Sociology of Health and Illness, 39*(5), 696–710. https://doi.org/10.1111/1467-9566.12546

Conroy, S. A., & O'Leary-Kelly, A. M. (2014). Letting go and moving on: Work-related identity loss and recovery. *The Academy of Management Review, 39*(1), 67–87.

Hagiwara, M., Dean, E. E., & Shogren, K., A. (2019). The self-determined career design model: Supporting young people with developmental disabilities and their families in home and community settings. In K. Scorgie & C. Forlin (Eds.), *Promoting social inclusion co-creating environments that foster equity and belonging, international perspectives on inclusive education* (Vol. 13, pp. 201–220). Emerald.

Land, R., Rattray, J., & Vivian, P. (2014). Learning in the liminal space: A semiotic approach to threshold concepts. *Higher Education, 67*, 199–217. https://doi.org/10.1007/s10734-013-9705-x

Leonard, H., Foley, K.-R., Pikora, T., Bourke, J., Wong, K., McPherson, L., Lennox, N., & Downs, J. (2016). Transition to adulthood for young people with intellectual disability: The experiences of their families. *European Child and Adolescent Psychiatry, 25*, 1369–1381. https://doi.org/10.1007/s00787-016-0853-2

Osgood, D. W., Foster, E. M., & Courtney, M. E. (2010). Vulnerable populations and the transition to adulthood. *The Future of Children, 20*(1), 209–229. https://doi.org/10.1353/foc.0.0047

Reid-Cunningham, A. R. (2009). Anthropological theories of disability. *Journal of Human Behavior in the Social Environment, 19*, 99–111.

Scorgie, K., & Forlin, C. (2019). Social inclusion and belonging: Affirming validation, agency, and voice. In K. Scorgie & C. Forlin (Eds.), *Promoting social inclusion co-creating environments that foster equity and belonging, international perspectives on inclusive education* (Vol. 13, pp. 3–16). Emerald.

Semon, S., Lane, D., & Jones, P. (2021). Introduction: A journey of collaborative practices and inclusion around the globe. In S. Semon, D. Lane, & P. Jones (Eds.), *Mapping collaboration across international inclusive educational contexts, international perspectives on inclusive education* (Vol. 17). Emerald.

Strnadová, I., & Cumming, T. M. (2016). *Lifespan transitions and disability: A holistic perspective.* Routlege.

Vincent, J. (2019). It's the fear of the unknown: Transitioning from higher education for young autistic adults. *Autism, 23*(6), 1575–1585. https://doi.org/10.1177/1362361318822498

SECTION 1

TRANSITIONS TO AND THROUGH SCHOOLING FOR ECE / PRIMARY / ELEMENTARY

EXHAUSTED, SCARED, ANXIOUS, STRESSED, FRUSTRATED, SAD, BUT HOPEFUL: TRANSITIONING TWO BOYS WITH AUTISM FROM HOME TO SCHOOL

Emma Barrett

ABSTRACT

Transitioning a child with Autism from home to school can be a very traumatic time. The process can be extremely challenging for not only the child but also the parent and the family. This is made even more challenging when a parent is transitioning more than one child at the same time. This chapter describes how one mum planned for and managed the transition for two boys, diagnosed with Autism, from home to school. This is her story and the impact it had on her family. It is full of a range of emotions as the family moves through this process.

Keywords: Autism; parent; transition; school; early intervention; disability

INTRODUCTION

I am the parent of four beautiful boys. Three of whom have autism. I am also a special education teacher working with young people who have high and profound special educational needs. I have been teaching for more than 15 years both within the Australian Government system and overseas in an international school. I have taught all years of schooling from early childhood to upper secondary students. I have a thorough understanding of the education system and the constraints that teachers and parents face.

Transition Programs for Children and Youth with Diverse Needs
International Perspectives on Inclusive Education, Volume 18, 3–8
Copyright © 2022 Emma Barrett
Published under exclusive licence by Emerald Publishing Limited
ISSN: 1479-3636/doi:10.1108/S1479-363620220000018001

I am currently on extended parental leave so that I can facilitate early inter-vention and transitions to school for my young children. I have been part of all facets of the transition process with my adult son and have recently begun the home to school transition process with my next generation of boys. I bring to this discussion a full understanding of exactly what the next 14 years of schooling entails.

TRANSITION FROM HOME TO SCHOOL IN THE EARLY YEARS

Although I will be writing about the transition from home to school, I feel it is important to give a quick insight of my knowledge and background of the education system as it serves to understand how I have come to view the importance of transitions and how, as a parent I can alter the way in which my children are seen, heard, and nurtured.

My oldest son was not the child that teachers requested to teach; I never got a phone call to tell me that it was a pleasure to have him in their class. I spent 14 years fighting to get my son's needs met while trying to respect the school system that I also worked within. There were many times I failed to receive the support my son needed but with each failure comes knowledge. The strength that I gained from this first journey has given me the knowledge strength and understanding of how to better navigate the school system and thus receive the best support for my younger boys who are just starting their first transitions into school.

I write this reflection one week before one of my boys starts kindergarten (kindergarten is part-time non-compulsory school education for children the year they turn four before July), and his older brother begins year one. Both have been diagnosed with Autism. I do this with a young baby, an adult child, and having experienced countless hours of early intervention therapy outside of school hours for my two young boys.

A PARENT'S THOUGHTS ON WHAT SCHOOL WILL BRING

I passionately believe the transition from home to school is the hardest transition a parent will make with their child. It's a leap of faith that every parent takes in the hope that an educator will see their child's strengths and positive character-istics and assist and nurture them into and through their schooling journey. The first time I took this leap into the unknown 16 years ago I was naive in the process and had no idea what challenges lay ahead. This time I head into it with eyes open, organized, and planned, prepared and probably overly assertive about what my children need.

My two young children have already attended school tours, visits with teachers and the environment, transition days and class visits with their peers; all planned and supported by the school as the "normal" transition process. This, however, doesn't begin to prepare my children for the challenges of this transition from home to school. I have spent time liaising with the school, setting up meetings, and discussions about my children. I am, nevertheless, sure that their teachers really do not have sufficient information to enable an easy transition for my boys.

At home we have visual schedules for daily events, each child having their teacher on their schedules long before school starts. I have attended meetings with teachers and the principal prior to the end of the previous year. I have provided as much paperwork as possible including diagnosis letters to ensure the school has been able to apply for funding to have an assistant available to support my children. My children will be in a regular class and the teachers will have a diverse group of students, many of whom will also have specific needs. At this stage no assistant has been allocated.

I have spent months planning with therapists and completing early intervention with my children so that they can have the best possible start to the year. We didn't spend the holidays just playing with friends; we attended therapy sessions, social skills groups, and practiced routines ready for the start of school. Nothing is left to chance and you certainly won't hear me saying "he'll be fine, the teacher will sort it out." I have thought of every possible scenario, worked out what could happen, and how I can provide support.

My biggest struggle as a parent, who is also an educator, is how to ensure I provide the teachers with all the information they require without undermining their knowledge or capabilities. This is a huge challenge as I know and understand my children's intricacies. I have completed a myriad of daily routines to ensure they are able to navigate the world safely. Yet how can I impart all this knowledge onto another person in one or possibly two brief meetings without them feeling threatened or labeling me as "the pushy parent"?

THE EARLY YEARS IN PREPARATION FOR TRANSITION

My children have been receiving therapy support for numerous years before they began this transition to school. I started when they were around two years old, noticing their different intricacies and how those were affecting their daily life. We have spent an incomprehensible amount of time undergoing therapy, travel, planning, meetings, organizing, and gaining support. The toll that this has taken on me as a parent is often overlooked or ignored. Returning to work for me becomes a distant ideal as therapy and early intervention takes over my life; particularly when I am managing more than one child through this process.

In Australia, Early Intervention is valued, supported, and provided for children with a disability. As a parent the responsibility of organizing, booking, attending, and ensuring that my children receive the support they require, nevertheless, falls solely on me. Although there is ample support for families who understand the necessary processes and seek support, there is no requirement for early intervention, nor is there a simple process to gain this support.

Transitioning my children to school looks vastly different from that of my friends who are transitioning their children. For them this is the first big experience where teachers will guide their children into becoming lifelong learners. For us and many families like mine, it's a huge change as we are transitioning years of knowledge and specialist therapists plans and practices over to a school, a teacher, a deputy principal, a principal, hoping that we have given them all the skills that we have learnt, but knowing that it's impossible to impart years of training, knowledge, trial and error, and success in a few short meetings. This makes me as a parent anxious and makes this process difficult because my personal feelings of stress and the potential for failure taint the process.

SPECIALIZED EARLY INTERVENTION THERAPY

As an educator I understand the importance of early intervention and so I prioritize this for my children. My boys will have on average 10–15 hours of therapy, in addition to attending school, each week. The reason I include therapy in the transition discussion is because I believe it is vitally important to ensure my young boys are not overloaded with expectations beyond that of their peers.

The hardest part of the transition process is discussing with the school how attendance will look different for my children. Most therapy takes place outside of the school environment. Unfortunately, this means that my children either attend full school plus full therapy or we need to plan and negotiate a transition program with the school. This is a difficult discussion because although the school management and staff understand the importance of early intervention there is no one size fits all model and so it falls on me to negotiate what I will need for my children.

Having negotiated with my children's school to ascertain the best programs for my children and decided to take a slow and initial part-time transition into full time schooling, I still feel that there needs to be an easier way to support them through intervention into transition to school. There is also no requirement for schools to participate in pre planning and transition for individual students, therefore, as a parent I have to understand that this is my job and make the arrangements for this to happen. Thankfully, this time I have the knowledge and understanding of the process and my children will have this vital early head start into the classroom.

Having negotiated a transition plan that will hopefully work for my boys starting school, it is now vital to develop transition plans for between home, therapy, and school. How will the skills my child is learning in therapy be transitioned into the classroom, so they have the best opportunity to learn? Our therapy model relies on teaching in isolation, then small groups, then transitioning into the school environment. This is a lengthy process and one which is often unable to be understood by the school system who often struggle to have enough support for all students' individual needs.

SOCIALIZATION

This is a fundamental part of the education system. It is impossible to expect a child to learn if their socialization is hindered. Both as a parent and an educator I believe this is critical to the success of my children's education.

My children have complex regulation difficulties, and these are heightened in the social environment. How do you transition from the home environment to the school environment when your basic regulatory system is overloaded? How do you support the school to understand how important this regulation is to ensure any learning happens at school? Particularly, when the school is bound by a curriculum, they need to teach within a set timeframe.

I believe that it is critical in this first transition to school that as a parent you bring specialized professionals that understand your child's needs into the school. I am using occupational therapists and educational psychologists to assist us in developing plans to support my boys (and my understanding) in gaining control of their regulation systems. Providing a detailed and focused plan which includes an escalation profile of my children and how they can become dysregulated, serves as a starting point for discussions with the school. This sounds like an easy task but any parent who has a child with challenging behaviors will attest that this is a long and complex procedure and the document taken to the school may have incorporated months and possibly years of formulation.

When meeting with the school parents need to impart years of knowledge and understanding in a short amount of time. There has been a shift in school processes over the years and the school my sons will be attending is luckily very receptive to gaining as much information from my therapists as they can. The difficulty for parents and staff is that this can only happen when a parent has had the foresight and forward planning to arrange and organize these documents. There is no requirement for any child entering school to have these documents in place. Often parents are unaware these services are available. My first time through as a parent my son had no diagnosis, no funding, and no support. This time my children are transitioning with every opportunity to succeed.

We can't discuss complex regulation difficulties without discussing outside play times. As a parent of children with these difficulties this is the time of the school day that worries me the most. My children struggle in small social settings with children and adults they know: how will they suddenly just cope with the traditional school model of everyone going to play with duty teachers? Even though I have provided every specialist report, plan, and document I can, having specialist one to one support in the playground is not considered a normal practice for schools. This is something that needs to be discussed with the individual school and teachers as part of transition. As a parent I advocate for my child to be supported in the playground more than in the classroom because I understand that being dysregulated socially will lead to an inability to access the curriculum but could also lead to catastrophic meltdowns in an outside unstructured environment. I also know that the transition from the classroom to the playground and vice versa is one of the most difficult parts of my child's day. This is where I need to be strong and advocate for my child's needs.

FINAL THOUGHTS

As school is about to begin in a few days, like all parents taking a child through this first transition, I have everything organized. School supplies bought and labeled, lunch boxes washed and ready, uniforms cleaned, and children prepped and knowing that school is about to begin. This is, however, where the similarities with other parents stops.

I'm not excited to be sending my children to school, I'm exhausted. All the background work I do with planning, organizing, meetings, therapy, and phone calls, are what makes this transition hard. I'm scared of what will happen when my child becomes dysregulated and doesn't make the right choices. I'm anxious for the phone calls to start coming telling me what my child did inappropriately each day. I'm stressed trying to drive two children to school (with a baby in tow) and attend extensive therapy and the normal community activities with their peers.

I'm frustrated because I know I should be excited about this huge step my children are about to make. I'm sad because my babies are growing up. But I'm also hopeful that this time will be different. That this time my knowledge and understanding of what lies before us is a strength and that I have used this knowledge to change the stakes for my children so that they will experience success greater than previous children before them. This time I believe that I am strong enough to ensure that this transition will be successful because I have made it so.

THE "NOW WHAT DILEMMA": AN EMIRATI PERSPECTIVE ON ISSUES RELATED TO TRANSITION OF LEARNERS WITH SEND FROM EARLY CARE TO PRIMARY EDUCATION

Rawhi Abdat and Eman Gaad

ABSTRACT

This chapter draws upon research conducted in the United Arab Emirates (UAE) on parents' perspectives of transition in early childhood intervention (ECI) for children with special educational needs and disabilities (SEND). The research followed a sequential exploratory mixed methods design to collect both qualitative and quantitative data. Data were collected from semi-structured interviews with 11 parents of children with different types of SEND, followed by a cross-sectional survey administered to (183) parents. Thematic analysis of interviews revealed that parents perceive the transition process as: "smooth," "stressful," and "blurring." Descriptive and inferential statistical analysis tests of the parents' responses to the cross-sectional survey showed significant differences among parents' perspectives toward transition with respect to parents' gender, education, type of child with SEND, and educational setting; no significant differences were found regarding children's gender. Implications for practice regarding transition from ECI to inclusive education are addressed through a transition framework introduced at the end of this chapter.

Transition Programs for Children and Youth with Diverse Needs
International Perspectives on Inclusive Education, Volume 18, 9–23
Copyright © 2022 Rawhi Abdat and Eman Gaad
Published under exclusive licence by Emerald Publishing Limited
ISSN: 1479-3636/doi:10.1108/S1479-363620220000018002

Keywords: Early intervention; transition; special education; inclusion; SEND; parents' perspectives

INTRODUCTION

Early childhood intervention (ECI) refers to "the provision of educational or therapeutic services" (Bruder, 2010, p. 339) to children with confirmed disabilities, those who are developmentally delayed or at risk of being disabled at some point in life (Massachusetts Department of Public Health, 2013), and their families (Zheng et al., 2016). These services are crucial for preventing disabilities or reducing their effects on children and their families and for helping the children to transition to the next stage of education with their peers in public schools (Rous, Myers, & Stricklin, 2007). For Guralnick (2001), ECI refers to designed programs that empower families to best promote children's developmental abilities, with specific emphasis on parent–child transactions and family experiences that help reinforce children's health. Meanwhile, ECI's main goal is to prevent or reduce any physical, cognitive, or emotional deterioration in young children who have environmental or biological risk factors (Odom et al., 2003).

There has been a growing interest in families as key partners in ECI programs, particularly the transition process after early interventions, because parents are the primary caregivers and have unique information about their children that can facilitate their development (Kohler, 1999). Parents of children with special needs are concerned about the acceptance of their children and their ability to cope in new educational settings after ECI, which have new staff, regulations, and procedures. They desire to share the detailed knowledge they have about their children and their experiences in early intervention in order to promote understanding of the effectiveness of the services provided in ECI (Starr et al., 2016).

The transition from ECI is an ongoing process, which starts at the pre-school stage. It requires a designed plan that includes all stakeholders to prepare each child for the subsequent phase of education (Siddiqua, 2014). Researchers have pointed out the importance of parents' participation in transition planning, particularly in their concern about their children's needs being met in the transition plans and their roles throughout the process. Their perspectives provide the staff with useful information to design rehabilitation plans to best suit their children's needs (Bruder, 2010; Zheng et al., 2016).

Researchers have studied the process of transition in ECI to identify components of effective parental involvement. Many studies showcase parents' concerns regarding transition as an important stage that needs specific measurements and support to reach the next educational placement (Trach, 2012). Others focus on the importance of collaboration with parents to achieve a seamless transition (Schischka et al., 2012), or on parents' roles and satisfaction regarding the transition process (Podvey et al., 2011).

In the UAE, considerable efforts are being exerted to achieve effective early intervention and smooth transition to inclusive education in collaboration with parents as essential partners in the process (KHDA, 2017; MOE, 2010). However, special education (SE) centers still exist and are receiving transitioned children from ECI after six years of age, particularly those with intellectual disabilities and autism (MOCD, 2015). This highlights the need for more in-depth research to understand parents' experiences during and after transition from ECI to other educational settings (Starr et al., 2016).

PARENTS IN THE ECI TRANSITION PROCESS

A review of the literature for this chapter detected a number of studies related to the transition process from ECI to other educational settings. An examination of these studies generated three main themes as they reflected the parents' perspectives during the transition. Accordingly, this section summarizes some key findings from the literature exploring parents' experiences in terms of their feelings, challenges they faced and strategies that promote effective transition.

Transition is Stressful to Parents and Families

Previous studies found that transition from ECI to schools and from home-based ECI to center-based preschools is stressful for families to the shift in service provider and place of service. Therefore, parents need support to adapt to these changes (Rous, Hallam et al., 2007).

In the USA, Rosenkoetter et al. (2009) reviewed family studies in early childhood transition published between 1990 and 2006. The researchers found that transition is a stressful stage for families, as it is a dynamic, not static process, so supporting families and building relationships with them can reduce their stress. Another study by Kruse (2012) focused on families' experiences during the transition process in ECI programs. Results of the interviews that conducted with mothers indicated that parents experienced conflicts with the overall system during transition that could be referred to as an imbalance of power between themselves and the system. Meanwhile, Guralnick (2017) emphasized the importance of social support as a fundamental protective factor for families of young children with special needs in addressing and reducing parent-related stress during the transition process. Moreover, Kyn et al. (2013) investigated differences in parental stress with an early intervention program in Norway. Parents reported that when given emotional support, information, and advice, their stress was minimized, and they dealt more confident in their parental roles.

To explore families' and service providers' experiences during the transition from ECI services to school education, Hanson et al. (2000) conducted a study focused on children's transition from the third year of age to the pre-school age. They found that some families expressed concern regarding the shift in service between the ECI and public schools, resulting in a hesitancy to move from one system to another, characterized as movement from the "known" to the "unknown." More recently, Leadbitter et al. (2020) focused on the discussion among parents of children with Autism Spectrum Disorder (ASD) about the transition to school and the difficulties they encountered due to a lack of routine-based structure in the new educational setting. The authors also noted the stressful feelings that parents experienced with extended family members regarding the lack of understanding and acceptance for their children, which made them avoid extended family activities and events.

Challenges Described by Parents during Transition

Kruse (2012) found that parents expressed their concerns regarding the lack of placement options for their children, explained their roles to advocate for their child and keep them progressing, and emphasized the need for external support. This is emphasized by Hanson et al. (2000) who found that families were given limited choices or no choices at all in regards to the new educational settings, as the professionals or other officials mainly made the choice of transition. Scaling up, parents explained that the transition of their children to inclusive settings had been affected by the readiness of the child and type of special needs, such as autism. Moreover, UNESCO (2017) reported that parents of children with SEND are too often forced to select between two only options, the first one is to meet their children's needs within SE schools, and the second is to ensure that their children get the same learning opportunities and rights similar to other peers through enrollment in mainstream education.

Janus et al. (2008) took into account the educational stage in which the child was currently enrolled. They found that families of children with SEND who were still in ECI were more satisfied with services than families of children transitioned to kindergartens, as those families reported to be less positive toward care procedures as a result of lower levels of communication with them following the transition. Gatling (2009) investigated obstacles and factors that assist transition through the perspectives of parents and service providers. The researcher found that factors that may obstruct smooth transition are: parents' worries about services, ambiguity during meetings with professionals to discuss the children's eligibility, they felt that they are not prepared or informed better about types of meetings and their roles in it.

Consistently, Schischka et al. (2012) explored stakeholders' views on the transition process from the ECI stage to public school placement. Thematic analysis indicated that parents expressed some concerns regarding their children's nature of disabilities and how teachers are able to response to their individual special needs in classrooms, as well as the scarcity of communication with parents as a result of a "closed door" policy by the schools after the transition. This was also emphasized by Fontil and Petrakos (2015), who found a number of challenges that faced parents of children with autism, such as communication and trust-building relations with the staff and a lack of support following the transition to public schools in comparison with support before the transition.

Similar results were found in Canada by Villeneuve et al. (2013). The authors reported that parents faced difficulties organizing frequent meetings with teachers to exchange knowledge about the transition process. They experienced a lack of communication with the staff, and they required more information about their children's needs as well as the new educational context. In Ontario, Siddiqua (2014) found that parents of transitioned children had negative perceptions about the public schools. They expressed their concern regarding a lack of information received from school about their children and available services, and limited communication between teachers and families, as well as regarding a disorganized services post-transition.

Some studies also found that the new educational settings and the lack of consistency in the stages of the transition are among challenges described by parents. Ahtola et al. (2011) found that the majority of parents of transitioned children did not receive sufficient information about the new school and even how their children were progressing. Starr et al. (2016) also pointed out the need for consistency throughout the transition process among all parties in the system, and the importance of early preparation for transition.

Strategies that Promote Effective Transition

The literature clearly demonstrates the importance of parental involvement in ECI, and confirms their satisfaction with the programs as success factors. Rous, Hallam et al. (2007) argued that encouraging families to take part in the transition and helping children to adapt to new settings led to achieving transition outcomes. Meanwhile, Rosenkoetter et al. (2009) claim that parents feel that they are effective in the transition process when they engage more in meetings and school activities. Moreover, Gatling (2009) introduced factors that may support a smooth transition, among them are parents' effective communication and participation, and providing them with sufficient knowledge.

Brown and Guralnick (2012) placed families at the center of a support approach that targets parents to facilitate their day-to-day interactions with needed social structures, and to ensure their children's optimal development by meeting their needs, and providing professionals with assistance and information that enlarge the children's learning opportunities. Guralnick (2017) also concluded that the ultimate goal of ECI is to empower the family intervention style, which includes strong relationships with the community, comprehensiveness, and consistency of services, and placing the family at the center of the process. Therefore, understanding how parents view the transition process and to what extent they are involved in it is highly important for evaluating ECI programs and providing feedback to specialists.

Pang (2010) investigated a family's needs and concerns regarding their child with special needs in early intervention. The results indicated that the utilization of family-centered practices helped the staff to understand family priorities and incorporate greater family engagement in transition. The study suggested encouraging families to provide input about the intervention strategies they wanted to follow, the child's placement, and the transition plan. Pang suggested that every family member should receive training and be included in the transition process.

Starr et al. (2016) interviewed parents of children with ASD to understand their perspectives toward the transition process. Results were categorized into four major themes: relationship-building, communication, knowledge, and support. This was concluded by Ahtola et al. (2011) that collaboration and communication between sending and receiving staff are highly helpful, particularly the written information shared between programs and the accommodations provided on the new curriculum. Meanwhile, Spencer-Brown (2015) examined parents' perspectives of children with special needs during the transition process. The majority of the parents interviewed indicated the importance of communication and cooperation between families and educators. They perceived their engagement as adding value to the outcome of the transition process, and providing them with needed information. On the same course, Siddiqua (2014) declared that parents provided with more information about the transition, resulting in more positive perceptions and satisfaction about the whole process.

It is worth noting that previous literature has focused on families of children who transitioned to inclusive education and their satisfaction (Burford, 2005). However, there is less information about the parents of children who transitioned to SE centers. In the UAE, laws and policies encourage moving toward inclusion (MOE, 2010); meanwhile, SE centers are still an available option to receive ECI children older than six years old (MOCD, 2015). The current study tried to bridge the gap by investigating parents' perspectives on ECI transition with regard to their children's educational status and other demographic variables.

METHODOLOGY

This chapter is based on a mixed-method research study (Qualitative and Quantitative) with exploratory sequential design that was used to investigate parents' perspectives as participants in the transition process from ECI to other educational contexts. In the first qualitative phase of the study, the researchers implemented semi-structured interviews on a purposive sample of (11) parents whose children have transitioned to different educational settings. Two of the children are with global developmental delay, three of them with intellectual disability, four with ASD, one with hearing impairment, and one with multiple disabilities. In the second quantitative phase of the study, the researchers conducted a survey with (183) parents whose children were enrolled in the Emirates' Early Intervention Program. The sample included parents of children with global developmental delay ($n = 66$, 36.1%), intellectual disability ($n = 49$, 26.8%), ASD ($n = 35$, 19.1%), multiple disabilities ($n = 20$, 10.9%), and sensory impairments ($n = 13$, 7.1%).

RESULTS AND DISCUSSION

The qualitative findings that emerged from the interviews are classified under three broad themes: (1) smooth transition, (2) stressful transition, and (3) blurring transition. The themes emerged during the interviews based on factors that shaped parental perspectives toward early childhood transition in the UAE. It is worth mentioning that parents' perspectives oscillated back and forth through a full spectrum of feelings. They changed according to the place to which the child was transitioned, whether to an inclusive setting or SE center. Parents' perspectives demonstrated change depending on the stage of transition and the types of challenges they faced at each stage.

Smooth Transition to the SE System

The interviewed parents explained that the transition went smoothly during the services provided in ECI stage, where children receive comprehensive rehabilitation programs, including family services. Thus, this approach creates a common ground with parents and strengthens their relationship with the ECI program. Siddiqua (2014), who explored parents' experiences during the transition, affirmed that parents had more positive perceptions and satisfaction about service pre-transition than post-transition. Likewise, Gavidia-Payne et al. (2015) agree that parents view the transition as a smooth process before the transition point.

Interviewees whose children have been transitioned to SE centers pointed out that the transition process went smoothly with their children. They believe that their children could make more progress in these centers than anywhere else. They added that the SE staff was more qualified and cooperative with them than regular school staff. Interviewees shared their positive perceptions toward the transition process when their children had transitioned to what they called "suitable educational settings." Parents experienced smooth and clear transition procedures since they consider SE centers the most appropriate placement for their children's abilities. McIntyre et al. (2007) explained how a suitable educational setting, which is one that meets the family's expectations and ambitions for a child, leads to a successful transition. Rimm-Kaufman and Pianta's (2000) Model of Transition emphasizes the importance of continuous collaboration between family and school, and seamless relationships among all parties to achieve effective transitions.

Stressful Transition to Regular Schools

The interviewees considered community attitudes as an obstacle to transition for students with SEND to inclusive education; therefore, some parents had preferred not to declare to the public that they had a child with special needs. This finding is in agreement with Rosenkoetter et al. (2009) that transition is a stressful stage and a complicated process for families. Therefore, they recommended providing support to families and building relationships with them in order to reduce stress, as well as building collaboration between sending and receiving educational settings, which promotes positive outcomes for the transitioned children. Spencer-Brown's (2015) also concluded that the interviewed parents asserted the importance of communication and cooperation between families and educators.

Further analysis emphasized that the interviewees viewed teachers and other staff in regular schools as not adequately qualified to receive students with SEND at regular schools and not supportive of inclusion, which makes the transition more difficult. This is in line with Fontil and Petrakos (2015), who found that trust-building relations with the staff after transition is a challenge parents face during the transition process. The 11 interviewees in this study shared the view that the transition to inclusive education settings is a stressful experience. They suggested that regular education facilities are not prepared to accommodate students with SEND, particularly in terms of staff attitudes, non-adapted curriculum, or the educational atmosphere in general.

A significant number of studies concur with the results of this study. For instance, Starr et al. (2016) found that parents of transitioned children are facing challenges in all ecological systems levels. Similarly, Schischka et al. (2012) pointed out that parents expressed some concerns regarding their children after the transition to public schools. Moreover, Walker et al. (2012) concluded that parents considered schools unprepared for children with SEND and often resisted to include them. In the UAE, Alborno (2013) documented the lack of support services to students with SEND in regular schools, and Alobeidli (2017) revealed that regular classroom teachers tend to have negative attitudes toward the inclusion of students with disabilities. However, this finding is different than Walker et al.'s (2012) study in Australia, where parents felt satisfied with the support provided to their children from their teachers. And, it is also inconsistent with Siddiqua (2014), where indicated that parents had positive perceptions toward teachers in Canada. The reason for the differences could be attributed to cultural differences, where inclusion and ECI had its deeper roots in these countries.

Parents in this study stated that they felt depressed when they were informed about the next educational transition setting. Almost half of them would have preferred to keep their children in ECI for a longer because they felt that their children were safe in the ECI program, whereas other educational settings were unknown to them, which caused stress. In line with this finding, Hanson et al. (2000) noted that parents preferred to keep their children in the ECI because they did not want to move their children from "known" settings to "unknown" settings in schools. Consistently, Villeneuve et al. (2013) voiced parents' concerns about their children in a new educational setting and their need for more information about it. And more recently, Carroll and Sixsmith (2016) found that parents felt fear and anxiety when they were informed about the transition to a new setting; they found it difficult to adapt to new professionals.

Blurring Transition Pathways after ECI

Most interviewees highlighted the lack of coordination and collaboration among stakeholders. They shared that, while ECI seeks to include some children in public education facilities by preparing them for the next stage, schools do not complement the role of the early intervention; they follow their own regulations. Guralnick (2001) suggested that the ECI mode requires a high level of collaboration between related government and community entities, and families. More recently, Connolly and Devaney (2018), Starr et al. (2016), and Curle et al.

(2017), all stressed the need for consistency and collaboration in the transition process between all parties in the system.

Interviewed parents expressed their concern about the future of their children after early intervention. They declared that transition pathways were not clearly portrayed, resulting in confusion about what to do with their children and the right educational course for each child. The parents voiced their desperate need to know about available educational pathways after the ECI stage. Podvey et al. (2011) stated that transition is not just an event that occurs with the child at the beginning of the program, but it is a process that starts with planning and setting goals in collaboration with the new placement to ensure consistency and the child's adaptation to the new environment.

These findings are consistent with a significant body of studies that found a lack of knowledge among parents in regards to the transition process (Gatling, 2009; Spencer-Brown, 2015; Villeneuve et al., 2013). In addition, other studies found that parents were concerned about the lack of knowledge regarding their children in general, the disorganized education system, and the services available to their children. The literature suggests that supporting parents' access to information is key in early intervention as it helps the family to shape an understanding about their children's future, including possible needs in the next stage (Siddiqua, 2014).

Interviewees also uncovered the need for their children to develop more skills during the early intervention stage. They felt that their children had not been sufficiently empowered for the next educational level, particularly inclusive education. Gaad and Thabet (2016) pointed out that students with SEND should be well prepared before they are included in regular schools to avoid unexpected situations. Armed with this knowledge, children in ECI should be provided sufficient time to receive the needed services before being referred to the next educational stage, especially when they're transitioned to inclusive settings. The success of the transition depends on sufficient preparation for the child and their family.

DIFFERENCES IN PARENTS' PERSPECTIVES

The quantitative findings from the cross-sectional survey have shown that there were significant differences between parents' gender in favor of fathers with regards to their perspectives toward the transition journey ($t = -3.649, p < 0.05$). Fathers were more positive in their views toward the transition journey ($M = 3.97$), they reported through the survey items, that the transition trajectory was clear and smooth for them when compared to mothers who had moderate views toward transition ($M = 3.04$). This may be because mothers usually undertake the responsibility of following up with their children with SEND, which is consistent with the fact that the vast majority of the employees in SE and ECI centers are female. In addition, children in early developmental stages are more attached to their mothers as a source to satisfy their basic needs while fathers are busy with their business outside the family. Thus, mothers' expectations about the provided services and transition options may be higher than fathers' who are not as deeply involved in the process. In a recent study in Ireland, Connolly and Devaney (2018) concluded the importance of involving parents, especially fathers, in their children's services. This is in line with Gaad's (2006) findings that the number of fathers of children with Down syndrome in the UAE participating in monthly meetings had decreased, as mothers usually spent more time with their child and responding to their needs.

In regard to children's gender, the t-test indicated that there were no statistical differences between the two groups ($t = -0.258, p > 0.05$). In ECI, parents are expected to follow up with their children and communicate with the staff to ensure the best services. Early education policies in the UAE emphasize ECI for all children with SEND without any gender-based discrimination, where both genders are following the same protocols and receiving the same services.

The results of parents' perspectives toward the transition with respect to educational level show higher mean scores among parents with basic reading and writing skills as well as parents with high school degrees. On the contrary, the results showed the lowest mean scores for parents holding a bachelor's degree or higher. One-way ANOVA and Scheffe post hoc tests revealed significant statistical differences between parents' educational level mean scores ($F = 26.228, p < 0.05$). These differences are between parents with basic literacy skills and parents with a bachelor's or above ($p = 0.000$), in addition to a statistically significant difference between parents with high school degrees and parents with a bachelor's degree or above ($p = 0.000$), indicating that parents with lower educational achievement demonstrated more positive perspectives regarding transition.

This may be because educated parents are expected to learn more about their children's status, and search for the best rehabilitation approaches as well as best practices in ECI and transition. Therefore, their perspectives toward transition might be associated with higher expectations about their children and their future. On the other hand, parents with lower educational levels who have basic literacy skills or are illiterate, tend to have more limited knowledge about global practices in ECI, transition and inclusion, which may result in them holding more positive perceptions about the transition process overall. With little opportunities for comparison, the services offered are sufficient and acceptable to them. This finding is inconsistent with Siddiqua (2014), who found parents' educational level did not significantly affect their perceptions toward transition. The reason for the difference could be attributed to social and cultural factors that are different from the UAE. Illiterate parents might have fewer opportunities to access information available in languages other than Arabic, or to enroll in training courses and obtain knowledge resources that improve their knowledge about ECI.

In terms of children's educational status, One-way ANOVA and Scheffe post hoc tests indicated significant statistical differences between children's educational status mean scores ($F = 30.737, p < 0.05$). The differences found between parents of children in ECI, SE centers and regular schools, indicated more positive perceptions of parents of children enrolled in SE centers and ECI centers. These centers follow the same policies of the Ministry of Community Development (MOCD) as they are affiliated under the same entity, which promotes consistency in services provided within these two types of centers. However, regular schools follow different regulations set by the Ministry of Education (MOE) and the Knowledge and Human Development Authority (KHDA) which often make it difficult for the parents to adapt to the new educational environments after the transition, in addition to the challenges associated with inclusive education in the UAE in general (Alborno, 2013; Alobeidli, 2017). Furthermore, ECI centers provide great attention to the family through counseling that meets their individualized needs based on family concerns and priorities. In addition, the quality standards in ECI allow children to receive more therapeutic sessions (MOCD, 2015). Janus et al. (2008) declared that families in ECI were more satisfied with services than families of transitioned children to kindergartens, and they become less engaged in the school stage due to limited student-related education activities such as IEP meetings they were invited to attend (Podvey et al., 2011).

One-way ANOVA test also showed statistically significant differences between the mean scores on parents of children with different types of SEND ($F = 4.887$, $p < 0.05$) and Scheffe post hoc test indicate that these differences are significant between parents of children with developmental delay, and parents of children with intellectual disabilities and ASD. Children with confirmed disabilities such as intellectual disabilities or ASD are stigmatized by the society (Alobeidli, 2017), and their families face community challenges more than families of children with developmental delay that have not yet been classified under disability categories. Transition to inclusive settings is also not encouraged for children with autism and intellectual disabilities by the MOCD that prefers to refer them to SE centers (MOCD, 2019). Interviewees who had children with sensory disabilities also described the transition as an easy process when compared with parents of children with other disabilities, such as ASD. These findings are also in line with the conclusion of the research done by Hanson et al. (2000), Leadbitter et al. (2020), and Starr et al. (2016) regarding challenges facing the transition of children with autism. Therefore, more focus should be directed toward parents of children with autism and intellectual disabilities to ensure successful transitions and create a supportive ecosystem for inclusion in the UAE.

A TRANSITION FRAMEWORK TO INCLUSIVE SETTINGS

Based on the study results, the researchers introduced a transition framework to ensure successful and smooth transition from ECI to inclusive settings. The transition framework suggests three main pillars, constructed based on the parents' views and the literature review, which are "Enablers, Stakeholders, and Inclusive Educational Settings."

The first pillar is the "Enablers" that consists of the ecosystem that children and their parents live in. These enablers support the child's transition to a later educational environment, and any deficiency in the system may lead to confusion regarding the transition process or feelings of stress, as the parents reported. Therefore, the family is considered as the core of the enablers, where family embraces the child and lead them to a safe transition (Hayes et al., 2017). So a trainings strategy in this pillar is needed to provide parents with the necessary knowledge about the available transition options and support them in making appropriate decisions, as well as their roles during it, to ensure their effectiveness throughout the transition process.

The second pillar of the suggested framework is the "Stakeholders" which also emphasizes the role of parents in the process of transition, particularly their written consent to the transition decisions. Senders and receivers must also agree on the transition steps and the ultimate goal. For example, the ECI program prepares the transition plan in cooperation with parents and the child's transitioned setting. ECI staff are well trained in forming transition plans, and applying them collectively in cooperation with the family in different settings. Accordingly, it is very important that the school team then follows the transition plans, establishes a method for continuous collaboration with the ECI to follow-up the child in the new setting, and ensures the proper implementation of it. This requires a training strategy for regular school teachers, on how to reflect transition plans in the form of suitable individual plans for transitioned students that can be applied in school settings.

The lack of proper coordination between concerned entities, as reported by the parents, has led to feelings of confusion during the transition. Therefore, ministries and local authorities responsible for education and ECI should agree on a unified transition plan and use it as an official document recognized and approved by all parties.

The third and final pillar is the "Inclusive Educational Setting" as a key factor in completing the transition process and ensuring its success, which depends on teachers' attitudes, teaching qualifications, and the schools' readiness to receive children with SEND. To ensure school environments are inclusive requires that all children should have the opportunity to learn regardless of their learning abilities and with adequate support when needed. Creating inclusive environments requires accommodations in physical and human elements, such as physical accessibility, curriculum accommodations, differentiated instruction, and teaching and assessment methods, as well as positive attitudes toward children by teachers and peers (UNESCO, 2017). Hayes et al. (2017) suggested a need for transformation in early learning environments with plentiful opportunities for children to become involved in the learning process, and to have access to different contexts with a flexible and responsive role of the educators.

One of the effective strategies that are already implemented in the ECI stage and needs to be extended to regular schools is the interdisciplinary teamwork that considers parents as integral part of it, this approach promoted greater collaboration with parents so that they participate in their children's educational plans, implement them in natural environments and review them with the team.

This framework might be effective in transition as it conforms with the parents' views on the basic principles of the transition process. They insured the community support, as well as active family participation through the exercise of their roles and responsibilities to achieve an effective transition. Parents also emphasizes the creation of an inclusive culture of inclusion in schools among teachers, staff and peers, and a unified coordination mechanism among the concerned parties that ensure policy consistency and implementation on common ground.

CONCLUSION

This chapter summarizes the findings of a study that produced insight into parents' experiences during the transition of their children with SEND from ECI to other educational settings. Parents viewed the transition in ECI stage from three different perspectives based on the place of transition, stages of transition, and the types of challenges they faced at each stage. Some parents indicated that the transition went smoothly when their children transitioned to SE centers; however, others felt that the transition was stressful when their children transitioned to regular schools. Meanwhile, parents considered the transition as a blurring stage when reflecting on the coordination between entities, transition pathways, or the need for information. In addition, statistically significant differences were found among parents' perspectives toward the transition pertinent to the gender of the parent, parents' educational level, child's educational status, and type of educational needs; however, no significant difference was found regarding a child's gender. Accordingly, the researchers introduced a UAE's transition framework to ensure successful and smooth transition from ECI to inclusive settings.

REFERENCES

Ahtola, A., Silinskas, G., Poikonen, P. L., Kontoniemi, M., Niemi, P., & Nurmi, J. E. (2011). Transition to formal schooling: Do transition practices matter for academic performance? *Early Childhood Research Quarterly*, 26(3), 295–302. https://doi.org/10.1016/j.ecresq.2010.12.002

Alborno, N. E. (2013). *The journey into inclusive education: A case study of three Emirati government primary schools*. Doctoral Dissertation. http://bspace.buid.ac.ae/handle/1234/512

Alobeidli, A. (2017). *An investigative study of the factors affecting the attitudes of female Emirati teachers toward the inclusion of students with intellectual disabilities in the government primary schools in Dubai, the United Arab Emirates*. Doctoral dissertation. http://bspace.buid.ac.ae/handle/1234/512

Brown, S., & Guralnick, M. (2012). International human rights to early intervention for infants and young children with disabilities: Tools for global advocacy. *Infants & Young Children*, 25(4), 270–285. http://dx.doi.org/10.1097/IYC.0b013e318268fa49

Bruder, M. B. (2010). Early childhood intervention: A promise to children and families for their future. *Exceptional Children*, 76(3), 339–355. https://doi.org/10.1177/001440291007600306

Burford, S. L. (2005). *Transition to kindergarten for children with disabilities: A survey of family experiences, appraisal and coping*. Doctoral dissertation. ProQuest Dissertations and Theses database. (UMI No. 3194535).

Carroll, C., & Sixsmith, J. (2016). A trajectory of relationship development for early intervention practice for children with developmental disabilities. *International Journal of Therapy and Rehabilitation*, 23(3), 131–140. https://doi.org/10.12968/ijtr.2016.23.3.131

Connolly, N., & Devaney, C. (2018). Parenting support: Policy and practice in the Irish context. *Child Care in Practice*, 24(1), 15–28. https://doi.org/10.1080/13575279.2016.1264365

Curle, D., Jamieson, J., Buchanan, M., Poon, B., Zaidman-Zait, A., & Norman, N. (2017). The transition from early intervention to school for children who are deaf or hard of hearing: Administrator perspectives. *Journal of Deaf Studies and Deaf Education*, 22(1), 131–140. https://doi.org/10.1093/deafed/enw067

Fontil, L., & Petrakos, H. (2015). Transition to school: The experiences of Canadian and immigrant families of children with autism spectrum disorders. *Psychology in the Schools*, *52*(8), 773–788. https://doi.org/10.1002/pits.21859

Gaad, E. (2006). The social and educational impacts of the first national Down syndrome support group in the UAE. *Journal of Research in Special Educational Needs*, *6*(3), 134–142. https://doi.org/10.1111/j.1471-3802.2006.00071.x

Gaad, E., & Thabet, R. A. (2016). Behaviour support training for parents of children with autism spectrum disorder. *Journal of Education and Learning*, *5*(1), 133–153. http://dx.doi.org/10.5539/ijef.v5n1p133

Gatling, V. (2009). *The transition from early intervention to early childhood special education programming: Three case studies*. Doctoral dissertation. https://vtechworks.lib.vt.edu/bitstream/handle/10919/26632/GatlingDissertationfinal.pdf

Gavidia-Payne, S., Meddis, K., & Mahar, N. (2015). Correlates of child and family outcomes in an Australian community-based early childhood intervention program. *Journal of Intellectual and Developmental Disability*, *40*(1), 57–67. https://doi.org/10.3109/13668250.2014.983056

Guralnick, M. (2001). A developmental systems model for early intervention. *Infants & Young Children*, *14*(2), 1–18. https://doi.org/10.1097/00001163-200114020-00004

Guralnick, M. (2017). Early intervention for children with intellectual disabilities: An update. *Journal of Applied Research in Intellectual Disabilities*, *30*, 211–229. https://doi.org/10.1111/jar.12233

Hanson, M., Beckman, P., Horn, E., & Sandall, S. (2000). Entering preschool: Family and professional experiences in this transition process. *Journal of Early Intervention*, *23*(4), 279–293. https://doi.org/10.1177/10538151000230040701

Hayes, N., O'Toole, L., & Halpenny, A. (2017). *Introducing Bronfenbrenner: A guide for practitioners and students in early years education*. London: Routledge.

Janus, M., Kopechanski, L., Cameron, R., & Hughes, D. (2008). In transition: Experiences of parents of children with special needs at school entry. *Early Childhood Education Journal*, *35*(5), 479–485. https://doi.org/10.1007/s10643-007-0217-0

Knowledge and Human Development Authority (KHDA). (2017). *Dubai inclusive education policy framework*. Dubai: Knowledge and Human Development Authority.

Kohler, F. W. (1999). Examining the services received by young children with autism and their families: A survey of parent responses. *Focus on Autism and Other Developmental Disabilities*, *14*(3), 150–158. https://doi.org/10.1177/108835769901400304

Kruse, A. D. (2012). *Understanding experiences of families and their partnerships as they navigate early intervention, transition, and early childhood special education*. Doctoral Dissertation. http://lib.dr.iastate.edu/cgi/viewcontent.cgi?article=3682&context=etd

Kyn, N., Ravn, I., Lindemann, R., Smeby, N., Torgersen, A., & Gundersen, T. (2013). Parents of preterm-born children; sources of stress and worry and experiences with an early intervention programme – a qualitative study. *BMC Nursing*, *12*(28), 1–11. https://doi.org/10.1186/1472-6955-12-28

Leadbitter, K., Macdonald, W., Taylor, C., Buckle, K., & Consortium, P. (2020). Parent perceptions of participation in a parent-mediated communication-focussed intervention with their young child with autism spectrum disorder. *Autism*, *24*(8), 2129–2141. https://doi.org/10.1177/1362361320936394

Massachusetts Department of Public Health (MDPH). (2013). *Early intervention operational standards*. http://www.mass.gov/eohhs/docs/dph/com-health/early-childhood/ei-operational-standards.pdf

McIntyre, L. L., Eckert, T. L., Fiese, B. H., DiGennaro, F. D., & Wildenger, L. K. (2007). The transition to kindergarten: Family experiences and involvement. *Early Childhood Education Journal*, *35*, 83–88. https://doi.org/10.1007/s10643-007-0175-6

Ministry of Community Development. (2015). *Annual report*. Dubai: UAE.

Ministry of Community Development. (2019). *Family journey guidelines in the Emirates early childhood intervention programme*. Dubai: UAE.

Ministry of Education. (2010). *School for all: General rules for the provision of special education programs and services (public & private schools)*. Dubai: UAE.

Odom, S. L., Hanson, M. J., Blackman, J. A., & Kaul, S. (2003). *Early intervention practices around the world*. Baltimore, MD: Brookes.

Pang, Y. (2010). Facilitating family involvement in early intervention to preschool transition. *The School Community Journal, 20*(2), 183–198. https://www.researchgate.net/publication/228459381_Facilitating_Family_Involvement_in_Early_Intervention_to_Preschool_Transition

Podvey, M., Hinojosa, J., & Koenig, K. (2011). Reconsidering insider status for families during the transition from early intervention to preschool special education. *The Journal of Special Education, 46*(4), 211–222. https://doi.org/10.1177/0022466911407074

Rimm-Kaufman, S., & Pianta, R. (2000). An ecological perspective on the transition to kindergarten: A theoretical framework to guide empirical research. *Journal of Applied Developmental Psychology, 21*(5), 491–511. https://doi.org/10.1016/S0193-3973(00)00051-4

Rosenkoetter, S., Schroeder, C., Rous, B., Hains, A., Shaw, J., & McCormick, K. (2009). *A review of research in early childhood transition: Child and family studies.* Technical Report #5. http://www.niusileadscape.org/docs/FINAL_PRODUCTS/LearningCarousel/ResearchReview-Transition.pdf

Rous, B., Hallam, R., Harbin, G., McCormick, K., & Jung, L. A. (2007). The transition process for young children with disabilities: A conceptual framework. *Infants & Young Children, 20*(2), 135–148. https://doi.org/10.1097/01.IYC.0000264481.27947.5f

Rous, B., Myers, C., & Stricklin, S. (2007). Strategies for supporting transitions of young children with special needs and their families. *Journal of Early Intervention, 10*(1), 1–18. https://doi.org/10.1177/105381510703000102

Schischka, J., Rawlinson, C., & Hamilton, R. (2012). Factors affecting the transition to school for young children with disabilities. *Australian Journal of Early Childhood, 37*(4), 15–23. https://doi.org/10.1177/183693911203700403

Siddiqua, A. (2014). *Exploring experiences of parents of children with special needs at school entry: A mixed methods approach.* Master Dissertation. https://macsphere.mcmaster.ca/handle/11375/16487

Spencer-Brown, A. (2015). *Parental expectations and perspectives as they relate to their children with special education needs (SEN) during transition from early intervention/Preschool to kindergarten.* Doctoral Dissertation. https://digitalcommons.brandman.edu/cgi/viewcontent.cgi?referer=https://www.google.ae/&httpsredir=1&article=1020&context=edd_dissertations

Starr, E., Martini, T., & Kuo, B. (2016). Transition to kindergarten for children with autism spectrum disorder: A focus group study with ethnically diverse parents, teachers, and early intervention service providers. *Focus on Autism and Other Developmental Disabilities, 31*(2), 115–128. https://doi.org/10.1177/1088357614532497

Trach, J. S. (2012). Degree of collaboration for the successful transition outcomes. *Journal of Rehabilitation, 78*(2), 39–48. https://www.researchgate.net/publication/289978738_Degree_of_Collaboration_for_Successful_Transition_Outcomes

UNESCO. (2017). *A guide for ensuring inclusion and equity in education.* Paris: The United Nations Educational, Scientific and Cultural Organization.

Villeneuve, M., Chatenoud, C., Hutchinson, N., Minnes, P., Perry, A., Dionne, C., ... Weiss, J. (2013). The experience of parents as their children with developmental disabilities transition from early intervention to kindergarten. *Canadian Journal of Education, 36*(1), 4–43. https://www.researchgate.net/publication/258312386_The_Experience_of_Parents_as_Their_Children_with_Developmental_Disabilities_Transition_from_Early_Intervention_to_Kindergarten

Walker, S., Dunbar, S., Meldrum, K., Whiteford, C., Carrington, S., Hand, S., ... Nicholson, J. (2012). The transition to school of children with developmental disabilities: Views of parents and teachers. *Australasian Journal of Early Childhood, 37*(3), 22–29. https://doi.org/10.1177/183693911203700304

Zheng, Y., Maude, S. P., Brotherson, M. J., & Merritts, A. (2016). Early childhood intervention in China from the families' perspective. *International Journal of Disability, Development and Education, 63*(4), 431–449. https://doi.org/10.1080/1034912X.2015.1124988

FRAMING THE FOUNDATIONS: A PRACTICE MODEL FOR TEACHING CHILDREN ON THE AUTISM SPECTRUM IN EARLY YEARS CLASSROOMS

Wendi Beamish and Annalise Taylor

ABSTRACT

Starting school is major educational transition for all children as it requires the forming of fresh relationships, settling into a new classroom environment, and engaging in more formal learning activities. For children on the autism spectrum, starting school is a stressful period due to the substantially changed conditions. With appropriate and flexible supports, however, these children can overcome their desire for sameness, belong to a community of active learners, and experience academic and social success. This chapter presents a practice model to support teachers seeking to successfully include and educate children on the spectrum in the early years of schooling. This Model of Practice comprises 23 practices aligned with the organizers of Belonging, Being, *and* Becoming *from the Australian Early Years Learning Framework. The practices are foundational in nature and enable teachers to identify and use them in their planning and instruction in order to respond effectively to specific children's needs. The model has been field tested by early years teachers from 23 schools across three Australian states. Perspectives provided by these teachers about the model and how they used it in their classrooms are woven into the chapter. Their perspectives highlight the usefulness of the model as a classroom resource for teaching not only children on the spectrum but also those with diverse learning needs. Reported perspectives also indicate that using the model may enhance teachers' autism-specific knowledge and*

Transition Programs for Children and Youth with Diverse Needs
International Perspectives on Inclusive Education, Volume 18, 25–35
Copyright © 2022 Wendi Beamish and Annalise Taylor
Published under exclusive licence by Emerald Publishing Limited
ISSN: 1479-3636/doi:10.1108/S1479-363620220000018003

confidence in working with children on the spectrum. The chapter concludes with recommendations made by teachers for using the practice model.

Keywords: Autism; early childhood teachers; inclusive education; mainstream classroom; model of practice; transition

INTRODUCTION

For all children, transition to school provides opportunity for more formal educational experiences, prospects for new friendships, and scope for increased independence. Yet, for children on the autism spectrum and their families, this crucial transition is fraught with challenges as they move into a new service system. To minimize the challenges and capitalize on the current circumstances, the transition process needs to be managed well by teachers. Responsive management can increase the likelihood of the child on the spectrum retaining learning gains achieved prior to school and adjusting to the changed routines, people, and learning demands. Sensitive management can support family engagement, coping, and well-being during this period. Finally, proactive management can reduce the work demands associated with educating and including children on the spectrum while building productive relationships with their parents.

Internationally, the majority of young children on the spectrum are commencing school in mainstream settings (approx. 80% Australia, ABS, 2018; approx. 98% United Kingdom, McConkey, 2020; approx. 91% United States, Snyder et al., 2016). Many mainstream teachers, however, have identified that they lack the specialized knowledge and skills to address the multifaceted educational needs of this student cohort (Ravet, 2018; Saggers et al., 2019). To fill this void, a variety of teacher-friendly online resources such as the Early Years Model of Practice (EY-MoP) have been developed by researchers in partnership with practitioners. This Australian practice model for classroom teachers supports pedagogical decision making when working with children on the spectrum in the early years of schooling (i.e., first 3 years of formal education). The model and its practices, supported by a range of videos, podcasts, and print material, can be accessed via *inclusionED* (www.inclusioned.edu.au). This online professional learning platform translates the research findings from several *Australian Cooperative Research Center for Living with Autism* research projects into teaching practices for use in inclusive classrooms and at home. Practices are drawn not only from the EY-MoP but also from the Middle Years Model of Practice (MY-MoP) as well as projects such as structured teaching, classroom acoustics, and social robotics clubs.

MODEL FEATURES

The EY-MoP is conceptualized as a framework comprising a set of research-supported educational practices. Several key features underpinned the design of the model to ensure that practices were relevant to and useable by early years teachers with limited understanding and specialized knowledge in autism. These features are the nature of the practices, the presentation of the practices, and the organization of the practices within the model.

Practices within the model are foundational in nature and constitute a range of core strategies and processes that teachers use in their daily work to plan and enhance the learning of young school-age children. Moreover, practice selection has taken into consideration the evidence that children on the spectrum learn and interact with people and the environment differently from many of their peers (Janzen, 2003). These children typically are concrete, visual learners; have good rote memory skills; and learn best in a predictable environment. Many find it challenging to attend to and process information. Additionally, they often experience difficulties with communication, social interactions, and managing emotions and behavior. Learning outcomes are increased when teachers use the practices within the model in conjunction with information on children's strengths, preferences, interests, and needs.

Each practice is written using teacher-friendly language and has a consistent Teacher–what–how structure (e.g., Teachers nurture students' emotional literacy by modeling, recognizing, and responding to expressed emotions), together with an abbreviated form (e.g., *Model emotional literacy*). In addition, each practice is supported by a 2-page practice brief to guide teacher understanding and class-room implementation.

The model is organized for use with 23 practices distributed across the framework in the areas of *Belonging, Being,* and *Becoming* (see Table 1) from the Australian Early Years Learning Framework (DEEWR, 2009). Practices are

Table 1. The Early Years Model of Practice.

Belonging	*Environmentally-focused practice area*	Interact with every student	Provide an organised classroom	Consistently use routines
		Provide feedback on learning and behavior	Give clear directions	Consistently use schedules
		Actively supervise class	Reinforce class rules	Prepare students for transitions
Being	*Socially-emotionally focused practice area*	Model positive interactions	Teach self-regulation	Conduct ABC analysis
		Teach friendship skills	Teach social problem solving	Modify environment to reduce behavior
		Model emotional literacy	Use peer-mediated instruction	
Becoming	*Instructionally-focused practice area*	Assess student knowledge	Monitor student progress	Teach literacy skills
		Provide systematic instruction	Teach communication skills	Teach self-help skills

presented within the model using their abbreviated forms. Environmentally focused practices that create an inclusive and structured classroom are aligned with *Belonging*. Socio-emotionally focused practices that support relationships and behavioral adjustment are aligned with *Being*. Instructionally focused practices that support child assessment and delivery of curriculum are aligned with *Becoming*. The model enables teachers to select relevant practices when children transition into and between classrooms.

MODEL DEVELOPMENT

The EY-MoP was the output of a 3-year, multi-stage research project funded by the *Australian Cooperative Research Center for Living with Autism*. Cycles of design–evaluate–redesign conducted by the research team in collaboration with classroom teachers were used to generate, validate, and field test the practice model. North American practice listings from early childhood special education and autism education were identified as sources for potential practices. Relevant practices were scrutinized and refined by the research team to form a working set of 31 practices, which was considered a manageable size for use by teachers (Beamish et al., 2014).

The working set of practices was validated using online surveys. First, a small group of educational experts provide feedback on practice content, which triggered wording revisions. A large group of over 100 early years teachers then provided feedback on the relevance and usability of the practices in mainstream classrooms. This feedback resulted in a model comprising 29 amended practices. Next, these practices were assigned abbreviations and embedded in the *Belonging–Being–Becoming* structure to form the EY-MoP. A supporting brief was then written for each practice. For a more details on this process, see Taylor et al. (2019).

Field testing of the EY-MoP was undertaken by early years teachers from 23 schools in metropolitan, regional, and rural locations across the eastern states of Australia. All participants taught in mainstream classrooms that included a child on the spectrum. The EY-MoP materials were uploaded to the project website to enable teacher access. The model was tested by teachers for an 8-week period, with online surveys and phone interviews being used to collect data prior to and after using the model. Teachers were asked to use the EY-MoP in ways that most enhanced their daily practice with regards to educating the child on the spectrum in their class. Following field testing, the model was amended to 23 practices on the basis of teacher evaluation and use.

MODEL AND TEACHER PERSPECTIVES

Participating teachers had much to say about their experiences using the EY-MoP. During interviews they shared impressions of the model, identified practices they used, and expressed feelings of knowledge and confidence at the end of the field-testing period. In this section, comments provided by teachers allow their "voice" to be heard and their contributions to be acknowledged. For more comprehensive reporting of our teachers' perspectives, see Beamish et al. (2020).

Impressions of the EY-MoP

Teachers' impressions of the EY-MoP revolved predominantly around the importance of the practices and the usability of the model. Taken together, these viewpoints provide broad teacher endorsement of the practices and signal viability of the model for classroom use.

Importance of the Practices

During interviews, teachers spoke about the importance of the practices from varying perspectives. Several teachers connected the practices to their daily work in classrooms and what they aspire to do. For example, one teacher said:

> These are the sorts of things we try our best to do. These are- I look at it, and I go 'these are the things I try my best to do all the time.' As a teacher, as an effective teacher, this is the stuff you're aiming for. (#13)

Many teachers commented on how the practices seemed to meet the needs of children on the spectrum. Comments included:

> I really liked how it incorporates everything to do with the, with an ASD student, so about them belonging, because these are all- like, I guess there's all, you can have needs in all 3 of these areas. So in *Belonging*, I really liked how, obviously, it's to ensure that the child feels like they belong in the grade, to develop themselves, which is then Being, and then also what they can become in terms of their curriculum, and, because, obviously, being a teacher, that's what we look at, what our focus is as well is they learn. So I thought it sort of comprises everything we want for, not just, I guess, ASD students, but also for any student in a class. (#16)

Moreover, approximately a third of the teachers remarked about the applicability of the practices for not only children on the spectrum but also other children in their class. One teacher stated:

> Well, when I read through it all, it all obviously made good sense. It is pretty much what we do every day. Obviously, you do your best to do most of it, but every day- you know, you can't cover everything every day, obviously, as much as you'd love to. No, it made sense, obviously, for all children, really, not just children with ASD, or with any other diagnosis of anything. It just, I think, helps you to, reminders of the inclusion in the classroom, and things that you, just remind you of things that you need to be thinking of and considering every day. (#7)

These presented comments highlight the importance our teachers attributed to the practices within the model. Comments also suggest ways in which the teachers saw the model as being useful in their classrooms.

Usability of the Model

Following use of the EY-MoP materials, teachers shared their thoughts on the value of the resource as a whole. They also shared how the model informed their practice and how it might support the practice of colleagues. First and foremost, teachers reported on the teacher-friendly nature of the resource. Typical comments were:

> I think that there's so much, there's so much in that model, and because it's so easy to access, you know, you just click on a hyperlink and it opens up, and there's a whole heap of ideas there, and links to other resources as well. I just think it's really, you know, very accessibly for teachers in that realm. (#20)

> The actual Model of Practice is very succinct, it's easy to understand, easy to read. If you do feel like you need a, you know, better understanding, you can click on the link, and it takes you in and takes you that bit further. (#13)

Teachers who actively used the model reflected on ways it positively impacted their practice. For example:

> I think this model works for me to organise my thoughts, like I said. It's a good, it's a good place to go, if I'm unsure, to find what it is that I'm struggling with, and to help me plan out my thoughts, because that's one thing that I really, really struggle with is that I get too distracted by something else that I'm thinking about, and I need to just pull it back and that, I find that really, really beneficial. (#19)

> I thought… yuck, just another thing, but in saying that, it's the best other thing that I've been asked to do, because it's benefited the children, it's benefited me, and I've got a great resource that's here, that's self-explanatory, easy to read. (#17)

A number of experienced teachers referred to using the model as a tool to reflect on their practice. Some also suggested that the model would be a valuable resource for preservice and early career teachers. One teacher recounted:

> So, I have found it helpful, and I would definitely give this to a graduate… I actually showed my student teacher, and she found it really helpful with when she had to teach my kids for eight weeks. So, she picked out what she felt was most needed for my ASD student. So, we worked on some strategies that met that, especially with providing instruction about what he needs to do, and what's expected of him. (#10)

These insights from teachers following field testing point to the key strengths of the EY-MoPs and its applicability for use in early years classrooms.

Most Frequently Used Practices

In general, practices implemented during the field-testing period were evenly distributed across the areas of *Belonging*, *Being*, and *Becoming*. It is worth noting that participating teachers reported using practices that specifically addressed the unique ways that children on the spectrum learn and interact with teachers, peers, and the classroom environment. Teachers' views on practice areas are now presented, together with brief summaries of the most frequently used practices.

Belonging Practices to Adjust the Learning Environment

Environmentally focused practices were a popular choice for use by participating teachers. Many explained that fostering a sense of belonging and creating a safe and supportive learning environment were fundamental to their daily practice.

One teacher said, "I think it's such a major thing that all children, but especially children who are on the spectrum, because their sense of belonging sort of, yeah, underpins like their attitude toward coming in the classroom, how safe they feel" (#4). This sentiment was extended by another teacher who stated, "I feel it's really important to build those practices from the beginning of the year, especially at Foundation level [first year of school]" adding "you need to make sure they're all feeling comfortable in their learning environment and that you build a positive space... for all students" (#8). The majority of teachers, however, identified that they focused on using the recommended practices related to routines, schedules, and transitioning between activities, which all provide structure and predictability for children on the spectrum. For example:

> I think the one I probably focussed on, or what I want some other ideas for, I guess, would be the *transitions*. You know, we do a lot of transitioning through the day, and any support or help that I could get, or different ideas. You know, you try your best, but you don't always prepare them [children on the spectrum] for a change, and sometimes in our busy school, changes come upon really quickly, so you don't always get time to prime them, either. (#9)

- *Consistently use routines*
  Teachers provide structure and consistency by establishing, teaching, and using routines (e.g., going to the toilet, taking a break).
  The consistent use of classroom and individualized routines provides children on the spectrum with a predictable and structured learning environment, which enhances engagement and independence. Visual supports enable changes to routines to be communicated to the child beforehand.
- *Consistently use schedules*
  Teachers ensure the learning environment is structured and predictable by preparing and consistently using class and/or individual schedules.
  Schedules support children on the spectrum by providing reliable time, event, and location information in an accessible format that facilitates their understanding and reduces teacher explanation. Schedules can be presented visually using objects, symbols, photos, or words.
- *Prepare students for transitions*
  Teachers provide structure and predictability by carefully preparing students for classroom transitions.
  Children on the spectrum should be prepared as early as possible for transitioning from one activity, learning space, or environment to another. Using visually supported transition routines can help to reduce stress and assist these children to transition in a smooth way.

Being Practices to Build Social Emotional Competence
The current emphasis on social-emotional learning in schools, resulted in these focused practices being regularly selected for use. As one teacher shared, "I really like the social-emotional learning, that's a big focus at our school... I just think the social-emotional learning is very important to me and my kids" (#26). Several teachers mentioned the importance of building the social and friendship skills of

children on the spectrum; "I've put in my plan for next week, to do a bit of scenario... encouraging friendships to develop" (#7). Additionally, many teachers commented on how practices in this area met the specific needs of their children on the spectrum. For example:

> Teaching the feelings and emotions is really important, particularly for these guys [children on the spectrum], and being able to identify them, and how they manifest in their bodies, what to do, how to self-regulate themselves when they're feeling angry you know, that sort of thing, because they come to particularly this school, and they've got to learn to get along with 119 others [year level cohort]... it can be quite a challenge. (#9)

As flagged in the above quote, teaching self-regulation, friendship skills, and social problem solving were the practices most often used most by participating teachers.

- *Teach self-regulation*
  Teachers foster self-regulation in students by providing systematic instruction.
  For children on the spectrum, the ability to regulate their feelings and behavior independently, without direct adult support, impacts positively on their engagement and learning. Teachers can foster self-regulation by modeling strategies and behaviors that can be used to manage feelings and behaviors during activities, routines, and transitions.
- *Teach friendship skills*
  Teachers build friendship skills by providing systematic instruction in play and social skills coupled with multiple opportunities for practice.
  Some children on the spectrum benefit from targeted instruction to build the skills required to initiate, develop, and maintain friendships with peers. Use of embedded instruction enables teachers to explicitly teach and provide opportunities for children to learn and practice these important skills.
- *Teach social problem solving*
  Teachers build student ability to solve social problems by systematically teaching the problem-solving process and encouraging its use when solving a social issue.
  Social problem solving involves the use of process-based strategies to analyze, understand, and respond effectively to everyday problems and conflicts. Instruction in this area benefits children on the spectrum because they begin to understand what a social problem is, the process they should follow when such a problem occurs, and the strategies they could use to solve it.

Becoming Practices to Deliver Effective Instruction

Instructionally focused practices were regarded by teachers as core business. One teacher commented, "there are so many different parts of the curriculum, and so different things that you need to due to make sure the children are progressing, and that you are catering for their needs" (#5). Yet, in this area, the practice related to teaching self-help skills was most frequently implemented; "The self-help skills is what we're really sort of working on for our little boy now... he pretends he can't do it, and I know that he can, so I want him to be proactive with it" (#6). Practices related to assessing student knowledge and providing systematic instruction were the next most frequently used. For example, one teacher noted, "I'm noticing that more and more we're needing to adjust assessments in order to give children on the spectrum the opportunity to show what they understand" (#4); while another teacher commented, "my student [on the spectrum] can be quite wriggly during introductions for lessons, so I need to make sure I'm being very clear and direct with the message of what they're expected to learn, and required to do during the task" (#10).

- *Assess student knowledge*
  Teachers use a variety of assessment materials and strategies to learn what their students know and can do and use this information to inform their planning.
  Data from formal and informal assessments provide insight into the knowledge and skills of children on the spectrum. Teachers can use these data to personalize learning experiences and inform the delivery of targeted instruction. Adjusting the assessment task and using visual and concrete materials may enable a more accurate picture of what the child knows and can do.
- *Provide systematic instruction*
  Teachers provide systematic instruction in what students need to know and do.
  Systematic instruction supports the learning of children on the spectrum because they know what they are expected to learn; prior learning is drawn on; instruction is logical and sequenced; and instructional feedback is consistently provided. When using this approach, content is presented in achievable chunks starting from what the child already knows and can do.
- *Teach self-help skills*
  Teachers cultivate independence by teaching self-help skills and providing frequent opportunities for practice.
  Children on the spectrum start school with varying degrees of self-help skills, with some needing additional support and instruction to develop these skills. A skill can be taught systematically by breaking it into chunks, teaching each chunk, and then teaching the chunks together. The use of modeling and visual supports may facilitate learning.

Feelings of Knowledge and Confidence

During the final interview, over half of the participating teachers reported that using the EY-MoP material during the field test had enhanced both their knowledge and confidence in teaching their child on the spectrum. These reported comments were supported by survey data, which showed small, statistically significant increases in teachers' perceptions of their knowledge and confidence (Beamish et al., 2021).

An early career teacher said, "I think I've gained a fair bit of knowledge about, like, a lot of things that... I wasn't aware of. So, yeah, I feel like I've gained a lot" (#2). By comparison, a more experienced teacher commented, "I definitely gained confidence and assurance that what I was doing was on the right track, and the importance of it all. So, yeah, just overall… it showed me that what I was doing was time well spent" (#11). Finally, a teacher who actively used the EY-MoP stated:

> The model's definitely strengthened my own practice, and it's boosted my confidence in catering for the needs of students on the spectrum… It's definitely made me feel more confident as a team member in my setting as well, to share what I've learned, and to share my experience. (#20)

RECOMMENDATIONS FOR USE

Three key recommendations for using the EY-MoP arose from teacher feedback. First, teachers indicated that practices should be selected on the basis of child need (e.g., *prepare students for transitions* for a child who gets upset when moving from one activity to another). In some instances, a practice may be selected on the basis of teacher need (e.g., *provide systematic instruction* for a teacher who feels that the child on the spectrum frequently cannot tell her what he is meant to be doing). Second, teachers suggested that collaborative use of the resource was likely to enhance teaching and learning outcomes. For this reason, *inclusionED* (www.inclusioned.edu.au) encourages users to network and collaborate with others when implementing specific practices. Third, teachers recommended that the EY-MoP would be a valuable resource for preservice and beginning teachers. Their recommendations included: "this model I think would be really good for our graduate teachers" (#9); and "I just wish I had something like this when I started teaching" (#11).

CONCLUSION

The EY-MoP is a flexible resource that provides early years teachers with a frame for making pedagogical decisions when working with children on the autism spectrum. The foundational practices within the model enable teachers to be responsive to the complex needs of these children upon transition to school while building professional capacity to nurture social-emotional and early academic learning. This model of practice is not a "one-stop shop" for educating young school-age children on the autism spectrum, but it does frame the foundations for teaching them in the first few years of schooling.

ACKNOWLEDGMENTS

The authors thank schools, teachers, and university colleagues who partnered with us to make this research possible. The authors also appreciate the contributions made by the broader Autism CRC Project 2.037 team.

This research is supported by the Cooperative Research Center for Living with Autism (Autism CRC) under Project No. 2.037. The authors acknowledge the financial support of the Autism CRC, established and supported under the Australian Government's Cooperative Research Centers Program.

REFERENCES

Australian Bureau of Statistics [ABS]. (2018). *Disability, ageing and carers, Australia: Summary of findings, 2018 (No. 4430.0)*. https://www.abs.gov.au/ausstats/abs@.nsf/mf/4430.0

Beamish, W., Bryer, F., & Klieve, H. (2014). Transitioning children with autism to Australian schools: Social validation of important teacher practices. *International Journal of Special Education, 29*(1), 130–142.

Beamish, W., Macdonald, L., Hay, S., Taylor, A., Paynter, J., & Tucker, M. (2020). A model of practice for building teacher capacity in educating young school-age children on the autism spectrum: User perspectives. *International Journal of Disability, Development and Education,* 1–17. https://doi.org/10.1080/1034912x.2020.1774046

Beamish, W., Taylor, A., Macdonald, L., Hay, S., Tucker, M., & Paynter, J. (2021). Field testing a model of practice for teaching of young school-aged students on the autism spectrum. *Research in Developmental Disabilities, 113*, 1–12. https://doi.org/10.1016/j.ridd.2021.10394

Department of Education Employment and Workplace Relations for the Council of Australian Governments [DEEWR]. (2009). *Belonging, being & becoming: The early years learning framework for Australia*. Commonwealth of Australia.

Janzen, J. E. (2003). *Understanding the nature of autism: A guide to the autism spectrum disorders* (2nd ed.). Therapy Skill Builders.

McConkey, R. (2020). The rise in the numbers of pupils identified by schools with autism spectrum disorder (ASD): A comparison of the four countries in the United Kingdom. *Support for Learning, 35*(2), 132–143. https://doi.org/10.1111/1467-9604.12296

Ravet, J. (2018). 'But how do I teach them?': Autism & initial teacher education (ITE). *International Journal of Inclusive Education, 22*, 714–733. https://doi.org/10.1080/13603116.2017.1412505

Saggers, B., Tones, M., Dunne, J., Trembath, D., Bruck, S., Webster, A., Klug, D., & Wang, S. (2019). Promoting a collective voice from parents, educators and allied health professionals on the educational needs of students on the autism spectrum. *Journal of Autism and Developmental Disorders, 49*(9), 3845–3865. https://doi.org/10.1007/s10803-019-04097-8

Snyder, T. D., de Brey, C., & Dillow, S. A. (2016). *Digest of education statistics 2015 (NCES 2016-014)*. National Center for Education Statistics, Institute of Education Sciences & U.S. Department of Education.

Taylor, A., Beamish, W., Tucker, M., Paynter, J., & Walker, S. (2019). Designing a model of practice for Australian teachers of young school-age children on the autism spectrum. *Journal of International Special Needs Education*. Advance online publication. https://doi.org/10.9782/18-00017

THE EXPERIENCES OF FIRST GENERATION LEARNERS DURING TRANSITION FROM A GOVERNMENT SCHOOL TO A PRIVATE INCLUSIVE SCHOOL IN A TRIBAL REGION OF MAHARASHTRA, INDIA

Ratika Malkani and Richard Rose

ABSTRACT

This chapter reports a study of school provision for first generation learners in a tribal community in Maharashtra, India. The chapter considers how a group of children transferred from a government school provision of poor quality into a new and inclusive privately funded school with a more child centered approach. It examines issues relating both, to access and the quality of education available to meet the needs of first generation learners. The main aim of this study was to investigate educational opportunities and the challenges of this change in provision from the perspectives of children and their parents. This study provides unique insights into the needs of first generation learners by presenting their own voices as a means of articulating their experiences through a process of transition.

Keywords: First generation learners; India; scheduled tribes; inclusion; transition; student perspectives

Transition Programs for Children and Youth with Diverse Needs
International Perspectives on Inclusive Education, Volume 18, 37–52
Copyright © 2022 Ratika Malkani and Richard Rose
Published under exclusive licence by Emerald Publishing Limited
ISSN: 1479-3636/doi:10.1108/S1479-363620220000018004

INTRODUCTION

Context and Background

This chapter reports research conducted into the experiences of a group of first generation learners during transition from a government school to a well-resourced private school in a tribal region of Maharashtra State, India. The research considered issues of access and the quality of education provided to students from an economically disadvantaged rural community and the impact of change, through the development of new educational opportunities. This study used qualitative research methods including semi-structured interviews and observations to investigate the experiences of 10 children, and to identify processes and structures that support or hinder the students from achieving their educational goals. The research recognized the complex nature of the circumstances and responsibilities the children have toward their families and how these influence and impact on their learning and progression through their school years.

The research study gathered generic data to identify good practice and areas needing improvement to help students successfully complete statutory schooling. Finally, using capability approach theory as a normative framework for the study, it allowed researchers to gain insight into the effectiveness of the support structures set up for students as they progressed through their schooling such as provision of a relevant and varied curriculum, counseling for students, the positive attitude of teachers working with these children, and support for parents to understand and navigate the school system. The study interrogated approaches to promoting education for all—in particular, the methods adopted to meet the needs of first generation learners. The application of Sen's capability approach used in an educational setting enabled the researchers to look beyond the economic value of education and simplistic interpretation of school attendance as a human right (Unterhalter & Brighouse, 2007). The main purpose of the research reported was to investigate educational opportunities and the influence of socioeconomic factors and change following transition from a state government school to a well-resourced private school from the perspectives of children and their parents.

In common with many Asian countries, the Government of India, as a signatory to international agreements (United Nations Educational, Scientific and Cultural Organisation, 1994, 2000, 2015), has developed a national education policy, which aims to promote a more equitable and inclusive approach to education (Ministry of Human Resource Development, 2009). Over the past 50 years, a range of initiatives aimed at addressing the needs of learners from disadvantaged and marginalized communities have been adopted, including the Integrated Education of Disabled Children (IEDC) (Ministry of Welfare, 1974), and the Project for Integrated Education for the Disabled (PIED) (Ministry of Human Resource Development, 1987). However, with the passing of the Right of Children to Free and Compulsory Education Act (RTE) (Ministry of Human Resource Development, 2009) a clear intention to identify disadvantaged groups that have often been excluded from mainstream education provision, can be seen to have influenced the most significant legislation in respect of promoting inclusive education to date. The RTE defines "compulsory education" as an obligation of government to ensure attendance and completion of elementary education to every child in the 6–14 years age group.

Acknowledging that many children in India continue to have difficulties accessing quality education, the RTE Act identifies disadvantaged groups including those from scheduled castes, scheduled tribes, socially and education-ally backward classes, or those placed at disadvantage as a result of social, cul-tural, economic, geographical, linguistic, gender, or other factors, as being in need of increased support and attention (Ministry of Human Resource Devel-opment, 2009, p. 2). Because of this legislation, a number of initiatives introduced by both State Governments and private enterprise have been implemented in order to achieve the objectives of increased educational opportunities for all learners. These initiatives include the introduction of a quota system whereby a mandatory provision to provide 25% reservation of school places for disadvan-taged children in private schools has been introduced.

The imposition of a quota has been highly controversial and was challenged in the Supreme Court by representatives of the private school sector (Dutta & Khan, 2016). The opponents of the quota argued that they had established a market-based right to education founded on priorities associated with academic learning outcomes, parental choice, and school autonomy and that government interference and the imposition of a quota was likely to erode the rights of parents who had chosen to send their children to fee paying schools (Gorur & Arnold, 2020). The objections were overruled and therefore the obligation of private schools to accept children from disadvantaged communities has been upheld. However, this section of the RTE remains contentious. Juneja (2014) suggests that education in India has been characterized by long held customs of social stratification and that traditions of privilege based upon a caste system have been jealously guarded by a privileged elite. As a result of this long-established form of discrimination, it has inevitably been difficult to implement the requirements of the RTE without significant opposition. The deployment of complex admissions procedures and the segregation of disadvantaged children from their peers once enrolled (Choudhary, 2014; Juneja, 2014) have resulted in many children being unable to gain their entitlement to schooling. Gorur and Arnold (2020) describe a significant discrepancy between the expectations of national government and the state-level implementation of the requirements of the RTE Act, which has "damaged efforts to organise the rights-based social world and given ammunition to opponents of the RTE Act to argue against its implementation" (p. 11).

There are instances in which the management of private schools have made significant efforts to ensure that previously marginalized children are provided with appropriate access and learning opportunities, though inclusion remains a largely ill-defined concept in the Indian education system (Rose et al., 2014). This chapter describes the findings from research into one such initiative led by private enterprise within a remote rural community by exploring the experiences of the young people and their families most closely affected by this system.

LOCATING THE RESEARCH

The study discussed in this chapter was conducted in Maharashtra State, which is located in the western peninsular region of the country and is the second-most populous state, and third-largest state by area in India. Research was conducted with a purposive sample from a tribal community within Maharashtra where the local language is Marathi (one of the authors is fluent in this language). The families within the sample are described officially as belonging to scheduled caste and scheduled tribes with an average family income below $3.50 per day, which officially classified them as living below the poverty line. The adults who participated in the research worked as daily wage laborers, their income coming from construction work, fishing, or food gathering from adjoining forests. The majority were not literate but had completed four years of primary schooling. Less than 10% of adults in the area had completed Secondary schooling.

Data were collected during field work from an NGO run school for rural children in an area about a 100 kilometers from the closest city in Maharashtra state. This school was built by a construction company, which was developing a new holiday town in this rural belt. This construction project has been controversial, with concerns about procurement of land from tribal farmers who had been granted it by the Indian State. Additional concerns have been expressed over potential harm to the environment by deforestation and quarrying in a UNESCO World Heritage Site known for its evergreen tropical forests. In response to negative publicity surrounding these issues, the construction company as a part of its corporate social responsibility strategy, provided funding to an international charitable organization to start a school in the area for the children whose families had been displaced from their homes to clear the area for development of the holiday village. The NGO that manages the school has a philosophy of providing education to underprivileged children and has schools in several parts of India and in other countries. They have adopted a holistic approach to supporting children, which in addition to providing education ensures the social welfare of children through the provision of meals and health care.

The students who were enrolled in this school lived in the local villages and had previously had access to education through a local Zilla Parishad (state government) school. At the time of the fieldwork undertaken for this research, there were approximately 100 pupils on roll at the newly built private school, all of whom had made a transition from the state funded school. A staff of eight well-qualified teachers and a number of specialists who provided lessons in music, physical education and art, and support for pupils with special educational needs had been appointed to the school, which follows the Maharashtra State Board examination syllabus and its associated curriculum. Some members of the local community who had their children enrolled at the school were deployed to provide additional classroom support.

METHODS

Research Design

The study used qualitative research methods within an ethnographic framework, including semi-structured interviews and non-participant observations to investigate the experiences of 10 children aged 10–14 years. The participants all of whom were currently enrolled in the non-government organization (NGO) run school, had transferred from the Zilla Parishad School two years earlier. A set of individual case studies based upon the experiences that were being investigated were developed and enabled comparisons to be made in respect of the individual experiences of students. The research focused on contextual factors related to the differences of provision made in the Zilla Parishad and NGO schools, and the perceptions and attitudes of students and families toward education through data collected from first generation learners, their teachers and their parents. This enabled the researchers to construct narrative case studies (Elliott, 2005) to understand the experiences of individuals in this period of critical change in their lives. In order to observe and study the children in their natural setting, it was decided to approach this set of individual case studies ethnographically (Le Compte & Boulder, 2010). As a result of its remote location, spending extensive periods of time in the community being studied was not feasible therefore, an ethnographic approach based upon short term field visits rather than ethnography in its truest sense was used in this research (Dennis & Huf, 2020).

Data Collection Procedures

Semi-structured interviews were designed for use with three sample groups, these being students, parents, and teachers. Questions were designed to avoid jargon and be easily understood, starting with questions about the present educational situation and moving on to others related to past experiences and aspirations for the future. Factual questions were interspersed with those seeking opinions throughout the interviews. All interviews were conducted in Marathi the local language of the community, though some respondents also spoke Hindi (see Table 1).

To facilitate discussions by students about the challenges and opportunities the school offers them, a fictitious situation often experienced by first-generation learners was presented as a focus for discussion (Wadhwa, 2018). This included the use of picture cards depicting scenes of everyday life relevant to their situation as the basis for discussing how education might influence change in their lives (Dreze & Sen, 1997). The students were asked to discuss this scenario with the help of related questions.

Parent interviews were also facilitated by first presenting situations often experienced by first generation learners. Literacy levels among adults in the community were very low, and it was therefore important to adopt interview procedures that drew upon their experiences in a respectful and supportive manner (Malkani & Rose, 2018). Discussion of the presented scenario was followed by a series of related questions planned to gain insights into their

Table 1. Interviews Conducted.

Student	Gender	Interview Time	Language
A	F	35 Minutes × 2 Days	Marathi/Hindi
B	M	48 Minutes × 2 Days	Marathi/Hindi
C	F	40 Minutes × 2 Days	Marathi/Hindi
D	F	32 Minutes × 2 Days	Marathi/Hindi
E	M	45 Minutes × 2 Days	Marathi/Hindi
F	F	40 Minutes × 2 Days	Marathi/Hindi
G	M	30 Minutes × 2 Days	Marathi/Hindi
H	M	28 Minutes × 2 Days	Marathi/Hindi
I	M	37 Minutes × 2 Days	Marathi/Hindi
J	F	42 Minutes × 2 Days	Marathi/Hindi
K	M	15 Minutes	Marathi/Hindi
L	M	10 Minutes	Marathi/Hindi
M	F	10 Minutes	Marathi/Hindi
N	F	12 Minutes	Marathi/Hindi
O	M	15 Minutes	Marathi/Hindi

Parent	Gender	Interview Time	Language
A	M	20 Minutes	Marathi
B	M	15 Minutes	Marathi
C	F	35 Minutes	Marathi
D	M	18 Minutes	Marathi
E	F	25 Minutes	Marathi
F	F	32 Minutes	Marathi
G	M	22 Minutes	Marathi
H	M	17 Minutes	Marathi
I	F	40 Minutes	Marathi
J	F	37 Minutes	Marathi
K	F	20 Minutes	Marathi
L	M	17 Minutes	Marathi
M	F	25 Minutes	Marathi
N	M	12 Minutes	Marathi
O	M	15 Minutes	Marathi

interpretation of the experiences of their children, and their aspirations for the future. This method was chosen because at times direct questions about issues in their own lives could have been difficult or embarrassing for them to discuss. This is a population that has often been discriminated against and may feel threatened by the presence of outsiders. The interviews were conducted in an informal and conversational manner in an effort to build a bond of trust, enabling them to be more comfortable when engaged in conversation.

Class teachers were interviewed to gain insights into how students were responding to the education being provided and to understand any adjustments that had been necessary to build student confidence and ensure their progress through the school curriculum.

OBSERVATIONS

Each of the sample students was observed in three contexts; these being

(1) where students were free to choose both their activities and their companion (e.g. playground);
(2) where large groups of students were relatively free to mingle within broad categories (e.g. assembly, lunch settings, communal setting);
(3) where small groups of children were in closeness, proximity (notably in classrooms, art and music lessons).

In addition, observations were conducted in student home settings to collect additional data, which would enable a better understanding of their life outside of school. Observations were managed as unobtrusively as possible, noting verbatim speech where appropriate and recording some key words/phrases that assisted with the analysis and interpretation of data collected.

Contextual Data

Documents from the NGO school regarding their policy on inclusion, individual education plans or extra help/tuition records, teaching and learning policies, attendance register, and health records were collected. The village government office and the Gram Panchayat (a Gram Panchayat is a system of local government with an elected administrator or Sarpanch as its elected head) was also visited to collect information about the social situation of the community with regards to the available government aid for education and health, and the economic condition of students and their families.

The contextual information along with information provided by families and the school enabled a profile for each student to be constructed. These profiles contained information about their family background and previous educational experiences, thereby facilitating a greater understanding of the choices they make regarding their education.

Ethical Issues

All ethical issues received due consideration and approval from a university ethics committee. Informed consent for conducting interviews and securing discussions with the children, parents, and other participants was obtained after information regarding the purpose of the research was provided to all parties. For parents who experienced literacy challenges information was read and verbal consent recorded. Anonymity of all participants was assured.

On completion of data collection through interview or observation this was discussed with the participants to avoid any misinterpretations. This gave them an opportunity to delete or change statements they felt that may have been misinterpreted or misunderstood. All interviews were transcribed, segmented, and subjected to thematic coding by the researchers, and a process of blind coding of a sample of transcripts was deployed to ensure trustworthiness of the data.

FINDINGS: EXPERIENCES, AMBITION, AND ATTITUDES

Important issues emerged from the interview data and were verified through observations. In particular, the students were eager to praise the provision being made for them in the new school, while bemoaning the lack of quality in their earlier educational experiences. It was evident that these students perceived their new educational status as affording opportunities that were still denied to their peers attending the state school, and that this had influenced both their ambitions and their attitudes.

Students during interview were keen to discuss their earlier experiences of education at the Zilla-Parishad school. Their views were often negative in respect of the quality of teaching and the general support provided. In some instances, the lack of encouragement to enjoy learning and the expectations of teachers was seen to have discouraged students from participation in education, as was apparent in these comments given in interviews.

> If there is someone who can help you study when you don't understand it makes it easier. At the Zilla Parishad School very often I would feel like shutting the book and not opening it again because it was so tough.

> At times, I felt like closing my book and not looking at it because it was so difficult.

> Because my sister failed (sic.) she now stays at home to help my mother because my father said it's no use going to school if you can't pass (Her sister was 14 when she dropped out of school).

Teacher attitudes were perceived by many students to be a major obstacle to learning and some reported the use of corporal punishment as a means of chastising under performance in class. Corporal punishment is illegal in Indian schools, but there is evidence to suggest that its use remains widespread (Ghosh & Pasupathi, 2016; Tiwari, 2019).

> I didn't like school because teacher got upset with me when I could not understand numbers. He even hit me if I did badly in the test.

> I left the Zilla Parishad school because I could not understand the lessons teacher taught and made mistakes when I had to do school work. If I did something wrong the teacher used to get angry and hit me.

Teacher absenteeism in government schools has been reported as a particular problem in rural areas of India (Duflo et al., 2012; Mooij & Narayan, 2010). The students interviewed recognized the impact of this behavior on their own learning opportunities and also commented on the injustice that they perceived to exist when double standards were applied in schools.

At the Zilla Parishad School my teacher used to get upset if I stayed absent from school, even though he did not come to school every day. We ended up playing with friends in school two or three times a week.

Last week my sister's teacher was not there for three days.

The students were eager to contrast their experiences in the NGO school with those experienced in the state system, and the impact that their changing situation had upon their lives. They reflected upon the positive attitudes of teachers and the welcome that they felt within a different school environment.

At this school teachers don't get upset if we don't do work at home. All they want is for us to come to school.

This is the only place where I can laugh.

Students felt confident that the teachers in the school would enable them to succeed and provide additional support when it was needed. Teachers were ambitious for their students who recognized increased opportunities to better their lives.

When I think that I might have to leave school, I get upset because I want to go to a university in the city to learn to be a teacher.

In addition to recognizing the support afforded by teachers at their new school, the students sometimes acknowledged a renewed respect for education on the part of parents.

My dad is pleased that I am so good at doing calculations. That is why I can do accounts for him and no one can deceive him.

This increased enthusiasm from parents was acknowledged by one mother who in talking about her daughter stated:

I don't want my daughter to get married early and do housework. I want her to study and be like Madam (the teacher at the school).

The children themselves recognized when their parents had positive attitudes toward the new educational opportunities that were being provided:

My siblings and I have to study hard or my father gets upset. He wants us to be better than him and to be able to read and write. He knows how essential it is to be literate.

Children perceived school to be an important social venue as well as providing academic opportunities.

I like to play in school because after I get home I have to do work and I never get to play.

When we go to school in the morning we are very hungry because most nights we don't have dinner. We really look forward to our breakfast and lunch, they give us as much as we ask for and the food in school is tasty.

I can't wait to come back to school after holidays because I love the food they give us.

Observations of children's lives outside of school confirmed the importance of the social interactions afforded within the school environment. On returning home, children were seen to have been allocated specific duties and tasks, such as caring for cattle or fetching water, which needed to be completed before they could contemplate further study or homework. The NGO school recognized the high level of commitment that students had to domestic work and made allowances for this when they struggled to deliver homework on time. While encouraging the students to study hard they acknowledged the need to balance the pressures from school with those associated with family responsibilities. The time for socialization and play was limited. The activities in which the students observed were engaged were clearly delineated, with boys expected to herd and feed cattle, collect firewood, and shop for food supplies, whereas the girls were mainly involved in preparing and cooking meals, washing utensils, and caring for younger siblings.

Parents were reticent in discussing the tasks allocated to their children on return from school and in some instances, it was apparent that parental aspirations in respect of education were limited. The children themselves recognized the dilemma faced by their parents. As one boy stated:

> I can earn up to Rs. 50 per day when I go and help my mother to sell fish at the evening market, which is a big help... I am the only son and I have a big responsibility to care for my family.

While acknowledging this situation and clearly understanding that his parent's perspective was based upon the traditional harsh realities of life in this community, he himself could perceive of a different way of supporting his family and suggested that:

> When I become an artist, I want to sell my art at exhibitions for a lot of money. I can use this to help my mother.

Education had provided this child with insights into a life that was very different from that of his parents and aspirations that were difficult for them to understand.

Many children attending the NGO school were clear about the impact it had upon their future potential for a life different from that experienced by their parents. They recognized that their opportunities had been increased and their horizons broadened by the experiences they were being given. The school regularly discusses the importance of continuing education beyond statutory school leaving age and encourages students to consider applying for places in further or higher education. This process has led to increased ambition on the part of many students as was the case of a boy who when asked about the future stated that he was going to be an astronaut in India's space program. When asked if he had an alternative career in mind he said,

> No, I have not, because I know I am going to be an astronaut.

While it is impossible to know whether this ambition might become a reality, it was apparent that the NGO school had instilled ambition and self-confidence in its students and given them a belief that if they worked hard at their education they could achieve their dreams.

The level of ambition was equally strong in girls who recognized that the priority given to the education of girls in India was often less than that afforded to boys (Jain et al., 2017; Nakray, 2017). Anxiety about the possibility of having to follow a traditional route of leaving school before completion of education and early marriage was apparent in some. As shown above when one girl indicated:

When I think that I might have to leave school I get upset, because I want to go to a university in the city and learn to be a teacher. That is why I come to school regularly.

While the students attending the NGO school had developed positive attitudes toward their own learning and their potential for life enhancement, there were aspects of their attitudes that were less positive. In some instances, they had developed attitudes of superiority over those who continued to either attend the Zilla Parishad School, or who had left school early. This at times led to tensions and was evident in the abusive and discriminatory language adopted by some of the NGO school students. For example, when one of the authors of this paper was observed in conversation with a student from the Zilla Parishad School she was told.

Don't talk to them, they don't know how to talk properly. They are like "junglies" (people who live in the jungle).

There were clear indications that these students felt in many ways superior to their peers, even when these were members of their own family. It is too soon within this educational experiment to gauge how these attitudes might impact on the future development of this community, or to see whether the school's ability to address prejudicial attitudes will prevail.

DISCUSSION
Quality of Education Provided

Within the Indian education system there is often a significant disparity between the quality of education provided in government and private sector schools (Bedi, 2018; Mander, 2015). This situation has emerged in part through a market driven approach to education in India, in which the emergence of a burgeoning population of middle class Indians have taken advantage of opportunities to pay for their children to attend what they perceive to be elite schools (Kingdon, 2020; Singh Gill, 2017). While efforts have been made through recent legislation to increase opportunities for those from discriminated and marginalized groups in India, the successes achieved toward creating a more equitable education system have been limited (Kumari, 2016; Srivastava & Noronha, 2016).

The data collected in this study from rural Maharashtra indicates that there are several reasons for the difficulties in creating a more inclusive and equitable education system. Not least of these is the long-established policy of dependence upon government schools that are inadequately resourced and often staffed by poorly qualified teachers (Mukherjee et al., 2016). The prospects of teaching in a poor rural environment with few of the material benefits available in cities or even relatively small urban environments does little to attract many of the best qualified teachers in the country.

The NGO school at the focus of this study was built partly as an act of community benevolence, but also to fulfill the need of a corporate organization to ensure a welcome in the district and to recruit a complicit workforce. The financial strengths of the corporation were important in enabling this school to provide a high-quality education to a proportion of the population. By ensuring that the school was well resourced it was possible to recruit well qualified and motivated teachers who were committed to improving the educational opportunities available to their students. The data collected clearly demonstrates that having well motivated and professionally qualified teachers impacts the whole community by.

Aspirations

In many agricultural communities in rural India, such as that discussed in this chapter, employment opportunities have been limited (Nair, 2014). Migration from rural communities to find employment in metropolitan cities has become a feature of the recent Indian landscape (Deshingkar, 2010; Mander & Sahgal, 2010). Increased mechanization and technology has changed the face of rural employment significantly and in recognition of this change many young people aspire to work in urban environments and in professions that were beyond the possibilities of their parents (Brown et al., 2017). The NGO school in this study has succeeded in raising the aspirations of its students, with many believing that their future will see them in well paid professional employment away from their current villages.

Whereas student commitment to attendance at the Zilla Parishad school was inconsistent, in the NGO school it was high. Students recognized that education can be a transformative process in their lives and they made clear their intentions to take advantage of this situation. This change of perception in respect of the possibilities afforded through education was similarly recognized by parents, including those who had limited experience of schooling and low levels of literacy.

It is too early to judge how many of the students interviewed for this research will achieve their stated ambitions. However, aspiration is an important factor in learning motivation, and it was apparent that those young people in this community who attended the NGO school had much higher aspirations than their peers at the Zilla Parishad school.

Relationships

Relationships are important in education. The students who participated in this research were positive about their relationships with their teachers in the NGO school, but often had a negative perception of those in the government school. There was a general belief on the part of students that the teachers in the NGO school respected them and wanted them to do well. Unlike in the Zilla Perishad school where poor academic performance was addressed through punitive measures, the NGO school provided structured support that students recognized as enabling them to improve their academic attainment. Another important factor was the teachers' understanding of family pressures, including those associated with domestic responsibilities, that impacted upon student approaches to their school work. High levels of empathy were in evidence and can be seen to have contributed significantly to the success of this innovation.

The relationship between the NGO school and parents was also important. In some instances, the school had provided parents with employment opportunities. Parents have been encouraged to attend the school to discuss their children's learning and to engage with social activities and school events. Some parents reported difficulties with participation at this level, feeling intimidated by a system of which they had limited personal experience or understanding. However, the school saw this as an important part of their mission and worked hard to build confidence in the parents and enabled them to participate at a level with which they felt most comfortable.

The impact of the NGO school on relationships between youth in the community is more nuanced. Evidence from the data suggests that students who were being given greater opportunities had in some instances developed negative attitudes toward their peers who remained in the Zilla Parishad school. With increased aspiration has come a belief that receiving a good quality education creates opportunities for social mobility and that this in some ways makes students superior to their peers. The impact of educational opportunity upon aspiration in India has been well documented (Morrow, 2013; Nathan, 2005; Ross, 2019), but less attention has been given to the potentially divisive situation in which some members of a family are provided with increased opportunity while others are not. This would appear to us as an obvious area in need of further research.

Sustainability

In any innovative development program, it is important to consider the potential for sustainability of the measures adopted. The motivations of the funders of this school were partly related to the need to acquire land and to employ local laborers for a private enterprise. The NGO that runs the school has experience of successful management of schools in similar contexts, which provides some confidence regarding the long-term future of the provision. The school is still in its early stages of development and its sustainability may well be influenced by the outcomes achieved for students. Previous research from India suggests that students in privately funded education significantly outperform those in the government run schools, making them a much more attractive proposition for parents (Singh & Sarkar, 2015). However, in rural areas such as that discussed in this chapter, parental choice is limited because of the poverty in which most families live, and even those who would desire a better education for their children have little control over the options open to them. In its current situation the school has been able to maintain a team of highly committed teachers and other staff. Teachers are well paid compared to most working in Indian rural communities, though retention in rural schools often presents a challenge in these districts that lack the facilities and opportunities afforded by metropolitan cities and may thus prove less attractive to many professionals (Chauhan, 2009).

CONCLUSION

The provision of a well-resourced school staffed by committed professionals has raised the aspirations and achievements of those students who have been enabled to enroll. Ultimately it seems likely that the life opportunities for these students will be considerably enhanced, especially when compared to the life chances of their peers who attend local Zilla Parishad schools. For a proportion of the children in the study area, inclusion in high quality schooling has become a reality. However, concerns must be expressed for the potential of this project to increase the gap between those who gain the social and economic advantages that come from improved education and those who do not have such opportunities. In the longer term, it will also be interesting to see whether those who gain a good education move away from the area thus denuding the community of a young population that would normally make a significant contribution to the local economy.

The model of provision here is one among many that are emerging with the intention of developing a more inclusive education system in India. This chapter has reported research which benefited from the presence of a researcher who was familiar with the language and the culture of the environment in which the investigation was conducted. As a small-scale study, its findings cannot be generalized but do contribute to an appreciation of how innovation can bring successful transition from a school that offers limited opportunities to an environment in which learners are encouraged and respected and expected to achieve well. The need for further research into the impact of such innovations is clear and should provide greater understanding of the approaches that are proving beneficial to previously disadvantaged learners, their families and communities. Such studies will need to have a longitudinal element to gauge the efficacy of projects that are at an early stage of development.

REFERENCES

Bedi, J. S. (2018). State of Punjab education: Analysis based on DISE data. In J. S. Bedi (Ed.), *Policy impacts on qualitative and quantitative aspects of Indian education. India studies in business and economics*. Springer.

Brown, T., Scrase, T., & Ganguly-Scrase, R. (2017). Globalised dreams, local constraints: Migration and youth aspirations in an Indian regional town. *Children's Geographies, 15*(5), 531–544.

Chauhan, C. P. S. (2009). Education for all in India: A second look. *International Journal of Lifelong Education, 28*(2), 227–240.

Choudhary, S. (2014). Right to education act 2009: Letting disadvantaged children down? *International Research Journal of Social Sciences, 3*(8), 1–7.

Dennis, B., & Huf, C. (2020). Ethnographic research in childhood institutions: Participations and entanglements. *Ethnography and Education.* https://doi.org/10.1080/17457823.2020.1722951. Accessed on June 20, 2020.

Deshingkar, P. (2010). *Migration, remote rural areas and chronic poverty in India.* ODI Working Paper 323/CPRC Working Paper 163. Chronic Poverty Research Centre.

Dreze, J., & Sen, A. (1997). *Indian development: Selected regional perspectives.* Oxford University Press.

Duflo, E., Hanna, R., & Ryan, S. (2012). Incentives work: Getting teachers to come to school. *American Economic Review, 102*(4), 1241–1278.

Dutta, I., & Khan, M. A. (2016). Educational and social inclusion of children admitted under RTE quota: A survey of private schools of Bhopal. *MIER Journal of Educational Studies, Trends and Practices, 6*(2), 138–154.

Elliott, J. (2005). *Using narrative in social research.* Sage.

Ghosh, A., & Pasupathi, M. (2016). Perceptions of students and parents on the use of corporal punishment at schools in India. *Rupkatha Journal on Interdisciplinary Studies in Humanities, 8*(3), 269–280.

Gorur, R., & Arnold, B. (2020). Regulating private sector schooling in the global south: The case of India. *Compare: A Journal of Comparative and International Education.* Published on line 22nd May. https://doi.org/10.1080/03057925.2020.1766947

Jain, P., Agarwal, R., Billaiya, R., & Devi, J. (2017). Women's education in rural India. *International Journal of Social Sciences and Humanities, 1*(1), 21–26.

Juneja, N. (2014). India's new mandate against economic apartheid in schools. *Journal of International Cooperation in Education, 16*(2), 55–70.

Kingdon, G. G. (2020). The private schooling phenomenon in India: A review. *The Journal of Development Studies.* https://doi.org/10.1080/00220388.2020.1715943

Kumari, J. (2016). Public–private partnerships in education: An analysis with special reference to Indian school education system. *International Journal of Educational Development, 47*(March), 47–53.

Le Compte, M. D., & Boulder, J. J. (2010). *Designing and conducting ethnographic research: An introduction.* Rowman and Littlefield.

Malkani, R. (2017). *Investigating the educational opportunities provided for first generation learners in rural Maharashtra, India.* PhD thesis, University of Northampton.

Malkani, R., & Rose, R. (2018). Learning from the voices of first generation learners in a remote community of Maharashtra, India. *International Journal of Whole Schooling, 14*(2), 104–127.

Mander, H. (2015). *Looking away.* Speaking Tiger.

Mander, H., & Sahgal, G. (2010). *Internal migration in India: Distress and opportunities, a study of internal migrants to vulnerable occupations in Delhi.* Centre for Equity Studies.

Ministry of Human Resource Development. (1987). *Project for integrated education for the disabled [PIED].* Government of India.

Ministry of Human Resource Development. (2009). *Right of children to free and compulsory education act [RTE].* Government of India.

Ministry of Welfare. (1974). *Integrated education of disabled children [IEDC].* Government of India.

Mooij, J. E., & Narayan, K. (2010). Solutions to teacher absenteeism in rural government primary schools in India: A comparison of management approaches. *The Open Education Journal, 3,* 63–71. http://hdl.handle.net/1765/20502. Accessed on June 22, 2020.

Morrow, V. (2013). Whose values? Young people's aspirations and experiences of schooling in Andhra Pradesh, India. *Children and Society, 27*(4), 258–269.

Mukherjee, A., Goe, R., & Middendorf, G. (2016). The efficacy of public education as a means of social mobility for the indigenous tribal populations of rural India. *Journal of Land and Rural Studies, 4*(2), 225–241.

Nair, I. (2014). Challenges of rural development and opportunities for providing sustainable livelihood. *International Journal of Research in Applied, Natural and Social Sciences, 2*(5), 111–118.

Nakray, K. (2017). Gender and education policy in India: Twists, turns and trims of transnational policy transfers. *International Sociology, 33*(1), 27–44.

Nathan, D. (2005). Capabilities and aspirations. *Economic and Political Weekly, 40*(1), 36–40.

Rose, R., Doveston, M., Rajanahally, J., & Jament, J. (2014). What is effective inclusion? Interpreting and evaluating a western concept in an Indian context. In C. Forlin & T. Loreman (Eds.), *Measuring inclusive education*. Emerald.

Ross, P. (2019). Occupation aspirations, education investment, and cognitive outcomes: Evidence from Indian adolescents. *World Development, 123*. https://doi.org/10.1016/j.worlddev.2019.104613. Accessed on June 2, 2020.

Singh Gill, A. (2017). State, market and social inequalities: A study of primary education in the Indian Punjab. *Millennial Asia, 8*(2), 194–216.

Singh, R., & Sarkar, S. (2015). Does teaching quality matter? Students learning outcome related to teaching quality in public and private primary schools in India. *International Journal of Educational Development, 41*, 153–163.

Srivastava, P., & Noronha, C. (2016). The myth of free and barrier-free access: India's right to education act–private schooling costs and household experiences. *Oxford Review of Education, 42*(5), 561–578.

Tiwari, A. (2019). The corporal punishment ban in schools: Teachers' attitudes and classroom practices. *Educational Studies, 45*(3), 271–284.

UNESCO. (1994). *The Salamanca statement and framework for action on special needs education.* UNESCO.

UNESCO. (2000). *The dakar framework for action, education for all. Meeting our collective commitments.* UNESCO.

UNESCO. (2015). *Education 2030: The Incheon declaration and framework for action for the implementation of sustainable development goal 4.* UNESCO.

Unterhalter, E., & Brighouse, H. (2007). Distribution of what for social justice in education? The case of education for all by 2015. In A. Sen (Ed.), *Capability approach and social justice in education* (pp. 67–86). Palgrave.

Wadhwa, R. (2018). Unequal origin, unequal treatment, and unequal educational attainment: Does being first generation still a disadvantage in India? *Higher Education, 76*(2), 279–300.

SECTION 2

TRANSITIONS TO AND THROUGH SCHOOLING FOR SECONDARY

A JOURNEY TO BELONGING: TRANSITIONING THROUGH SCHOOL WITH AUTISM

Annetta Galer

ABSTRACT

This chapter provides an insight into how one family managed the challenges their son faced going through school. Identified with Autism at aged six years, Ben has experienced a range of transitions throughout his school life in inclusive classrooms and programs. One of the most challenging was the transition from primary into secondary school. Now in his final year of secondary schooling, the chapter explores Ben's educational experiences, family reflections on schooling, and post school opportunities.

Keywords: Autism; transitions; early intervention; inclusive schooling; post school transition; peer relationships

INTRODUCTION

We are a family of six, currently living on the Gold Coast in Queensland. We have also resided in North Queensland and Toowoomba, which is more inland. I have four children – a daughter who is in her third year of an education degree; a son, Ben, who has Autism, and is in grade 12; another son in grade eight; and a son in grade six in primary school.[1] My husband is a secondary teacher and he and our children are all at the same school. I am currently working as a supply teacher while I complete a master's degree.

Our family has faced a number of transitions with moving between cities and schools. But for Ben, transitions have also included transitioning across various school levels – into and between Kindy, into formal schooling, from primary to high school – and transitions between different teachers. Ben is now in his final

Transition Programs for Children and Youth with Diverse Needs
International Perspectives on Inclusive Education, Volume 18, 55–62
Copyright © 2022 Annetta Galer
Published under exclusive licence by Emerald Publishing Limited
ISSN: 1479-3636/doi:10.1108/S1479-363620220000018005

year of schooling and looking forward to another transition, out of school into the big wide world. He has, for the most part, coped well and taken change in his stride. As I reflect on Ben's schooling, a number of situations and components that have shaped the transitions he has experienced come to mind.

BEN'S EARLY YEARS

Throughout Ben's early years it just seemed as if a number of things were amiss. These centered mostly around communication, language, peer relationships, and play. For example, when I took him to playgroups, I often felt like a Jack-in-the-box as I would be up and down, sorting out what he was getting into. That's when I started thinking that he might not be developmentally where his peers were. He often seemed more demanding, and if he wasn't getting along with friends, I would have to step in to intervene. He was a very active boy. If he was climbing a tree, he would try to climb to the top. But he would also play with things differently from how they were typically used, such as the swings at the park. He preferred running to the boundaries of parks.

Probably his communication and speech were the biggest reasons for me to seek help for him initially, because I knew language difficulties could potentially hold him back. When he was a couple of years old and should have been saying his first words, he was very delayed. When he first started talking, he struggled with speech. His vocabulary was also limited. I learnt some baby sign language and taught him simple things like eat and drink and more and thank you. That seemed to help communication and reduce frustration. As Ben grew older his friends also had difficulty understanding him, and he seemed frustrated with talking to anyone in general, which could have been a reason why he didn't try and talk much at all. He ended up grunting.

When he was about three or four, I sought out specialists to determine what was going on. Though I worked in disability at the time, I didn't know much about Autism. I went to the community health center to a pediatrician, occupational therapist, and child psychologist for assessment. I would say things like, he avoids eye contact and is just in his own little world most of the time, and finds it hard to get along with peers his own age. The pediatrician didn't seem to click onto Autism, but she referred me to a speech therapist. This turned out to be most useful because it addressed Ben's speech issues. Even now at age 17, his speech is not always the clearest, but at least everyone can understand him.

Kindy

When Ben started Kindy a few days a week, he had an excellent teacher. She was also the first person who vocalized the word Autism to me. I took Ben to a pediatrician, and though the doctor told me that he could detect "autistic tendencies," he was reluctant to diagnose Ben as he thought he might "grow out of" these behaviors. Ben, therefore, was not officially diagnosed until almost two years later. This resulted in him missing opportunities for early intervention that might have been helpful in his transition to Kindy. During Kindy, I often left the classroom in tears, because I was so regularly informed about what Ben had done that day that was bad or wrong. In hindsight, due to the lack of assessment and information, the interventions that might have been most helpful to Ben at that time were unavailable.

SCHOOL TRANSITIONS

Primary Schooling

Ben's school experiences have been strongly shaped by his teachers and the support services that he has received. He has attended two regular private schools in Queensland; the first for prep and grades one and two, and the one he is currently at since grade three. He received some support in his first school as they had a learning support unit. The head of learning support was very proactive and got Ben support aids such as cushions for him to sit on to help him self-regulate and keep attention, and ear plugs when he had to go to Chapel as he found the music too loud and would often put his hands over his ears to try to block out the noise. In addition, his prep teacher was very accommodating and when she noticed he was not coping, she would send him over to a quiet area in the reading corner. The following year, grade one, the teacher utilized fewer intervention strategies and seemed somewhat stressed by having Ben in her class.

When we moved, I was nervous about Ben transitioning into a larger school and having team teachers for grade three. But they were most supportive of him and though there were some challenges, he coped quite well. Ben was assigned a teacher to help him on school camps too.

Secondary Schooling

Transitioning from primary school to high school was probably the biggest transition for Ben. Suddenly there were so many more teachers, classes, and students. Ben found this overwhelming at times, especially sensory-wise with a lot more noise going to and fro, and large events like assemblies and chapels at school. He has coped better as he has gotten older and become more verbal, which also allows us more insight into what he is thinking and feeling.

The high school has a learning support unit, and they made the first contact with me to set up a meeting when Ben transitioned between primary to high school. For the first year in high school, they set up a new individual education plan (IEP) for Ben, which included needed supports and interventions. The difference between primary school was that the high school had a specific unit which coordinated supports, and took effort to introduce students and parents to new protocols. For example, they had a day where all the new students for the following year visited the high school and received help and information from older students and teachers. They learned how to use the lockers with the large padlocks and combination codes. They had sessions where students could ask questions about high school, and Ben was able to meet the support teachers he was going to have. To help his transition, the school printed out pictures of the lockers and classrooms and a list of his teachers so Ben would have an example of what it looked like before he arrived.

The high school has also assigned the same teacher aide to Ben several years in a row. With all the other yearly changes – new teachers, new classes, and new subjects – to have the same teacher aid across a number of years has provided a measure of consistency. There is someone in the school who Ben knows and trusts, and someone who knows Ben. They know his quirks, they know his humor, they know how to get him to laugh, how to bring down his anxiety and make him feel at ease in the midst of all the hustle and bustle at school.

It has also helped Ben to have a sister who was already in high school, especially since they have vertical pastoral care classes where siblings are in the same PC class together. So, he had his sister there waiting for him when he started high school and that also provided consistency and a safe zone for him each day. In the last few years, Ben has taken an active role in his PC. First by collecting the roll bag while still in middle school, a job he has now passed onto his younger brother, and as a senior leading the younger students in morning devotions.

Expressing Anxiety

It was hard to gauge Ben's thoughts during his first years of high school as he was quite closed and didn't share a lot. If I would persist, he would get frustrated, so I would have to pick my moments to try to get anything out of him. We were fortunate that my husband also worked at the high school, so sometimes Ben's teachers would bail him up in the staffroom corridor to let him know how things were going; but rarely would we hear it from Ben.

Ben has always had a fair degree of anxiety, but he is generally resilient and just keeps on trying. He is one of these kids with Autism who is quiet and compliant at school and does the right things, so his teachers may not see the anxiety building. If he had a really bad day, he would come home which is his safe place, and then let it all out through having a verbal outburst or getting into arguments with his siblings. This, though, was more prominent in the early years of high school when he had difficulty verbalizing his feelings. He is now more able to express himself to the point of the rest of us not getting much of a chance to talk over dinner.

Homework

Homework has always been a challenge for Ben. I think that Ben finds homework difficult because he is so exhausted from having to manage the school day – the noise, the brushing past other students, getting to class, keeping focused attention, and all the executive functioning skills that are required for learning, such as planning, organization, and problem-solving. I think school is just so draining for him every day that when he comes home, he needs time and space to just recoup and recharge.

When he was in primary school, every afternoon I would make a cup of tea and sit beside him at his desk in his room and help him. When the other children were born, however, it became harder to spend that one-on-one time with him. After he was diagnosed with Autism, he received funding for a teacher aide, which was especially helpful to address his learning and homework needs. Since he has been in high school, they have actually written into his IEP that he doesn't even have to attempt homework. This has spared us a lot of heartache all round.

School Sport

Choosing a school sport for Ben was also challenging. I was uncertain about how Ben would fit into a team sport as negotiating play was difficult for him. In team sports, if children have doubts about your ability to perform, they often don't pass the ball to you in touch, footie, or basketball. So, when Ben started at his new school for grade three, he would receive coaching in after school tennis lessons. He used to play tennis for interschool sports in both summer and winter. Tennis seemed to work well for him. There was no one touching him and the noise levels were low. He learnt to hit the ball and actually got quite good at it. The physical activity and exercise were a benefit, and it provided a shared interest with his sister who also enjoyed tennis for school sport.

Friendships

The social aspects of school have also had some challenges. Ben often communicates that he doesn't care about what others think of him, or about fitting in, but on the other hand, of course he does and this comes out in a round-about way, often at the dinner table when he is down on the way the other students act at school. Ben wants to have friends and be accepted, but he doesn't really know the best way to go about making friends. He tells us he has tried with some peers at school over the years but says they don't seem interested. He feels that they just tolerate him. However, he has made a couple of friends in Youth group, which has been wonderful, though they are a little bit younger. Ben loves going to Youth because he feels accepted for whom he is. He says they don't judge him so he can just be himself and have fun.

PREPARING FOR POST SCHOOL TRANSITION

Ben is finishing Grade 12 this year, which involves another transition. I am somewhat nervous about how he is going to fill his days when formal schooling, which has been the focus of his weekly schedule for the past 12+ years, is completed. To that end, I am grateful for the career advisor and the industry liaison officer at the school who seek out pathways in consultation with students who are not attending university or taking a full-time job at the completion of grade 12. One benefit is that they have helped to identify Ben's strengths and interests.

Ben is very much into computers, and he has tried subjects, such as engineering, and all the "fab lab" type subjects which incorporate the use of 3D printing as they match his interests. His marks, though, reflect where he struggles academically. Due to his struggle with English, even though he enjoys the content, he is often unable to complete the assignments. For example, he took courses in Physics, Engineering, Design and Digital Solutions, and even though he loved the content, loved designing things, he found it difficult to come up with new ideas and write these up into assignments.

The school career advisor, after meeting with Ben and exploring his interests, told us that he could do a Tertiary and Further Education (TAFE) course at school during Year 11. Ben agreed and completed a Certificate III, in screen and media in Year 11. He enjoyed having one day a week off school to go to TAFE. This year he is working on a Certificate III in business as part of a school-based traineeship, so every Friday he gets to work at an organization, mostly on a computer doing projects like updating their website and using design software. He receives support, mentoring, and feedback from a trainer, as well as a small payment. He also has a job at Red Rooster for one shift a week, and is performing well. So, he has had some wins and successes which has boosted his self-confidence and bit by bit is forging a path into post schooling around his interests.

As we move forward, I realize how important it is for us to place more activities into Ben's schedule. I also need to look into obtaining some funding to provide additional opportunities for him. The concern is that, without scheduled activities, Ben will spend more time on his growing passion for computer games. I do realize that many children on the Autism spectrum are into computer gaming because they do not have to interact or socialize with other people. Now that he's nearly 18, Ben plays online with friends and others, and he would happily spend additional time playing games. So, the need to find additional activities for him to engage is a critical step during transition from formal schooling.

REFLECTIONS ON SCHOOLING

As I reflect on Ben's 12 years of schooling, a number of considerations come to mind that might have improved his overall experience. The first is related to the process of getting a diagnosis. For example, I wish I had known there was an Autism package that I could have accessed when Ben was younger. I also wish I had known that funding and support were available that would have provided additional assistance and intervention for Ben in his early years. Information is essential for parents when a concern is detected.

Another consideration has to do with teacher preparation that enables them to plan and adapt instruction to the meet strengths and needs of students with a range of learning challenges. Typically, providing support for students like Ben in the classroom has been placed on teacher aides. While these personnel have positive influences and are essential to learning outcomes, they also tend to be the least qualified and trained. Students are often pulled out of the classroom for instruction in support units, which reflects a deficit model of education, when what they need most is a teacher who has received training to remove barriers to learning, implement innovative pedagogy geared to the individual student, and craft a truly inclusive learning environment. I would like to see the school explore the concept of co-teaching where a teacher who has more experience with students with complex needs is placed in a classroom with a newer, younger, or less experienced teacher to provide mentoring and demonstrate creative ways to design and implement lessons. In addition, professional development might be provided to all staff at the school, including counselors, chaplains and others.

Professional development regarding how to plan and deliver lessons according to each student's learning strengths would, I believe, also address the issue of grades. For example, when Ben gets a D on his report card, the implication is that he is responsible for the grade due to a lack of effort. That has been really discouraging and heartbreaking, because grades can determine a student's livelihood, and affect what pathways are available to them post school. What might be acknowledged is that grades are also a reflection of the support available to the student at school. The focus might be on increasing support when needed to attain desired outcomes.

An area that might be explored is support for social involvement, such as clubs at lunch time. Ben often spent lunch breaks wandering around the playground aimlessly or sitting with a group of students who might not have been the best choice for him. It would have been helpful for him to have had support socializing and mixing with other children, making friends for whom he is, rather than having them view him as "a kid with Autism."

The final reflection is more unique to our situation and is related to the fact that Ben's father taught at the school, and I also worked there to varying degrees as a relief teacher. This made it more difficult at times to connect to Ben's teachers, either to avoid the perception of overstepping boundaries or be seen as taking advantage of our ties to the school. As I look back, I wonder how I might have better navigated interactions to be both respectful and forthright.

CONCLUSION

In the coming year, Ben is going to be transitioning to the big wide world and his foremost desire is to be treated just like anybody else. He wants to be a valued member of society. To do what makes him spark joy, to put his hand to it and make sufficient income so that he can support himself. He wants to be a contributor. He does not want anyone to feel sorry for him.

To me, the most important component in transition for children with Autism or those with other disabilities is that they are viewed as a person first, a child first; they are not seen as a label, or a diagnosis. This is what all students who are making transitions through life need. We may have to make accommodations for some children and consider the unique needs of students like Ben. But, while we may need to make an extra effort, it is important to not treat them differently, because they do not want to feel different. They want to feel like everyone else, they want to be included. They want to belong.

As far as Autism goes, I think it is time to move on from society becoming aware of Autism, to a society truly inclusive of those who are Autistic. Like Ben, they are awesome people who have so much to offer the world to make it a better place. To that end, perhaps it's time to promote a transition in society, to become a community where all are welcome, valued, and belong.

NOTE

1. The pseudonym, Ben, has been used to protect identity.

TRANSITION FROM PRIMARY TO SECONDARY SCHOOL: A COLLABORATIVE INTERVENTION BETWEEN SIX SOUTH AFRICAN SCHOOLS SITUATED IN SOCIOECONOMICALLY CHALLENGED CONTEXTS

Ansie Elizabeth Kitching, Robert Tubb Carstens and Petra Engelbrecht

ABSTRACT

The transition from primary school to secondary school is viewed globally as a crucial period in students' lives and a challenging transition can have both short-term and long-term consequences for the wellbeing of students. Despite primary-secondary transition being so important, it is a neglected area of research in general in most countries including South Africa. By smoothing the transition from primary to secondary school challenges that are related to students' disengagement with education, school failure (school dropout), and continued social inequality can be addressed. In this chapter, the value of a transition intervention based on peer mentoring to ease the transition of students in five primary schools in an area of the country where the context is characterized by socioeconomic challenges is discussed. A lack of resources and funding make it difficult to provide individual support to all these students. In response to this challenge, a peer-mentoring approach has been applied to develop an intervention aimed at preparing the students with

Transition Programs for Children and Youth with Diverse Needs
International Perspectives on Inclusive Education, Volume 18, 63–76
Copyright © 2022 Ansie Elizabeth Kitching, Robert Tubb Carstens and Petra Engelbrecht
Published under exclusive licence by Emerald Publishing Limited
ISSN: 1479-3636/doi:10.1108/S1479-363620220000018006

insight into the challenges that awaits them. The intervention encompasses a workshop attended by a representative group of 20 Grade 7 students, selected based on the leadership skills as demonstrated in their interactions with adults and peers. Following the workshop, they are given the opportunity to give feedback to their Grade 7 peers and also avail themselves for individual discussions with their peers. In this chapter, we critically reflect on the value of this peer-mentored approach for socioeconomically challenged school contexts.

Keywords: Holistic wellbeing; school transition; collaborative problem solving; participatory collaboration; peer support; peer mentoring

INTRODUCTION

The transition period from primary to secondary school is a critical time in a student's life, making it a social and academic turning point for students (Hanewald, 2013). This transition period also coincides with the onset of early adolescence, a developmental phase in which students have to establish their own identity, accept increased responsibility, and make personal and social adjustments. Effects that this move across school settings can have include students' sense of emotional and intellectual wellbeing, e.g., they can feel marginalized, unwelcomed, stressed, and not respected or valued by others leading to underachievement or even eventually dropping out (Boone & Demanet, 2020; Symonds, 2015; Van Rens et al., 2018; Waters et al., 2012). It is therefore evident that students' experiences during this transition period can have an impact on their intellectual, social, and psychological wellbeing. The transition experience in this phase should, as a result, be understood as intensely emotional and social in nature (Pereira & Pooley, 2007). This impact should be addressed if we intend to protect the overall wellbeing of students.

In a recent literature review of research on transition from primary school to secondary school, Bharara (2020) found that globally, school transition research has mainly focused on the negative academic impact of school transitions with less emphasis on the development of more generalized support interventions. The implication is that little is known about interventions that can support students to cope better overall with transitions. Van Rens et al. (2018) as well as Hanewald (2013) also indicate that there is limited evidence of interventions that focus on a collaborative partnership between teachers, students, and their parents even though research indicates that well designed and implemented transition interventions that promote interpersonal relationships can assist in the process of making this transition period a positive experience for all involved. These findings resonate with current research in the South African context.

In the South African context, the transition from public primary school (Grade R to Grade 7) to public secondary school (Grade 8–12) involves transition to a different and more formal school environment between Grade 7 and Grade 8. A policy brief released in 2018 by the National Education Evaluation and Development Unit (NEEDU) states that transition from primary to secondary school can be a positive step forward in a student's educational journey and the foundation for success throughout their schooling. Contrary to this, students can find transition very difficult if they are not guided to manage the disruption caused when they move from Grade 7 in primary schools to Grade 8 in secondary schools. The policy brief emphasizes the importance of preparing students academically and socially to be able to deal with the secondary school curriculum and the school culture. The problem observed is that in practice, schools are left with the responsibility to ensure that students are prepared for the transition. As stated earlier, the emphasis often remains on academic preparation, with limited attention to the preparedness for the social and ecological challenges that students will encounter (e.g., Engelbrecht et al., 2002; Loebenstein, 2005).

The socioemotional impact of the adaptation to a new environment can add to the disruptions if one considers the findings of research on the associations between adolescents' interpersonal relationships, school well-being, and academic achievement during educational transitions (Kiuru et al., 2020). Pyhältö et al. (2010) found that adolescents experience social interactions within the school community both rewarding and challenging. Maintaining supportive relationships with school friends and teachers and a dynamic, reciprocal relationship with their school environment can play a critical role in countering the social impact of transition (Longobardi et al., 2016). Furthermore, the combined direct and indirect influences of socioeconomic contexts must be acknowledged (Hanewald, 2013). Limited attention to social support from peers, teachers and parents can have serious consequences for students who are vulnerable due to the serious challenges associated with the socioeconomic deprivation in their environments.

In this chapter we will

- Discuss the embeddedness of preparation for transition in a holistic wellbeing approach to ensure attention to socio-ecological challenges.
- Describe a brief transition intervention that has been implemented over a period of 4 years in six South African public schools which serve families and students who face serious socioeconomic challenges.
- Critically reflect on the contribution of this brief intervention and briefly present guidelines for adapting the intervention to be more accessible to Grade 7 students in this unique South African school context.

EMBEDDING THE PREPARATION FOR TRANSITION IN A HOLISTIC WELLBEING APPROACH

In an analysis of international literature, several key factors that can either contribute to transition to secondary schools in a positive or negative way have been identified (Bhahara, 2020; Hanewald, 2013; University of Dundee, 2019; Van Rens et al., 2018; West et al., 2010). Cumulative evidence from international research, despite being characterized by a wide variety of perspectives and methodologies, indicates that different systems within an individual's social contexts including the school, peer, family, and neighborhood contexts are interdependently involved in supporting or hindering transition and the overall wellbeing of students (Haneveld, 2013; University of Dundee, 2019; Reupert, 2017; Rimm-Kaufman & Pianta, 2000; West et al., 2010).

By placing transition within a socio-ecological approach based on Bronfenbrenner's bio-ecological (2005) and Rimm-Kauffman's and Pianta's ecological and dynamic model of transition (2000), it can be posited that transition to secondary schools takes place in an environment defined by reciprocal, multi-faceted, and complex relationships between individuals and their contexts (Swart & Pettipher, 2016). In concurrence with the socio-ecological approach, the transactional model describes adolescent development as a result of the continuous dynamic interactions between adolescents and the experiences as provided by their social settings (Sameroff, 2010).

Theories that explain the complex dynamic interactive processes between human beings in general and educational contexts in particular present a basis for understanding the need for a more integrative process-orientation approach to the implementation of interventions than the traditional linear-casual programmatic approaches (see Stacey, 2007; Radford, 2008). An understanding of the inherent complexity in these processes enables those responsible for the development and implementation of these processes to value ongoing reflections and adaptations to ensure the efficiency and sustainability of the process (Kitching & Van Rooyen, 2020).

The development of interventions aimed at preparing students for the transition from primary to secondary school therefore needs to adopt an approach that acknowledges the transition ecology and the dynamic social interactive processes. Evans and Prilleltensky (2007) informed by the ecological models, developed a holistic wellbeing model that proposes an integrative approach to the promotion of wellbeing. This approach emphasizes the importance of simultaneously attending to three levels of wellbeing namely individual, relational, and collective levels to ensure that the diverse needs in a community are addressed (Prilleltensky, 2005, 2012).

Taking the signs of wellbeing as described by Evans and Prilleltensky (2007) into consideration, transition from a holistic well-being perspective should entail the following on each of the following levels. On individual or personal level, the provision of opportunities such as attending career exhibitions and psycho-social support that may encompass the development of self-knowledge in groupwork will enhance their sense of self-determination, self-control, and self-efficacy. Students should also be granted a "voice" in making decisions regarding aspects of his/her physical and/or emotional wellbeing that will advance their sense of mastery and self-control. On relational wellbeing level, students should be engaged in conversations with those who have an impact on their transition to elicit respect for one another, a sense of belonging, acceptance of each other, trust, mutual respect for each other, caring behavior toward one another. On a collective wellbeing level, understood as the co-construction of enabling spaces in which equality and justice are appreciated and enhanced, students themselves have to be involved in the decision-making processes to ensure the equitable allocation of bargaining powers, resources, and obligations.

A SOUTH AFRICAN INTERVENTION

Contextualizing the Intervention

South Africa has a history of educational inequality attributed to the racist policies that originated in the colonial era and fully realized under apartheid (McKeever, 2017). Despite the abolishment of these policies in 1994, inequality continues to be determined by socioeconomic factors. In view of this persisting inequality, the support of vulnerable students, enabling them to successfully navigate their way through the education system is of the utmost importance (McKeever, 2017).

It is important to note that the schools that are involved in the wellbeing initiative serve a majority of families and students who have been impacted by these historical disparities in education (Kitching, 2019). All public schools are categorized for funding purposes based on the relative poverty of the communities surrounding the schools and categorized according to a quintile system which includes five categories (Western Cape Education Department, 2006). Quintile one is considered the 'poorest," and are non-fee paying schools while quintile five is the "least poor" and fee paying. The school communities in our discussion with the exception of one school, are categorized as quintile one schools. The implication is that students from these schools have limited resources and opportunities including limited access to additional psycho-social support services that might be accessible to their more privileged peers in quintile four and five schools where parents can afford to pay high school fees. One of the more serious challenges associated with these socioeconomic conditions are the abuse of substances such as alcohol and marijuana – by both students and parents. Another major concern reported nationally is absenteeism and a high dropout rate which is evidently associated with a lack of motivation among students. Some schools experience a lack of parental interest in their children's school career that can also be ascribed to the fact that some parents have to commute vast distances or work late hours. Despite the adversities faced by these communities, all the schools involved in this discussion provide their learners with access to a school library and a computer room, thereby providing students with access to books, computers, and the Internet. The schools further have qualified personnel who are dedicated and hard working.

Between 2015 and 2017, a holistic wellbeing approach was applied to develop an integrative process that could strengthen the capacity of the participating schools to facilitate the promotion of wellbeing in their contexts (Kitching, 2019). The promotion of wellbeing within this approach advocates for the inclusion of as many role-players as possible in the promotion of wellbeing, a focus away from the ameliorative toward the transformative and the embeddedness of interventions into a comprehensive process to avoid a fragmentation (Kitching, 2019; Prilleltensky, 2012).

Wellbeing support teams were established in every school in 2015 to facilitate the development of the process. These wellbeing support teams were equipped through the overall participatory action research and action learning approach as developed by Zuber-Skerritt (2018) to take ownership of the wellbeing of all the members of the school community on individual, relational, and collective levels. One of the most important ongoing tasks of these teams has been to identify the needs of all the members (including staff, parents, and students) on the three levels of wellbeing and initiate interventions framed within a holistic wellbeing approach to address the identified gaps. The need for an overall wellbeing coordinating committee (WBCC) that collaborates across the school boundaries, was identified and the committee was established 4 years ago. The overall Wellbeing Committee (WBCC) comprises of staff members and parents from all six schools. The project has been sustained following the completion of the research conducted by Kitching (2019) and is continuing to contribute to the development of these schools' capacity to take ownership of the mental health and wellbeing of all their members.

Approximately 500 students from the four public primary schools annually transition to the two secondary schools in the town as well as to other public secondary schools in the school district. Following a brief survey, the WBCC became aware of the Grade 7 students' concerns about the transition to secondary school. The WBCC decided to adopt a peer-support approach in response to the concerns expressed regarding the concerns expressed regarding the challenges students experience in transitioning to secondary schools the WBCC decided to adopt a peer support approach. A peer support approach implies that a selected group of students will be involved in the process and enabled to provide support to other students during the transition process with a view to promoting social and emotional wellbeing (Brady et al., 2014).

Selection of the Peer Support Group

The Grade 7 peer support group included 20 students (4 from each primary school). The students from each school were invited to participate in the peer support training based on the following criteria: (1) a demonstrated ability to understand and communicate knowledge, skills with a positive attitude that will impact on their peers, and (2) positively influence their fellow-students to engage with them.

Structure of the Intervention

The aim of this ongoing intervention since 2017 has been to equip a group of students with the necessary skills to not only manage the way in which they personally cope with the transition process but also to provide peer support to other students. The intervention comprises three phases, namely a one-day workshop collaboratively developed by the wellbeing coordinators from each school; an interactive session between students who attended the workshop and their peers; and ongoing informal engagements among students and between students and adults involved in the process.

Presenting the One-Day Workshop

For the past 3 years, the one-day workshop has been presented on a Saturday to ensure that academic time is not affected. The attendees included the selected Grade 7 group of 20 students. All the wellbeing coordinators attended the workshops in 2017 and 2018. And, since 2019, parents who are members of the WBCC also attended the workshop. In addition, a group of 10 Grade 8 students from the two secondary schools were identified by the Life Orientation subject teachers and were invited based on their leadership qualities. Also, since 2019, the head leaders of the Student Representative Councils from the two secondary schools in the area have been invited.

The workshop commences with an introduction of the ASPIRE principles (agency, safety, positivity, inclusion, respect, and equity) developed by Roffey (2017). The aim of these introductory engagements is to enhance a sense of connectedness between the groups involved. This forms a basis for understanding the importance of connecting with one another to strengthen relationships, resilience, and responsibility. Each principle has been introduced by one of the committee members through an experiential learning exercise selected to demonstrate the principle.

Following the introduction of the ASPIRE principles, the Grade 7 students work together in smaller groups to formulate questions regarding their concerns about entering secondary school. A few major concerns and anxieties have been identified as indicated in the facilitators' reflexive notes for the period 2017–2019. The content of these questions reflects research findings in the literature that separate dimensions associated both with the formal school system (e.g., academic demands) and informal social system which are playing a major role in facilitating the transition of young adolescents to secondary school (Anderson et al., 2000; West et al., 2010). Important questions related to the informal social system continue to be how they would be able to fit in and find friends. Furthermore, concerns about whether they will be able to cope with peer pressure and bullying in the secondary school context, in view of all the negative reporting on the use of social media in this regard, continue to be expressed year by year.

Once the questions are formulated, the Grade 8 students work through the questions and then engage in smaller groups with the Grade 7 group to discuss the concerns expressed through the questions. They present their advice by drawing on their own knowledge and experiences within their own school communities. They are allowed to engage with their peers and to provide the most suitable response to the questions without interference from the adults in the room. This allows for an authentic student-to-student experience during which the Grade 8 students acknowledge their sense of mastery regarding their own transition to secondary school and retain their authentic voices. Following the presentation, the Grade 7 students then have the opportunity to request further clarification when needed or ask other questions that were triggered through the various conversations between students within the session.

Engaging with Their Peers

Upon conclusion of the workshop, each primary school's peer mentors are presented with a Well-being Support Buddy badge to ensure that they will be recognized by their peers as a source of information and support and to cultivate a feeling of pride for the role that they were trained to fulfill in their school community.

During the weeks following the workshop, the wellbeing coordinators negotiate times for the Grade 7 peer mentors to engage with their fellow peers. These arrangements are made according to available time slots within the school day and best suited for their school's particular context. In these time slots, the Grade 7 wellbeing support buddies share what they have learnt with their peers and answer questions. They also explain that they will be available for further discussions with fellow students at suitable times. Their availability continues into Grade 8 where they are supported by the wellbeing team coordinators at the secondary school. It is important to note that they already met with these teachers in Grade 7 since the teachers also attended the workshop.

Adaptations during the COVID-19 Pandemic

In March 2020, the COVID-19 pandemic changed the situation, and it became impossible to present the workshop in the previous format. The WBCC, instead of terminating the interventions, participatively compiled a brochure with information that will assist learners with the transition based on previous experience. The brochure includes students' questions from previous years as well as questions received from the current Grade 7 group. The secondary school teachers requested input from the Grade 8's who contributed advice. The WBCC's assistant collated all the input and designed a brochure. Every Grade 7 learner received a brochure at the end of 2020. In 2021, the Grade 8's who did not attend one of the primary schools involved in the wellbeing-initiative will receive this brochure and the wellbeing coordinators in the two secondary schools will follow it up.

THE EVOLUTION OF THE INTERVENTION OVER A PERIOD OF 4 YEARS

The contents have been revised and adapted annually based on the reflexive engagements between the committee members and the documentation received from students during the workshop (e.g., questions and feedback from the students).

In 2017–2018, only the wellbeing coordinators and the selected Grade 7 and Grade 8 groups were involved. Minor changes to the experiential learning exercises were made so that these exercises are more relevant based on the feedback from students and coordinators. Coordinators also reflected on the process with their colleagues in their individual schools. In 2018, a group of parents joined the wellbeing coordinating committees, following volunteer support training that prepared them to take responsibility for their school community. These parents became co-presenters during the workshop. Their involvement facilitated a deeper understanding of the need to prepare students for Grade 8. It also enhanced these parents' understanding of the impact of transition on their own children and enabled them to share their understanding with other parents in their own community contexts.

Another advancement was the inclusion of leaders of the student representative council from the two secondary schools. These school leaders specifically focused on expectations regarding rules in the school contexts as well as access to formal support.

CRITICAL REFLECTION ON THE INTERVENTION

Transition from primary to secondary school can be described as a developmental process that involves tension between change and stability and adjusting to new challenges within a range of complex multiple settings (Rimm-Kaufman & Pianta, 2000). The incorporation of the described intervention clearly raised the awareness of the importance of addressing these transition issues within the six school communities.

The overall limited access to support services in vulnerable contexts in South Africa (e.g., Nel et al., 2016) led to the decision to develop a brief intervention to address the concerns expressed by learners in Grade 7. Due to the lack of availability of more general programs, the WBCC decided to design their own intervention. This deliberate decision to steer away from the few available programs that tend to focus on academic demands based on linear prescriptive models was informed by an applied complexity perspective on human relating and interacting. This implies ongoing reflexive engagement on how to improve the intervention processes rather than on traditional monitoring and evaluation practices and in this way also enhances sustainability and ownership. By doing so, the WBCC developed their own broad outline for engaging students in conversational processes in the preparation for the transition from Grade 7 to Grade 8. Recognizing the emergent nature of the process allowed them to adapt the process over time, which continues to enhance the sustainability of the intervention. The COVID-19 adaptation of the intervention, for example, provides an indication of this ability to adapt to circumstances rather than give up on a valuable intervention. In the process, the WBCC realized that the brochure can be used in the future to complement what has been done before to ensure the inclusion of students who might not reach out to their peers who were equipped as Wellbeing Support Buddies.

Reflecting on the intervention with consideration of the essential components of an effective transition intervention as described by Anderson et al. (2000) reveals that the deliberate and efficient planning by a functioning team that is representative of all stakeholders in the process (members of both primary and secondary schools as well as parents) is critically important. In this case, the planning team succeeded in involving the students as well as the parents as active agents in the transition process. A supportive network that enhances a sense of belonging and connectedness including the development of collaborative partnerships between the schools has been developed (Topping, 2011). Departing from a holistic wellbeing perspective enabled the planning team to establish effective lines of communication that make the ongoing exchange of information and collaboration possible between parents, students, and their peers in different school communities as proposed by Van Rens et al. (2018, p. 53).

By applying a holistic wellbeing approach, the intervention addresses developmental as well as ecological challenges more effectively. The focus on relationships ensures that the students are well on an individual level by engaging them in conversations that allow them to address their specific concerns and have access to peers and supportive adults. On a collective level, the fact that the students are given a strong voice in the process and are equipped to engage with their peers enhances their capacity to take responsibility.

By combining the support from peers and teachers, a space is created in which peers who have taken part in the workshop and become mentors and teachers can come together with a specific focus according to Brady et al. (2014, p. 244). This focus encourages discussion of transition issues and development of supportive relationships with other students. Although peer support is not the only solution to the challenges experienced during transition to secondary school, peer mentors are uniquely placed to understand the challenges experienced by their peers and make a valuable contribution to their overall wellbeing of their peers (Brady et al., 2014). The intention with this input continues to be to equip the students with a better understanding of dealing with challenges that will enable them to rely on their relationships, develop a sense of belonging and take responsibility. Through agency they develop the courage to let their voices be heard in their new environment. The ASPIRE principles applied in the workshop also guide their engagement with their peers.

The overall contribution of the wellbeing initiative has furthermore been to improve collaboration between the receiving secondary schools and their feeder primary schools. It is clearly a vital tool in school improvement efforts. This is characterized by increasing voluntary participation, shared responsibility, shared accountability, joint decision-making, trusting and respectful relationships, and mutual support in the transition process as evidenced in the reflexive engagement in the process by all role players. One should not underestimate the leadership role of the WBCC in the development of these collaborative partnerships. It is an interactive dynamic within the overall school system that is socially constructed in and from context (Engelbrecht & Muthukrishna, 2019).

Seeing That This Intervention Is Work in Progress, a Few Critical Pointers for Future Implementation Has Been Identified

First, the concept of feedback is central to the further development and sustainability of the intervention. A feedback loop as a "circular arrangement of causally connected elements in the transition process so that each element has an effect on the next until the last feeds back into the first" (Walby, 2007, p. 464) should be created. A positive feedback loop strategy will enable the WBCC to identify small changes in the process and drive change onwards that could lead to larger effects in a non-linear way and escalate change within the intervention process as well as in the wider school communities (Walby, 2007). By developing a feedback loop, individual school characteristics, the resultant differences between these schools, and the feedback loop's influence on the transition process could also possibly be identified.

The adaptation of the intervention due to COVID-19 has provided the WBCC with the first step in endeavoring to ensure in a more pro-active manner that all students are included in the conversational processes. As a result, students who could be more vulnerable in making poorer transitions and who can provide additional important information regarding transition concerns can be included in the process in future.

Due to the lack of research on innovative approaches to transition interventions in South Africa, the WBCC should consider the ongoing longer-term collection of data to monitor the impact of the intervention on academic achievement as well as on the social-emotional wellbeing of students. Some theoretical suggestions have been posited on how interpersonal relationships, school well-being, and academic achievement may be related (Sameroff, 2010), but little is known about the reciprocal dynamics between the quality of interpersonal relationships and school wellbeing, and how these dynamics contribute to academic achievement. A better understanding of how quality of interpersonal relationships and school wellbeing work together to affect academic achievement during educational transitions is crucial, since successful adaptation during these critical transitions has long-term impacts on youth's academic and mental-health outcomes (Upadyaya & Salmela-Aro, 2013). By collecting longer term data, a valuable contribution to much needed research will be made.

CONCLUSION

Against the background of an inconsistent and incomplete data base of interventions in South Africa that focuses on facilitating a successful transition from primary to secondary school, this chapter focused on an innovative and collaborative intervention in a socioeconomic challenged context. By embedding the intervention in a holistic wellbeing approach that acknowledges transition ecology and dynamic social interactive processes, the need for more social and personal interventions that promote the interpersonal relationships with peers and the sense of belonging at secondary school was addressed.

The overall contribution of the intervention in the six school communities to the promotion of personal, relational and collective wellbeing of students, teachers and parents during the transition period was discussed and the pivotal agential role of the WBCC and team coordinators in every school described. It is important to note that this intervention forms part of the ongoing overall contextually relevant facilitation of holistic wellbeing in the six school communities and should not be regarded as a standalone process. By continuously revisiting the overall wellbeing of school communities including the transition process through regular conversations with all members of their school communities, this intervention can be described as the unfolding of a flexible natural process instead of a top-down approach to transition (e.g., Kitching, 2019).

By advocating a holistic wellbeing approach and collecting longer term data, this specific transition intervention can contribute to increasing the awareness of school leaders and policymakers of the importance of involving a wider group of teachers, students, and parents as equal partners in decision-making and the development of successful transition interventions.

REFERENCES

Anderson, L. W., Jacobs, J., Schramm, S., & Splittgerber, F. (2000). School transitions: Beginning of the end or a new beginning? *International Journal of Educational Research, 33*(4), 325–339.

Bharara, G. (2020). Factors facilitating a positive transition to secondary school: A systematic literature review. *International Journal of School & Educational Psychology, 8*(Suppl. 1), 104–123.

Boone, S., & Demanet, J. (2020). Track choice, school engagement and feelings of perceived control at the transition from primary to secondary school. *British Educational Research Journal, 46*(5), 929–948.

Brady, B., Dolan, P., & Canavan, J. (2014). What added value does peer support bring? Insights from principals and teachers on the utility and challenges of a school based mentoring programme. *Pastoral Care in Education, 32*(4), 241–250.

Bronfenbrenner, U. (Ed.). (2005). *Making human beings human, bio-ecological perspectives on human development.* Sage.

Engelbrecht, P., Howell, C., & Bassett, D. (2002). Educational reform and the delivery of transition services in South Africa: Vision, reform, and change. *Career Development and Transition for Exceptional Individuals,* April 2002. https://doi.org/10.1177/088572880202500105

Engelbrecht, P., & Muthukrishna, N. (2019). Inclusive education as a localised project in complex contexts: A South African case study. *South African Review of Education, 25*(1), 107–124.

Evans, S. D., & Prilleltensky, I. (2007). Youth and democracy: Participation for personal, relational, and collective well-being. *Journal of Community Psychology, 35*(6), 681–692. https://doi.org/10.1002/jcop.20172

Hanewald, R. (2013). Transition between primary and secondary school: Why it is important and how it can be supported. *Australian Journal of Teacher Education, 38*(1), 62–72.

Kitching, A. E. (2019). The development of an integrated, multi-level process to facilitate the promotion of holistic wellbeing in school communities. In I. Eloff (Ed.), *Handbook of the quality of life in African societies* (pp. 45–69). Springer Nature AG.

Kitching, A. E., & Van Rooyen, B. (2020). Key aspects for the sustainable coordination of a process to facilitate holistic well-being in South African schools. *Health Promotion International, 35*(4), 692–701. https://doi.org/10.1093/heapro/daz060

Kiuru, N., Wang, M. T., Salmela-Aro, K., Kannas, L., Ahonen, T., & Hirvonen, R. (2020). Associations between adolescents' interpersonal relationships, school well-being, and academic achievement during educational transitions. *Journal of Youth and Adolescence, 49*(5), 1057–1072.

Loebenstein, H. (2005). *Support for learners with intellectual disabilities in the transition to secondary school.* Unpublished PhD thesis, Stellenbosch University.

Longobardi, C., Prino, L. E., Marengo, D., & Settanni, M. (2016). Student-teacher relationships as a protective factor for school adjustment during the transition from middle to high school. *Frontiers in Psychology, 7*, 1988.

McKeever, M. (2017). Educational inequality in Apartheid South Africa. *American Behavioral Scientist, 61*(1), 114–131.

National Education Evaluation and Development Centre (NEEDU). (2018). *Schools that work: Advocacy policy brief*s. Department of Basic Education.

Nel, N. M., Tlale, D., Engelbrecht, P., & Nel, M. (2016). Teachers' perceptions of education support structures in the implementation of inclusive education in South Africa. *Koers, 81*(3), 1–14. http://dx.doi.org/10.19108/koers.81.2.2249

Pereira, A. J., & Pooley, J. A. (2007). A qualitative exploration of the transition experience of students from a high school to a senior high school in rural Western Australia. *Australian Journal of Education, 51*(2), 162–177.

Prilleltensky, I. (2005). Promoting well-being: Time for a paradigm shift in health and human services. *Scandinavian Journal of Public Health, 33*(5), 53–60. https://doi.org/10.1080/14034950510033381

Prilleltensky, I. (2012). Wellness as fairness. *American Journal of Community Psychology, 49*(1–2), 1–21. https://doi.org/10.1007/s10464-011-9448-8

Pyhältö, K., Soini, T., & Pietarinen, J. (2010). Pupils' pedagogical well-being in comprehensive school–significant positive and negative school experiences of Finnish ninth graders. *European Journal of Psychology of Education, 25*(2), 207–221.

Radford, M. (2008). Prediction, control and the challenge to complexity. *Oxford Review of Education, 34*(5), 505–520.

Reupert, A. (2017). A socio-ecological framework for mental health and well-being. *Advances in Mental Health, 15*(2). https://doi.org/10.1080/18387357.2017.1342902

Rimm-Kaufman, S. E., & Pianta, R. C. (2000). An ecological perspective on the transition to Kindergarten: A theoretical framework to guide research. *Journal of Applied Developmental Psychology, 21*(5), 491–511.

Roffey, S. (2017). The ASPIRE principles and pedagogy for the implementation of social and emotional learning and the development of whole school well-being. *International Journal of Emotional Education, 9*(2), 59–71. https://files.eric.ed.gov/fulltext/EJ1162077.pdf

Sameroff, A. (2010). A unified theory of development: A dialectic integration of nature and nurture. *Child Development, 81*(1), 6–22.

Stacey, R. (2007). The challenge of human interdependence. Consequences for thinking about the day to day practice of management in organisations. *European Business Review, 19*(4), 292–302. https://doi.org/10.1108/09555340710760125

Swart, E., & Pettipher, R. (2016). A framework for understanding inclusion. In E. Landsberg (Ed.), *Addressing barriers to learning* (pp. 3–28). Van Schaik.

Symonds, J. (2015). *Understanding school transition: What happens to children and how to help them.* Routledge.

Topping, K. (2011). Primary-secondary transition: Differences between teachers' and children's perceptions. *Improving Schools.* https://doi.org.10.1177/1365480211419587

University of Dundee. (2019). *Primary-secondary transitions: A systematic literature review.* University of Dundee.

Upadyaya, K., & Salmela-Aro, K. (2013). Development of school engagement in association with academic success and well-being in varying social contexts: A review of empirical research. *European Psychologist, 18*(2), 136.

Van Rens, M., Haelermans, C., Groot, W., & Van den Brink, H. M. (2018). Facilitating a successful transition to secondary school: (How) does it work? A systematic literature review. *Adolescent Research Review, 3*, 43–56.

Walby, S. (2007). Complexity theory, systems theory, and multiple intersecting social inequalities. *Philosophy of the Social Sciences, 37*(4), 449–470.

Waters, S., Lester, L., Wenden, E., & Cross, D. (2012). A theoretically grounded exploration of the social and emotional outcomes of transition to secondary school. *Australian Journal of Guidance and Counselling, 22*(2), 190–205.

Western Cape Education Department. (2006). 424 Western Cape schools consider 'No Fee' status. Media Release, March 23, 2006. https://wcedonline.westerncape.gov.za/

West, P., Sweeting, H., & Young, R. (2010). Transition matters: Pupils' experiences of the primary-secondary school transition in the West of Scotland and consequences for wellbeing and attainment. *Research Papers in Education, 25*(1), 21–50.

Zuber-Skerritt, O. (2018). An educational framework for participatory action learning and action research (PALAR). *Educational Action Research, 26*(4), 513–532. https://doi.org/10.1080/09650792.2018.1464939

TRANSITIONING FROM SPECIAL SCHOOLS OR SETTINGS INTO INCLUSIVE SCHOOLS: EXPECTATIONS AND REALITIES FOR STUDENTS WITH COMPLEX NEEDS

Chris Forlin and Joanne Deppeler

ABSTRACT

With the move toward a more inclusive educational system across most jurisdictions, the expectation is that students with the most complex needs who have previously attended special schools, will gradually transition into inclusive schools. This expectation raises issues regarding the practicality of this move and the capacity of inclusive schools in being able to provide appropriate support and curriculum for these learners. Examples of transition programs across different countries are discussed to establish the most effective processes, support structures, and initiatives that have been employed to facilitate this transfer. The role of collaboration between schools and a review of support models that are provided for learners with high support needs in inclusive settings are discussed. Compared to the expectations for this move, and to understand the reality of it, perceptions of teachers, parents, and students are considered.

Keywords: Transition; inclusion; special schools; inclusive schools; collaboration; complex needs

Transition Programs for Children and Youth with Diverse Needs
International Perspectives on Inclusive Education, Volume 18, 77–90
Copyright © 2022 Chris Forlin and Joanne Deppeler
Published under exclusive licence by Emerald Publishing Limited
ISSN: 1479-3636/doi:10.1108/S1479-363620220000018007

THE MOVE FROM SPECIAL SCHOOLS TO INCLUSIVE SCHOOLS

Inclusive education is generally applied in a broad sense as "education for all" that considers the needs of any potentially marginalized students and the removal of barriers or obstacles that prevent them from accessing education. This definition of inclusive education adopts an approach where the focus is on inclusive practice that supports all learners regardless of ability, status, background, or any other special need (Ainscow et al., 2011). The move from a former segregated dual system to an inclusive education approach has had a tremendous influence on education systems worldwide, schools, and all stakeholders involved in education (Forlin, 2019). High quality schooling for all students, including those with complex needs, is now considered vital to ensure improved quality of life.

School policies and practices play a pivotal role in improving student outcomes and promoting greater effectiveness. Over the past two decades, there has been a substantial increase in the diversity of students who attend regular schools, which has corresponded with the worldwide development of an inclusive education approach to schooling. Inclusive education school systems have necessarily been required to change school policies and practices to provide both *equitable* access and *high*-quality schooling for *all* students (Chambers & Forlin, 2021; Deppeler et al., 2016). Recommendations from the research literature are broadly in agreement that for children and youth with various disabilities supported transitions are beneficial (see for example Cantali, 2019; Neal et al., 2016).

Students transitioning from special schools whose needs are complex will require additional support to achieve and participate at the same levels as others in an inclusive environment (Forlin & Deppeler, 2018). Decisions regarding the provision of support for the inclusion of students with complex needs transitioning from special to inclusive schools must be taken seriously to ensure that family support is positive.

Where students are simply "placed" in the regular classroom without effective support or provision, this can lead to negative family attitudes toward the process of inclusion based on their child's experiences of schooling (Chmiliar, 2009). With families' experiences of inclusion being formed quite early in a child's schooling, they may struggle to have the child's areas of difficulty realized and appropriate early interventions made (Isaksson et al., 2010). Being able to find an inclusive school which parents consider would meet their child's needs is a challenge that can highly influence a child's social inclusion and academic achievement (Forlin et al., 2019). Failure of the school or an individual teacher to respond appropriately to student's learning challenges sufficiently early in schooling can lead to longer term learning challenges and tensions between the school and families.

EXAMPLES OF TRANSITION PROGRAMS FOR STUDENTS IN DIFFERENT COUNTRIES: PROCESSES, SUPPORT, EXPECTATIONS

There remains a lack of international research literature on children and youth with disabilities who move from specialist provision into a mainstream school to inform "good" practices. Studies are frequently focused on a single specific disability and often have small samples of participants and therefore the authors typically caution against generalizing their findings to wider populations. However, these studies do add to the scarce research literature on potential factors influencing successful transition from a special school to a mainstream setting.

Special Classes

Special classes within regular schools have been proposed to support the transition of students with ASD (Carter et al., 2014). Grindle et al. (2012) reported on an Applied Behavior Analysis (ABA) intervention within a special class in a mainstream school. As students' skills developed, they moved from one-to-one instruction to small groups, and then to mainstream classes. The satellite class is another special class example of supported inclusion in which specialist support is provided in a small class within a mainstream school to enable students to gradually transition to the mainstream setting. Longer transition periods into mainstream classrooms are believed to be potentially better in terms of providing more opportunities for social interaction with peers and thus the development of social skills (Keane et al., 2012), and greater access to academic stimulation and the broad curriculum (Deppeler & Loreman, 2015). While there has been limited systemic or comparative reviews of the satellite class model (Carter et al., 2014, 2019; Keane et al., 2012), the model has been used extensively in NSW, Australia where it began in the 1990s, and internationally in New Zealand (Ministry of Education, n.d.) and the UK with reported success. Studies in the UK (e.g. Croydon et al., 2019) and in Australia (e.g. Martin et al., 2021) have reported on satellite classroom models as advantageous for students with ASD transitioning to a mainstream education setting. Success, nevertheless, is reported as being dependent on the attitudes and the quality of the preparation of the mainstream schools, the skills and expertise of the satellite support teachers, ongoing support, professional development for staff, and strong home-school partnerships (Martin et al., 2021).

COLLABORATION BETWEEN SPECIAL AND REGULAR SCHOOLS DURING TRANSITIONS

Transition from a special education environment to a mainstream school is a complex process that involves students, their families, special education teachers, mainstream classroom teachers as well as a range of allied health professionals and school administrators. Collaboration is, therefore, a critical component of the process.

Collaboration with families is an essential aspect of ensuring positive and effective inclusion that can establish strong foundations for supporting learners with high support needs. While collaboration is used effectively across many areas of education, it has the least amount of supporting evidence in transition programs for students with disabilities (Rowe et al., 2014). Talapatra et al. (2018) further drew attention to the critical need for increasing the involvement and contribution of psychologists in transition services for students with intellectual disabilities who require the highest levels of support. While collaboration may be deemed to be a valuable component, it may not be easily and successfully achieved among teachers and other allied health professional without clearly articulated roles and responsibilities for the various professionals, leadership support, and training, to develop the participants' collaborative skills (Plotner et al., 2017).

Collaboration can take the form of generic school-based special education support where there is often reliance on teacher aide support (Carter et al., 2018; Sharma & Salend, 2016). Alternatively, highly specific forms of collaborative support can be offered, such as the *Autism Spectrum Disorder Inclusion Collaboration Model* (Simpson et al., 2003). This collaborative consultation framework supports classroom teachers to work with specialist professionals in a number of specific areas including environment and curricula modifications, classroom support and instruction, student social support, and home-school collaboration (Simpson et al., 2003).

Malapela et al. (2020) reported that parents from sub-Saharan Africa felt unprepared to handle the transition of their adolescents from special school into community life. Early planning and a multidisciplinary approach involving families and healthcare workers and community leaders was reported to be necessary to support parents and their children to successfully transition to productive members of the community. Shephard's (2020) longitudinal research study with ASD students with intellectual disabilities in England highlights the importance of attending to the diversity and complexity of young people's experiences of transition from special to further education. She argues that institutions need to take greater responsibility in modifying transition programs that support a diversity of students to navigate change. Hart (2021) echoes this view and emphasizes the importance of giving voice to young people with disabilities in these processes.

Transition from special school to post school options and further education has along with transition from special school to other stages of schooling, been under researched and these studies reinforce the importance of future research in this area.

As proposed by Hart (2021),

> Inclusivity is paramount, but so too is society's willingness to listen. Transition involves everyone; a willingness to invite all perspectives into the fold of diversity that makes for a robust and socially-just society. (p. 13)

ACTIVE PARTICIPATION OF CHILDREN AND YOUTH WITH DISABILITIES

Active participation of children and young people with disabilities in transition planning and decision-making is also considered critical for success. Listening to the voices of students and their families is emphasized by researchers as an important way to ensuring this happens. Chandroo et al.'s (2018) systematic review of research on the involvement of students with ASD in the transition process, reported the strong impacts of self-determination, knowledge, and skills on their participation. Similarly, Cumming and Strnadová (2017) single case study reports on an Australian *Flexible Integration Model*, a person-centered approach which was designed to support students with emotional and behavioral disabilities to transition from special school to various mainstream education settings. The focus of the model was providing students with choices of different subjects and "hands-on" learning activities that were of interest to them at the mainstream setting, and that were not available at the special school sites. The findings indicated that when transition planning incorporates student choice, it can have positive effects on appropriate behavior and attendance, and simultaneously provide positive role models in the mainstream settings.

Aligned with the research discussed in this chapter are studies that have listened to the views of children and youth with disabilities who have experienced school exclusion and placement in alternative educational provision and what factors were supportive of their return to mainstream schools (Atkinson & Rowley, 2019; Goodall, 2019; Trotman et al., 2019). These three areas are also key to successful transition from special school to a range of educational contexts. Findings from these studies recognize the value and effectiveness of the following:

(1) Listening to the perspectives of children and youth with disabilities along with their families and other relevant professionals
(2) Understanding the importance and impact of the relational context (e.g., family, the school, and the community), and
(3) Collaboration that includes the children and youth with disabilities, the family and interprofessional expertise, and approaches.

MODELS OF SUPPORT FOR INCLUDING LEARNERS WITH HIGH SUPPORT NEEDS IN REGULAR SCHOOLS

Models of support for students with high and profound support needs, who are most likely to be those transitioning from special schools, focus on placement, personnel, and the student (Fig. 1).

(1) *Placement* models of support – These involve the provision of alternative physical arrangements either on a temporary or permanent basis. This can be changes to classroom placement, withdrawal, or other segregated facilities.
(2) *Personnel* models of support – These involve the provision of a range of personnel in addition to the teacher. This can include support teachers, assistants, psychologists, or speech therapists.
(3) *Student focused* models of support – These describe support provided at three levels. The first level of provision is within the regular classroom based on modification of the existing curriculum by the class teacher; the second level

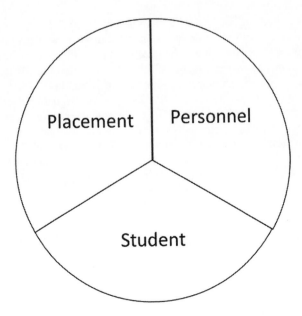

Fig. 1.   Models of Support for Transitioning.

is intermediary support provided by additional school-based personnel or
itinerant teachers and can include individual or small group work; the third
level provides an alternative educational pathway offering a separate curriculum which may or may not be offered within the regular classroom or
through withdrawal.

Placement Models

While international education systems typically promote an inclusive approach to
placement as a first-choice option; they may also provide a range of alternative
facilities specifically designed to support those students whose needs are not being
served in the regular classroom. Many of these systems have developed a continuum of placement options for students with high needs that range from fully
inclusive models to placement in a segregated specialist facility designed to cater
specifically for the needs of students with the most complex intellectual, physical,
medical, or health conditions. For example, in NSW, Australia, the state education system web pages promote its commitment to inclusive education principles and schooling. The site also outlines a continuum of provision, ranging from
a placement in fully inclusive schools (with adjustments and itinerant support
teachers if required) to various forms of specialist "allied health support services";
"specialist support classes" and "Schools for specific purposes" (SSPs). "SSPs are
schools that support eligible students with a diagnosed intellectual or physical
disability, Autism Spectrum Disorder, mental health considerations, sensory
processing disorder or behavior disorders" (NSW Government Education, 2021).

Personnel Models

Personnel models of support involve a wide range of allied health and peripatetic staff including educational psychologists, teaching assistants, school counsellors, social workers, mentors, speech-language pathologists, physiotherapists, itinerant teachers, and in-school learning support teachers. While the intention of the support that they offer may be similar by way of training, their actual involvement in schools in supporting learners with complex needs varies considerably both between and within countries. Previously, the involvement of paraprofessionals was by direct engagement with students, usually in a withdrawal mode providing structured but limited interventions. In recent years, though, there have been considerable and rapid changes in the education of students with special needs, predominantly within the whole school movement which has been a major drive in the changing role of support staff (Forlin & Chambers, 2020). A wide range of professional and non-professionals now work to support students with high needs in schools. These staff are employed under a variety of working conditions involving consultancy directly with students in schools and classrooms and within a single school or acting in an itinerant capacity across schools. Increasingly peripatetic staff are finding that they are providing support to the teacher rather than to the child.

A wide range of support staff, either employed within a school or acting in an itinerant capacity, appear to be involved in supporting the education of students requiring additional support when placed in an inclusive school. Of major consequence, would seem that those who spend most time with these students within the regular school system and who are expected to provide the differentiation to curriculum using effective pedagogies are the least well-trained. Most common are the variously named teaching support staff or assistants e.g. learning support assistant, teacher aide, integration aide, special needs assistant, and indigenous education assistants and/or officers that are present in many inclusive classrooms. In general, these staffs propose that they are inadequately prepared to support students, like those transitioning from special schools, who have complex needs (Cockroft & Atkinson, 2015). Within regular schools the qualified staff such as psychologists, speech-language pathologists, counsellors, and social workers, especially when employed in a part-time capacity, all seem to be able to spend only minimal time supporting individual students and in an ad hoc way. Itinerant paraprofessionals indicate that time pressures prohibit them from providing what they consider to be essential and intensive interventions or support. This is particularly noticeable for supporting learners with the most complex needs and undoubtedly contributes to the more rapid placement of such students into alternative options outside of the regular classroom or school.

Student-Focused Models

A range of support structures are evident within schools depending on the local context, and these are organized to provide for individual student's particular learning needs. These structures are, however, primarily designed to support students with mild to moderate learning challenges. For students who experience greater challenges, three layers of student focused support are identified namely, those that occur within the existing regular school system; those that offer an intermediary for reintegration into the regular school; and finally, those that provide an alternative educational pathway. These layers of support are grounded upon the principle that intensive assessment and team decision making must involve all stakeholders and families before options for support are determined and offered to individual students.

For supporting students in the regular school system intervention is provided within the existing resources of a school, and it is expected that the student will respond to these. For students transitioning from a special school where they have experienced intensive individual support, this level of support is not going to be sufficient. Students requiring complex interventions are more prone to be offered an alternative placement within a special class or resource center, where more intensive support can be provided by specialists. Although students with high support needs may attract higher levels of financial support in some systems, regular schools do not always have the manpower to be able to provide this within the regular classroom (Forlin & Deppeler, 2018).

Reviewing models of practice, the key approach in regular schools seems to focus on two stages of whole-school practice and in-class support (Fig. 2).

Both stages are closely intertwined as quality teaching practices in the classroom require support and school-wide collaboration. The role of school leaders is a key ingredient for providing this support and in cultivating quality teaching in school staff (Chambers & Forlin, 2021). For both types of support, nevertheless, there is a lack of evidence-based data on the impact of these practices on changes in learning outcomes for students with multifaceted needs for a disability (Forlin et al., 2013).

Peer support for students who experience more severe learning challenges in inclusive classrooms has also proved to be highly effective and beneficial to their learning (Bradley, 2016). Peer support programs encourage personal and social growth but can also have a positive impact on school ethos regarding accepting students with disabilities. Although paraprofessionals provide extensive support

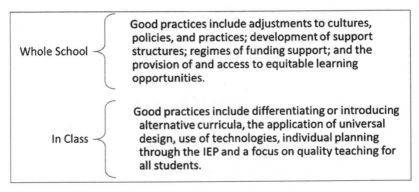

Fig. 2.   Levels of Support Provided in Regular Schools.

for students with severe disabilities, their continual presence can hinder peer social interactions (Carter et al., 2016).

Examples of good practice include interventions that involve the child, family, and school in a multisystemic approach. The most effective models of support identified by Urbis Pty. Ltd. involved three overlapping intervention approaches:

(1) The use of universal programs. Ones that focused on prevention and include classroom-based approaches; included changes to the school environment; and involved the family and community.
(2) The use of selected interventions for students at risk for developing emotional or behavioral disorders; including group approaches.
(3) Interventions that were targeted for individual students who have been identified as having an emotional or behavioral problem or a mental health disorder.

(Adapted from Urbis Pty. Ltd, 2011, August, p. 140)

LINK BETWEEN EXPECTATIONS AND REALITY

For students with the most complex needs, it was previously considered that they would require continued support through an alternative program outside of the regular education system. This is what led to the establishment of special schools and the dual system of special and regular education which is evident in most regions. The expectation to transition these students into mainstream schools and provide a curriculum that will meet the requirements of individual students with the most challenging needs, is challenging. While the move toward relocating students from special schools into inclusive classrooms is becoming an important aspect of confirming an inclusive approach to education, the reality is that in every system there still exist special schools that cater for students with the most challenging and complex disabilities (Chambers & Forlin, 2021).

To make this transition more viable, in recent years, systems have started to establish stronger links between special and regular schools through creating co-sites. These allow for new buildings to incorporate both regular classrooms and specialist areas where more intensive support can be provided. The setting in which students with complicated needs are educated will impact upon expectations and the curriculum that may be offered (Forlin & Chambers, 2017). If students with the most complex needs are to be educated successfully in regular classrooms, however, then to be effective inclusive practice will need to:

... ensure that teacher education, resources, policy, and processes, are made available at all levels and stages of execution to enable inclusion to move beyond rhetoric. If classrooms of the future are going to continue to accommodate an increasingly diverse group of learners, then governments must adopt a more proactive and realistic role to establish policy and to provide support for practices that address the fundamentally different needs of all learners. (Forlin & Chambers, 2017, pp. 567–568)

A lack of appropriate support, acceptance or understanding within regular schools, for including learners with multiple and complex challenges, will continue to trigger the need for more alternative placements. Inclusive schools will also have to compete with their inability to provide the extensive range of support options generally found in special schools. As special schools have become well established in communities, they have been able to offer regular and intensive support in areas such as occupational therapy, speech therapy, and physical therapy often providing therapeutic pools, spas, sensory rooms, and a wide range of life skills areas to accommodate the specific needs of learners and to prepare students for post school living. With parental choice being at the forefront of education, it will be seen whether parents will be prepared to give up these excellent facilities to move their child to an inclusive school, where such facilities are unlikely to be offered. Inclusive schools will need to provide evidence that what they have to offer by way of inclusion will far outweigh the facilities and support offered in special schools if parents are going to support this move.

Transitioning students from special schools into regular schools will undoubtedly be affected by the differing models of support offered between government and non-government systems and will depend upon the context, geographical access, and the availability of personnel. Although most systems actively promote inclusive education as an expectation, there remains, in reality, students with high needs that reportedly are not able to be catered for within an inclusive school. Alternative specialist placements continue to be a commonly accepted approach for supporting students identified with high needs across all jurisdictions.

To ensure any transition from a segregated special school to an inclusive school is effective, lessons learned from families of children with high support needs highlight a number of areas for specific focus (Forlin et al., 2019). These include but are not limited to the following recommendations:

- Better educator preparation for curriculum modification and pedagogical approaches for effective inclusion,
- A stronger focus on social inclusion to enable a sense of belonging and achievement,
- Safe learning and social environments that meet the high needs of students from special schools,
- Support and information networks for parents providing advice and assistance in locating suitable schools,
- Honor the knowledge of parents and families in having in-depth understanding about their child's needs and "what works,"
- Adopt a collaborative approach between schools and parents, mutual sharing within a positive and supportive environment, maintaining regular contact and opportunities to review and reflect upon programs and practices.

(Adapted from Forlin et al., 2019, p. 102)

Unless trained professionals are given sufficient time and adequate resources to support learners with high needs within inclusive classrooms, then the transition to inclusive schooling for these students is going to be particularly challenging to maintain. Physical placement of students from special schools to a regular school, by itself will not lead to them being included and engaged in regular classes. Of extreme importance is also the necessity to provide an environment that will incorporate social inclusion where students with the most challenging needs can feel that they belong and are welcomed and valued members of the school (Scorgie & Forlin, 2019). This would require a transformation of attitudes and beliefs within many school communities, as presence alone will not guarantee social inclusion. As social institutions, developing an ethos of belonging for all students should underpin a school's philosophy for becoming inclusive. The reality of a change of physical placement under the rubric of inclusion, while meeting a system's expectation for practice, may not result in the desired effect. If teachers are unable to provide the expected resources and support that parents received for their students when in a special school, and if they are unable to meet the learning needs of students with complex issues, then these students may simply continue to be educated in a segregated classroom.

CONCLUSION

Internationally a continuum of placement options from full-time placement in a regular classroom to full-time placement in a segregated specialist school have mostly been retained. In general, four options are provided including full-time placement in inclusive regular schools, a special class within a regular school, a special center on or off site of a regular school, and a separate specialist facility. All systems have their own set of criteria for access to these differing placement options. Placement options tend to more readily available in government systems with nongovernment systems or schools relying heavily on placement within the regular school. With increased parental options in many regions, decisions for school placement are now made in collaboration with parents, rather than solely determined by the system. To move students from well-resourced special schools to regular schools where support will be limited may not be accepted as a positive way forward by parents.

With an expectation by education systems, nevertheless, that more learners are to be moved from special to inclusive schools in the future, successful and collaborative approaches to transition planning will continue to be crucial if students with the most complex conditions and requirements are to realize positive success both socially and academically (Forlin & Deppeler, 2018). Inclusive schools that aim to accommodate the multifaceted needs of learners will need to provide both a curriculum that can meet their academic needs, and also establish a culture which supports authentic belonging where care and respect are valued (Mcilroy, 2019). Schools will further need to ensure that social inclusion is foremost in their practices by providing an environment underpinned by positive and accepting attitudes of all members of a school's community in which students with the most challenging needs can feel that they belong and are welcomed contributing members.

REFERENCES

Ainscow, M., Dyson, A., Goldrick, S., & West, M. (2011). *Developing equitable education systems.* Routledge.

Atkinson, G., & Rowley, J. (2019). Pupils' views on mainstream reintegration from alternative provision: A Q methodological study. *Emotional and Behavioural Difficulties, 24*(4), 339–356. https://doi.org/10.1080/13632752.2019.1625245

Bradley, R. (2016). 'Why single me out?' Peer mentoring, autism and inclusion in mainstream secondary schools. *British Journal of Special Education, 43*(3), 272–288.

Cantali, D. (2019). Moving to secondary school for children with ASN: A systematic review of international literature. *British Journal of Special Education, 46*(1), 29–52. https://doi.org/10.1111/1467-8578.12258

Carter, E. W., Asmus, J., Moss, C. K., Biggs, E. E., Bolt, D. M., Born, T. L., & Fesperman, E. (2016). Randomized evaluation of peer support arrangements to support the inclusion of high school students with severe disabilities. *Exceptional Children, 82*(2), 209–233.

Carter, M., Stephenson, J., Clark, T., Costley, D., Martin, J., Williams, K., Bruck, S., Davies, L., Browne, L., & Sweller, N. (2019). A comparison of two models of support for students with autism spectrum disorder in school and predictors of school success. *Research in Autism Spectrum Disorders, 68*, 101452.

Carter, M., Stephenson, J., Clark, T., Costley, D., Martin, J., Williams, K., et al. (2014). Perspectives on regular and support class placement and factors that contribute to success of inclusion for children with ASD. *Journal of International Special Needs Education, 17*, 60–69. https://doi.org/10.9782/2159-4341-17.2.60

Carter, M., Stephenson, J., & Webster, A. (2018). A survey of professional tasks and training needs of teaching assistants in New South Wales mainstream public schools. *Journal of Intellectual & Developmental Disability*, 1–10. https://doi.org/10.3109/13668250.2018.1462638

Chambers, D., & Forlin, C. (2021). An historical review from exclusion to inclusion in Western Australia across the past five decades: What have we learnt? *Education Sciences, 11*(119), 1–15. https://doi.org/10.3390/.educsci11030119

Chandroo, R., Strnadová, I., & Cumming, T. M. (2018). A systematic review of the involvement of students with autism spectrum disorder in the transition planning process: Need for voice and empowerment. *Research in Developmental Disabilities, 83*, 8–17.

Chmiliar, L. (2009). Perspectives on inclusion: Students with LD, their parents, and their teachers. *Exceptionality Education International, 19*(1), 72–88.

Cockroft, C., & Atkinson, C. (2015). Using the Wider Pedagogical Role model to establish learning support assistants' views about facilitators and barriers to effective practice. *Support for Learning, 30*(2), 88–104.

Croydon, A., Remington, A., Kenny, L., & Pellicano, E. (2019). 'This is what we've always wanted': Perspectives on young autistic people's transition from special school to mainstream satellite classes. *Autism & Developmental Language Impairments, 4*, 1–16.

Cumming, T. M., & Strnadová, I. (2017). Transitioning back to mainstream education: The Flexible Integration Model. *Australasian Journal of Special Education, 41*(1), 51–67.

Deppeler, J. M., Forlin, C., Chambers, D., Loreman, T. J., & Sharma, U. (2016). Equity and quality: Inclusive education in Australia for students with disabilities. In J. Deppeler & D. Zay (Eds.), *Inclusion through shared education* (pp. 63–81). (Inclusive Education and Partnerships). Deep University Press.

Deppeler, J. M., & Loreman, T. (2015). Teaching and learning for all. In J. M. Deppeler, T. Loreman, R. Smith, & L. Florian (Eds.), *Inclusive pedagogy across the curriculum, international perspectives on inclusive education* (Vol. 7, pp. 1–10). Emerald.

Forlin, C. (2019). Teacher education and inclusion in the Asia-Pacific region. In J. Lambert (Ed.), *The Oxford research encyclopedia of education*. Oxford University Press. https://oxfordre.com/education/view/10.1093/acrefore/9780190264093.001.0001/acrefore-9780190264093-e-570

Forlin, C., & Chambers, D. (2017). Catering for diversity: Including learners with different abilities and needs in regular classrooms. In R. Maclean (Ed.), *Life in schools and classrooms: Past, present and future* (pp. 555–572). Springer. https://doi.org/10.1093/acrefore/9780190264093.013.1214

Forlin, C., & Chambers, D. (2020). Diversity and inclusion and special education. In U. Sharma (Ed.), *Oxford encyclopedia of inclusive and special education*. Oxford University Press. https://doi.org/10.1093/acrefore/9780190264093.013.1214

Forlin, C., Chambers, D., Loreman, T., Deppeler, J., & Sharma, U. (2013). Inclusive education for students with disability: A review of the best evidence in relation to theory and practice. Report to the Australian government department of education, employment and workplace relations & Australian research alliance for children and youth, Canberra. https://www.aracy.org.au/publications-resources/command/download_file/id/246/filename/Inclusive_education_for_students_with_disability_-_A_review_of_the_best_evidence_in_relation_to_theory_and_practice.pdf

Forlin, C., & Deppeler, J. (2018). Supporting learners with high support needs in inclusive schools: Does this interconnect with career planning and transition into post-school options? *Hong Kong Journal of Special Education, 20*, 73–91.

Forlin, C., Scorgie, K., Strikwerda, H., Walker, J., Donnelly, M., Jane, S., & Aragon, A. (2019). "He seemed a little lost soul": Family insights into the reality of realizing inclusive education for a child with a disability. In C. Forlin & K. Scorgie (Eds.), *Promoting social inclusion Co-creating Environments that foster Equity and belonging, international Perspectives on inclusive education* (Vol. 13, pp. 80–93). Emerald.

Goodall, C. (2019). More flexibility to meet my needs. *Support for Learning, 34*(1), 4–33. https://doi.org/10.1111/1467-9604.12236

Grindle, C. F., Hastings, R. P., Saville, M., Hughes, J. C., Huxley, K., Kovshoff, H., Griffith, G. M., Walker-Jones, E., Devonshire, K., & Remington, B. (2012). Outcomes of a behavioral education model for children with autism in a mainstream school setting. *Behavior Modification, 36*, 298–319. https://doi.org/10.1177/0145445512441199

Hart, S. M. (2021). Agentic ethnography: Inclusive interviews of young adults with significant disabilities on the transition from school. *International Journal of Research & Method in Education*. https://doi.org/10.1080/1743727X.2021.1881057

Isaksson, J., Lindqvist, R., & Bergström, E. (2010). Struggling for recognition and inclusion: Parents' and students' experiences of special support measures in school. *International Journal of Qualitative Studies on Health and Well-being, 5*(1), 1–11.

Keane, E., Aldridge, F. J., Costley, D., & Clark, T. (2012). Students with autism in regular classes: A long-term follow-up study of a satellite class transition model. *International Journal of Inclusive Education, 16*, 1001–1017. https://doi.org/10.1080/13603116.2010.538865

Malapela, R. G., Thupayagale-Tshweneagae, G., & Mashalla, G. (2020). Transition of adolescents with intellectual disability from schools for learners with special educational needs: Parents views for the preparedness. *Journal of Applied Research in Intellectual Disabilities, 33*, 1440–1447.

Martin, T., Dixon, R., Verenikina, I., & Costley, D. (2021). Transitioning primary school students with Autism Spectrum Disorder from a special education setting to a mainstream classroom: Successes and difficulties. *International Journal of Inclusive Education, 25*(5), 640–655. https://doi.org/10.1080/13603116.2019.1568597

Mcilroy, A.-M. (2019). Assessment, curriculum, and literacy practices to develop and support social relationships in a New Zealand primary school. In K. Scorgie & C. Forlin (Eds.), *Promoting social inclusion co-creating environments that foster equity and belonging, international perspectives on inclusive education*, (Vol. 13, pp. 139–150). Bingley: Emerald.

Ministry of Education, New Zealand. Satellite units on host school sites. (n.d.). https://www.education.govt.nz/school/property-and-transport/school-facilities/learning-support-and-special-school-related-facilities-property-entitlement/specialist-schools/satellite-units-on-host-school-sites/

Neal, S., Rice, F., Ng-Knight, T., Riglin, L., & Frederickson, N. (2016). Exploring the longitudinal association between interventions to support the transition to secondary school and child anxiety. *Journal of Adolescence, 50*, 31–43.

NSW Government Education. (2021). Inclusive learning support. https://education.nsw.gov.au/parents-and-carers/inclusive-learning-support/support-and-adjustments/available-support/schools-for-specific-purposes-ssps

Plotner, A. J., VanHorn Stinnett, C., Rose, C., & Ivester, J. (2017). Professional characteristics that impact perceptions of successful transition collaboration. *Journal of Rehabilitation, 83*(2), 43–51.

Rowe, D. A., Alverson, C. Y., Unruh, D., Fowler, C., Kellems, R., & Test, D. W. (2014). A Delphi study to operationalize evidence-based predictors in secondary transition. *Career Development and Transition for Exceptional Individuals, 38*(2), 113–126. https://doi.org/10.1177/2165143414526429

Scorgie, K., & Forlin, C. (2019). Social inclusion and belonging: Affirming validation, agency and voice. In K. Scorgie & C. Forlin (Eds.), *Promoting social inclusion co-creating environments that foster equity and belonging, international perspectives on inclusive education* (Vol. 13, pp. 3–16). Emerald.

Sharma, U., & Salend, S. (2016). Teaching assistants in inclusive classrooms: A systematic analysis of the international research. *Australian Journal of Teacher Education, 41*(8), 118–134. http://dx.doi.org/10.14221/ajte.2016v41n8.7

Shepherd, J. (2020). Beyond tick-box transitions? Experiences of autistic students moving from special to further education. *International Journal of Inclusive Education*. https://doi.org/10.1080/13603116.2020.1743780

Simpson, R. L., de Boer-Ott, S. R., & Smith-Myles, B. (2003). Inclusion of learners with autism spectrum disorders in general education settings. *Topics in Language Disorders, 23*, 116–133. https://doi.org/10.1097/00011363-200304000-00005

Talapatra, D., Roach, A. T., Varjas, K., Houchins, D. E., & Crimmins, D. B. (2018). Promoting school psychologist participation in transition services using the TPIE Model. *Contemporary School Psychology, 22*(1), 18–29.

Trotman, D., Enow, L., & Tucker, S. (2019). Young people and alternative provision: Perspectives from participatory–collaborative evaluations in three UK local authorities. *British Educational Research Journal, 45*(2), 219–237. https://doi.org/10.1002/berj.3495

Urbis Pty. Ltd. (2011, August). *The psychological and emotional wellbeing needs of children and young people: Models of effective practice in educational settings*. Final Report. Prepared for the Department of Education and Communities.

"IT DOESN'T JUST HAPPEN": TRANSFORMING SCHOOLS FOR EFFECTIVE TRANSITION

Michelle Ralston and Kerry Dally

ABSTRACT

Planning for transition to a new educational setting, such as changing grades or moving from primary to high school, is important for all students but particularly for those who may require additional support for their individual needs. Research shows that transition planning and implementation for students with disability are best supported through collaboration and information sharing among all stakeholders. In Australia, the Disability Standards for Education (DSE) (2005) mandate consultation between education providers, students with disability, and their carers as part of the process of enrollment so that reasonable adjustments to support a student's progress can be identified and implemented. This chapter reports on two innovative approaches to the organization of transition and support systems for students with disability. The findings reveal that effective transition "doesn't just happen" and that school leaders need to establish effective mechanisms for consultation and collaboration.

Keywords: Collaboration; transition; support systems; disability; leadership; educational settings

INTRODUCTION

Preparing students for transition to new learning environments can optimize learning (Lincoln et al., 2016; Strnadová & Cumming, 2014). Transition preparedness also serves the staff who will be working with new students (Lincoln et al., 2016). A well-developed transition plan ensures that staff are equipped with

Transition Programs for Children and Youth with Diverse Needs
International Perspectives on Inclusive Education, Volume 18, 91–107
Copyright © 2022 Michelle Ralston and Kerry Dally
Published under exclusive licence by Emerald Publishing Limited
ISSN: 1479-3636/doi:10.1108/S1479-363620220000018008

information about student academic and social needs, and necessary resources (Strnadová & Cumming, 2014; Towns, 2018). This in turn ensures successful outcomes for students (Dockett, 2018; Forlin et al., 2019; Lincoln et al., 2016; Towns, 2018).

In this chapter, we focus on the transition of students with disability in mainstream settings and adopt a broad definition of transition. Based on Strnadová and Cumming's (2016) notion of transition as a period of change, we define transition in the school setting as the process of adapting to change, such as moving from a class, stage, school, or environment to another. Transition involves a process of preparing for, and adjusting to, new contexts such as curricula, pedagogy, environment, and relationships between peers and staff (Lincoln et al., 2016). This may include a student working with a new teacher because their current teacher has gone on leave, moving to a new class at the beginning of the school year, or moving into primary or high school. Transitions do not just happen for the student (Forlin et al., 2019). All aspects of the school environment must undergo preparation for change as the school prepares for and proactively responds to the experiences and expectations of new students and their families (Dockett, 2018).

The Organisation for Economic Co-operation and Development (OECD) (2017) states that transitions must be "well-prepared and child centered, managed by trained staff collaborating with one another, and guided by an appropriate and aligned curriculum" (p. 13). Quality transition programs ensure information and strategies pertinent to the specific student's strengths, interests, and needs are shared with new teachers and support staff (Neal & Frederickson, 2016; Tso & Strnadová, 2017). Information about student progress, "what works and doesn't" (Towns, 2018, p. 44) is also shared in order to guide decisions about priority of needs, adjustments to curriculum, teaching and learning experiences, and assessment. Collaboration during transition ensures continuity in learning and support while simultaneously supporting adaptation to change (Dockett, 2018; Lincoln et al., 2016). Collaboration between all stakeholders optimizes opportunities for learning (Strnadová & Cumming, 2014, 2016). During the transition period, communication between the personnel in the student's present environment and the environment they will be moving into are considered critical (Pitt et al., 2019).

The student and the family are key stakeholders who remain consistent across all transitions in the student's life. Family involvement is therefore essential for the student to build confidence and trust in the new setting (Neal & Frederickson, 2016). Student input into decision-making, when this is age appropriate, has also been found to have positive outcomes for the student and school (Knesting et al., 2008; Rodriguez et al., 2017).

Other key stakeholders identified in research as essential in transition programs are the personnel beyond the school who provide ongoing support to the student (Strnadová & Cumming, 2016). Professionals such as occupational therapists can assess the new setting and provide advice on adjustments needed to the physical environment to ensure access to learning, while speech pathologists and psychologists can provide information on developmental progress, long-term goals, and effective pedagogy.

Teachers and support staff in the new setting can be more effective and efficient in providing essential support when well informed by the student, family, previous teachers and support staff, and interagencies who have been involved in the learning and support of that student (Strnadová & Cumming, 2016). In addition to this knowledge, teachers and support staff need empathy, skills and commitment to the student (Beamish et al., 2012; Lightfoot & Bond, 2013).

Thus, the research shows that successful transitions for students with disability require collaboration, teamwork and good communication between home, school and at times, external professionals, to ensure the needs of students are being recognized and addressed. The other common aspects that are pertinent to transitions for students with disability include policies, school leadership, and the skills, knowledge and attitudes of teachers and support staff. In this chapter, we first review the national standards governing the enrollment and participation of students with disability in Australian schools and then examine two innovative approaches to facilitate the transition and inclusion of students with disability.

TRANSITION PLANNING IN THE AUSTRALIAN CONTEXT

As there is no legislative requirement or national education policy that requires the development of transition plans in Australia, the Australian Disability Standards for Education (DSE) (2005) will be used as a framework.

The DSE (2005) mandate consultation between education providers, students with disability and their carers as part of the process of enrollment so that reasonable adjustments are identified and implemented (DSE, 2005). Transition planning is not explicitly mentioned in the DSE (2005) but can be inferred from the mandated procedures for consultation, enrollment, determining reasonable adjustments, ensuring access to services, complaints handling, and learning and development programs.

The purpose of transition planning inferred from the DSE (2005) is the provision of adjustments that ensure students with disability have choices, opportunities and learning experiences on the same basis as a student without a disability so that students with disability can participate in education and training, achieve learning outcomes, and achieve independence.

The DSE (2005) establishes the expectation that education providers will establish mechanisms, such as policies and procedures, to ensure the objectives of the DSE (2005) are achieved. Consultation is a mandatory procedure where the education provider is expected to establish a formal process for consultation and decision-making with all key stakeholders. This is particularly important during enrollment and other periods of transition as the ongoing interchange of information and opinions will influence what and how adjustments are implemented. In addition, the process of consultation assists the education provider to meet its legal obligation to "ensure staff have sufficient information and expertise"

(Disability Standards for Education 2005 Guidance Notes, 2006, p. 10) to design equitable learning opportunities for their students.

According to the DSE (2005), clear mechanisms are necessary to ensure and facilitate accessible, fair, and accountable consultation. Information about student needs must be provided to those working with the student and reasonable adjustments must be "negotiated, agreed and implemented" (DSE, 2005, Part 5.3(c)). Learning Support Team meetings where Individual Education Plans (IEPs) and Transition Plans (Strnadová et al., 2017) are collaboratively devised are examples of such mechanisms.

Consultation is not restricted in the DSE (2005) to a mere exchange of information. The discourse implies an interactive dialogue that seeks consensus while valuing the perspectives of each party. Words and phrases such as "negotiate[d] ... agree[d]" (DSE, 2005, Part 5.3(c)), "review" (DSE, 2005, Part 5.3(b)), "facilitate [d]" (DSE, 2005, Part 7.3(b)), and "collaborative arrangements" (DSE, 2005, Part 7.3(b)), suggest interaction and working together to achieve agreed goals.

Consultation can involve each person working in isolation, and one person appointed as the leader. While this approach facilitates the collation of information and guides decision-making, the principles outlined earlier suggest that the DSE (2005) supports *collaborative* consultation whereby the parties work together toward an agreed purpose (Idol et al., 2000; Leko et al., 2015). Andreozzi and Pietrocarlo (2017) define collaborative consultation as "reciprocal adaptation" (p. 127) where all participants develop new competencies in the context of a shared project. Collaborative teams that exercise trust and mutual respect while working together share expertise and develop a new "collective intelligence" (Zundans-Fraser & Bain, 2016, p. 136). Collaborative consultation demands a high level of participation from all individuals (Zundans-Fraser & Bain, 2016) and a shift from the traditional practice of consultants working in isolation. Collaboration during transition develops genuine partnerships and respectful, reciprocal relationships as personnel work toward supporting a student to achieve learning outcomes in the new environment.

The advantage of collaboration over consultation is that through the collaborative process team members experience professional growth (Deppeler, 2006; Dockett, 2018) as the interactions lead to new thinking, perspectives, and actions (Zundans-Fraser & Bain, 2016). As each member works through different opinions and values the expertise and input of all involved, new meaning and actions are devised that are unique to a particular student and team members. Thus, collaboration results in a new collective intelligence shared between team members. In the school context, this leads to increased quality and effectiveness of teaching and learning experiences (Dockett, 2018; Friend et al., 2010; Leko et al., 2015). Establishing mechanisms for collaboration is therefore a worthwhile investment. The process leads to a better-quality product and increased capability of staff. In Zundans-Fraser and Bain's (2016) research about collaboration in schools, staff reported the interactive benefits of collaboration to include feelings of ownership and consistent implementation of teaching programs. Staff also reported feeling less isolated because the development of trusting relationships and mutual learning provided them with a support framework.

According to multiple studies reviewed by Zundans-Fraser and Bain (2016) and Mangano (2015), efficient and effective collaborative practice requires a collaborative culture, organizational management, and staff who have the skills for collaboration. In the remainder of this chapter, we examine how two schools have modified their existing inclusion support systems to facilitate the transition of students with disability into new educational settings.

ENROLMENT AND TRANSITION PROCESSES IN MAINSTREAM SCHOOLS

The findings reported in this chapter were part of a larger research project that explored the extent to which DSE (2005) principles are being implemented in mainstream schools in one Australian state, as well as what (or who) influences that implementation. The larger study employed a two-phase mixed-method design whereby school staff (teachers, principals, learning support officers (LSOs, otherwise known as Teaching Assistants) and school counsellors) were asked to complete an online survey at the end of which they were invited to participate in an interview. A total of 449 people completed the surveys and 12 people were interviewed. The survey results are reported elsewhere, and the findings reported here focus on two case study schools which had recently introduced innovative systems to facilitate transition processes and inclusion support for students with disability. In order to maintain anonymity, the two schools are referred to as Senior High and Secondary High. The data for these two schools were obtained primarily from the semi-structured staff interviews supplemented by an analysis of school documents and survey results from any participants who identified the relevant school name in their survey. Survey results from six staff from Senior High and 10 staff from Secondary High were available for analysis and in each school the interviews were conducted with the principal, and three teachers.

Senior High

Senior high school catered for students in Year 11 and 12 who sought an alternative pathway to achieving the Higher School Certificate (HSC) while transitioning from school to the workplace. Typically, students undertook school-based traineeships or apprenticeships while simultaneously completing the HSC. This private school was a Registered Training Organization (RTO) accredited through the Australian Skills Authority (ASQA). Students could complete Stage 1 apprenticeship or achieve a full year of credit toward a Certificate II trade qualification such as mechanic, electrician, or carpenter.

This small school had 240 students aged 16–19 years and the equivalent of 12.2 full-time teachers. Some teachers specialized in HSC subjects such as Maths and English, while others were Vocational Education and Training (VET) teachers who were qualified tradespersons with teacher qualifications. No LSOs were employed. School records revealed that just over 20% of their students experienced disability as reported in the Nationally Consistent Collection of Data (NCCD). A new principal moved to the school during the year prior to this research and assessed practice in relation to adherence with the DSE. The principal identified transition into the senior school setting for students with a disability, as a priority area for change within the school.

Historic policy and procedures were problematic. After a student commenced at the school an IEP was created by a curriculum coordinator, but not disseminated to staff. The principal noted that the IEPs "sat on the shelf and nothing much happened. They were not communicated to teachers." Adjustments to assessment were considered a major issue as the school was registered to sign off on student competency against national RTO Standards. The principal noted that a student's failure to meet the required standards was often not due to a student's lack of ability, but rather, because the staff did not have adequate knowledge or support to make necessary adjustments. This sentiment was echoed in comments from staff who recognized their lack of expertise to adequately support students. While a Learning Support Team existed, its role was restricted to applying for disability provisions for HSC exams.

All interviewees from this school noted attitudinal problems among some staff. Informal staffroom conversations were reported to often revolve around teachers complaining about what a student could not do, rather than about what the teacher could due to ensure student achievement. The reluctance to make adjustments was typified in this reported comment:

> "I don't know why I am having to do this, just to get this particular kid through the course. Why do I have to make any changes just for him? This is not what I signed up for." When offered suggestions these same teachers would complain that they did not have time.

Recognizing the attitudinal issues, limitations to policy and procedures, and lack of compliance with the DSE (2005), the principal observed, "it doesn't just happen." The principal therefore assumed responsibility for establishing systems that enabled staff to fulfill their legal and ethical obligations. This involved reviewing and writing policy and procedures that guided, supported, and monitored staff implementation.

An experienced and qualified Learning and Support Teacher (LaST) was employed to facilitate collaboration between students, families and staff in the development and implementation of IEPs. The role of a LaST is to provide additional support to classroom teachers in planning and implementation of adjustments, team teaching, mentoring opportunities, and accessing resources. The LaST at Senior High described her role as:

> Taking policy and helping teachers put it into practice in the regular classroom. Working alongside everyone else, not having special classes that separate teachers and students.

All interviewees mentioned that the school implemented a targeted approach to change the culture of the school for students, families, and staff during enrollment and transitions to higher grades.

The enrollment policy and process were improved to be better aligned with the DSE (2005), including the opportunity for consultation with the student and parent/guardian about any adjustments that may be needed to complete the enrollment process and participate in school curriculum activities. New procedures enabled staff to informally interact with prospective students and families during three information evenings where information about the school, courses, and enrollment process were explained. The LaST and administrative staff were available to assist families to complete forms that sought to obtain information about the student's learning difficulties, needs or an existing IEP. All enrollment forms were reviewed before entrance testing, and families were consulted about any necessary adjustments to ensure the student was given the best opportunity to demonstrate their knowledge, skills, and ability during the English and Maths exams. This new procedure resulted in an increase in the number of students with disability successfully achieving enrollment at Senior High.

Once students had been offered a place in the school, the LaST initiated further contact with the student and family to establish a transition program and IEP relevant to the new school. Interviewees noted the benefit of viewing IEPs from the student's previous location. One teacher commented:

> It is good to know what they are used to. For example, having an LSO in most lessons. If they are used to an LSO they can feel out of their depth here [because there are no LSOs at this school]. (T47)

Ideally, collaborative planning with the students' previous school was viewed as beneficial. However, not all schools agreed to this process. Where possible, adjustments used in the previous setting were continued, if appropriate. The LaST disseminated the IEP and personally spoke to each teacher about the adjustments needed and supported teachers to modify lesson content, activities, and assessments. During the first few weeks at the school, the LaST prioritized developing independence skills with those students who had previously had in-class support from an LSO.

While changes to the enrollment and transition process were deemed as important, both the principal and deputy recognized that "consistent and sustainable practice needs systems that do not rely on one person." At this early stage, they recognized the burden of change was falling disproportionately on the LaST. They sought to establish systems that supported all staff to do their jobs well, so the staff could then support the students. Knowledge and skills were needed, along with a commitment to equity. The Deputy described this as a "teacher's heart." Policies were revised with the intention to guide and support teachers. For example, the Literacy and Numeracy policy embedded the need for adjustments. Implementation was supported with a curriculum-based budget for adjustments such as additional resources. The policy also prioritized Learning and Development for staff, with mentoring and co-teaching opportunities with the LaST.

Despite these policies, some teachers remained reluctant to implement these practices. The principal saw compliance as an opportunity to improve practice and influence attitude. While providing training to staff on mandated requirements, she would ask them, "How can this regulation/requirement benefit us?" The mandatory requirements include the DSE (2005), Nationally Consistent Collection of Data (NCCD) (Australian Government Department of Education and Training (DET), n.d.), and Australian Professional Standards for Teachers (Australian Institute for Teaching and School Leadership (AITSL), 2015). For example, she claimed the NCCD enabled the identification of more students who would not otherwise have been identified, and the range of support in the school broadened. The Deputy explained the four steps they used to persuade reluctant staff to change their behavior from compliance to commitment.

(1) Mandates – it's the law. We have to do it. Making adjustments *are* what we signed up for. They are our professional responsibility.
(2) Adjustments are the right thing to do so that all the kids in your class have the opportunity to learn.
(3) The changes/adjustments benefit all of the kids you have in front of you.
(4) They make the teacher a better practitioner. [A teacher who can] understand students, differentiate better, ... and validate assessment tasks in a manner that suits Australian Skills Quality Authority.

(Deputy)

To further strengthen positive attitudes, the principal changed the Learning and Development policy. Complementing the new enrollment and transition policy, and in alignment with the DSE (2005), the revised professional learning policy recognized that training needed to be timely in order to address student needs and provide adequate support to staff. Staff were now encouraged to seek and participate in learning opportunities in Term 1 to gain disability specific knowledge and skills related to newly transitioned students.

Integral to all policy revisions was helping teachers gain awareness, strengthen their attitude, and build personal knowledge and skills to include students with disability in their classrooms. Procedures (within the policy) were considered essential "as they make sure the policy isn't just an archival document, but that it lives" (Deputy). Procedures included Learning and Development of staff, collaboration with key stakeholders, accessing resources, evaluating student progress and suitability of adjustments, and monitoring implementation of adjustments by staff. The Deputy expressed a pragmatic approach, "Some teachers are more willing to adapt than others. Some teachers are vigilant, others try not to get caught." Monitoring systems were standardized across policies and curriculum areas within the school. Teachers needed to document and provide the following to their curriculum coordinator: Record of adjustments in class programs for individuals, aligned with the IEP; Register of completed program activities; and Assessment marks or competencies achieved for all students, with examples of student achievement at low, middle, and high levels.

Describing the school as still in a "reactive phase" the principal expressed a need to manage change gradually. Effective transition required systems to build staff capability through cultural change of attitude and learning and development. School capacity could then be enhanced through policies and procedures that informed, guided, supported, and regulated implementation.

Secondary School

Secondary School was a large co-educational high school catering for approximately 1,200 students from years 7 to 12 (aged 12–19 years). Secondary School employed the equivalent of 85 full-time teachers. School records show that in 2016 the school was allocated three special education teachers for the 200 students who had IEPs. Each special education teacher had responsibility for approximately 66 students. Appraisal of the effectiveness of this Learning Support model for students, teachers, and parents involved staff, student, and parent surveys and comparison of NCCD and National Assessment Program – Literacy and Numeracy (NAPLAN) data.

Whole school evaluation found that quality partnerships with parents, ongoing consultation with service providers, and monitoring of adjustments across each student's eight teachers from different curriculum areas, were not being achieved consistently for students with disability. The planning of individual goals and adjustments was occurring predominantly by the designated special education teachers, but these teachers did not have responsibility for teaching those students in the mainstream classroom. The impact of this historic structure was minimal ownership of responsibility or sharing of expertise across faculties within the school.

The school review process also identified the desire of staff to have more support and expertise in the classroom to meet diverse learning needs. Concern was raised that the expertise in the school remained limited to three full time special education teachers who did not have the time to adequately assist the numerous teachers or their students. This model had been used in the school for many years but the capacity of the school as a whole had not increased. The review highlighted that a different approach was required. A system that facilitated development of teacher knowledge and commitment to individual students, with time allocation.

The principal and his leadership team were challenged to develop a new model that was cost neutral. That is, no extra funds were available to employ more staff or support the cost of any change. The school embarked on a Case Management Model.

Two of the designated full time (FT) special education positions were converted to 10 Case Manager (CM) positions at 0.2 FT equivalent (1 FT = 5 teachers @0.2). The conversion of one FT position is illustrated in Fig. 1. The third FT position was converted to four positions, with one of those allocated 0.2 additional release for a Case Management Coordinator's position. In summary, the previous three positions were converted into 14 positions, with each teacher managing approximately 15 students.

The role of Case Manager (CM) allowed 0.2 release for quality planning time with students, parents and teachers at the start of each year. This facilitated transition from year to year, class to class, teacher to teacher. The CM convened

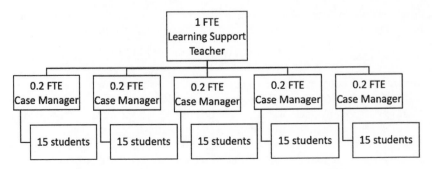

Fig. 1.   Conversion of One Full Time Equivalent (FTE) Teacher to Five Case
Managers.

meetings to develop and review IEPs with all key stakeholders. There was a focus on establishing current goals and adjustments at the beginning of the school year to ensure relevance and equity in classrooms as soon as possible.

Key to the CM role was consultation and collaboration with all stakeholders. Already established within the school were teams who addressed post-school options, aboriginal and Torres Strait Islander support, and student wellbeing. Services such as pastoral care and school counseling were also available. Regional support from the specialist intervention teams was available on request from the school. External providers such as physiotherapists and speech pathologists played consultative roles on request. The CM facilitated provision of these services in a coordinated manner so that these services were no longer working in isolation but collaboratively supporting the student.

The ongoing release from face-to-face teaching allowed for regular consultation, monitoring and evaluation of adjustments and learning gains throughout the year. The CM was responsible for tracking student data by analyzing all available results, reports and information provided by teachers, parents and students. Regular Teacher Team Briefings held between CMs and other teachers who worked with that student ensured communication of IEPs and provisions from each stakeholder, supporting staff to implement adjustments consistently. This was further facilitated by a centralized data base that utilized technology to ensure easy access for all staff to IEPs, assessment data, and specialist reports. The CM was the main point of contact for staff about further advice in relation to adjustments to learning and assessment activities, and for students and their parents in relation to feedback about effective adjustments and progress toward achieved goals.

Several criteria were identified for the selection of staff for the Case Manager positions.

- Formal expressions of interest were sought from all staff. Personal willingness to participate, and commitment to improving outcomes for students with disability, in collaboration with colleagues, were essential.

- Representation of the broad spectrum of faculties in the school was sought. For example History, Mathematics, Creative and Performing Arts and Physical Education. The goal was for each faculty to be represented across the 14 CMs. This created a structure to facilitate regular dialogue about quality learning and adjustments, beyond the Learning Support Department, in every faculty and across all curricula.
- Appointment to the position was for two years, when new CMs would be appointed. The Principal's vision was to build the capacity of the school by supporting *all* staff to make adjustments for all students with disability and individual support needs. The transition of staff into and out of the roles of CM on a rolling basis established a network of support and expertise. As new CMs were selected, they were trained by the outgoing CMs and mentored throughout the year by the ongoing CMs. As the outgoing CMs remained (mostly) on staff, they were also able to provide collegiate reciprocal learning.

The allocation of students to each CM was also carefully considered. As much as possible, the CM taught the students allocated to their caseload, within their regular classes. This provided the opportunity for authentic dialogue between the other seven teachers who taught the same student about adjustments that worked, and what might be tried. In this sense, collaboration was embedded into the school structure. The eight teachers of the same student had an invested interest in optimizing teaching and learning opportunities in their classrooms. The structure enabled the development of genuine partnerships and respectful, reciprocal relationships as they worked toward supporting the student to achieve learning outcomes in new environments. The structure also disrupted the traditional work practice of working in isolation, embedding ongoing supportive opportunities for teachers to develop new competencies in the context of their collective intelligence.

While undertaking the same responsibilities as the other CMs, the Case Management Coordinator had the additional responsibility of overseeing and supporting the implementation of the new model. The school organizational chart depicted in Fig. 2 illustrates the role each case manager had in supporting Key Learning Area (KLA) staff with shared students, and the Coordinator role with allocated additional time (0.2 FTE). The Coordinator's role included monitoring curriculum adjustments across year groups by collating data from all IEPs and providing targeted Learning and Development to staff based on this data.

The school planned a staged transition to the new model. Prior to commencement, CMs were given targeted professional learning from school and regional staff who specialized in diversity. Professional learning included: The DSE – the legal and moral imperative for inclusion; Consultation and collaboration for personalized planning; Incorporating student voice in planning and review processes of adjustments; Transition planning; Literacy and reading; Response to Intervention; Differentiation of instruction and assessment; and Case management policy and procedures. In addition, collaborative learning

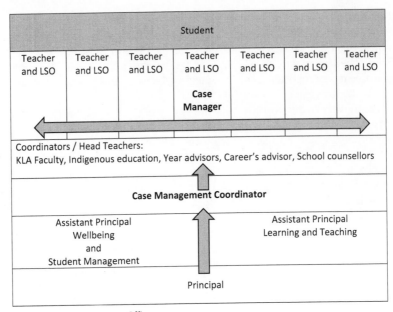

Fig. 2.   Organizational Chart.

among the team of CMs occurred every three weeks during term one, with the introduction of Case Manager Forums, chaired by the Case Management Coordinator.

Several systems were established to evaluate the CM system. Schedules and procedures were developed to review and assess: Transition plans and IEP review (Term 1 and 4); IEP implementation and relevance (at least once per term); Student satisfaction survey about teacher understanding of needs and adjustments (Term 2); and, Staff, student, parent satisfaction survey (Term 4). A formal review of the case management system in 2019 found that over the three year period of operation the number of staff trained and experienced in case management had risen from three to 21. Students reported that their needs were being met with effective adjustments more consistently across subject areas. The connection with the CM established both formal and informal opportunities to provide timely feedback when needs changed or adjustments required modification. Students believed that their goals were more personalized and relationships with staff more positive. Parents noted improved collaboration with the school, highlighting the effectiveness of one point of contact, and knowing that the CM had dedicated time off class for that communicative process.

Teachers reported an increase in cross-curriculum dialogue with colleagues and that having a CM in their faculty facilitated deeper collaboration. Teachers reported that having the CM teach the same student as they taught created authentic knowledge and achievable adjustments in the context of motivated teams. Teachers reported gaining new knowledge about skill-based learning, as opposed to a rigid content focus, that could be generalized across all curriculum subjects. In addition, teachers reported an increased knowledge about specific students, their needs and effective strategies to help them learn. CMs reported a growth in expertise in adjustments, collegial support, and collaboration. The CM coordinator found the system enabled a more efficient and effective ongoing partnership with regional personnel and specialist teachers.

School data indicated improved student outcomes. For example, suspension and welfare referral rates decreased. National Assessment Program – Literacy and Numeracy (NAPLAN) results for Year 7 showed a decrease in the percentage of students in the bottom two bands for reading from 2013 to 2017. Teachers attributed these outcomes to increased capacity to differentiate and meet student need.

At this school, the CM system established a clear mechanism to ensure and facilitate accessible, fair and accountable consultation and collaboration between all stakeholders. This increased school capacity to respond to the needs of unique students, expanded teacher capability, and increased student learning. Teachers gained the support they desired through time allocated collaboration. Expertise was increased, organized and accessible across all staff.

DISCUSSION

In Australia, the DSE (2005) mandates the principles and standards that should underpin the delivery of educational services to students with disability. Enshrined within the DSE (2005) is the principle that students with disability should be provided with opportunities and learning experiences *on the same basis* as students without disability so that equitable educational outcomes for all may be possible. McMaster (2015) noted that educational inequality can originate within schools, not because a student has an impairment, but because the internal organization and procedures of a school can be disabling. As the case studies reported in this chapter reveal, changes to an organizational environment can build the capacity of a school and the capability of staff within it, thus, making the goal of equitable access to education more achievable.

While the inclusion and educational attainment of a student with disability in one setting or class may be successful, the transition to a new setting may serve to disrupt a student's progress if it is not effectively executed. As the case studies revealed, changes can be implemented to establish more effective communication channels, at no additional expense to schools or education systems.

The role of the school principal has been described as the two complimentary functions of leadership and management (Andreozzi & Pietrocarlo, 2017). As leaders, principals create the conditions that enable staff to do their jobs effectively (Bai & Martin, 2015). Most notably, principals influence the culture of a school. Culture can be defined as a system of "ideas and images that orient and bind the behaviours of all relationships within and beyond the school"

(Andreozzi & Pietrocarlo, 2017, p. 128) such as those with students, staff, teachers, families, and inter-agencies. Andreozzi and Pietrocarlo (2017) argue that the culture of a school can either propel or prevent innovation.

Both principals in the case study schools expressed strong commitment to equity in access, participation, and achievement for students with disability. Both expressed the opinion that the educational success or failure of students with disability was not due to student capability. Rather, it was the challenge and responsibility of teachers to evaluate their practice to ensure that learning activities were accessible and responsive to ensure participation. The principals reported awareness of a discrepancy between "what is and what could be" (Bai & Martin, 2015, p. 1231) in their schools. They sought to "influence people's actions and, indeed, the thinking that informs those actions" (Ainscow & Sandill, 2010, p. 403) within the school context.

While both schools were different in size and transition practices, both underwent transformative processes that sought to build the capacity of the whole school to ensure that students with disability could participate in all aspects of school life. The principals targeted transition points of enrollment and the start of a new school year, as times when teachers might be more motivated and aware of the need to know their students well, in order to teach them. The principals' goal was to support teachers in providing appropriate adjustments within a reasonable time and thereby facilitate positive experiences and influence cultural attitudes. Both schools embedded systems to support teachers within school policies and procedures. These included time-allocation for collaboration, targeted learning and development, and regulatory processes. Clearly articulated statements from each principal about fundamental values, such as inclusion and equity underpinned these systems.

The management role of the school principal is significant. The verbs used in the DSE (2005) reveal that people in authority in schools have the mandate to *decide, determine, assess, develop, ensure, establish, design, provide, facilitate, and implement.* These causative verbs emphasize the role and responsibility school leaders have in causing action to be undertaken in their setting. The imperative verb "ensure" accentuates the expectation that people in authority in schools have the capacity and responsibility to effect change and influence outcomes in relation to compliance with the DSE (2005). The findings from our study confirm Webster's (2019) assertion that a principal's actions directly impact what happens across the whole school, in classrooms and extracurricula activities.

After initiating school wide reviews, both principals revised policies to influence practice. Ainscow and Sandill (2010) warn that changes to policy and procedures, alone, do not change practice. A social reorientation is essential. The two schools included clear statements at the beginning of each policy of the legislation, regulations, and values on which decision processes would be based. The revised policies informed staff of expected actions and guided them with procedures to follow. A collaborative culture was embedded into policy, with teachers supporting one another in developing new responses to diversity. This resulted in more consistent implementation of adjustments and improved student outcomes. Capability of staff was enhanced with authentic collaboration that resulted in the development of trusting relationships and learning opportunities through mentoring (Dockett, 2018).

Targeted learning and development were also embedded into policy. This supported staff and assisted the schools in meeting their obligation to ensure staff had sufficient information and expertise. Although not directly addressed by the two schools, Dockett (2018) suggests the need to educate principals, teachers, and LSOs about the collaborative process. Effective collaboration must be built on a shared commitment to generate new knowledge, strategies, and skills in the context of equal partnerships and a shared vision (Dockett, 2018).

The implications from our study indicate that for transitions of students with disability to be successful, collaborative procedures need to be established within schools to ensure that teachers and support staff are given the information they require to understand the specific strengths, abilities, and needs of the students, and the kinds of pedagogy that have been found to be effective. These systems need to be sustainable, so that transition programs do not just take place when students leave and enter new schools, such as primary to secondary, but that these systems are in place for transitions from year to year, teacher to teacher, support staff to support staff.

CONCLUSION

This chapter has drawn attention to the potential for improved transition processes for students with disability. Effective transition between and within schools does not "just happen." School principals play a critical role in establishing school culture and sustainable collaborative systems for effective transition. Efficient collaboration enables effective practice, positive staff attitudes, skill development, and student learning. Systems that enable collaboration have the potential to generate new knowledge and skills that ensure equitable access to learning for all students.

REFERENCES

Ainscow, M., & Sandill, A. (2010). Developing inclusive education systems: The role of organisational cultures and leadership. *International Journal of Inclusive Education, 14*(4), 401–416. https://doi.org/10.1080/13603110802504903

Andreozzi, P., & Pietrocarlo, A. (2017). Educational inclusion and organization. In F. Dovigo (Ed.), *Special educational needs and inclusive practices* (pp. 119–142). Sense Publishers.

Australian Government Department of Education and Training (DET). (n.d.). Nationally consistent collection of data school students with disability: Frequently asked questions. 2014. http://www.schooldisabilitydatapl.edu.au/other-pages/faq

Australian Institute for Teaching and School Leadership (AITSL). (2015). Australian professional standards for teachers. https://www.aitsl.edu.au/australian-professional-standards-for-teachers/standards/list

Bai, H., & Martin, S. M. (2015). Assessing the needs of training on inclusive education for public school administrators. *International Journal of Inclusive Education, 19*(12), 1229–1243. https://doi.org/10.1080/13603116.2015.1041567

Beamish, W., Meadows, D., & Davies, M. (2012). Benchmarking teacher practice in Queensland transition programs for youth with intellectual disability and autism. *Journal of Special Education, 45*(4), 227–241.

Deppeler, J. (2006). Improving inclusive practices in Australian schools: Creating conditions for university-school collaboration in inquiry. *European Journal of Psychology of Education, 21*(3), 347–360. https://doi.org/10.1007/BF03173421

Disability Standards for Education 2005 Guidance Notes. (2006). Commonwealth of Australia. https://www.legislation.gov.au/Details/F2005L00767/Supporting%20Material/Text

Disability Standards for Education. (2005). Commonwealth of Australia. https://docs.education.gov.au/node/16354

Dockett, S. (2018). Transition to school: Professional collaborations. *The Australian Educational Leader (AEL), 40*(2), 16–19.

Forlin, C., Scorgie, K., Strikwerda, H., Walker, J., Donnelly, M., Aragon, A. B., & Aragon, S. J. (2019). "He seemed a little lost soul": Family insights into the reality of realising inclusive education for a child with disability. In K. Scorgie & C. Forlin (Eds.), *Promoting social inclusion: Co-creating environments that foster equity and belonging* (pp. 93–103). Emerald Publishing Limited. https://doi.org/10.1108/S1479-363620190000013008

Friend, M., Cook, L., Hurley-Chamberlain, D., & Shamberger, C. (2010). Co-teaching: An illustration of the complexity of collaboration in special education. *Journal of Educational and Psychological Consultation, 20*, 9–27. https://doi.org/10.1080/10474410903535380

Idol, L., Nevin, A., & Paolucci-Whitcomb, P. (2000). *Collaborative consultation* (3rd ed.). Pro-ed.

Knesting, K., Hokanson, C., & Waldron, N. (2008). Settling in: Facilitating the transition to an inclusive middle school for students with mild disabilities. *International Journal of Disability, Development and Education, 55*(3), 265–276.

Leko, M. M., Kiely, M. T., Brownell, A., Osipova, A., Dingle, M. P., & Mundy, C. A. (2015). Understanding special educators' learning opportunities in collaborative groups: The role of discourse. *Teacher Education and Special Education: The Journal of the Teacher Education Division of the Council for Exceptional Children, 38*(2), 138–157. https://doi.org/10.1177/0888406414557283

Lightfoot, L., & Bond, C. (2013). An exploration of primary to secondary school transition planning for children with down's syndrome. *Educational Psychology in Practice, 29*(2), 163–179. https://doi.org/10.1080/02667363.2013.800024

Lincoln, M., Hagon, M., & Paxton, C. (2016). Transition partnerships: Embracing opportunities for innovation. *The Australian Educational Leader (AEL), 38*(4), 38–42.

Mangano, M. (2015). Teacher views on working with others to promote inclusion. In D. Chambers & C. Forlin (Eds.), *Working with teaching assistants and other support staff for inclusive education. International perspectives on inclusive education* (Vol. 4, pp. 117–132). Emerald Group Publishing Limited. https://doi.org/10.1108/S1479-363620150000004005

McMaster, C. (2015). "Where is ____?": Culture and the process of change. *International Journal of Whole Schooling, 11*(1), 16–34.

Neal, S., & Frederickson, N. (2016). ASD transition to mainstream secondary: A positive experience? *Educational Psychology in Practice, 32*(4), 355–373.

Organisation for Economic Co-operation and Development (OECD). (2017). *Starting strong V: Transitions from early childhood education and care to primary education.* OECD Publishing. https://doi.org/10.1787/9789264276253-en

Pitt, F., Dixon, R., & Vialle, W. (2019). The transition experiences of students with disabilities moving from primary to secondary schools in NSW, Australia. *International Journal of Inclusive Education.* https://doi.org/10.1080/13603116.2019.1572797

Rodriguez, C., Cumming, T., & Strnadová, I. (2017). Current practices in schooling transitions of students with developmental disabilities. *International Journal of Educational Research, 83*, 1–19. https://doi.org/10.1016/j.ijer.2017.02.006

Strnadová, I., & Cumming, T. (2014). The importance of quality transition processes for students with disabilities across settings: Learning from the current situation in New South Wales. *Australian Journal of Education, 58*(3), 318–336.

Strnadová, I., & Cumming, T. (2016). *Lifespan transitions and disability: A holistic perspective.* Routledge.

Strnadová, I., Cumming, T., & O'Neill, S. (2017). Young people transitioning from juvenile justice to the community: Transition planning and interagency collaboration. *Current Issues in Criminal Justice, 29*(1), 19–38. http://www.austlii.edu.au/au/journals/CICrimJust/2017/10.html

Towns, S. (2018). A sense of belonging: Why it matters for successful transition into secondary school. *Australian Educational Leader (AEL), 40*(2), 43–45.

Tso, M., & Strnadová, I. (2017). Students with autism transitioning from primary to secondary schools: Parents' perspectives and experiences. *International Journal of Inclusive Education, 21*(4), 389–403.

Webster, A. A. (2019). Translating theory to practice for principals working within inclusive education policy. In K. Trimmer, R. Dixon, & Y. Findlay (Eds.), *The Palgrave handbook of education law for schools* (2nd ed., pp. 257–280). Palgrave Macmillan. https://doi.org/10.1007/978-3-319-77751-1

Zundans-Fraser, L., & Bain, A. (2016). The role of collaboration in a comprehensive programme design process in inclusive education. *International Journal of Inclusive Education, 20*(2), 136–148. https://doi.org/10.1080/13603116.2015.1075610

GENUINE ENGAGEMENT WITH CHILDREN: A PRINCIPAL'S REFLECTION ON CREATING A LEARNING ENVIRONMENT WHERE EQUITY IS UPHELD, AND DIVERSITY EMBRACED

Simon Reid

ABSTRACT

This chapter presents the reflections of a principal in his experiences of supporting and transitioning the inclusion of learners with diverse needs into both primary and secondary schools. His extensive experience has led him to challenge established practice to find alternatives that support all learners. His journey has guided him on a path to broaden the definition of education from developing intellect and attaining knowledge to one that also includes emotion, connection, invention, and innovation. The purpose of education for all children is encouraging them to be thinkers, doers, and to embrace opportunities to develop their competence. This chapter includes his reflective approach to learning with a strong emphasis on the need for supporting students with diverse needs as they transition through the often-complex schooling arena.

Keywords: Inclusion; principal; transition; parents; collaboration; innovation

Transition Programs for Children and Youth with Diverse Needs
International Perspectives on Inclusive Education, Volume 18, 109–123
Copyright © 2022 Simon Reid
Published under exclusive licence by Emerald Publishing Limited
ISSN: 1479-3636/doi:10.1108/S1479-363620220000018009

INTRODUCTION

In my time as principal for 29 years I have worked in remote aboriginal, isolated rural, mining, low socioeconomic, high growth suburbs, high socioeconomic, primary, and secondary schools. What I know to be true is that post code does not discriminate when it comes to students with diverse needs. In the schools I have led they have all had upwards of 10 students funded for having a disability. As a high school principal there were more than 40 in my school and in my present primary school, in a high socioeconomic environment, we have had upward of 20 students each with quite diverse needs.

In each of these schools, I have worked to create learning communities that are vibrant and dynamic and deliver outcomes for all students. My philosophy for students with diverse needs, as with all students, is "see the student." We belong to one community, and we need to learn to live with, and have empathy for each other, and this can occur through having a gradual release model that schools create. Individual accountability and responsibility are gradually increased through planned designated steps with achievement markers used as sign posts to progress to the next step. Students transition over time from being in an environment that is very controlled to being autonomous. I have learned a lot along the way and especially the critical importance of identifying and supporting transition processes through a philosophical belief in putting the child central to any decision-making and working collaboratively to ensure the input of all stakeholders. My way to do this is to create an environment where children's safety and wellbeing is at the center of thought, values, and actions of all in the school. Every child is everyone's responsibility.

THE SCHOOLING PROCESS: CREATING INCLUSIVE COMMUNITIES

The schooling process is not just about learning academics; it is about learning to be part of a community. It starts small in kindergarten and progressively gets larger and more complex as the student moves through school until they eventually leave after Year 12 and enter the community at large. Through this journey, students learn academic skills and knowledge; however, I believe they have the opportunity to learn something far more important such as the soft skills and knowledge that enables them to be functioning and engaged members of the community. It is hoped that all children are given the same rights and opportunities and importantly leave with an inherent belief system that the world is a place of opportunity, and effort is the driver of progress. It is everyone's responsibility to support this. It is for these reasons that schools need to closely resemble the real society, by teaching empathy and understanding explicitly, role modeled, and importantly experienced.

Creating a school environment where all children enthusiastically engage in learning experiences and cultural values of safety, wellbeing, connection, inclusion, and personal best are entrenched, is aspirational and requires high level skills and commitment by all. We know what this should look like and the research lays out the "how" and the "what"; the question is why isn't every school like this? The answer is, it's hard! Schools are complex and complicated organizations and to achieve these ideals requires sophisticated thinking, skills, and behavior. It starts with clarity of moral purpose and investing in people. This, coupled with trusting people, establishing a culture of high expectations, a solid understanding of teaching and learning practice, and a belief of "what we stand for," provides the foundation for a successful school. The big challenge for schools in integrating students with diverse needs is the development of a philosophical framework of competency, autonomy, growth, and progress, which is embraced by all. This is extremely difficult as anchored biases and belief systems held by individuals and systems create constant challenges. Transition processes are the key strategy for actioning this philosophy, and they are the nuts and bolts for students, staff, and parents. Stakeholder involvement in their establishment is critical. That involvement is a safe way for biases, fears, and beliefs, to be acknowledged, challenged, and appropriate learning and accommodations implemented.

My Favorite Woollen Jumper

What is a school? Build it better! It is important to create places where everyone has a place where they belong. I have a saying that I share with all new parents into my school, "We strive to create a place where it feels like your favorite woollen jumper, the one that you want to put on each day." It is a bit cliché and could be construed as trite by some. For me, though, it is a metaphor for having responsibility for leading a school where children feel safe, secure, and thrive. Schools are more than buildings, beautiful grounds, and academic results. They are communities and are in essence a microcosm of society where children learn about life, living, and what really matters. What they experience everyday creates a blueprint on their beliefs, values, and behaviors. Given the opportunity, students can participate in learning communities within their schools and neighborhoods, and be ready to assume constructive roles as workers, family members, and citizens in a global society (Saravia-Shore, 2008).

Nurturing Children with Diverse Needs

It is widely recognized, empirically and epistemologically, that the characteristics of a civilized society/community are based around safety, affinity, unity, responsibility, friendliness, cooperation, and adherence to rules and general order. Schools as communities are no different. If children experience these each day both toward themselves and others, then, they will imitate them as a means of connecting, engaging, and belonging to their social environment. Nelson Mandela is quoted as saying "History will judge us by the difference we make in the everyday lives of children" (2002). This is a poignant statement for all adults. Children need to be nurtured in a supportive environment, in which parents and other caregivers provide positive guidance. The quicker and more efficiently a child can demonstrate the mores and behaviors of their environment the more effective their inclusion into the social fabric of the classroom or the playground. This in my experience is the greatest challenge for students with diverse needs. Our social society is complex and the skills to navigate it for many are intuitive, but for students with diverse needs, they need to be supported with time and patience to learn, rehearse, and practice these skills. This highlights the importance of having efficient and effective transition processes and welcoming inclusive environments throughout a child's schooling.

Transition into Preschool Years

The transition of children from a home or childcare environment into a school is a critical time, especially for those with additional needs. The preschool years are foundational for teaching children the fundamentals of social interaction – sharing and compromise, cooperation, and verbal communication. Consistency is the key for all students, day in day out, year in year out. The creation of patterns and routines from the outset of schooling that are consistently adhered to throughout schooling, enables the young child to learn within an environmental context to see patterns and then can formulate reliable predictions for learning academic, social, and behavioral skills. This is so important for a child with diverse needs as they need opportunities to see, feel, hear, and do across multiple settings and contexts for habits to be formed. To achieve this requires all adults, teachers, support staff, and parents to work toward making a difference to children with diverse needs by making their lives consistent, routinized, and predictable. Further reason for, and the imperative of transitions.

TRANSITIONING THE COMPLEXITY OF PRIMARY AND SECONDARY SCHOOLS

The following two case studies highlight my personal experiences with a primary and a secondary student's progress through school. Even though decisions are not always effective, both cases demonstrate the importance of continued flexibility and a willingness to keep trying. They also underscore the vital importance of safeguarding consistency across the various transitions that a child must cope with during their school life, through a collaborative approach.

The valuable lesson learned from David's journey is that it is important to have a team approach with the right people, an individual approach for each child, and educators who demonstrate a willingness to learn and adapt. It is critical for all to stay consistent, especially once an effective approach has been established and as the child transitions into further years.

The key learning from Raymond's story is that it is never too late to make a difference to a student's journey in education. Transitioning between schools can provide an opportunity to reframe the direction a child is taking and help them refocus to become fully included in school life. Consistency in approaches, and a clear understanding of how to support the numerous transitions a student must deal with are essential components to success.

David* is a student with Autism and has been in the school since Kindy and he is now in Year 4. His journey is the classic tale of our approach and transition processes being successful, going off the rails, and then getting back on track. David entered our school in Kindy and with the support of our Student Services team and the tremendous work of our Kindy teacher and teacher assistant he made an excellent transition into schooling. By the end of his Kindy year, he had established routines and was grasping the curriculum.

The next step in his schooling was where I went wrong and decided to place him with a teacher whom I thought would continue with the agreed plan. As an experienced teacher, though, they aimed to implement their own previously effective strategies. Unfortunately, these did not meet David's needs. This had a significant impact on his well-being, inclusivity, and education, as well as creating a great deal of confusion for the parents. Because of the experience and high regard, the teacher was held by the community, the parents just followed. It quickly became apparent that other parents and his peers were becoming very unsettled by his behavior. It became a particularly challenging year for all concerned because the teacher would not change their approach and David became more and more a polarizing figure in the classroom and the parent community. Both student and parent became isolated and marginalized.

At the end of the year as David was to transition into Year 1, we reset with an experienced teacher of students with diverse needs. Transitioning David into a new structure in Year 1 when entrenched beliefs by parent and child had been established, was a very difficult task: a lot more than I thought it would be. We were forced to go back to the beginning. It was a difficult year for all; however, by the end of the year David was back on track, his behaviors were far from consistent, and his learning was not where we were comfortable with. Once we had re-established a consistent approach that met his needs, David's transition to Year 2 was excellent and so was Year 3 and again in Year 4. David is now an accepted member of his cohort and the school. The progress David has made socially and academically is summed up in one action. David wrote a card and presented it to me in my office requesting to organize a fund raiser for "Genes for Jeans Day"** and explained why he wanted to. I wrote back and approved it. He was so excited that he immediately showed his teacher and then classmates who all responded positively. He then returned quietly back to his seat and continued working. A remarkable transformation.

Note: Pseudonyms are used for all case study names.

**Note:* A fund-raising activity to support people with genetic disorders.

Raymond's story is a secondary student's story. Raymond is Autistic and transitioned into my last school in Year 7 (first year high school). He was 13 years old and came with a very large file from the primary school of behavior infractions and case conference notes, with a reoccurring theme of conflict between the school, parents, school psychologist, and the child. On enrolling in the school, the parents made a point of having a meeting with me and I listened. It was more of a plea for help than a meeting. For over an hour they poured out their thoughts, feelings, and experiences. We created a plan and an approach to support Raymond. In a high school it can be more challenging for a student with Autism, and for the staff. With so many different year level teachers, it is also difficult in ensuring a coordinated approach. However, the mechanism I had used previously in a primary school setting I used in the secondary setting with the same positive outcomes.

From day one, Raymond started to demonstrate patterns of behavior that were entrenched and destructive to him being accepted and gaining an education. With teenagers, relationships are the key. The school was organized around teams of teachers working together to support students rather than just being subject based. This meant for students like Raymond the planned approach remained consistent as the student transitioned between lessons, between semesters, and between each year level. Predictability and consistency were the mantra.

Raymond was in my home group and as a result I saw him every day and I was able to ensure that Raymond transitioned into the day the same way. I was his home room teacher for all six years of his schooling. In that time, I witnessed Raymond grow into a young man, become confident in processes and learning, get a part time job, and become a high functioning member of the high school. He became a student who enjoyed school, went on camps, participated in significant events such as socials, the Debutante Ball, and successfully achieved positive learning outcomes in completing his Victorian Certificate of Education achieving entrance to his university course of choice. The highest achievement for Raymond came from his acceptance by his peers to an extent that he became a House Leader in Year 12.

EVERY CHILD IS EVERYONE'S RESPONSIBILITY

Every child is everyone's responsibility and as a principal my role is to support this through the establishment of transparency in processes, pedagogy, curriculum, and student management. Staff and students need to have a school environment that is so consistent that the school day is as predictable as the sun rising and setting. For this to occur it requires a high level of empathy by all adults in the school. All decisions in the school need be prefixed with "What is the impact on the child/ren?" I will often pose this scenario to guide people to move to a place of empathy for students.

> Imagine you are taking a journey in your car from home to a place seven suburbs away. Each suburb has a different set of traffic rules. There is no doubt that your journey would be very stressful. This is what it is like for children if we don't have a classroom and playground environment that is consistent and predictable. As teachers in a school, it is essential that we understand the predicaments children face each day transitioning from different environments, classrooms, events and or learning activities. This is particularly important for the child with diverse needs.

The Home – School – Home Transition

John Bowlby (1969), a British psychologist, was the first theorist to describe connectedness between human beings as lasting, known as Attachment Theory. In my experience Attachment Theory extends beyond the home and includes the school environment for students with diverse needs. It also makes the connectedness between home and school a crucial transition point. When children are frightened or anxious, they will seek proximity from their primary caregiver to receive both comfort and care (Cherry, 2019). How this translates for a student with diverse needs is, if they are stressed, do not feel safe and secure, learning cannot happen. For these reasons, smooth consistent predicable transitions for students with diverse needs are essential. This applies to all transitions, home to school and school to home, be it between lessons, movement between classrooms, or more significant transitions from one year level to another. The transitions must be well thought out, planned, understood, and supported by all, and most importantly consistently implemented.

The transition process that often gets missed, however, is the one that carries the greatest weight in terms of impact on the student and that is the one with the parent at the beginning and end of each school day. A successful transition to and from school enables the student to form predictable routines and creates favorable conditions for success. This transition process cannot be taken for granted, it must be understood, rehearsed, and adhered to. When daily transitions are consistently implemented, positive constructs are developed around expectations, connection, and genuine collaboration between the student, parent, and teacher. In my current school we have established a model which has become accepted practice that all students are met and greeted at the door each day. This is to ensure that every child is welcomed into the day and the teacher makes an immediate connection by making each child feel valued. For students with diverse needs, we go one step further by making the transition a connection with the child and the parent. This is a powerful symbol of unity around common desires of success for child, parent, and teacher. The transition at the end of the day is equally important. All classes have a plenary to conclude the day. The plenary reviews all the learning intentions for the day, and it is also a time for the students to highlight what they have learnt and teachers to recognize effort. For students with diverse needs, this time provides a framework in the transition process with the parent when the day concludes, by asking the child to communicate what they have learnt. It is a positive and engaging process around success and connection to transition to going home.

The following case studies illustrate parental perspectives of the importance of schools establishing effective transition processes to support families transition their children into school.

Parent One

The valuable lesson for me here was the reminder to listen to the parent. Not just hear the words but also hear the emotion behind the words and to listen to the words without forming judgment. As principals we can get cornered by policy and procedure. In this case I listened to what my gut instincts were saying. The conversation with the parent was measured. The parent was not running away from their responsibilities nor were they shopping around to find a school that would give them what they wanted; it was a genuine plea for help. They knew their responsibilities; they loved their child and needed a school that supported their child to learn.

My child has been diagnosed with Autistic spectrum disorder/Severe mental disorder.

Having had very damaging experiences at two other local primary schools, our current primary school was the third school our children attended in under 12 months. The genuinely inclusive culture at this school was a game changer, not just for our kids, but for our whole family. As the principal said to me at the end of our very first meeting "All you want, is to be able to send your kids to school and know they'll get the care and education they need." The principal and his staff have certainly delivered on this, beginning with a smooth transition into the school then supporting and empowering our kids throughout their primary school journeys.

From our experiences, having the opportunity to engage in open and frequent communication with all pertinent staff has been absolutely essential in achieving mutual understanding and facilitating the best possible outcomes for our kids. This open dialogue has always made our kids' transitions through the school very smooth and given staff valuable information to help accommodate our kids' needs. Our children have thrived at this PS in a supportive environment where every child matters and kids with additional needs are not treated like they are a burden on the school. Rather, they are celebrated just that little bit more and made to feel like they truly belong.

Our son is 11 years old and was prenatally diagnosed with Klinefelter's Syndrome (47 XXY). While he has achieved physical development milestones he is socially withdrawn and has demonstrated anxiety from an early age. He did not achieve speech and language milestones and started speech therapy at two years of age. He has been to several schools during his short life and is now in his fourth school.

He started preschool at four and a half years old. He enjoyed the company of other children, but it was evident early on that he was not able to cope with the classroom learning. He would often sit under the desk, be disruptive, and sit in the corner. We applied to have him transferred for Grade 1 to a private school, dedicated to speech and language development. He settled well but socially he was not happy. Visual clues were extensively used to support his learning and classrooms were minimally decorated to reduce visual stimulation. Unfortunately, he was unable to complete Year one at this school when our family had to relocate. He was not permitted to transfer to a speech and language school. We then enrolled him in an independent school hoping that a small school environment would provide the supports he required. When that teacher left, and he had a new one the outbursts and the frequency of them increased so we decided to remove him and we moved him to our local government catchment school.

The school model for him now consists of an education assistant learning support, a nurturing teacher, and an inclusive school. With this combination for the first time, we have seen him finally thrive at school. One of the biggest changes we have seen in him is his new positive behavior toward school, and it has been his enthusiasm every morning to get to school early and to want to stay back and play with the kids. This year he transferred to a Year 5 class, and we are very pleased that he has not faltered once in accepting the change to the new teacher. A great achievement for the team at this school for a smooth transition. The two Deputy Principals have provided him with great support when he has escalated and is unable to self-regulate. They have taught him to signal to teachers when he needs a moment to calm himself. We have discussed this approach at home to reinforce the school's agreement with him. We are very happy with this collaborative approach. He sees the consistency between school and home and knows that he's always supported and always receiving the same messages.

From my personal experience it has been the sharing of experiences from other families in research papers that have helped us govern our son's journey. His current school has been such a fabulous support network for our son and we need to shout that from the rooftops.

Parent Two

The insight gained from this example underscores the importance of a school's culture to facilitating inclusion. A commitment to inclusion should be evidenced from the point at which the student and the parent enter the school. Students want to fit in and belong, and when surrounded by other students whose actions and words represent inclusive principles, new students quickly adapt. Consistency in implementing predictable and reliable processes for all students leads to the establishment of a culture of safety and trust. To promote effective transitions for students with diverse needs, schools as a moral imperative must establish and maintain a culture that values and supports inclusive practices.

STRATEGIES FOR CREATING AN INCLUSIVE SCHOOL COMMUNITY

Cultivate an Environment for Social Inclusion

School is about more than academics. It is a social community that incorporates valuing and belonging for all students. It is a place where students acquire skills for social interaction and where they seek social inclusion. Establishing structures and routines that facilitate social inclusion is essential to building a community where students feel safe and secure. This may be particularly important during times of transition, especially for students with diverse needs.

Patterns for social inclusion should be consistently and explicitly modeled by teachers. Through classroom activities and interactions, students can learn about each other, their similarities and differences, their strengths and shared interests – information that can be used to establish friendships and enable students to support one another within the learning environment. When students learn to value and respect one another as individuals they develop attitudes and skills that promote relationships building, rather than distancing.

View Teachers as Enablers

In my experience, teacher practice both in and outside the classroom is a key attribute to a child with diverse needs' success – socially and educationally. It can be an enabler or an inhibiter. It is an unfortunate truth, in many cases, that the attention a student receives is negative or critical because of belief systems held by the teacher, reinforced by school norm and practice. This attitude toward students inhibits teachers from forming effective and supporting relationships with their students and can create a distance between the teacher and the student. In turn, this creates a class norm and may alienate the students with diverse needs, causing resentment, frustration, anger, and an unresponsive attitude to learning in the classroom.

In many cases, classroom norms and expectations flow over to the playground. This belief then tends to form part of the transition narrative as the child moves from one year level to the next, resulting in potential isolation, deregulation, and disengagement become the prevailing experience for the child. Teachers need to position themselves as enablers, and view children with diverse needs as just "children,", not challenges, but children deserving of care, and support.

Quality teaching by teachers with positive attitudes is extremely important. This is demonstrated when teachers employ instructional strategies in the classroom that facilitate learning for all students. Quality teaching may require an innovative approach to incorporating a willingness to adapt lesson planning and delivery to each child's strengths so that optimal outcomes can be achieved. According to Alton-Lee (2003):

> Evidence internationally is that what happens in classrooms through quality teaching and through the quality of the learning environment generated by the teacher and the students, is the key variable in explaining up to 59%, or even more, of the variance in student scores. This finding of the far greater magnitude of influence on outcomes of teachers and classes than schools has been evident for different outcome measures and different educational systems across a range of studies and countries. (Alton-Lee, 2003, p. 2)

Promote Collaboration and Teambuilding

Much has been said about getting the right people into your organization; however, in my experience, it is all about creating the right environment so that people will step into the role of being the right person. I believe in investing in people through trust and quality professional learning. By giving people training in the right approach using empirically researched best practice, providing direction, tools, and support, along with autonomy, it is my experience that a school becomes full of the right people. An important factor is establishing a genuine collaborative culture, staff wanting each other to succeed and wanting all children to thrive and where adherence to pedagogy and process is expected and celebrated.

As a principal, one of my main goals is to establish processes where internal and external professional development are directly connected to the school goals and direction. Through professional development, teaching staff are able to see how their own learning will have a positive impact on the students they teach and how enacting what they have learned will support the school to achieve its student learning goals. Staff by-in is achieved when professional development is viewed as relevant, engaging, and targeted.

One of the major agencies for change is supporting performance and development of staff. Establishing a culture that encourages individuals to critically review their present practice and assume accountability for personal performance, school priorities, and their professional growth needs is important. Learning teams and the allocation of financial resources through the appointment of teaching and learning coaches, investing in, and training of team leaders, and allocating meeting time, are all useful mechanisms for disruptive innovation to embrace change. What results is the development of agreed standards and protocols to encourage the sharing of ideas to provide positive and constructive feedback.

Teaching can be a very insular profession, for significant periods of time teachers are alone in their classroom with the children. To address this isolation, I invest highly in the establishment and development of teams; professionally, financially, and personally, through relationships and coaching. All teachers are grouped in professional learning teams, vertically Kindy to Year 6 as well as a separate year level team. Teams are used to develop a culture of collaboration and collective responsibility. Teachers take responsibility for improving instructional practices to achieve gains in learning for all their students. Genuine team-based work implies more than the simple act of working alongside colleagues. It involves teachers working in a spirit of openness and critical reflection, sharing their experiences, ideas, and expertise with each other, and engaging in an ongoing process of inquiry that promotes deep team learning. The work of teams is guided by a clear and systematic model of problem-solving and learning, one that encompasses a learning → application → refinement → application cycle.

Highly effective learning also comes from establishing processes for visiting classrooms for peer observation and the provision of feedback. Success comes from respect and familiarity, in this case through knowing each other and knowing the needs of children in the school. This enables teachers to share effective strategies for learning, which can be especially important during times of transition for students with diverse needs as each teacher views their responsibility to support and build on the efforts of previous teachers.

Provide Feedback and Hold High Expectations

The establishment of team and learning norms leads to the development of practices that have significant impact on students with diverse needs, i.e., feedback and high expectations. I hold firmly to the belief that you cannot have one without the other. When teachers hold high expectations of themselves and their students, successful outcomes naturally flow. To have high expectations teachers must accurately know their students, value them as learners, and understand how to support their learning through quality and timely feedback. In the classroom, teachers can do this by challenging their students and encouraging continuous improvement through promoting high expectations by engaging in ongoing and meaningful classroom interactions with their students. Teachers' beliefs about their students influence how they teach and interact with them.

The role of the principal is to provide the same for the teachers, i.e., high expectations, support, and feedback, with the addition of a framework of assistance, guidance, and data, so progress can be measured and celebrated. One of the difficulties teachers may experience is the feeling that the child is their responsibility alone. My role as principal is to provide clarity regarding the teacher's role as well as the ongoing supports provided by other professionals, and the assurance that all parties will work together to craft a unified plan and a united approach to education. It is a well-worn quote, but it is so true, the journey of education "is a marathon not a sprint." The role of the principal is to be a mentor and motivator to stay the course, and to maintain consistent and reliable partnerships.

Promote a Whole School Approach

School processes for transition need to be inclusive of teachers, students, and parents and should encompass a belief of creating the conditions for success. For this to occur all the people in each student's education are required to have ownership of the processes in the school, take responsibility for their role, and be actively involved in the student's education. This must occur not only when they are directly involved in teaching them, but also in the transition processes when receiving the student and when delivering the student. This incorporates all transitions, with another teacher, whether it be to a specialist teacher, preparation for a relieving teacher, including a new student to the school, or a student leaving, or transitioning to the next year level. Success as a whole school comes from teachers embracing transitioning as an essential component of school, not a "nice to have." This can be achieved through many strategies, but none of them are successful without the whole staff having and accepting high expectations for themselves and colleagues. This individual and collective accountability means the plans and the processes actually work because they are not pieces of paper and talk, they are actioned, and people hold themselves and others to account.

A CHILD-FOCUSED MODEL

Throughout this chapter, I have focused on the "why" and the "how" of transitions. I have deliberately left discussing the "what" to last. In my experience the "what," more simply put as the education plan for the student, is the glue that clarifies roles, has targets to aim at, and has common reference points that define progress. The planning process for students with diverse needs begins from the outset of the student entering the school. It is essential that the family feel welcomed, supported and listened to. The listening to the parent and the child is the important first step. For people to be equal partners and feel valued they need to be heard. It is not our place to start by telling people who know their child better than we will ever know them, how things are going to go. Trust comes from being equal partners where all members of the team equally contribute to a plan that will provide for the unique needs of the student. Effective plans come from having comprehensive information about the student, qualitative and quantitative data. It is the merging of all this information that can lead to the development of a comprehensive plan and approach.

Fig. 1 outlines the approach that I have developed with teams of teachers over my career, and which has proven highly successful. The development of a plan for each student has in equal measure inputs from the stakeholders, parents, the child, Teachers/Student Services Team, and external providers. Integrating these inputs with the following: learning intention, strategies, progress points, and review processes in learning/curriculum, pedagogy, health and wellbeing, and student management ensures there are clear roles, responsibilities, and progress markers. Part of the plan which I believe makes a real difference is the explicit planning and ongoing review of transition strategies to be implemented.

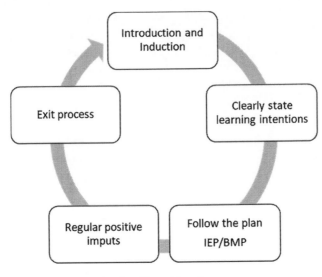

Fig. 1.   Transition Process.

The core process for our transition strategy for all transitions is illustrated in Fig. 2. The joining arrow to the right of the diagram is to illustrate the plan and how the transition processes are constantly monitored and adjusted as the student makes progress and advances through the school. The plan and the transition

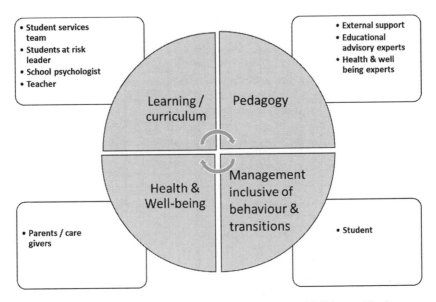

Fig. 2.   Individual Planning Process for Students with Diverse Needs.

strategy are designed keep us on the path and ensure that we as a school maintain the consistency in programming and delivery essential to achieving intended outcomes.

CONCLUSION

To bring this all together, I believe that all students have a need to be empowered to learn and achieve in the care of high-quality teachers as people and in practice. Students with diverse needs must experience the best conditions for learning which equip them with the knowledge, skills, and dispositions for being a member of not only the school community but also to be able to engage and shape the world around them outside the school environment. All growth comes from the same inputs, consistency, predictability, safety, and nurture. Our challenge is to remain focused on these outcomes.

I believe transition processes are instrumental in developing a culture that embraces a whole school community approach to adult-student relationships involving all school and community members that students interact with in the school. As a principal of the school, I play a key role in ensuring that transition practices and behaviors support all students and staff, and that there is a widely supported set of values and principles as a common thread in daily interactions. For students with diverse needs every interaction requires a carefully planned transition. My role is to maintain a shared vision for a safe learning environment that creates genuine opportunities for empowerment and growth.

REFERENCES

Alton-Lee, A. (2003). *Quality teaching for diverse students in schooling: Best evidence synthesis.* Ministry of Education, Term Strategy Policy Division. ISBN 0-478-18742-4.

Bowlby, J. (1969). *Attachment and loss.* Basic Books.

Cherry, K. (2019). What is attachment theory? The importance of early emotional bonds. https://www.verywellmind.com/our-editorial-process-4778006

Mandela, N. (2002). *Address by Nelson Mandela at luncheon hosted by United Nations* (UN) General Secretary Kofi Annan, New York, United States. http://www.mandela.gov.za/mandela_speeches/2002/020509_kofi.htm

Saravia-Shore, M. (2008). Diverse teaching strategies for diverse learners. In R. W. Cole *Educating everybody's children* (Chapter 2). Association for Supervision and Curriculum Development (ASCD) Publications.

SECTION 3

TRANSITION TO POSTSECONDARY EDUCATION AND VOCATIONAL OPPORTUNITIES

CAREER INTERVENTIONS WITH AN INCLUSIVE PERSPECTIVE FOR INDIVIDUALS WITH DISABILITIES AND VULNERABILITIES

M. Cristina Ginevra, Sara Santilli, Ilaria Di Maggio and Laura Nota

ABSTRACT

Individuals with disabilities and vulnerabilities often experience a series of interventions that are of little benefit in terms of career development, resulting in uncertainty, career barriers, disinvestment in the future and school, a lack of knowledge regarding current reality, and a tendency to delay important life decisions, which can limit their ability to imagine and plan for the future. Based on the most recent and accredited approaches in the field of career guidance, this chapter explores a number of innovative programs and interventions designed to support children, adolescents, and adults with and without disabilities in planning their educational and professional futures in an inclusive perspective. Emphasis is given to actions and interventions to enable individuals with and without disabilities to develop critical consciousness, awareness, and reflection regarding the contextual variables and conditions that may represent career barriers to their future, to support them in aspiring to an inclusive and sustainable future, and to help them to acquire the strategies and skills needed to pursue what is close to their heart.

Keywords: Career guidance; career interventions; inclusive perspective; social justice; children; adolescents

Transition Programs for Children and Youth with Diverse Needs
International Perspectives on Inclusive Education, Volume 18, 127–141
Copyright © 2022 M. Cristina Ginevra, Sara Santilli, Ilaria Di Maggio and Laura Nota
Published under exclusive licence by Emerald Publishing Limited
ISSN: 1479-3636/doi:10.1108/S1479-363620220000018010

INTRODUCTION

In today's volatile environment, those who aim to help people, at any age, with disabilities and vulnerabilities to plan their educational and professional future and enter the world of work must consider a high number of crises and global challenges that are shaping the future of humanity. Examples of such challenges include increasing social injustice, the polarization of wealth and work, and the increase in population movements, with rising migration rates that are affecting the destruction of natural resources (Nota et al., 2020). Moreover, the recent COVID-19 pandemic, in addition to constituting a health emergency, may represent one of the most serious crises for the economy and labor market on a global scale since the Second World War, with potential for profound repercussions in terms of career design for all individuals.

These new phenomena add further complexity to the landscape of existing challenges, such as globalization, global economic recession, automation of jobs, deregulation of markets, and increase in atypical and precarious working patterns. Professionals who work with career guidance and career counseling must adjust their training and interventions to account for the multiple changes in the nature of work and in the demands of the labor market. These challenges have profound consequences for the design processes of a future career, especially for young people (Nota et al., 2020).

Current changes in the world of work also accentuate disparities between people with and without disabilities in their work, requiring the need to consider social justice a priority for professionals who support people in career design. Having a disability, especially during childhood, often involves undergoing a series of interventions that are of little benefit in terms of career development, resulting in greater difficulties and professional barriers in acquiring and maintaining a competitive job (Ginevra et al., 2019).

Lack of career development interventions for people with disabilities and vulnerabilities may result in uncertainty, career barriers, disinvestment in the future and school, a lack of knowledge regarding current reality, and a tendency to delay important life decisions, which can limit the ability to imagine and plan for the future. Career guidance plays an essential role because of its focus on professionally designed programs and on ensuring active participation in educational, social, and vocational contexts. As career guidance programs consider the right to work a foundational right for all, an important component involves the opportunity to identify, develop, and create a professional identity, also for people with vulnerabilities and disabilities.

Career practitioners are called upon to act from an inclusive perspective to help people with disabilities craft personal and professional identities. Specifically, they are called to bypass standardized counseling patterns, or the implementation of late interventions carried out during transitional stages and focused largely on diagnosis, to considering the examination of entry requirements for education and jobs, and the formulation of predictions concerning one's aptitude to adapt to educational and professional conditions (Nota et al., 2020). Even with the necessary adaptations related to personal peculiarities (and this also applies to typically developing individuals), career practitioners are called to refer to theoretical models that are more in line with current times and to the same constructs and resources on which particular attention has recently been placed in the world of work. To that end, career practitioners should assure that individuals with disabilities have access to the same career development activities, instruments, and interventions developed and tested for peers without disabilities (Ginevra et al., 2019).

Career practitioners also have to act on the life contexts of people, most especially those with disabilities, to identify the organizational and managerial changes needed so that the various educational, social, and professional contexts can allow everyone to obtain a high-quality professional life (Shogren et al., 2016).

Following an analysis of the role of career guidance from an inclusive and life-long perspective, this chapter will explore a number of innovative programs and interventions designed to support children, adolescents, and adults in planning their educational and professional futures. Particular attention will be paid to the recent changes in the field of career guidance to assist and support people with the highest vulnerability and marginalization levels. It is considered particularly relevant to enable individuals with and without disabilities to develop critical consciousness, awareness, and reflection regarding the contextual variables and conditions that may represent career barriers to their future. It is also relevant to encourage and support them to envision future possibilities, and to guarantee their rights to participate in training and professional contexts, reducing the "weight" of experiences of failure, difficulties, and discomfort (Hooley et al., 2017).

CAREER GUIDANCE FOR AN INCLUSIVE AND SUSTAINABLE FUTURE

There is a growing consensus within the international literature suggesting that career development is a significant component for positive development. A special issue published in 2015 by the *International Journal of Educational and Vocational Guidance* (Watson et al., 2015) clearly highlighted the close relationship between various developmental areas such as cognitive, emotional, social, linguistic, and physiological. Though each has unique traits, they are all linked together and dependent on each other, and contribute to the positive functioning and development of an individual.

The interplay between these different developmental areas is in line with the Positive Youth Development approach (Lerner et al., 2009), which emphasizes people's strengths and the complex relationship between an individual and his/her life settings. Positive trajectories in the life span result from beneficial mutual relationships between a person who is in a specific developmental stage and the elements in his/her context that provide support and promote personal growth, benefiting both the individual and his/her social system. Among the models proposed within the positive development approach that received strong empirical support is the Five C's model (Competence, Confidence, Connection, Character, and Caring). This model was theorized by Eccles and Gootman (2002), and by Roth and Brooks-Gunn (2003) and operationalized by Lerner and his collaborators (Lerner et al., 2009). Competence is associated with having a positive outlook on one's actions in defined domains, such as social, cognitive, academic, and vocational (Phelps et al., 2009). Confidence is displayed by a largely positive sense of self-worth and self-efficacy (Phelps et al., 2009). Connection is demonstrated through valuable and encouraging relationships with other individuals and institutions including school, family, and peers. Character indicates respect for rules and an understanding of right and wrong. Caring is explained as the manifestation of sympathy and empathy for someone else. It has been reported that youth exemplifying higher levels of the Five Cs are more likely to be on a positive and beneficial developmental trajectory for both themselves and their contexts and thus contribute to their own positive growth, as well as that of their family, their community, and society.

In the career guidance field, the Life Design International Research Group (Savickas et al., 2009), based on social constructivism's epistemology, clearly recognizes career development as highly contextualized and individualized. It highlights that all the life spheres are significant for the person, and all have to be considered in the construction of career and life projects. Moreover, it conceptualizes an individual as an active agent and actor of his/her own personal and career development, and of his/her present and future, through designing personal life stories or narratives and formulating coherent life aims and plans (Pouyaud, 2015). According to this paradigm, the individual is not shaped by the context but rather person and context are interdependent. This means that the individual develops within a specific social and cultural context, including organizations, societal policies, and practices, that can affect human functioning. As a result, career guidance should focus on how these multiple nonlinear interactions can positively impact career and life results (Hirschi & Dauwalder, 2015).

Recently, particular attention has been given to inclusion and sustainability, human rights, and social justice in career and life interventions for the construction of personal and professional projects, especially for those who experience career barriers such as individuals with disabilities and vulnerabilities (Guichard, 2018; Nota et al., 2020). In particular, because of the global threats that the socio-economic context is currently facing, it is essential to support people's future design from an inclusive and sustainable perspective. Career interventions, therefore, should incorporate individual and collective reflections to promote collective empowerment and critical consciousness development to enable individuals with and without disabilities and vulnerabilities to design their lives (García-Feijoo et al., 2020; Nota et al., 2020). In this sense, it is essential to promote an individual's ability to critically analyze both the challenges of today and those that might be encountered in the near future, fostering awareness of contextual factors that might represent barriers to human life and development, as well as to the design of the future. It is also essential to foster critical awareness, critical thinking, and sensitivity to the inequalities and oppression that maintain, if not increase, disparities in educational, social, and work contexts. In addition, it is increasingly important to develop one's abilities to take individual or promote collective action to foster, through one's educational and professional choices, social change to benefit the wellbeing of all (Fernández et al., 2018; Hooley et al., 2017).

IMPLEMENTING CAREER INTERVENTIONS IN AN INCLUSIVE PERSPECTIVE

From a life-long perspective, people with and without disabilities and vulnerabilities should be guided to identify the future they wish to have, aspire how to achieve it in an inclusive and sustainable way, and specify the societal or global challenges they wish to face and/or tackle and the skills they would like to acquire. These actions reduce the risk of creating a future that strongly depends on the past or present, or on a range of often inhibiting personal and contextual determinants.

In line with Blustein et al. (2019), we believe that career interventions should be implemented throughout various developmental stages, with a focus on specific educational goals and on fostering a greater sense of awareness, reflectivity, sharing, social responsibility, and aspirations for a better world, through the use of workshop activities that encourage active participation and the process of co-creating (Nota & Rossier, 2015). This is in contrast to the more simplistic strategy of asking children to think about "what to do or be when you grow up."

In planning career guidance interventions, it is essential to incorporate certain objectives and strategies, which are discussed next.

Include Ways to Involve People Actively

Active involvement requires that participants are properly introduced to, familiarized with, and motivated to engage in career planning activities at the outset in a way that engages open participation, which differs from typical educational activities that focus on evaluation. In presenting career interventions, it is useful to initially promote an innovative career guidance culture that moves beyond an approach that centers on research, or offering suggestions, advice, or "the right places to the right people" or that advertises "successful" competence profiles, budgets, or employability rates. It is also appropriate in the first meeting of the career intervention to draw up a "career guidance contract" in which the professional commits to carefully and scrupulously considering the expectations and needs of the participants, and the participants commit to collaboration and active participation.

Identify the Goals to Pursue, in Terms of Knowledge and Skills Improvement

To create a career intervention that incorporates a valuable experience for everyone, it is necessary to clearly determine the goals that are to be pursued and the projected outcomes that will be reached, by providing a description of the growth and improvement of the specific abilities of the people participating in the career intervention program (Nota et al., 2020). Each goal should describe the expected results and the responsibilities that are connected with the actions of professionals needed to achieve the goal.

Incorporate Personalization Forms

Personalization involves the differentiation of factors as requests, stimuli to offer, working material, and so on, developed considering the preferences of those who led the activity and of the participants' traits, including the presence of a disability and/or poor language skills (Nota et al., 2020). The customization of goals, activities, and material to meet unique learning strengths and preferences is fundamental since it allows everyone who takes part in the activity to benefit from effective teaching strategies, resulting in personal growth and improvement.

Effectively Manage Teaching and Learning Processes

When designing specific career guidance interventions, we believe in the importance of incorporating three components or stages that are separate, and yet connected and interdependent. First, attention should be focused on the modalities of support required to achieve the identified goals. This stage is of paramount importance, and requires sensitivity and precision. It centers on the need to provide optimal conditions for engaging in the activities that involve teaching and learning. For example, particular attention should be given to the detection, recall, and assessment of the prerequisite skills and knowledge needed in order to participate in an active way in each component. In addition, identifying the reasons that determined the decision to incorporate a specific intervention into the training program links each activity with a specific outcome.

The second stage, cues for teaching and learning incentives, requires participants to plan teaching actions and measures that are customized and differentiated, in order to maximize the learning probability of each participant. These incorporate a range of educational actions, such as instructions and exemplifications, modeling, role-play, exercises, feedback, and reinforcements. This stage also involves the planning of short presentations on the constructs or topics that are especially relevant and require more focused attention. Participants might then be invited to discuss the various constructs and their importance or relevance for designing an inclusive and qualitative future, and the materials required to incentivize the quantitative and qualitative reflections about the construct under consideration. Participants can also be asked to give personal reflections regarding the contribution that a specific construct might provide when drafting out perspectives and purposes and identifying commitments and objectives. Moreover, using these actions, participants have the possibility to choose freely to favor the beginning of a personalized guidance path for the future.

The third stage focuses on "closure." This is a delicate phase, as it implies the task of leading operations of assessment and modality choice to ensure the maintenance and generalization of the learning process such as the use of tests, creation of situations that allow one to "directly observe" learning, and "homework" assignments.

Career guidance should be integrated into activities throughout the developmental periods. The next section provides examples of a number of innovative and effective programs to use with children, adolescents, and young adults that focus on ways in which career interventions can prepare individuals to understand the increasing complexities in the world of work and, at the same time, to address current issues facing society.

CAREER INTERVENTIONS FOR CHILDREN

Given the early nature of career development and its close connection to other areas of positive development, numerous researchers (e.g., Hartung, 2015; Watson et al., 2015) emphasize the need to implement career interventions, as soon as possible, from early childhood. These career interventions should offer opportunities for all children to envision positive career paths, stimulate understanding and acquisition of competencies and resources crucial for career planning, and contribute to quality of life and psychosocial wellbeing. This training should also apply to children with disabilities who tend to be at greater risk in their career planning processes and to be more at risk of being excluded during adulthood from the world of work (Chen & Chan, 2014; Lee et al., 2015).

Particular emphasis should be given to knowledge of the world of work, the issues of decent work, equity, and work inclusion, especially as the beliefs about the world of work and occupations begin during childhood and are crucial for career construction (Hartung, 2015). Children should be stimulated to have a cooperative vision of the world of work; to recognize that diversity and collaboration among diverse individuals make the work contexts more meaningful and efficacious. In addition, as suggested by Brownlee et al. (2019), children should be encouraged to acquire democratic values, rights and responsibilities toward the well-being of self and others, to be whistleblowers in their future work contexts; in other words, to give the alert for the presence of any "fake actions," discrimination, and/or injustice that they may observe in their future work contexts.

In this regard, we recall the intervention program proposed by Hawkins (2014) with preschoolers, through a Participatory Action Research approach. Children were presented with and read books that told stories incorporating issues of iniquity, prejudice, injustice, and stereotypes about various areas of social life. At the end of the reading, a discussion was started with brief guidance on the specific issue of social justice that the text raised. This was followed by questions that favored dialogue among children and between children and adults, highlighting the skill of critically reflecting on the structural issues connected with social justice and, by doing so, identifying and questioning one's own prejudices.

With the aim of encouraging a critical reflection of the world of work, we have developed a career education program "They are working. What are they doing? First steps toward the knowledge of the world of work." It is an example of career intervention that can be implemented as early as kindergarten in schools with children with and without disabilities. This program consists of 10 didactic units, and each step lasts about 35 minutes and involves a small group of about five children. It aims to foster a greater knowledge of occupations, reduce stereotypical beliefs about the world of work, and promote job analysis, that is, the systematic analysis of the places, tasks, actions, and instruments for each occupation.

The first eight meetings focus on 16 occupations (2 for each meeting), the ninth meeting examines the kindergarten teacher and children's parents' jobs, and the final lesson focuses on occupations familiar with children's everyday life. Specifically the occupations discussed in previous didactic units are described and represented in the neighborhood where children live. For each occupation, actions, tools, and workplaces are discussed, as well as its contribution to the community and economy. In addition, the importance of education is emphasized in order to acquire the competencies needed to obtain the job. All occupations are presented using both male and female terms and with images and video clips of both men and women to avoid stereotypical beliefs. Moreover, some clips of cartoons very popular among children are also used to show occupations throughout the training. These can be selected from free online movies, cartoons, and pictures to reduce costs and or edited using free and user-friendly apps and programs.

To evaluate the effectiveness of the career education program, in a preliminary study we involved 133 kindergarten children with a mean age of 5 years and randomly assigned them to the experimental or the control group. The analyses carried out showed a significant deeper occupational knowledge for the experimental group. Specifically, on the post-test, the experimental group showed a greater knowledge of actions and instruments in all occupations considered. Overall, the career intervention suggested the need and the concrete possibility of working in favor of early career development in an inclusive perspective. In this developmental age, practitioners do not seek an early identification of a school or work choice, rather they promote positive developmental trajectories useful to prepare children to be citizens and workers of the future.

CAREER INTERVENTIONS FOR ADOLESCENTS

During preadolescence and adolescence, it is crucial to systematically analyze current social conditions and the ability to reduce societal inequalities to design in an inclusive and sustainable future. Studies in the career guidance field suggest that adolescents with vulnerabilities who have a high ability to systematically analyze current social conditions and the perceived capacity to reduce societal inequalities are characterized by a feeling of hope for their vocational future (Diemer et al., 2016; Nota et al., 2020). This relationship allows them to implement career and educational choices and/or to continue an educational and professional course, despite the career barriers they experience (Diemer et al., 2016).

With this perspective, several programs in the literature that aim to increase critical awareness are especially informative for professionals in career guidance and professional design. These professionals could utilize and adapt such programs to their intervention groups' specificities and uniqueness (for more information, refer to Heberle et al., 2020).

For example, we present the culturally sensitive social–emotional learning school program called "Fulfill the Dream," proposed by Slaten et al. (2016), which was designed to promote social justice and support critical consciousness development among youth with vulnerabilities related to poverty. The program includes 10 intervention sessions and, through the utilization of a critically conscious approach oriented to social justice, aims to stimulate adolescents to define and redefine their goals and dreams for the future. The program includes a debate, creative writing assignments, small-group activities, and the critical analysis of multimedia pertaining to the culture of the youth to allow adolescents to reflect and understand such concepts as community contexts, barriers, and supports. This is designed to motivate participants to think about their dreams, and the strategies and future plans they would like to achieve and, in relation to this, to encourage them to think about what they value.

Based on the Life Design International Research Group, and in line with recent suggestions from the international scientific community that emphasize the need for adolescents to imagine and design their future in an inclusive and sustainable perspective, Santilli et al. (2020) developed the school program called "Looking to the Future and the University in an Inclusive and Sustainable Way." The program involves secondary school students with and without disabilities and/or learning difficulties. The goal is to train young people to imagine and design the future, starting from the challenges and emergencies that they want to face to then move on to intentions, knowledge and skills that they will have to acquire and strengthen to achieve their goals. They will also have to learn and strengthen the conditions, as well as the educational and professional goals they have to pursue, with the tenacity to face specific identified challenges.

The intervention includes five didactic units, of two hours each, once weekly, for 5 weeks in total. In the first didactic unit, adolescents are invited to reflect on and discuss the five areas of crucial importance for humanity and the planet identified by the United Nations [UN] (People, Planet, Prosperity, Peace, and Partnership). In the same meeting, adolescents are encouraged to analyze these issues related to their hopes and concerns for the future. In the second didactic unit, the 17 Sustainable Development Goals set by the UN are introduced and explained to foster a global perspective and develop students as global citizens exposed to a range of views on globalization. Adolescents are then asked to select a number of objectives that are of interest to them and explain why they have been chosen. During this didactic unit, there is also a discussion about the significance of education for the future. In the third and fourth didactic units, adolescents are invited to reflect on their possible future mission and callings considering social challenges and goals. By identifying the mission, participants are encouraged to imagine future activities and occupations through which people, with the help of other professionals, address one of the most concerning challenges for their future.

In the last didactic unit, adolescents are helped in the discovery of jobs and professions that are connected to their missions, and the potential formation processes that can help them achieve the appropriate knowledge and skills to perform them. Adolescents are invited to reflect about the purpose of education to accomplish their missions and the role that instruction and training could give concerning the pursuit of the objectives, and the management of the various situations detected.

The study conducted by Santilli et al. (2020) showed, overall, that students who participated in the five didactic units – compared to students who participated in a traditional career guidance activity – have obtained higher levels in career adaptability, the skill of adapting to the unforeseen requirements related to changes in the world of work and working conditions, and a higher tendency to invest in the future and in postgraduate education. Furthermore, participants in the experimental group have reported more careful aspirations concerning future challenges (for example: "In the future, I would like to be involved with the challenges regarding the constant wars among countries, poverty, and inequality"; "In the future, I would like to achieve my goals taking into consideration the contribution I could give with my work to the challenges") and toward the development of a fair and sustainable future (for example: "In the future, I would like to carry out a satisfying professional activity but I also want to help others thanks to my job"; "In the future, I would like to merge my passion for cooking with the well-being of the planet, trying to combat food waste and to detect ways to find raw materials avoiding the exploitation of resources"). Lastly, considering the social validity, participants have evaluated the whole intervention as important to reflect on specific dimensions regarding their future, deal with future transitions, and develop their educational and professional projects.

CAREER INTERVENTIONS FOR YOUNG ADULTS

In young adults with and without disabilities, career interventions aim to promote their career development and career transitions into the world of work.

An example of an activity in the professional sphere that corresponds with the goals that we value is the program proposed by Watts et al. (2011), which aims to promote a collective identity and critical reflection on the issue of inequality in young adults in various areas including the professional one. Participants are supported to develop a collective identity through recognizing the elements they have in common with other participants and highlighting what is unique about their various experiences, about the historical and social factors that underlie specific individual and collective challenges (Seider et al., 2015). Specifically, the group leader presents a social issue close to the participants' reality (e.g., poverty or unemployment). Through Socratic questioning, young adults are engaged in a collaborative dialogue to challenge commonly and stereotypically assimilated knowledge related to social issues. The goal is to distance from individualistic conceptions of poverty and unemployment, such as laziness, lack of persistence, and recognize what can be considered a structural barrier to solve social problems (e.g., job shortages, low wages, and discriminatory policies in work settings).

Critical reflection on social issues is applied through various means such as analysis of films, books, music, and examples from participants drawn from their daily experience in educational and community settings.

More recently, Blustein et al. (2019) proposed the MPOWER program to promote investment in young adults' future purposes to increase their intrinsic motivation and, ultimately, their investment in a college education. In general, the MPOWER project is designed to provide students with a set of exercises ranging from group experiential activities, individual reflection, and group activities. Group sharing guides them in exploring the "4 Ps" that together shape the goal: (1) supportive persons (significant adults, such as parents, extended family members, and teachers.); (2) prosocial benefits (students are motivated to pursue their purpose because of the benefits it may have for others); (3) propensity (specific skills and traits that students perceive as relevant to their chosen purpose); and (4) passion toward the goal. The workshops, of 3 hours each, are scheduled over six weeks. During the workshops, aspects of collective identity and reflection are explored and developed along with twenty-first-century skills such as communication, teamwork, and critical thinking. Furthermore, workshops incorporate experiential group activities, individual reflection, and group sharing focused on helping young adults to identify their professional goals, values, strengths, and desired social impact through a future profession.

Finally, we would like to mention the intervention proposed by the Larios Laboratory for young adults with and without vulnerabilities during the period of the COVID-19 pandemic. The intervention stems from the realization that the pandemic appears to be having a "devastating and disproportionate impact on young adults" employment. Young adults constitute the pandemic principal targets' including social and economic consequences (International Labor Organization, 2020). There is a danger that they will be affected throughout their working lives - leading to the emergence of a "lockdown generation." The COVID-19 crisis created more barriers for young people with disabilities to find or retain employment, who are already at greater social exclusion risk in the current labor market (Chan et al., 2020).

The project "Thinking about work and the future in the era of Covid-19" was held online with a group of unemployed young adults in April 2020 during the first COVID-19 lockdown in Italy. The goal of the intervention was to promote a future design that includes a shared sense of solidarity with others and the tendency to establish partnerships for a decent job and a better future. Through individual and group counseling activities, the project provided space and time to reflection, critical thinking, and learning conceptual, emotional, and behavioral tools useful for understanding the present. It also supported participants to imagine and build an inclusive and sustainable future, giving them a voice and allowing them to outline their own "mission possible," intentions, purposes, and plans. Specifically, the project involved 12 people looking for employment and consisted of five online meetings, two of which were individual and three small group meetings. Online career counseling is in line with the principles of the Life Design International Research Group. It aimed to promote career adaptability, resilience, orientation toward the future, and the propensity to identify inclusive and sustainable projects in the future.

Quantitative analysis performed to assess pre and post-intervention changes suggested that the unemployed people participating in the online career counseling group showed greater career adaptability, resilience, and orientation toward the future. The qualitative analysis examined reflections made at the end of each group meeting and the concerns, pre and post the intervention, regarding the participants' thoughts about the future and the years ahead. Those who participated in the intervention progressively produced less individualistic reflections with more attention to others and the context. Furthermore, more inclusive and sustainable thoughts about the future were observed in post-intervention than pre-intervention.

CONCLUSION

In this chapter, we have explored examples of career interventions for children, adolescents, and young adults with and without disabilities that can be implemented to support their career planning in an inclusive perspective. Based on the most recent and accredited approaches in the field of guidance, we proposed interventions that help people "reflect" on the contextual factors that can influence the design of a dignified future, that support them in aspiring to an inclusive and sustainable future, and that aim at acquiring the strategies and skills needed to pursue what is close to their heart.

In conclusion, we want to mention that, as suggested by Sultana (2018) and Nota et al. (2020), career practitioners, in addition to acting directly on clients with and without disabilities, should be able to implement multiple levels of intervention (micro, meso, and macro), acting on people's life contexts.

At a micro level, career practitioners can involve the parents of people with disabilities, training them to recognize their children's rights to educational and professional choice. It could be useful to expose parents to successful models of individuals with disabilities at school and work to expand their range of options available to their children. Parents could be involved in the school interventions and events dedicated to career issues to establish advantageous partnership, and encouraged to engage their children in volunteering internship and job shadowing to increase their knowledge of occupations (U.S. Department of Education, 2010).

At a meso level, intended as an institutional level that involves schools, organizations, and workplaces, career practitioners can act to foster the recognition and respect of the differences and uniqueness between individuals. For instance, in school contexts, career practitioners can arrange educational activities for teachers to build awareness of the theme of inclusion and acknowledge the work rights and educational rights of people with disabilities. This will encourage teachers to become capable of fostering the development of skills and resources considered useful for professional design and for an inclusion in the labor market of all of their students, with an inclusive perspective.

Career practitioners can expand their educational and advocacy work to employers, in order to make sure that they become conscious of their duties toward all the employees, with a special focus on those with disabilities. Training and advocacy with colleagues are of the utmost importance. These should be carried out with the purpose of preventing negative attitudes and prejudices that can mutate into new career barriers for those who risk the most (McManus et al., 2010). In this regard, it is necessary to foster activities and interventions that address issues of diversity in general, with a focus toward workers with vulnerabilities in the company. A main focus should be to increase knowledge of the skills and strategies that could be useful for colleagues to promote inclusion in professional activities.

At a macro level, the influence of career practitioners should reach policies and social culture, through actions such as public debates, dedicated spaces on websites, petitions, manifests, conferences and congresses focused on the above-mentioned themes. Joint commitments in international, national, and regional networks gain significance, because they can affect the political contexts in which people make decisions that involve educational and professional life, especially for those who live in a condition of disability (Nota et al., 2020). In this regard, we would like to recall the Manifesto for Inclusion and the Charter-Memorandum of Orientation and Career Counseling for a decent, inclusive and sustainable development for all (Soresi et al., 2019). These documents are the result of the reflections of almost 600 scholars, researchers, professionals, and managers who foster inclusive work environments and career guidance services, which aim to promote school, social and work inclusion, and the quality of all people's personal and professional lives. The overall objective of these documents and the various career programs explored in this chapter are to create a better future–for all.

REFERENCES

Blustein, D. L., Kenny, M. E., Di Fabio, A., & Guichard, J. (2019). Expanding the impact of the psychology of working: Engaging psychology in the struggle for decent work and human rights. *Journal of Career Assessment, 27*(1), 3–28.

Brownlee, J. L., Walker, S., Wallace, E., & Scholes, L. (2019). Doing the right thing in the early years of primary school: A longitudinal study of children's reasoning about right and wrong. *Australian Educational Researcher, 46*, 863–878.

Chan, F., Tansey, T. N., Iwanaga, K., Bezyak, J., Wehman, P., Phillips, B. N., Strauser, D. R., & Anderson, C. (2020). Company characteristics, disability inclusion practices, and employment of people with disabilities in the post COVID-19 job economy: A cross sectional survey study. *Journal of Occupational Rehabilitation*, 1–11.

Chen, C. P., & Chan, J. (2014). Career guidance for learning-disabled youth. *International Journal for Educational and Vocational Guidance, 14*(3), 275–291.

Diemer, M. A., Rapa, L. J., Voight, A. M., & McWhirter, E. H. (2016). Critical consciousness: A developmental approach to addressing marginalization and oppression. *Child Development Perspectives, 10*(4), 216–221.

Eccles, J., & Gootman, J. (Eds.). (2002). *Community programs to promote youth development*. National Academy Press.

Fernández, J. S., Gaston, J. Y., Nguyen, M., Rovaris, J., Robinson, R. L., & Aguilar, D. N. (2018). Documenting sociopolitical development via participatory action research (PAR) with women of color student activists in the neoliberal university. *Journal of Social and Political Psychology*, *6*(2), 591–607.

García-Feijoo, M., Eizaguirre, A., & Rica-Aspiunza, A. (2020). Systematic review of sustainable-development-goal deployment in business schools. *Sustainability*, *12*(1), 440.

Ginevra, M. C., Soresi, S., Nota, L., Ferrari, L., & Solberg, S. (2019). Career guidance for persons with disabilities. In J. A. Athanasou & H. N. Perera (Eds.), *International handbook of career guidance* (2nd ed.). Springer.

Guichard, J. (2018). Life design interventions and the issue of work. In V. CohenScali, J. P. Pouyaud, M. DrabikPodgorna, G. Aisenson, J. L. Bernaud, … J. V. Guichard (Eds.), *Interventions in career design and education: Transformation for sustainable development and decent work* (pp. 15–28). Springer, Cham.

Hartung, P. J. (2015). Life design in childhood: Antecedents and advancement. In L. Nota & J. Rossier (Eds.), *Handbook of life design. From practice to theory and from theory to practice* (pp. 89–101). Hogrefe.

Hawkins, K. (2014). Teaching for social justice, social responsibility, and social inclusion: A respectful pedagogy for twenty-first century early childhood education. *European Early Childhood Education Research Journal*, *22*, 723–738.

Heberle, A. E., Rapa, L. J., & Farago, F. (2020). Critical consciousness in children and adolescents: A systematic review, critical assessment, and recommendations for future research. *Psychological Bulletin*, *146*(6), 525–551.

Hirschi, A., & Dauwalder, J. (2015). Dynamics in career development: Personal and organizational perspectives. In L. Nota & J. Rossier (Eds.), *Handbook of life design. From practice to theory and from theory to practice* (pp. 27–39). Hogrefe.

Hooley, T., Sultana, R., & Thomsen, R. (2017). *Career guidance for social justice. Contesting neoliberalism*. Routledge.

International Labour Organization. (2020). Global survey on youth and COVID-19. https://www.ilo.org/wcmsp5/groups/public/ed_emp/documents/publication/wcms_753026.pdf

Lee, I. H., Rojewski, J. W., Gregg, N., & Jeong, S. O. (2015). Postsecondary education persistence of adolescents with specific learning disabilities or emotional/behavioral disorders. *The Journal of Special Education*, *49*(2), 77–88.

Lerner, R. M., von Eye, A., Lerner, J. V., & Lewin-Bizan, S. (2009). Exploring the foundations and functions of adolescent thriving within the 4-H study of positive youth development: A view of the issues. *Journal of Applied Developmental Psychology*, *30*(5), 567–570.

McManus, J. L., Feyes, K. I., & Saucier, D. A. (2010). Contact and knowledge as predictors of attitudes toward individuals with intellectual disabilities. *Journal of Social and Personal Relationships*, *28*(5), 579–590.

Nota, L., & Rossier, J. (Eds.). (2015). *Handbook of life design. From practice to theory and from theory to practice*. Hogrefe.

Nota, L., Soresi, S., Di Maggio, I., Santilli, S., & Ginevra, M. C. (2020). *Sustainable development, career counselling and career education*. Springer International Publishing.

Phelps, E., Zimmerman, S., Warren, A. A., Jeličić, H., von Eye, A., & Lerner, R. M. (2009). The structure and developmental course of positive youth development (PYD) in early adolescence: Implications for theory and practice. *Journal of Applied Developmental Psychology*, *30*, 571–584.

Pouyaud, J. (2015). Vocational trajectories and people's multiple identities: A life design. In L. Nota & J. Rossier (Eds.), *Handbook of life design. From practice to theory and from theory to practice* (pp. 59–74). Hogrefe.

Roth, J. L., & Brooks-Gunn, J. (2003). What is a youth development program? Identification and defining principles. In F. Jacobs, D. Wertlieb, & R. M. Lerner (Eds.), *Enhancing the life chances of youth and families: Public service systems and public policy perspectives. Handbook of applied developmental science: Promoting positive child, adolescent, and family development through research, policies, and programs* (Vol. 2, pp. 197–223). Sage.

Santilli, S., di Maggio, I., Ginevra, M. C., Nota, L., & Soresi, S. (2020). 'Looking to the future and the University in an Inclusive and sustainable Way': A career intervention for high school students. *Sustainability*, *12*(21), 9048.

Savickas, M. L., Nota, L., Rossier, J., Dauwalder, J.-P., Duarte, M. E., Guichard, J., Soresi, S., Van Esbroeck, R., & van Vianen, A. E. M. (2009). Life designing: A paradigm for career construction in the 21st century, *Journal of Vocational Behavior, 75*(3), 239–250.

Seider, S. C., Clark, S., & Soutter, M. (2015). A critically conscious approach to fostering the success of college students from underrepresented groups. *Journal of College and Character, 16*(4), 253–262.

Shogren, K. A., Wehmeyer, M. L., Schalock, R. L., & Thompson, J. R. (2016). Reframing educational supports for students with intellectual disability through strengths-based approaches. In M. L. Wehmeyer & K. A. Shogren (Eds.), *Handbook of research-based practices for educating students with intellectual disability* (pp. 25–38). Routledge.

Slaten, C. D., Rivera, R. C., Shemwell, D., & Elison, Z. M. (2016). Fulfilling their dreams: Marginalized urban youths' perspectives on a culturally sensitive social and emotional learning program. *Journal of Education for Students Placed at Risk, 21*(2), 129–142. https://doi.org/10.1080/10824669.2015.1134331

Soresi, S., Nota, L., & Santilli, S. (2019). *Il contributo dell'orientamento e del counselling all'agenda 2030* [The contribution of guidance and counselling to the Agenda 2030]. Cleup.

Sultana, R. G. (2018). Precarity, austerity and the social contract in a liquid world: Career guidance mediating the citizen and the state. In T. Hooley, R. G. Sultana, & R. Thomsen (Eds.), *Career guidance for social justice: Contesting neoliberalism* (pp. 63–76). Routledge.

U.S. Department of Education (ED). (2010). *A blueprint for reform: The reauthorization of the elementary and secondary education act.* Office of Planning, Evaluation and Policy Development.

Watson, M., Nota, L., & McMahon, M. (2015). Child career development: Present and future trends. *International Journal for Educational and Vocational Guidance, 15*(2), 95–97.

Watts, R. J., Diemer, M. A., & Voight, A. M. (2011). Critical consciousness: Current status and future directions. *New Directions for Child and Adolescent Development, 2011*(134), 43–57.

FALLING BETWEEN TWO STOOLS? POST-SECONDARY TRANSITION PLANNING FOR STUDENTS WITH INTELLECTUAL DISABILITIES IN THE REPUBLIC OF IRELAND

Joanne Banks, Des Aston and Michael Shevlin

ABSTRACT

Over the last decade, there has been a significant increase of students with intellectual disabilities attending mainstream primary and secondary-level education in the Republic of Ireland (McConkey et al., 2017). Despite this increase, it appears that comparatively few of these students successfully transition to further/higher education and/or employment opportunities. This chapter examines typical transition support/guidance provided to students with intellectual disabilities as they prepare to complete their post-primary education in a mainstream setting. Using data from a study of school principals and school personnel responsible for career guidance and transition planning, the findings show guidance is limited for students with intellectual disabilities. Instead of being the responsibility of career guidance counsellors, guidance and transitions planning for students with intellectual disabilities are viewed as being the role of other personnel such as the school SENCO. By assigning this responsibility to special education roles in the school, students with intellectual disabilities may run the risk of having narrow and limited career options presented to them. This study raises serious questions about the effectiveness of mainstream schools in facilitating this critical transition stage for students who have intellectual disabilities.

Transition Programs for Children and Youth with Diverse Needs
International Perspectives on Inclusive Education, Volume 18, 143–158
Copyright © 2022 Joanne Banks, Des Aston and Michael Shevlin
Published under exclusive licence by Emerald Publishing Limited
ISSN: 1479-3636/doi:10.1108/S1479-363620220000018011

Keywords: Intellectual disability; special educational needs; inclusive education; transitions; post-secondary; Ireland

INTRODUCTION

It is well established that the employment and educational outcomes for students with disabilities are worse than their peers in mainstream education (Almalky, 2020; Pearson et al., 2020). Research shows that these students are more likely to be unemployed when they leave school, they are at a greater risk of living in poverty and dependent on social welfare as a source of income (Watson et al., 2017). Many students with intellectual disabilities leave school without "knowledge, skills and experiences" that are necessary to successfully find employment (Gibbons et al., 2015, p. 81) or progress to further education (Grigal et al., 2011; Newman et al., 2009). They are, therefore, significantly underrepresented in the workforce and often face limited educational options when they leave school with many destined for specific vocational or rehabilitation programs often funded by health departments or disability support services (Aston et al., 2021; Baer et al., 2011).

Given the dramatic changes in the profile of students in mainstream education over the past two decades, there is now increased attention on the adequacy of school supports such as guidance counseling in meeting the needs of increasingly diverse student populations. While diversity is welcome, little is known about the nature and quality of guidance or support that is offered to this cohort, in comparison to their non-disabled peers, or the extent to which students with intellectual disabilities are academically and socially prepared for life after school. The aim of this chapter is to examine school guidance and transition planning for students with intellectual disabilities in the Irish second level school system. Using data from a study of school personnel, it explores the nature and quality of guidance provision and examines the extent to which existing guidance structures are suited to the (changing) student population.

BARRIERS TO SUCCESSFUL POST-SECONDARY TRANSITIONS FOR STUDENTS WITH INTELLECTUAL DISABILITIES

Transition is defined as the process of moving from the protected life of a child to the autonomous and independent life as an adult (Leonard et al., 2016). It is at this stage that young people often make important life decisions with many deciding on their education and career goals. Critical transition periods, such as leaving second level education, can prove difficult for people with intellectual disabilities and their families with research highlighting the failure of this group to move from school to employment, training or further, and higher education (Pearson et al., 2020). Where students with intellectual disabilities do progress to employment, they are more likely than their peers to progress to sheltered or supported employment rather than the competitive labour market (Baer et al., 2011). Research shows that the issues that arise during the transition from school to adult life for students with intellectual disabilities can be "complex and multi-faceted" (p. 151) (Dyke et al., 2013) with multiple stakeholders involved (Jacobs et al., 2020) and often, students with intellectual disabilities excluded from the decision-making process (Kirk, 2008).

Problems can include a lack of transition planning for students before leaving school, limited or no coordination between schools and services or a lack of adequate services to meet local needs (Pearson et al., 2020). Research shows that decisions around post-school options for students with intellectual disabilities are often structured early on in their school career suggesting the need for guidance and transition planning to begin in their first or second year of secondary education. Some studies have, however, highlighted how some choices may already be shaped for these students who are more likely to have an "alternative" or reduced curriculum thus limiting post-school options (Hanreddy & Östlund, 2019). This is particularly problematic where students with intellectual disabilities are educated in special classes or units or settings separate from the mainstream class (Banks et al., 2016; McCoy et al., 2014).

In most schools, guidance counsellors are the experts in postsecondary planning, but for students with disabilities and those with Individual Education Plans, research has shown that this task often falls to special education teachers despite having no training in this area (Benitez et al., 2009). Despite the importance of professional guidance for this group of students, studies show that some students rely on informal networks for information about their post-school options due to a lack of awareness among school guidance counsellors. Where supports are lacking in school, transition planning to "atypical education/employment initiatives" can often fall to the families and parents of students with intellectual disabilities (Beresford, 2004; Hughes, 2012).

In these circumstances, students and their families can struggle to gain information about the types of courses on offer, the supports available and the suitability of the program causing increased stress and anxiety (Griffin et al., 2010; Marriott, 2008). Stress associated with this period can often be exacerbated by a lack of access to information about possible post-school pathways and the likely decrease in supports when the young person leaves formal education. Studies have also highlighted broader cultural barriers impacting progression from school such as low expectations among educators and guidance professionals around possible transitions to education or employment (Grigal & Hart, 2010). Given these failures, some now call for school transition services to be guided by the principles of the United Nations Convention on the Rights of Persons with Disabilities (UNCRPD) with the rights of the young person to freedom and choice are considered (Pearson et al., 2020).

FACTORS THAT SHAPE POSITIVE TRANSITIONS FROM SCHOOL

International research has highlighted some of the factors that shape positive transitions from school to post-secondary education (Bell et al., 2017; Björnsdóttir, 2017). Studies tend to focus on two main areas: guidance while in school and the availability of supports for these students when they enter post-secondary education. It is perhaps not surprising that guidance provision for students with disabilities is improved where schools have adopted an inclusive ethos and difference and diversity among the student population is welcomed. Studies have highlighted the importance of schools having an inclusive ethos as a major factor influencing successful post-school transitions for students with intellectual disabilities (Baer et al., 2011).

International and national legislation can also influence approaches to guidance provision and encourage professionals to move beyond simply providing guidance to the "mainstream" but to consider alternative pathways for students with different levels of need and ability. The role of the UNCRPD in shaping inclusive practices, should, in principle impact on guidance provision as well as placement, teaching, and learning for students with disabilities. At national level, legislation can also impact choices provided to students with intellectual disabilities and improvements can be seen in higher education entry for this cohort in the United States for example with the introduction of the Higher Education Opportunity Act (2008) (Gibbons et al., 2015). These improvements in progression can also be seen in other countries particularly where students with intellectual disabilities enter higher education to take certain specifically designed programs or vocational diplomas (Björnsdóttir, 2017; Gibbons et al., 2015).

Despite failures in school level guidance for students with intellectual disabilities, widening participation and increasing the numbers of students from "non-traditional" backgrounds is now a major policy initiative in further and higher education institutions around the world. These initiatives often target socioeconomic inequalities in our education system by increasing the number of students from marginalized groups and those experiencing socioeconomic disadvantage. More recently, however, further and higher education providers have begun to focus their Equality, Diversity and Inclusion (EDI) policies and the ways in which they can increase participation for students with disabilities. Some countries have gone further by introducing programs which enable students with intellectual disabilities to undertake specifically designed programs.

POST-SECONDARY TRANSITIONS FOR STUDENTS WITH INTELLECTUAL DISABILITIES IN THE REPUBLIC OF IRELAND

In line with countries internationally, there has been a dramatic shift in education policy in the Republic of Ireland, which has led to a significant increase in students with disabilities, including intellectual disabilities, attending mainstream primary and post-primary education. The introduction of national legislation such as the Education for Persons with Special Educational Needs Act (2004) marked the beginning of inclusion of students with special educational needs (SEN) in Irish mainstream schools. It is important to recognize that this Act is now 17 years old. Young people with intellectual disabilities who entered mainstream education system at the time of enactment are now reaching the age at which they will be transitioning out of the compulsory school system. Despite these changes to the profile of the mainstream school population, little is known about the types of guidance and transition planning available to this cohort of students while in school.

Similar to international research, Irish studies also show that students with intellectual disabilities are more likely to have negative transitions and post-school outcomes compared to their peers. Research suggests that there are insufficient pathways to tertiary education and/or employment opportunities for young people with intellectual disabilities (O'Brien et al., 2009; Scanlon & Doyle, 2018; Walk, 2015). In line with international research, Irish students with intellectual disabilities struggle to find meaningful employment opportunities, with 6% of the population in paid employment in the Republic of Ireland (Government of Ireland, 2017); they are at an increased risk of living in poverty (Watson et al., 2017); and have little expectation of progressing to higher education (Health Reseach Board, 2019; Hourigan et al., 2017).

The system of guidance provision in Irish mainstream education is outlined in the Education Act (1998) which stipulates that schools are obliged to "ensure that students have access to appropriate guidance to assist them in their educational and career choice." More recently, the Department of Education has indicated that a "whole-school approach" should outline the school's "approach to guidance generally and how students can be supported and assisted in making choices and successful transitions in the personal and social, education and career areas" (Department of Education and Skills, 2017; NCGE, 2017). Guidance counseling is provided for all students in mainstream schools regardless of their post-school choices however research indicates that current provision tends to emphasize academic pathways with a particular focus on entry to higher education (Smyth et al., 2011).

For students wishing to take alternative paths post-school, formal guidance at school is often unavailable, leaving them to access their own channels of information at home (Smyth & Banks, 2012; Smyth et al., 2011). There is little understanding on who is responsible for the post-school transition planning process for students with intellectual disabilities in mainstream schools (or students with disabilities generally), although recent research from Scanlon and Doyle (2018) shows that parents of students with intellectual disabilities, who typically play a much more significant role in their child's decision-making, would prefer post-school options and information to be provided to their child via the guidance service within schools (Scanlon & Doyle, 2018).

LIMITATIONS OF GUIDANCE PROVISION

The findings of this paper come from a broader mixed methods study of second-level school personnel (Aston et al., 2021) which highlights a number of key issues around the post-school transition process for students with intellectual disabilities in the Republic of Ireland. This research explored the nature and extent of guidance and transition planning available to the general student population. A multi-mode survey (postal and online) was sent to over 700 second-level school principals between November 2019 and February 2020 with a response rate of 15%. Given the low response rate, the findings in this paper are based on qualitative or open-ended survey questions completed by school principals as part of the broader survey in addition to data from in-depth qualitative interviews carried out with a sample of nine school personnel. The larger survey sample was used to select a smaller sample of nine interviewees (including guidance counsellors and special educational needs coordinators) working in Irish second-level schools. Due to the COVID-19 Pandemic, the interviews took place in March and April 2020 via Zoom and a semi-structured interview schedule used to gather opinions and perspectives from respondents.

FINDINGS

Data show that schools operated a robust process of transition planning, led by the Guidance Counselor but this appeared to be heavily centered around the Leaving Certificate examination, the Central Application Office (CAO) points system and entry to higher education and university. Principals surveyed provided a range of guidance for students in the mainstream including one-to-one guidance, classroom guidance, opportunities to go to open days, and interaction with parents about post-school transition. For students with intellectual disabilities however, transition planning and guidance provision was limited. Although the Special Educational Needs Coordinators (SENCO) and the Guidance Counsellors expressed confidence in ensuring students with intellectual disabilities are included socially within their schools, they highlighted a lack of adequate guidance and post-school transition planning for this cohort of students. Most participants ranked their schools as average or below average when it comes to supporting post-school transitions. In some cases, participants admitted much of their workload is over prescribed with the volume of work associated with the traditional pathways to post-secondary education:

> I don't do anything about transitioning for additional needs or students with additional needs [intellectual disabilities]. (Emily, Guidance Counselor)

During the interviews, Guidance Counsellors noted that the lack of career guidance for students with intellectual disabilities was often attributed to the major cutbacks to guidance provision since Ireland's economic recession in the late 2000s. They felt that their school principals expected them to assume more teaching and classroom-based responsibilities. Interestingly, in the survey of school principals, they stressed the need for improved guidance and access to appropriate information, in order to support students in their transition from school.

Lack of Clarity About Who Is Responsible for Guidance Provision

There is no clear indication of who was professionally responsible for supporting students with intellectual disabilities to plan their post-school transition, with much of the research nationally and internationally pointing toward the responsibility falling to families, and parents in particular. This study shows a clear ambiguity around whose responsibility it is in schools for supporting this cohort of students to transition to post-school destination. The findings highlight a contradiction between policy which promotes a whole-school approach to guidance including young people with special educational needs and the practice on the ground. Although school principals surveyed reported that the responsibility for guidance and transition planning is the responsibility of the school Guidance Counselor, the qualitative interviews painted a very different picture. Interviewees, both SENCO and Guidance professionals (bar one Guidance Counselor), explained that the SENCO in the school was "better equipped" to make those decisions:

> I don't make the judgement, I just say, "These are the options." I don't feel qualified or equipped to...
>
> [The SENCO] is better at saying, "Absolutely not." (Aoife, Guidance Counselor)

There were major differences in the extent to which the role of transition planning was conducted by SENCO's in differing schools with many favoring an individualized transition plan for students with intellectual disabilities. SENCO's placed value in an equity-focused approach to supporting students with special educational needs, which requires a very personalized relationship with the individual. This approach means that many SENCO's found it difficult to relinquish some of the responsibility around guidance and transition planning to their colleagues, who may not know the individual as well as they do:

> To be honest, I would find it difficult to hand over maybe some of that, like, in my mind to hand over some of that work to other people .... (Olivia, SENCO)

It was acknowledged by participants that transition planning for students with intellectual disabilities is a specialized area, given the limited number of students identified as having an intellectual disability that would be enrolled in any given year group. This meant the Guidance Counsellors, and SENCO's, felt these post-school pathways were atypical and would vary widely depending on the individual's needs. Despite this, there was very little variation in the typical destinations that these students would progress to after they complete school. Quite often, students would be linked in with health-based disability support services in the locality, or rehabilitative training initiatives in the area. It was evident that while Guidance Counsellors were obviously highly skilled in career guidance, the SENCO was recognized as an expert in matters pertaining to disability, and so, would be better suited to advise students, and their parents on disability services for after school, with little focus on potential post-school training or education opportunities that would lead to a meaningful career.

Perceived Transition Obstacles

Principals, SENCOs and guidance counsellors all agreed on the risks for students with intellectual disabilities moving from a highly supported and structured school environment to a more challenging situation in further or higher education which demands a higher degree of self-reliance. This gap in support as students moved from one educational setting to another was a key cause of concern among those surveyed:

> [Students] had SNA [Special Needs Assistant] access in school ... but that ceases once school stops .... TCPID School Transitions Survey (Aston et al., 2021)

School principals surveyed also described how these transitions from school often fail for students with intellectual disabilities, due to the lack of "proactive support networks ... that have existed at secondary school." Despite these fears, the study highlights a lack of data on school leavers with intellectual disabilities in relation to where they go and the levels of retention when they get there:

> I don't think there's any real follow-up...really it's once they're off the books, they're gone. (Frieda, SENCO)

The qualitative interviews identified a common theme of managing expectations among the school professionals. This "unwritten" job specification appeared across professional roles in terms of managing the expectations of both students and their parents.

For example, one participant spoke about a student who set their mind on a specific career goal that they, the educator, perceived to be totally unsuitable and they feared the student was being set up for failure, and future disappointment. In this case, the SENCO was concerned that the student wasn't being appropriately supported to explore different options and they queried whose responsibility it was to manage unrealistic expectations:

> Whose job is it to tell them really that course might not be for you or that career path isn't for you? (Eileen, SENCO)

Furthermore, according to the interviewees, parents had their own expectations of their child's abilities and where they expected their child to transition to after school. This expectation was often not aligned with the beliefs of the interviewees working in the school system. SENCO's and Guidance Counsellors explained how they felt an obligation to inform parents that their high expectations may not be realistic or naive. This realization of the extent to which their son/daughter is heavily supported in secondary school and the reality that those supports do not automatically transfer to adult education, is often identified during the final year of school. The consciousness of the complexity of applying for appropriate post-school supports can lead to panic and anxiety for students and their parents and can potentially cause tension between the family and the school.

I think that's a huge shock to parents when they realise in the sixth year that that's the case. (Freida, SENCO)

At this late stage in their final year of school, students and parents are coming to terms with the fact that their post-school transition is not going to be as straight forward as they had once imagined. They are likely to seek information on the appropriate supports and suitable education/training placements available to them once they leave school. In line with the limited literature, this study has highlighted a complete lack of knowledge of alternative educational/training options that would be accessible to, and suitable for, students with intellectual disabilities (Aston, 2019; Doody, 2015; Newman et al., 2009; Pallisera et al., 2018). There was a myriad of intersectional obstacles that prevented guidance professionals in particular from proactively seeking information on alternative pathways. The most prominent barrier was the hegemonic CAO system and the paperwork associated with the narrowly focused access route to higher education in the Republic of Ireland. The over-reliance on this traditional high-stakes exam leaves very little resources to focus on alternative pathways for "non-traditional" students.

The Importance of an Inclusive School Ethos

The extent to which a school has an inclusive ethos or follows the principles of inclusive education are shown in the literature to impact on all aspects of the school, including school culture, teaching and learning, and student-teacher relationships. The survey sought to investigate school principal's perception of inclusive education and how they constitute inclusion in their school. Principals felt their school had an inclusive philosophy "to a great extent." Additionally, 80% of the respondents reported using Individual Education Plan's (IEP), yet less than 50% of those respondents reported using the IEP for the purpose of transition planning. In respect to questions on inclusive teaching strategies, and more specifically, the use of Universal Design for Learning (UDL), 65% of principals stated they use UDL "to some extent" in their school. The in-depth qualitative interviews confirmed this finding, with respondents identifying inclusive teaching methodologies that fit into the UDL framework. However, respondents did not explicitly name "Universal Design for Learning."

Inclusive leadership was identified by interviewees as school principals, or deputies who had an understanding, or life experience in the area of special needs or disability – often a connection through a family member. Educators who claimed they had an "inclusive philosophy" within their school also claimed that they had strong support from inclusive leaders within their school. In one case, Aoife (Guidance Counselor) witnessed change in how their school had improved their inclusive practice over the past six years, which coincided with a change in staff and a new deputy principal who had worked as a SENCO in their previous school:

> I think it's just built up and built up with a couple of changes of staff and management. That's changed things ... She's [deputy principal] really, really pushed it as well ... (Aoife, Guidance Counselor)

With this change in leadership came increased attention to the concept of inclusion within the school. Additionally, new staff entering employment in the school under an inclusive leader fostered an inclusive ethos within the school.

Many of the SENCO's that participated in the study described feeling a disconnect between their personal vision for inclusion in the school and the understanding of the concept of inclusion held by their principal and their colleagues from across the school – often acting as a sole advocate promoting inclusion within the school:

> I would rather someone professional came in, because teachers just see me and they're like, "Here she goes on again." (Olivia, SENCO)

TRANSITION PLANNING: DISCUSSION AND CONCLUSIONS

People with intellectual disabilities are more likely to be unemployed/underemployed, at risk of poverty, and dependent on social welfare than their peers who do not have an intellectual disability (Watson et al., 2017). This cohort of young people are significantly underrepresented within further and higher education and the workforce in Ireland. Formal career guidance and supported transition planning are essential elements for all students to make successful progression into post-school settings (McGuckin et al., 2013). However, there is limited evidence about the type of career guidance or transition planning that students with an intellectual disability receive in school, or their progression pathway from school to post school settings. This study takes place within the context of a noticeable increase in students attending mainstream schools over the last decade (McConkey et al., 2017). Many factors are responsible for these increased numbers including significantly enhanced support provision within mainstream schools, combined with a desire from parents to have their children educated in mainstream settings. This study examined what if any transition planning to post-school settings was available for students who have an intellectual disability within mainstream schools. It also addressed the extent to which current guidance provision in schools prepares these students for post-secondary education, training, employment, and adult life more generally.

Transition processes for all students can be complex, however, this process is particularly problematic for students who have an intellectual disability. Four key themes that emerged from this study: (1) the nature and extent of existing transition planning, (2) responsibility for transition planning, (3) barriers to effective transition planning and (4) the presence (or not) of an inclusive school ethos.

The Nature and Extent of Existing Transition Planning

It is generally accepted that well established transition planning exists for students without an intellectual disability within mainstream schools. As a result, transition pathways to post-school settings are supported by expertise from guidance personnel, and information about post-school options is readily available and easily accessed. However, it is fair to say that students who have an intellectual disability experience a very different form of transition planning and face the reality of very limited choices on leaving school. Undoubtedly, this situation has arisen as traditionally these students were not expected to follow similar transition pathways alongside their non-disabled peers. Instead, this cohort were offered limited options including adult day centers or local vocational training centers mainly funded by health services. While some more options have emerged over the past decade, there is little evidence of a coherent alternative pathway to the traditional offering and as a result the system is quite fragmented and often opaque (Scanlon & Doyle, 2018). Dyke et al. (2013) observed that compared to their non-disabled peers, transitions for young people who have an intellectual disability took longer and involved fewer opportunities to participate in learning and activities designed to prepare them for adulthood.

There was little evidence of guidance provision informing the transition planning process for students with intellectual disabilities. Planning for these students often took place on a case-by-case basis. Transition planning for students who have a disability and/or special educational needs is recommended to take place at the age of 14 this is legislatively mandated in the United States, where approximately three-quarters of students have begun transition planning by this age (Newman et al., 2009; Wagner et al., 2014). There was no evidence to suggest that school personnel were aware of the need to begin the planning process at this age.

It is generally accepted that personal transition plans are essential to meet the transition needs of students who have an intellectual disability (Pallisera et al., 2018; Scanlon & Doyle, 2018). This personal transition plan would be designed with the young person centrally involved and target key skills such as decision-making, problem-solving, goal-setting skills, developing self-awareness, self-determination, and self-advocacy (Newman et al., 2009; Pallisera et al., 2018). These enhanced skills would be essential to enable the young person to achieve social and labor market inclusion (Pallisera et al., 2018). There was little evidence that school personnel were aware of the importance of developing personal transition plans for this student cohort.

Responsibility for Transition Planning

There was uncertainty about who took responsibility for post-school planning for this student cohort within schools. While it was clear that guidance personnel took responsibility for non-disabled peers and those with disabilities intending to apply for further and higher education students with an intellectual disability did not appear to be under their remit. Instead, there was strong evidence that the SENCO took overall responsibility for transition planning for this cohort.

A parallel system of transition planning has emerged in schools which mirrors the traditional parallel systems of mainstream and special education.

This blurring of professional roles has significant consequences for the quality of guidance available to this cohort of students as these students are missing out on guidance expertise when making critical life choices that will profoundly influence the future direction of their lives. Post-school transition for students with intellectual disabilities is atypical and it is not always a straightforward process for them and their families to access the requisite knowledge of alternative educational/training options (Aston, 2019; Doody, 2015).

There appeared to be an assumption among guidance personnel that students with intellectual disabilities progressed seamlessly into adult day services/ vocational training centers organized by the health service. Having chosen the mainstream school for the education of their children, families increasingly expect that mainstream pathways will be available for their children alongside their non-disabled peers and there is increasing evidence that these students and their families are less than satisfied with the limited options on offer (Scanlon & Doyle, 2018).

Also, parents of students with intellectual disabilities would prefer transition planning to be provided by the guidance personnel within mainstream schools (Scanlon & Doyle, 2018). Guidance personnel in this study were very concerned about their lack of specific training on transition planning for this student cohort and their limited knowledge about the availability of post-school placements. Similar findings were reported by McGuckin et al. (2013), when guidance personnel identified the need for tailored Continuing Professional Development designed to address their shortcomings in knowledge about transition planning for students with disabilities. In the absence of coherent transition planning within schools for this student cohort SENCOs assume responsibility for transition planning, along with the parents of those students who have an intellectual disability. There was an absence of any formal tracking system to monitor the progression of students with an intellectual disability into post-school settings, though some enquiries were made on an informal basis.

Barriers to Effective Transition Planning

Significant barriers to achieving successful post-school transitions were identified in this study, including the fear that appropriate supports would not be available in post compulsory education settings, a perceived shortage of places in appropriate settings for students with intellectual disabilities; and a lack of knowledge, information, and awareness of what is available after school for this student cohort. These barriers highlight the limited transition pathways for these students, in comparison to their non-disabled peers.

Transition planning is often ad hoc, based on limited information and takes place too late in their school careers to make a significant difference to their post-school life trajectory. School personnel and parents were fearful that adequate supports were not readily available to enable successful transitions to post-school settings within further and higher education. School personnel were very aware that these students were receiving significant levels of support within schools and were not certain about the availability of appropriate supports to enable progression. Similar concerns were expressed in the study by McGuckin et al. (2013), which investigated progression pathways for students who have disabilities and/or SEN into further and higher education. Supported transition models for students who have an intellectual disability in special schools have emerged, though these are not widespread (Scanlon & Doyle, 2018) they have proved to be very successful in bridging the gap between school and post-school settings, including employment.

Participating meaningfully within educational environments by young people who have an intellectual disability is often determined by expectations from school personnel, families and the wider community (Shevlin et al., 2020). Stereotypical attitudes within society have often led to a consistent underestimation of the capabilities of these young people and often undermined efforts to enable them to engage meaningfully within their local communities. School personnel were anxious to manage parental expectations regarding post school destinations for their children and often spoke of the need for "realistic choices" and avoiding "unrealistic expectations." It is always difficult to determine whether "realistic choices" as perceived by school personnel are the result of the overall limited expectations for this student cohort or whether it is a reflection of the reality of limited choices within existing transition pathways.

The Presence (or Not) of an Inclusive School Ethos

Research has shown that a school's culture and the expectation it holds for students can shape or influence the educational decision-making regarding post-school pathways (Smyth & Banks, 2012). Within this study, school personnel regarded whether an inclusive school ethos existed within their school as a critical factor in how provision for students who have an intellectual disability was structured and delivered within the school. School leaders generally described their schools as having an inclusive ethos, though some school personnel added caveats to this description. School leaders play a crucial role in deciding priorities for resource allocation, the level of guidance provision made available and the curricular programs on offer in the school. All of these decisions have a significant impact on the school experiences of students who have an intellectual disability.

Inclusive schools are usually characterized by a school leader who takes a whole-school approach, promotes collaboration, and includes all marginalized students in all aspects of the school experience (Lyons et al., 2016). Schools that adopted a whole-school approach in this study tended to have higher levels of cooperation and coordination among staff in transition planning for students with intellectual disabilities. There was evidence of a shared responsibility among school staff in helping these students to plan for their future.

CONCLUSION

While it is very evident that Irish government policy and enabling legislation has been designed to strengthen the development of inclusive learning environments in Irish schools, it is equally clear that there are serious shortcomings regarding the inclusion of children and young people who have an intellectual disability. Increasing numbers from this cohort are attending mainstream schools and there is evidence that school support provision has responded to this increase. However, these young people are not meaningfully included in post school transition planning at the same level as their peers.

Lowered expectations for this cohort of young people within the wider community results in the limited development of viable options for them on leaving school apart from the traditional offering of day services or vocational rehabilitation. Focused transition planning in schools is essential to raise expectations and help to forge new, exciting pathways for these young people enabling them to make the transition to a meaningful adulthood within their community alongside their peers.

REFERENCES

Almalky, H. A. (2020). Employment outcomes for individuals with intellectual and developmental disabilities: A literature review. *Children and Youth Services Review, 109*, 104656.

Aston, D. (2019). *Higher education opportunities for students with intellectual disabilities in the Republic of Ireland-a national response*. Inclusive National Higher Education Forum.

Aston, D., Banks, J., & Shevlin, M. (2021). *Post-school transitions for students with intellectual disabilities in the Republic of Ireland*. [online]. Dublin: Trinity College Dublin. http://www.tara.tcd.ie/handle/2262/94978. Accessed on July 25, 2021.

Baer, R. M., Daviso, A. W., Flexer, R. W., Mcmahan Queen, R., & Meindl, R. S. (2011). Students with intellectual disabilities: Predictors of transition outcomes. *Career Development for Exceptional Individuals, 34*, 132–141.

Banks, J., McCoy, S., Frawley, D., Kingston, G., Shevlin, M., & Smyth, F. (2016). *Special classes in Irish schools phase 2: A qualitative study*. NCSE/ESRI.

Bell, S., Devecchi, C., McGuckin, C., & Shevlin, M. (2017). Making the transition to post-secondary education: Opportunities and challenges experienced by students with ASD in the Republic of Ireland. *European Journal of Special Needs Education, 32*, 54–70.

Benitez, D., Morningstar, M. E., & Frey, B. (2009). A multistate survey of special education teachers' perceptions of their transition competencies. *Career Development for Exceptional Individuals, 32*, 6–16.

Beresford, B. (2004). On the road to nowhere? Young disabled people and transition. *Child: Care, Health and Development, 30*, 581–587.

Björnsdóttir, K. (2017). Belonging to higher education: Inclusive education for students with intellectual disabilities. *European Journal of Special Needs Education, 32*, 125–136.

Department of Education and Skills. (2017). *Guidance plan*. DES.

Doody, H. (2015). *Inclusive education: Challenges and barriers for people with intellectual disabilities accessing further education*. Master of Education.

Dyke, P., Bourke, J., Llewellyn, G., & Leonard, H. (2013). The experiences of mothers of young adults with an intellectual disability transitioning from secondary school to adult life. *Journal of Intellectual and Developmental Disability, 38*, 149–162.

Gibbons, M. M., Justina, H., Cihak, D. F., Wright, R., & Mynatt, B. (2015). A social-cognitive exploration of the career and college understanding of young adults with intellectual disabilities. *ASCA | Professional School Counselling, 19*, 80–91.

Government of Ireland. (2017). *Make work pay for people with disabilities*. Government of Ireland.

Griffin, M., Mcmahon, E., & Hodapp, R. (2010). Family perspectives on post-secondary education for students with intellectual disabilities. *Education and Training in Autism and Developmental Disabilities, 45*, 339–346.

Grigal, M., & Hart, D. (2010). *Think college! postsecondary education options for students with intellectual disabilities* (1st ed). London: Paul H. Brookes Publishing Company.

Grigal, M., Hart, D., & Migliore, A. (2011). Comparing the transition planning, postsecondary education, and employment outcomes of students with intellectual and other disabilities. *Career Development for Exceptional Individuals, 34,* 4–17.

Hanreddy, A. A. Ö., & Östlund, D. (2019). Alternate curricula as a barrier to inclusive education for students with intellectual disabilities. *International Electronic Journal of Environmental Education, 12,* 235–247.

Health Research Board. (2019). *National ability supports system (Nass).* HRB.

Hourigan, S., Fanagan, S., & Kelly, C. (2017). *Annual report of the national intellectual disability database committee 2017 main findings.* HRB.

Hughes, C. A. C. E. (2012). *The new transition handbook.* Paul H. Brookes Publishing Co.

Jacobs, P., Macmahon, K., & Quayle, E. (2020). Who decides? Transitions from school to adult services for and with young people with severe intellectual disabilities. *Disability & Society, 35,* 1058–1084.

Kirk, S. (2008). Transitions in the lives of young people with complex healthcare needs. *Child: Care, Health and Development, 34,* 567–575.

Leonard, H., Foley, K., Pikora, T., Bourke, J., Wong, K., McPherson, L., ... Downs, J. (2016). Transition to adulthood for young people with intellectual disability: The experiences of their families. *European Child & Adolescent Psychiatry, 25*(12), 1369–1381.

Lyons, W., Thompson, S., & Timmons, V. (2016). 'We are inclusive. We are a team. Let's just do it': Commitment, collective efficacy, and agency in four inclusive schools. *International Journal of Inclusive Education, 20*(8), 889–907.

Marriott, J. (2008). Post-16 education and disabled learners: A guide for schools, colleges and for information, advice and guidance workers. Action on Access [online]: The National Coordination Team for Widening Participation.

Mcconkey, R., Keogh, F., Bunting, B., Garcia Iriarte, E., & Flatman Watson, S. (2017). Relocating people with intellectual disability to new accommodation and support settings: Contrasts between personalized arrangements and group home placements. *Journal of Intellectual Disabilities, 20,* 1–12.

Mccoy, S., Banks, J., Frawley, D., Watson, D., Shevlin, M., & Smyth, F. (2014). *Understanding special class provision in Ireland.* NCSE/ESRI.

McGuckin, C., Shevlin, M., Bell, S., & Devecchi, C. (2013). *Moving to further and higher education: An exploration of the experiences of students with special educational needs.* [online]. Dublin: National Council for Special Education.

NCGE. (2017). *A whole school guidance framework.* National Centre for Guidance in Education.

Newman, L., Wagner, M., Cameto, R., & Knokey, A. (2009). *The post-high school outcomes of youth with disabilities up to 4 years after high school: A report from the national longitudinal transition study-2 (NLTS2).* National Centre For Special Educational Research.

O'Brien, P., Shevlin, M., O'Keefe, M., Fitzgerald, S., Curtis, S., & Kenny, M. (2009). Opening up a whole new world for students with intellectual disabilities within a third level setting. *British Journal of Learning Disabilities, 37,* 285–292.

Pallisera, M., Vilà, M., Fullana, J., Díaz-Garolera, G., Puyalto, C., & Valls, M. (2018). The role of professionals in promoting independent living: Perspectives of self-advocates and front-line managers. *Journal of Applied Research in Intellectual Disabilities, 31,* 1103–1112.

Pearson, C., Watson, N., Gangneux, J., & Norberg, I. (2020). Transition to where and to what? Exploring the experiences of transitions to adulthood for young disabled people. *Journal of Youth Studies.* doi:10.1080/13676261.2020.1820972

Scanlon, G. A., & Doyle, A. (2018). *Progressing accessible supported transitions to employment (PASTE): Navigating the transition from school – voices of young people and parents.* [online]. Dublin: Dublin City University.

Shevlin, M., Kubiak, J., O'donovan, M., Devitt, M., Ringwood, B., Aston, D., & Mcguckin, C. (2020). Educated and work ready: Effective practices for helping students transition to work. In U. Sharma (Ed.), *Oxford research encyclopedia of education.* Oxford University Press.

Smyth, E. A., & Banks, J. (2012). High stakes testing and student perspectives on teaching and learning in the Republic of Ireland. *Educational Assessment, Evaluation and Accountability, 24*(4), 283–306.

Smyth, E., Banks, J., & Calvert, E. (2011). *From leaving certificate to leaving school a longitudinal study of sixth year students.* Liffey Press.

Wagner, M., Newman, L., & Javitz, H. (2014). The influence of family socioeconomic status on the post–high school outcomes of youth with disabilities. *Career Development and Transition for Exceptional Individuals, 37,* 5–17.

WALK. (2015). *Accessing mainstream training: Barriers for people with intellectual disabilities.* WALK.

Watson, D., Lawless, M., & Maître, B. (2017). *Eemployment transitions among people with disabilities in Ireland, an analysis of the quarterly national household survey, 2010–2015.* ESRI.

PREPARING STUDENTS TO TRANSITION TO EMPLOYMENT: TEACHER PERSPECTIVES AND STUDENT OUTCOMES OF THE CALIFORNIA WORKABILITY 1 PROGRAM

Tamai A. Johnson

ABSTRACT

Work experience helps develop skills necessary for life after high school. The California WorkAbility 1 (WA1) Program was developed to improve post-secondary outcomes for students with disabilities by providing temporary employment to students. Teacher experiences and perspectives reveal benefits and challenges of the WA1 Program. Success of the program is measured by how many student participants are hired by the employer after internship hours are completed. Challenges include funding and development of an equitable process for student selection. This chapter discusses strategies and recommendations for developing an effective work-experience program, including, acquiring and appropriating funds, staff placement, collaboration, equitable access, and education of all stakeholders.

Keywords: Special education jobs; special education employment; post-secondary transition; student work experience; vocational training; vocational transition

Transition Programs for Children and Youth with Diverse Needs
International Perspectives on Inclusive Education, Volume 18, 159–169
Copyright © 2022 Tamai A. Johnson
Published under exclusive licence by Emerald Publishing Limited
ISSN: 1479-3636/doi:10.1108/S1479-363620220000018012

INTRODUCTION

Transition to adulthood can be challenging for any student. Students generally begin to question what life after high school will be like, and they may become concerned about supporting themselves, college, and/or finding employment. While this transition can be difficult for any student, it is more challenging for students with disabilities (Chambers et al., 2009; Dee, 2006; Johnson, 2018; Winn & Hay, 2009). Research suggests that when students with disabilities transition from adolescence to adulthood, employment is closely related to psychological health (Galambos et al., 2006) and an improved quality of life (Stodden & Mruzek, 2010). Alternately, unemployment for individuals with disabilities results in a loss of financial independence, poor quality of life, and abbreviated growth for society as a whole (O'Day & Stapleton, 2009; Wisman, 2010).

Winn and Hay (2009) indicated that the barriers impeding successful transition from high school to adulthood include the lack of connection between service agencies to support transition and the need for a comprehensive transition plan in high school. Establishing a comprehensive transition plan for students at the high school level, therefore, is essential to promoting optimal post-secondary outcomes (Johnson, 2018; Roffman & Brinkerhoff, 2007). Transition programs should also incorporate development of skills associated with workplace success, such as communication with others and teamwork. Carter et al. (2012) found that young adults with disabilities who had little or no trouble communicating with others had three to four times greater chance of employment after high school than those who had difficulty communicating with others. In addition, students who rated high in classroom social skills, classroom behavior, and self-advocacy during high school, and those who could travel independently, were more likely to be employed after high school. An additional component that has been connected to effective transition programs is the opportunity to engage in an actual work experience (Castellano et al., 2003; Carter et al., 2011).

Carter et al. (2009) explored early work experiences of youth with severe disabilities including intellectual disabilities, autism, and multiple disabilities using data from the National Longitudinal Transition Study-2, which examined how various student-, family-, school-, and community-level factors were related to waged work experiences during high school. The factors most associated with paid work were participation in internship, tech prep, and entrepreneurship programs. Students in this study who had vocational goals written into their Individualized Education Program (IEP) plans were more likely to have had a paid work experience. In addition, having access to work experience during high school was a precursor to job attainment in students' post-secondary lives.

Another commonly cited barrier to employment opportunities for students with disabilities is workplace prejudice toward hiring people with disabilities (Winn & Hay, 2009). Winn and Hay (2009) stated,

> It is recognised that it requires more than just schools to facilitate a positive transition but also employers to reconceptualise the notion of disability to one of individuals with ability and the contribution all people can make to the workplace. (p. 1)

Kaye et al. (2011) suggested several reasons why employers are reluctant to hire workers with disabilities, including lack of awareness of disability, lack of awareness of accommodations, cost concerns, and apprehension about legal and liability issues. Effective school to work partnership transition programs, therefore, should incorporate information and skill building for employers, which can change their perspectives regarding hiring, and result in a shift of focus from disability to ability. Work experience programs can allow employers to identify and appreciate a student-worker's strengths and how those strengths might be used in and for the benefit of their company.

The *Individuals with Disabilities Education Act* of 2004 [IDEA] is the federal law in the United States that outlines the educational rights of students with disabilities. Transition mandates were incorporated into the law because young adults with disabilities experienced reduced post-school integration, high drop-out and unemployment rates, low rates of post-secondary education enrollment, and reduced independent living and community participation (Flexer et al., 2011). IDEA describes transition services as:

> ... a coordinated set of activities for a child with a disability that ... is designed to be within a results-oriented process that is focused on improving the academic and functional achievement of the child with a disability to facilitate the child's movement from school to post-school activities, including post-secondary education, vocational education, integrated employment (including supported employment), continuing and adult education, adult services, independent living, and community participation. (See 20 US.C. 1401(34) and 34 CFR §300.43(a))

The state of California addresses employment goals for students with special needs through its WA1 program. The purpose of this chapter is to examine the WA1 program in California, through exploring the perceptions and experiences of special education transition teachers who have been involved in the program, and to document both strengths and areas for growth to achieve optimal student transition and employment outcomes.

THE CALIFORNIA WORKABILITY 1 PROGRAM

California's WA1 program was developed by the Department of Education in 1981. It is a school-based transition program, which offers students with disabilities, ages 14–22, an opportunity to participate in work experiences through participation in a comprehensive pre-employment education program, scaffolded employment opportunities, and follow-up services.

The WA1 program is funded and administered by the California Department of Education through its Special Education Department (California Department of Education). It was initiated as a pilot project to investigate work experience for youth with disabilities. Its charge is to promote the involvement of students, families, educators, employers, and agencies in planning and implementing an array of services that will assist with successful student transition to post-secondary employment, lifelong learning, and a better quality of life.

There are several collaborators of WA1 at the local level. The transition teacher is either a special education classroom teacher that works on campus with students, or an out-of-the-classroom special education teacher who may also have the title of Job Coach. Classroom transition teachers are focused on preparing students for college and careers. They teach lessons on resume writing, personal statements, and completing job applications. They survey student career interests using a commercial assessment or informal interviews with students, and complete other tasks related to transition instruction. Most importantly, these teachers are usually responsible for selecting which students participate in paid work experiences. A Job Coach prepares community employers (i.e., store managers) for working with students with disabilities and informs them of the program and how it works. Once students are accepted as interns, the Job Coach will meet with employers and student workers to check on student progress. Counselors provide students with opportunities to learn which post-secondary educational institutions have majors or fields of study that encompass student interests.

Community employers participate in WA1 by allowing students to work at their establishments as they train the student, and the school district pays the student's wages. Employers treat students the same as other employees and make accommodations as needed based on the student-worker's disability. Community employers may hire the student after the district internship expires. Parents collaborate with teachers and other school staff in IEP and Individualized Transition Plan (ITP) meetings. They work with their children to support and encourage self-advocacy. Parents might also provide transportation to the job site when possible. Students participate through exploring interests, demonstrating excellent work attendance, learning new job skills, expressing needs, and collaborating with coworkers.

The WA1 program grants money to school districts to pay student employees for working in businesses within their communities. Community businesses are offered free labor in exchange for training students for the duration of their placement, which includes a predetermined number of hours. An intended outcome of the WA1 program is that employers hire students after the program hours are completed.

The California Department of Education views WA1 as an effective program, because the students who participate in this program are *employable*. Unfortunately, employable does not mean employed. Research indicates that unemployment rates are significantly higher for youth with disabilities (16–23) than for their non-disabled peers, even for those who have participated in a vocational program in high school, such as WA1 (The National Collaborative on Workforce & Disability for Youth and Workforce Strategy Center, 2021).

Johnson (2018) conducted a study of the WA1 program in a large urban school district in Southern California to explore employment outcomes of students who participated in the WAI program. Student data was collected from the WA1 website, which contained information on employment of 291 students who had participated in the WA1 program and who were 2 years out of the program, or post-graduation. Of the 291 student participants, only eight (2.74%) were considered *direct hires*, that is, they were hired by the businesses where they completed the WA1 program. Students who were direct hires had worked 20 hours per week or more, were 18 years of age or older, and had a disability categorized as a specific learning disability versus a physical or emotional disability.

Another component of the Johnson (2018) study was qualitative. The data explored the perceptions, beliefs, and ideas of participants in this study. It determined the benefits and challenges of the WA1 program for students and teachers. Through thematic analysis, responses were categorized in themes that indicated major findings from the research. To further explore the strengths and areas of need in the program, Johnson (2018) gathered information from special education transition teachers who provided transition-related instruction (i.e., post-secondary employment/education) to high school students with special needs in a specific school district in southern California. Fifty-nine teachers in the District Office of Transition Services (DOTS) completed a survey about instructional methods and their influence on student direct hires during the 2013–2014 school year. In addition, focus group discussions were conducted with nine teachers (who had also completed the survey) exploring teacher perceptions about the WA1 program. Through open-ended survey responses and teacher input from the focus group meetings, Johnson (2018) delineated teacher perceptions of both benefits and challenges associated with the WA1 program and effective instructional practices employed to achieve student outcomes, which are reported next.

TEACHER EXPERIENCES AND PERSPECTIVES REGARDING THE WA1 PROGRAM

Teacher perspectives of the WA1 program derived from both survey and focus group responses highlighted internal and external benefits to both students and educators involved, effective instructional practices connected to the program, and a number of challenges that might be addressed. These are discussed further next.

How the California WA1 Program Benefited Students

Teachers spoke of both internal and external benefits experienced by the students they mentored through the WA1 program. Internal benefits included three categories: acquiring new skills, building relationships, and enhanced feelings and self-perceptions. For example, through participation in the program students acquired work-oriented skills such as learning how to write a resume and participate in an interview, as well as the importance of time management, such as being on time and taking breaks. They also were introduced to various workplace environments, including retail, food service, etc.

Relationship building was introduced through activities such as participating in role-playing that incorporated various workplace scenarios involving supervisors, co-workers, customers, and other personnel to build understanding of appropriate communication within a workplace environment. Skills for building community within a work setting were also introduced and practiced both prior to and within work placements.

Another internal benefit described by teachers was associated with perceptions of student growth in self-esteem and self-worth, with respect to both school and the work environment. Students expressed greater confidence in themselves as potential workers and were more focused on future life opportunities and outcomes than prior to their involvement in the program.

External student benefits of the WA1 program were related to the financial opportunities and outcomes of working or being employed. The ability to earn a paycheck enhanced motivation and a feeling of reward. Students acquired money management and financial literacy skills through learning how to set up and manage a bank account, and felt pride and satisfaction when they were able to purchase things for themselves or their family members. Transition teachers reported that student attendance increased once they deposited their first paycheck into their own accounts, highlighting the role of accountability to self and others.

Teacher Outcomes and Instructional Practices

Teacher responses included descriptions of how involvement in the WA1 program affected them personally and of the instructional practices they utilized with both students and teacher colleagues throughout the program. For example, teachers felt satisfaction and rewarded when students in the program were able to secure a job placement following completion of the program, especially when employed in an area of personal interest.

Teachers also described positive outcomes of collaborating with and supporting peer teachers to enhance information and skill building related to employment for all students. For example, the program allowed WA1 teachers to co-teach and co-plan with other teachers, both in special education and general education classes, to build skills such as incorporating employment vocabulary, interviewing skills, resume construction and completing job applications into general education class content. This opportunity resulted in a perception of greater unity and consistency within educational programming for students in the WA1 program.

Teachers also addressed instructional strategies utilized in their work with students and employers prior to, during, and after job placements. For example, prior to employment placement, teachers described use of lessons that emphasized effective work habits, workplace interpersonal skills, including behavior expectations and communicating with supervisors and coworkers. They also worked with students to identify interest areas and highlight strengths. During placement, teachers offered support by assisting students with paperwork, including helping students fill out timesheets, review paycheck stubs, and educating students about bank accounts; and with "soft skills," including communicating with others, understanding appropriate job behaviors, and learning to resolve conflict. Some students also received support to travel to and from their placement positions, which included using public transportation.

Teachers also provided support by meeting with employers regularly to get feedback on student progress to provide additional instruction. And when a job placement did not seem to be a good fit with student abilities and interests, teachers provided information to assist the student to modify or adjust responsibilities and activities within a work setting, or to seek placement at a jobsite that was more aligned to the student's interests, and that might lead to a direct hire.

Supports for students after WA1 work experiences consisted mostly of obtaining feedback from employers, teaching students to write resumes, and assisting students with job searches if they were not Direct Hires There was an overwhelming sense that transition teachers believe that supports are needed post-WA1 work experience. These supports should focus on identifying student strengths and experiences, applying for employment with another company, or obtaining additional education or training required to achieve personal vocational goals.

CHALLENGES ASSOCIATED WITH THE CALIFORNIA WORKABILITY 1 PROGRAM

In the data gathered through the open response survey questions and focus group participation, teachers identified a number of challenges connected to the WA1 program, including the criteria used for student selection for participation in the program, job availability with respect to location and employer willingness to participate, and the need to educate teachers, families and community members about the WA1 program. Though teachers participating in the study strongly supported the effectiveness of the program, they were aware of a number of areas that might be addressed to improve the program.

Student Selection Criteria

Teachers stated that there were no stated uniform requirements for student selection for the WA1 program; rather it was up to the transition teacher to determine who might be invited to participate. Teachers, however, indicated that quite often selection criteria seemed to be based on good attendance, good grades, good behavior, or positive student attributes. Students who were identified by a classroom teacher, or those who self-identified an interest in the program were also more likely to be involved. The downside of this was that students who may have also benefited from the program might have been overlooked. Given that the work experience seemed to be connected to student motivation for school in general, providing access to the WA1 program to additional groups of students, including those who may have been previously identified as not possessing the assumed criteria for participation, might provide unanticipated beneficial outcomes.

Job Availability: Location of Job

Participants believed that the location of the work site was essential when placing students for work experiences through WA1. They also suggested that this was one of the challenges of the program. Teachers felt the ideal placement for a work experience was near a student's home or school. However, many teachers in the district were working with students from urban, low-income areas where local jobs either were not available or were outside of a student's interest area. In such instances, transportation had to be included in the work schedule, which required teachers to factor in the amount of additional time it took to walk to a job site or use public transportation. In some neighborhoods safety was also a consideration when travel was required.

Job Availability: Employer Willingness to Accept Students for WA1 Training

There was strong agreement among transition teachers that one major challenge of the California WA1 program was the willingness of employers to participate by accepting and training students with disabilities. This typically was related to employer concern for any liability issues or the need to receive approval from corporate headquarters often located in other areas prior to involvement in the program. This, at times, resulted in limited job opportunities, or opportunities that did not align with a student's personal goals or aspirations.

The Need to Educate Others about the WA1 Program

Transition teachers identified one of the challenges of the WA1 program as a lack of education about the program among parents, teachers, and community employers. When essential stakeholders understand and affirm the program and its value, the transition through different points of the program, from selection, to identifying interests, to involvement, to securing job opportunities and potential placements is much smoother and better coordinated. Parents must have an understanding about how earnings from WA1 affect other financial support they may receive for their child with a disability. General education teachers need more information about how to deliver transition lessons to students when only a small number of students with disabilities are in their classrooms. Employers may need education on the risks and liabilities for participating in WA1. They may also need education about how to accommodate employees with disabilities on the work site. One way to ensure the education of all stakeholders would be to have Local Education Agencies (LEAs) conduct workshops with transition and WA1 topics for targeted audiences.

STRATEGIES FOR DEVELOPING AN EFFECTIVE WORK TRANSITION PROGRAM

Researchers who have found that student work experiences are positive indicate that working during high school or secondary years can lead to higher self-esteem, increased independence, and greater academic success (Geel & Backes-Gellner, 2012; Light, 2001; McWhirter et al., 2013). When students are provided opportunities for work experience, they can experience growth emotionally, socially, financially, and academically. Findings from the literature and from the research conducted with educators who participated in the WA1 program in a school district in southern California suggest a number of important components and strategies for designing an effective work transition program for students with disabilities at the secondary or high school level (Johnson, 2018).

When developing a work transition program such as WA1, it is important to determine funding resources and decide how much is needed to pay teacher salaries, as well as student salaries. To accomplish this, teachers should determine how much time is needed for students to benefit from a paid internship, and consider funding at least 100–300 hours per student. This would allow students to work 1 month to approximately 1 full semester depending on the amount paid per hour and the amount of time worked weekly. One might also consider a process for student selection. Once funding and student selection are completed, Job Coaches will go to local businesses and acquire internships for students. Students would then apply for these internships submitting cover letters and resumes that their transition teachers have helped them develop. Communication is key to a healthy WA1 Program. As soon as a student is hired as an intern, there should be weekly or bi-weekly collaboration meetings between the Transition Teacher, Job Coach, College and Career Counselor, Student, Employer, and Parent. These check-ins should be student centered and focus on student progress, supports, goals, strengths, and areas of need. These teams should also determine next steps for the student after the internship expires (e.g., Does the employer plan to hire the student? Can skills learned from this work experience transfer to future work experiences?).

RECOMMENDATIONS FOR ACTION

Based on the literature reviewed for this chapter, the following recommendations are suggested. Because students with physical and emotional disabilities tend to be significantly underrepresented in WA1 programs, the first recommendation is to allow equitable access to work experience for students with all disability types. Transition teachers should be provided uniform procedures for the equitable selection of students with varying disabilities for placement in work experiences. When more students are provided opportunities for work experience, it opens opportunities for growth emotionally, socially, financially, and academically (O'Day & Stapleton, 2009; Stodden & Mruzek, 2010; Wisman, 2010). Schools should expand current demographics of their student participants in work experience by reaching out to significantly more students with varying disabilities. Additionally, LEAs should strongly consider allowing student work experiences to occur during extended school breaks such as summer or winter break. Allowing students to work during these times might alleviate the pressures of simultaneously working and studying. Another suggestion resulting from the Johnson (2018) study is for local education agencies to promote placing students in work experiences that match their career interests. These placements could be based on the results of required career assessments administered by transition teachers to students in the special education program. Students are more motivated to participate in work when the job matches their interests.

Education is also strongly recommended. Johnson (2018) indicated the need for education about WA1 for both government officials and parents as well. One way to ensure that all stakeholders receive education related to WA1 would be to have LEAs conduct workshops related to transition and WA1 topics for targeted audiences. For example, one workshop might be created to discuss internal and external rewards of work experiences with students and parents to motivate them to participate in WA1 work experiences. Another workshop might be used to discuss the positive effects on teacher experiences to secondary teachers who need to collaborate with transition teachers. This may pave the way for teachers to be willing collaborators from the beginning of the academic year. There should also be a workshop or professional development meeting for transition teachers held at the beginning of the school year to help clarify student requirements for work experience. This may help eliminate a wide variance of criteria for student selection. LEAs might consider creating a coordinator position that is dedicated to job development and creating connections with community employers as a means to educate them on the topic of WA1. Educating employers may help alleviate issues with job availability for students. This might be in the form of periodic seminar workshops for employers that focus on themes related to employees with disabilities.

CONCLUSION

While developing a transition program, it is important to create student-centered goals remembering that the success of the program leads to positive outcomes for students. These goals might include identifying student strengths, researching vocational programs that lead to jobs in the field of student interests, scheduling work hours around classes or family responsibilities, completing yearly career assessments, or other employment related tasks. There are various positive outcomes for students involved in work programs, including financial rewards, a sense of independence, increased social connections, and an increase in self-confidence (Carter et al., 2011; Geel & Backes-Gellner, 2012; Johnson, 2018).

Successful transition from secondary education to adulthood requires the collaboration and input of multiple stakeholders. Programs such as California WA1 can help facilitate effective transition, through building life skills, enhancing self-determination, and promoting greater independence for students with disability, for the benefit of all.

REFERENCES

California Department of Education. https://www.cde.ca.gov/sp/se/sr/wrkabltyI.asp

Carter, E., Austin, D., & Trainor, A. (2011). Factors associated with the early work experiences of adolescents with severe disabilities. *Intellectual and Developmental Disabilities, 49*(4), 233–247. https://doi.org/10.1352/1934-9556-49.4.233

Carter, E., Austin, D., & Trainor, A. (2012). Predictors of postschool employment outcomes for young adults with severe disabilities. *Journal of Disability Policy Studies, 23*(1), 50–63. https://doi.org/10.1177/1044207311414680

Carter, E., Trainor, A., Ditchman, N., Sweeden, B., & Owens, L. (2009). Community-based summer work experiences of adolescents with high-incidence disabilities. *The Journal of Special Education, 45*(2), 89–103. https://doi.org/10.1177/0022466909353204

Castellano, M., Stringfield, S., & Stone, J. (2003). Secondary career and technical education and comprehensive school reform: Implications for research and practice. *Review of Educational Research, 73*(2), 231–272. https://doi.org/10.3102/00346543073002231

Chambers, D., Rabren, K., & Dunn, C. (2009). A comparison of transition from high school to adult life of students with and without disabilities. *Career Development for Exceptional Individuals, 32*(1), 42–52. https://doi.org/10.1177/0885728808323944

Dee, L. (2006). *Improving transition planning for young people with special educational needs.* Open University Press.

Flexer, R., Daviso, A., Baer, R., Queen, R., & Meindl, R. (2011). An epidemiological model of transition and postschool outcomes. *Career Development for Exceptional Individuals, 34*(2), 83–94. https://doi.org/10.1177/0885728810387922

Galambos, N., Barker, E., & Krahn, H. (2006). Depression, self-esteem, and anger in emerging adulthood: Seven-year trajectories. *Developmental Psychology, 42*(2), 350–365. https://doi.org/10.1037/0012-1649.42.2.350

Geel, R., & Backes-Gellner, U. (2012). Earning while learning: When and how student employment is beneficial. *Labour, 26*(3), 313–340. https://doi.org/10.1111/j.1467-9914.2012.00548.x

Individuals with Disabilities Education Act [IDEA] of 2004, 20 U.S.C. § 1401 et seq. (2017).

Johnson, T. (2018). *WorkAbility1: A California transition program evaluation* (Publication No. 13427458). Doctoral Dissertation, Azusa Pacific University. ProQuest Dissertations LLC.

Kaye, H., Jans, L., & Jones, E. (2011). Why don't employers hire and retain workers with disabilities? *Journal of Occupational Rehabilitation, 21*(4), 526–536. https://doi.org/10.1007/s10926-011-9302-8

Light, A. (2001). In-school work experience and the returns to schooling. *Journal of Labor Economics, 19*(1), 65–93. https://doi.org/10.1086/209980

McWhirter, E. H., Valdez, M., & Caban, A. R. (2013). Latina adolescents' plans, barriers, and supports: A focus group study. *Journal of Latina/o Psychology, 1*(1), 35–52. https://doi.org/10.1037/a0031304

O'Day, B., & Stapleton, D. (2009). *Transforming disability policy for youth and young adults with disabilities* (Research Brief 09-01). Center for Studying Disability Policy.

Roffman, A., & Brinkerhoff, L. (2007). *Guiding teens with learning disabilities navigating the transition from high school to adulthood.* The Princeton Review.

Stodden, R., & Mruzek, D. (2010). An introduction to postsecondary education and employment of persons with autism and developmental disabilities. *Focus and Autism and Other Developmental Disabilities, 25*(3), 131–133. https://doi.org/10.1177/1088357610371637

The National Collaborative on Workforce & Disability for Youth and Workforce Strategy Center. (2009). *Career-focused services for students with disabilities at community colleges.* Workforce Strategy Center.

Winn, S., & Hay, I. (2009). Transition from school for youths with a disability: Issues and challenges. *Disability & Society, 24*(1), 103–115. https://doi.org/10.1080/09687590802535725

Wisman, J. (2010). The moral imperative and social rationality of government-guaranteed employment and reskilling. *Review of Social Economy, 68*(1), 35–67. https://doi.org/10.1080/00346760902968405

THE REGIONAL LEARNING COLLABORATIVE: SUPPORTING SUCCESSFUL TRANSITIONS TO AND THROUGH COLLEGE FOR ALL STUDENTS

Nazanin Zargarpour and Susan R. Warren

ABSTRACT

This chapter recounts the story of the Regional Learning Collaborative (www.rlcollab.com) and its powerful positive impact, beginning in one urban region and expanding gradually. It first sets forth the challenges that gave birth to its vision. It introduces the intersegmental solutions and strategies innovated to address the challenges that thousands of students faced in advancing across the education transitions. The chapter next provides significant student achievement data in evidence of the Regional Learning Collaborative's proof of concept in supporting over one hundred thousand (113,000) primarily low-income and largely first-generation students to successfully transition across their academic and career pathways. Finally and importantly, the rigorous collaborative community approach and framework that continue to generate the Collaborative's equity outcomes are introduced and discussed.

Keywords: Intersegmental; collaboration; partnerships; PK-12-post-secondary; equity-focused; education transitions; data-driven

Never doubt that a small group of thoughtful, committed, citizens can change the world.

Indeed, it is the only thing that ever has.

Margaret Mead

–(Donald Keys, 1982)

Transition Programs for Children and Youth with Diverse Needs
International Perspectives on Inclusive Education, Volume 18, 171–189
Copyright © 2022 Nazanin Zargarpour and Susan R. Warren
Published under exclusive licence by Emerald Publishing Limited
ISSN: 1479-3636/doi:10.1108/S1479-363620220000018013

THE CHALLENGE

Why Do Today's Education Transition Challenges Call for Intersegmental Collaboration?

It was toward the end of an extensive and comprehensive, stakeholder-driven, and research- and evidence-based strategic planning process in a large, low-income, urban pre-kindergarten through 12th grade (PK-12) school district in Southern California ("District"), in 2015 (*Note*. A US school district is a special-purpose district that operates local public primary and secondary schools within a geographic area. Primary or elementary schools generally serve students in pre-school through 5th or 6th grades, generally ages 3–12. Secondary schools consist of middle schools with students in grades 6 or 7 through 8, ages 12–14, and high schools with students in grades 9 through 12, ages 14–18. School districts can be very small with only one school or extremely large with over 10,000 schools). The District Superintendent introduced a new data file for inclusion in the environmental scan that was being conducted to inform the District Strategic Plan (*Note*: In the United States (US), a superintendent of schools is an administrator or manager in charge of a number of public schools or a school district, a local government body overseeing public schools in a geographic area. All school principals (heads) in a respective school district report to the superintendent). He had received the data from the President of a community college at an intersegmental event, in which the community college had invited all of its feeder PK-12 school districts to discuss the challenges of student transitions from 12th grade in high school to the college (*Note*. Community colleges in the US are 2-year government-supported, nonresidential colleges that offer an associate degree and other certifications to people living in a particular area. They provide affordable postsecondary (post high school) education as a pathway to a four-year degree) (*Note*: US high schools are the final required schooling for students. These secondary institutions serve students in grades 9–12, generally ages 14–18). Successful completion of high school results in a diploma upon graduation. The Claremont Evaluation Center (CEC) team at Claremont Graduate University (Research Partner), which was leading the strategic planning activities, conducted an analysis of the data and found staggering results. Nearly 9 out of every 10 students (86%) who entered the community college after graduating high school in this district were dropping out of the college without earning any college credit (*Note*: Some of the data in this chapter are unpublished but have been presented at conferences and other professional and academic venues. Additional data about the RLC may be found at www.rlcollab.com). Further research would show that, while both segments of the education pipeline – the high school and the community college – were carrying out their educational duties responsibly, the low student retention rate was a function of structural misalignment across the transition between these two segments of the education pipeline.

Community colleges offer the most affordable means of higher education for many low-income and vulnerable students, as reflected in a Pell Institute study. The study found that students from lower SES families are much less likely to attend college, and if they do enroll, they are much more likely to attend a two-year college rather than a four-year university due to the greater affordability (Yamashita et al., 2018). Accordingly, a Pew Research Center study revealed that of the dependent undergraduate students at US community colleges, that is, students who receive some financial assistance from parents or other family members, 27% are in poverty and 50% are nonwhite (Smith, 2019).

The Strategic Plan environmental scan identified other significant challenges encountered by the approximately 23,000 students in the District, nearly 85% of whom are low-income, one-third (33%) English language learners (*Note*: Refers to students whose primary language is not English. These students are identified as having a level of English language proficiency that requires language support to achieve standards in grade-level content in English), 86% Hispanic/Latino, and 5% Black. Between 2012 and 2015, only 58% of the District's 12th graders ("seniors") attempted to enroll in a postsecondary college or university directly after high school, down from about 63% between 2005 and 2011 (*Note*: Refers to the two- or four-year education institutions that follow successful completion of high school or secondary education which is the last required schooling in the US Most students are 18 years of age at the end of high school). Among these college and university attempters, only 18.5% completed a postsecondary degree in four years, with an additional 9% in five years. Moreover, nearly two-thirds (63%) of high school seniors did not complete the high school academic courses required for entry into most 4-year institutions of higher education in California, barring them from California State University and University of California systems – the most affordable university options. For these students, community college becomes the most viable option. Yet, a staggering 86% of students who entered the college were dropping out without earning college credit.

The scan further showed that among the adults in that city, 31% did not graduate high school (HS), compared to 17% across the state of California, and only 18% completed college, compared to 33% statewide (US Census Bureau, 2019). These are stark realities, particularly in light of research by Georgetown University's Center on Education and the Workforce, predicting that by 2027, 70% of all jobs will require some education beyond high school – 40% will require a bachelor's degree (*Note*: A bachelor's degree or baccalaureate is an undergraduate academic degree awarded by colleges and universities after completing a 3–7-year course of study. The two most common bachelor's degrees are the Bachelor of Arts and the Bachelor of Science), or higher and 30% will call for some college or associate degree (Blumenstyk, 2020) (*Note*: An associate degree is an undergraduate degree awarded after a two-to-three-year course of post-secondary study. It is a level of qualification between a high school diploma and a bachelor's degree). Unfortunately, in the United States, low-income students are 10 times less likely to complete college, a phenomenon that perpetuates the cycle of poverty for many of our most vulnerable students. United States President Harry Truman's, 1947 Commission on Higher Education warned of the dangers of a system of education that perpetuates inequities of race and class:

> If the ladder of educational opportunity rises high at the doors of some youth and scarcely rises at the doors of others, while at the same time formal education is made a prerequisite to

occupational and social advance, then education may become the means, not of eliminating race and class distinctions, but of deepening and solidifying them.

Based on the data, the environmental scan flagged secondary-to-postsecondary transition as a significant challenge for the students of the region and an urgent priority for the District Strategic Plan. To identify and design evidence-based strategies addressing these obstacles in the District's 5-Year Strategic Plan, the Research Partner conducted root cause analysis of the challenges students were encountering. Root cause analysis consisted of review of extant research and triangulated qualitative inquiries at the district and college levels, including administrator interviews, student focus groups, and document and policy reviews.

The Research Partner discovered that, upon entry into community college, a large majority of students were being placed in a stacked series of three to four developmental (remedial), non-credit courses in English and/or Mathematics, all of which they were required to pass before they would be allowed to enroll in college level courses for credit and begin to work toward a post-secondary degree, the very purpose for which they had enrolled in college. For many students, this widely accepted practice led to a downward spiral of failure in their courses, leaving them psychologically demoralized and financially depleted, and eventually leading them to drop out. Further exacerbating matters, the placement decision in many colleges was based on one singular data point – a standardized placement exam determined by the college and administered in high school (*Note*. Later, in 2017, California state legislation (AB 705) was introduced to change this practice requiring that community college districts or colleges maximize the probability that a student will enter and complete transfer-level coursework in English and math within a one-year timeframe and use, in the placement of students into English and math courses, one or more of the following: high school coursework, high school grades, and high school grade point average). This singular assessment opportunity, which was administered at the end of 12th grade, tested learning objectives most students had learned in 6th grade. It was not a surprise, then, that students felt hopeless when faced with this system, and 9 out of 10 dropped out of community college before they ever earned a chance to enroll in a credit-bearing, college level course.

Further research on the target population provided evidence to dispel traditionally propagated myths about reasons for underperformance among low-income student populations and student populations of color. A CEC-conducted longitudinal study of 2,000 District high school students indicated that over 90% of 9th graders plan to complete college, eliminating low student aspirations as a potential root cause of low college persistence and completion rates. CEC-conducted evaluation studies also dispelled myths about student capacity. Low-income students who received academic, structural, social, and financial support attended, persisted in, and completed college at significantly higher rates than demographically matched peers; and some closed the *achievement* gap (Zargarpour, Martin et al., 2015; Zargarpour, Wanzer et al., 2015), as also evidenced in extant research (Cahalan et al., 2020; Yamashita et al., 2018).

What were the causes and obstacles that prevented 86% of the District's students who entered the community college from successfully enrolling in credit-bearing courses and navigating through college to degree completion? The CEC team identified three key systemic causes: (1) misalignment of policies and practices across segments, (2) lack of rigorous triangulation in measures used for student placement, and (3) insufficient student support. An urgent need emerged for articulation, alignment, and advising as students transitioned across pipeline segments (see Fig. 1) (Zargarpour, Donaldson et al., 2015a).

THE SOLUTION: INTERSEGMENTAL COLLABORATION

These striking challenges in the transition between high school and community college beckoned urgent systematic and structural solutions. However, the Research Partner was hesitant to include intersegmental solutions in a segmental District Strategic Plan. As the problem was situated in the transition space between the two segments, so too would the solution require cross-segmental action. What was needed was a *cross-segmental strategic plan*, with shared responsibility for planning, implementation, monitoring, and evaluation across the segments. In the same way that identification of the problem had required collaboration across the segments of the education pipeline, with transparent data sharing by the college with the district, identification of solutions would also require transparent and courageous data sharing and collaborative innovation between the segments. The parties were amenable to such collaboration.

In 2015, with the full engagement, support, and shared leadership of the District and College Practice Partners, the Research Partner at Claremont Graduate University's Evaluation Center founded the Regional Learning Collaborative (RLC). The RLC education pipeline Practice Partners include executive decision-makers, administrators, and students at the following education pipeline institutions:

- The Anchor School District
- Community College Partners

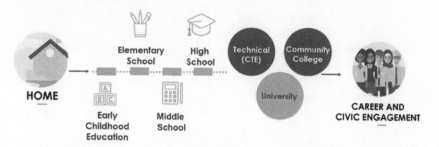

Fig. 1. Segments of the Education Pipeline. *Note:* This figure is reproduced, with permission, from the Regional Learning Collaborative website (www.rlcollab.com).

- University Partners
- Honorable Mayor of the City
- Regional Education-Focused Organizations
- State and National Partners as additional content experts.

The institutions of higher education that form the RLC represent over 50% of the District's college-going students. That is, over half of the District's students who go on to college attend one of the RLC Partner institutions (see Fig. 2).

Many PK-12 districts have partnerships with local colleges. The District in this study also had many strong initiatives with its postsecondary partners. However, prior to the founding of the Regional Learning Collaborative, never had all partners, across all the segments of the pipeline, come together to collaborate toward a shared vision and to meet regularly to co-create and advance one shared pipeline strategic plan.

The Research Partner built on the strength of existing relationships to convene the Practice Partners and engage all stakeholder groups in a shared, pipeline strategic planning process. It is important to note that student voices and perspectives were and continue to be systematically included in the RLC decision-making processes, planning, implementation, and reflexive monitoring. In fact, in developing the mission of the RLC, it was the student voices that rang the loudest in setting the north star. Students expressed that while they appreciate the firm belief that the adults in the system have faith in students' capacity to enroll in and complete college, they also need the adults to consider the realities of their lives – that not all may want to go to college full-time directly after high school; some

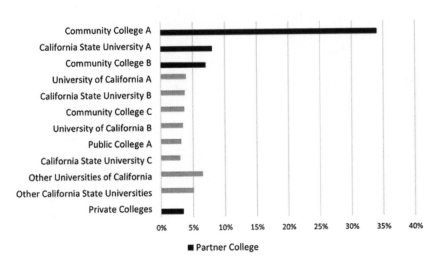

Fig. 2. Institutions of Higher Education Attended by the District Students. *Note:* This figure is reproduced, with permission, from the Regional Learning Collaborative website (www.rlcollab.com).

may need to couple work with college; some may need to take a gap year or two, and some may want to pursue a career technical education pathway. It was students who emphasized the need for multiple pathways to degree completion and career attainment.

Building on the valuable and insightful input of students, the mission of the RLC is to utilize innovative, research-driven, evidence-based, and collaborative approaches to restructure the education pipeline for successful student transitions across segments – elementary, middle, high school, technical training, community college, university, and career. The RLC's vision is for 100% of its students to attain postsecondary education and life-sustaining, fulfilling careers.

OUTCOMES AND STRATEGIC PRIORITIES
What Has the Regional Learning Collaborative Achieved toward Student Education Transitions?

Proof of Concept
The RLC initially prioritized the high school to college transition and identified developmental education reforms to address the 86% attrition rate for district students enrolling in the college. Within only the first 2 years, from 2016 to 2018, the RLC Partners collectively achieved proof of concept on this innovative framework for addressing challenging student transitions, with significant outcomes. The RLC reversed the ratio of success in the transition from high school to community college. Whereas previously nearly 9 out of 10 students (86%) dropped out without earning college credit, now nearly 9 out of 10 students (85%) were placed in credit-bearing, college-level courses, earning credits toward college degree completion and/or transfer to higher levels of education. This was achieved through the RLC's first strategic priority area – Developmental Education Reform – and two key associated high-impact strategies: the use of *multiple measures* to inform college course placement decisions and the provision of *corequisite education* – academic course support opportunities to assist students with the rigors of credit-bearing college courses.

The RLC's significant two-year outcomes in student academic achievement is of particular note, given extensive research on collective impact initiatives indicating that the average time between inception and impact ranges from 4 to 24 years. Researchers summarize that it usually takes considerable time to create real change in collaborative efforts (Stachowiak & Gase, 2018). Relationships must be developed; trust generated; consistent systems for engagement put in place; priorities identified; effective strategies developed and implemented; and processes and outcomes continuously measured.

Effective Expansion
Having achieved proof of concept in unprecedented time, the RLC Research Partners at the CEC next engaged RLC Practice Partners in a needs assessment and prioritization process to guide expansion of RLC efforts. The RLC identified

a second key impact priority for its Pipeline Strategic Plan – *Dual Enrollment (DE) courses* – to assist students with the transition from high school to post-secondary. Dual enrollment consists of innovative partnerships between public or charter secondary schools and local community colleges to offer college courses that allow students to earn college credit while still in high school (California Department of Education, 2021). Dual enrollment also introduces students to the rigors of college coursework early and provides students with an opportunity to develop college-going mindsets (Lile et al., 2017) and sense of belonging in college (Vargas et al., 2017), while still in high school. National research has shown that students who participate in high quality dual-enrollment programs are more likely to graduate from high school and get a college degree (Freedberg & Tadayon, 2020). Dual enrollment is a powerful strategy for achieving equity, as research shows that students who are most likely to benefit are those from low-income families, first-generation college students, and students of color – the most underrepresented in higher education (Career Ladders Project, 2019).

Again, within only two years of strategy implementation, in its dual enrollment strategic priority, the RLC achieved significant outcomes. The RLC achieved 500% increase in student participation in DE courses across the District. Prior to RLC intervention, dual enrollment had been offered at only one District high school, which served primarily high-income students. Within two years, from 2016 to 2018, dual enrollment courses were expanded to serve a broader range of low-income students and students of color across three of the District's seven traditional high schools. More specifically, participation of low-income students in DE courses nearly doubled, from 45% to 85%. Participation of Hispanic/Latinx students increased by 300%, and African American, female, and foster student participation in DE increased beyond Districtwide representation for each group.

Building on these significant advances in student achievement and education equity, the next two years of implementation focused on further expansion of dual enrollment opportunities to all students in the District. By the end of 2020, dual enrollment was expanded to all seven traditional high schools. In the 2019–2020 academic year, DE students earned 1,237 college credits with mean completion and pass rates of 87% and 98% respectively. Remarkably, today in one of the District's high-needs high schools serving 936 low-income 9th–12th grade students, over 60% of students graduate with college credit (see Fig. 3).

Further, a survey of 71 DE seniors in 2018–2019 reported positive qualitative impacts of DE participation in the RLC district:

- More realistic expectations of college (87%)
- Increased confidence to attain college success (86%)
- Increased confidence to attain life success (89%).

The RLC has succeeded in vastly broadening DE participation and college credit attainment in high school, for low-income and low-performing students, as suggested above, with the aim of increasing postsecondary outcomes.

Baseline 2016:

- DE at 1 high school
- Majority high-income, high-performing students

2018:

- DE at 3 high schools
- 500% increase in overall participation
- 300% increase in Latinx participation
- 200% increase in low-income participation
- Black and Female participation representative of District population
- 192 college credits earned through DE
- 96% completion rate
- 88% pass rate

2021 (despite pandemic effects)**:**

- DE at all 7 high schools
- Continued growth in DE participation districtwide and within each race/ethnicity
- 88% of DE students are low-income
- 1237 college credits earned through DE
- 87% completion rate
- 98% pass rate

60% of seniors at low-income high school graduate with college credit

20% higher college enrollment rate than non-DE students

Fig. 3. RLC Dual Enrollment Outcomes. *Note:* This figure is reproduced, with permission, from the Regional Learning Collaborative website (www.rlcollab.com).

The positive outcomes of RLC dual enrollment efforts validate findings from early studies on DE, which indicate that DE participants, on average, are more likely to graduate from high school, persist in postsecondary education, accumulate more college credits, and less likely to take basic skills courses in college than comparison students (Hughes et al., 2012). Further, RLC dual enrollment findings build on the extant research by validating group differences in DE outcomes, whereas previous studies did not disaggregate by student characteristics. Disaggregation of data by student groups is particularly important for those who have been historically under-represented in college attainment and who benefit from high expectations and strategies which inspire and support college readiness (Anderson et al., 2020).

Broader Impact

The RLC is nationally recognized for its groundbreaking outcomes in addressing racial equity in postsecondary education. In a national webinar hosted by California Competes on July 29, 2020, the panelists, ECMC Foundation president Peter J. Taylor and State of California Senior Policy Advisor for Higher Education Lande Ajose, PhD, consistently called for intersegmental collaboration as the next frontier of educational innovation needed for closing racial equity gaps (California Competes, 2020). Having effectively pioneered this work, with five years of consistent and committed participation from its over 90 intersegmental partners and four years of significant student outcomes in closing the income and race equity gaps, the Regional Learning Collaborative was recognized by ECMC President Peter J. Taylor as "the kind of change we need in California."

The Regional Learning Collaborative Partners continue to build on the RLC's successes with additional research-based, high-impact strategies that target evidence-based student supports in the spaces between the various segments of the education pipeline: elementary school to middle school, middle school to high school, high school to community college, and community college to university and careers (see Fig. 4). For example, bridge courses assist with transitions across segments, and the RLC's transfer strategies support student transition from

RLC Plan: Working in the Transitions...

HOME → Early Childhood Education · Elementary School · Middle School · High School · Technical (CTE) · Community College · University · CAREER AND CIVIC ENGAGEMENT

Fig. 4. Education Segments and Transitions. *Note:* This figure is reproduced, with permission, from the Regional Learning Collaborative website (www.rlcollab.com).

community college to university, with the aim of degree completion for all students, particularly among low-income students.

Importantly, all RLC strategies, once incubated and validated with rigorous proof of concept, are then implemented institution-wide by each RLC partner to support all of the student body, beyond students from the anchor District, thereby expanding the impact of RLC innovations to well over 113,000 students in the region annually. This scale of impact is further broadened when considering the numerous other pipeline collaboratives that have been created based on the impetus and approach pioneered in the region by the RLC. Further, RLC partners continuously present and publish on RLC strategies, approaches, and outcomes, for further broadening of impact on national and international scales (see Fig. 5).

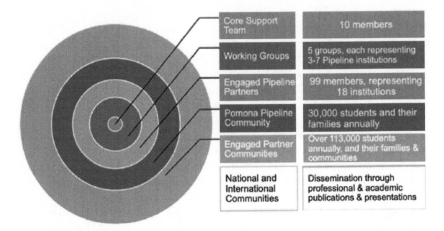

Core Support Team	10 members
Working Groups	5 groups, each representing 3-7 Pipeline institutions
Engaged Pipeline Partners	99 members, representing 18 institutions
Pomona Pipeline Community	30,000 students and their families annually
Engaged Partner Communities	Over 113,000 students annually, and their families & communities
National and International Communities	Dissemination through professional & academic publications & presentations

Fig. 5. The Regional Learning Collaborative Structure. *Note:* This figure is reproduced, with permission, from the Regional Learning Collaborative website (www.rlcollab.com).

RIGOROUS COLLABORATIVE COMMUNITY APPROACH

How Does the Approach of the Regional Learning Collaborative Lead to Equity for Diverse Students?

Committed Community Engagement

During the District strategic planning process, when the Research Partner and District Superintendent first approached the President of the community college to propose the idea of building into the District Strategic Plan an intersegmental collaborative of education partners, the college President was supportive yet skeptical. He intimated that such a partnership had not succeeded despite many past attempts. Nevertheless, the college President well understood and appreciated the need for such collaboration, having himself held regular, meaningful, and productive bi-segmental gatherings with his feeder districts. He committed his support and suggested that the collaborative work toward a shared strategic plan for the pipeline education community, above and beyond the District Strategic Plan that was already in progress.

The Research Partner took on the President's recommendation and, together with the powerful support of the District Superintendent, called on all of the district's pipeline partners, along with key business partners, to participate in a planning meeting that would launch the Regional Learning Collaborative. The Research Partner also called on its education-focused clients and partners in the community to engage in the Collaborative's efforts. These included college attainment programs and the Mayor of the City. Importantly, to ensure access to data and expertise from beyond its own region, the Research Partner also invited state, national, and international experts to engage in and help shape the discourse of the Collaborative. In all, 40 partners participated in the first RLC Convening, hosted and facilitated by the Research Partner at Claremont Graduate University. For the first time in the region's history, all Pipeline Partners and key Community Partners were engaged under one umbrella organization, collaborating in one seamless process as led by the Research Partner, to create a shared pipeline strategic plan to benefit all students in the region, particularly the most vulnerable.

Over time, engagement in each of the above-mentioned partner categories increased. New Pipeline Partners, Community Partners, and Content Experts joined the efforts and dedicated their resources to the work and mission of the Collaborative. Further, the enduring commitment of RLC Partners and the significant and unprecedented student outcomes that resulted from their sustained and dedicated efforts attracted the attention of Funding Partners. At the time of this writing, over 100 partners are engaged in developing and implementing the Regional Learning Collaborative's shared Pipeline Strategic Plan. And the Research Partner has evolved into a robust Core Support Team that serves as a backbone entity. The Core Support Team (CST) leads the RLC's research-informed strategic planning process, facilitates plan implementation, coordinates and bridges communication, monitors progress, engages Partners in reflection on experience and learning, and disseminates knowledge and learning locally as well as internationally through joint research and publication efforts with RLC Partners.

Core Support Approach

Partnerships across education sectors are vital to achieving college and career attainment, particularly for low-income students (Asera et al., 2017; Henig et al., 2016). A platform for communication, alignment, and collaboration across segments provides for a more seamless educational pipeline and facilitates development of shared vision and coherent practices to positively affect educational outcomes (Regional Education Laboratory, 2017). This is the work that backbone organizations take on in countless collective impact efforts and that the RLC Research Partner – the Core Support Team of dedicated graduate students and professionals from Claremont Evaluation Center and Capacity To Impact, Inc. – fulfills in the cross-segmental work of the Regional Learning Collaborative.

Yet, collaboration across multiple, complex systems, with differing needs and organizational processes, can be challenging (Bryson et al., 2015; Henig et al., 2015). As such, cross-segmental and multi-sectoral collaborations require diligent coordination, with cultural sensitivity, ongoing and transparent communication, and mutually trusting relationships. Only then can these diverse systems co-create and incubate innovations, generating new learning and producing new systems, structures, and processes that are able to bridge coherently across various sectors, segments, and institutions.

The effectiveness of the Core Support Team approach lies in its capacity to apply the evidence-based rigor of state-of-the-art research methods, to engage the systematic science of evaluation thinking and evaluation procedures, and to harness the immense power of committed and caring professional relationships toward a shared vision of postsecondary and career attainment for all students, detached from individual agendas and inclusive of all group identities (see Fig. 6). This approach is founded in the underlying core belief of the Core Support Team's leadership, namely, that every young person and every adult has unique capacities and critical contributions to make toward the betterment of society and that this potential can be fulfilled through quality education and positive developmental opportunities.

> Regard man as a mine rich in gems of inestimable value. Education can, alone, cause it to reveal its treasures, and enable mankind to benefit therefrom. (Bahá'u'lláh, 1983, p. 260)

The RLC's theory of change builds on this foundational belief. First and foremost, it holds the potential in youth and young adults among the most powerful reservoirs of society. Aiming to reveal and mobilize the positive potential latent in this reservoir, the RLC invests the collective resources and expertise of all its Partner organizations to foster the development and advancement of all students, and particularly underserved youth. The RLC thereby generates enhanced systemic capacity and outcomes, which in turn contribute to the advancement and prosperity of students of all diverse backgrounds, impact family and community wellbeing, and promote social justice, leading to the betterment of society as a whole.

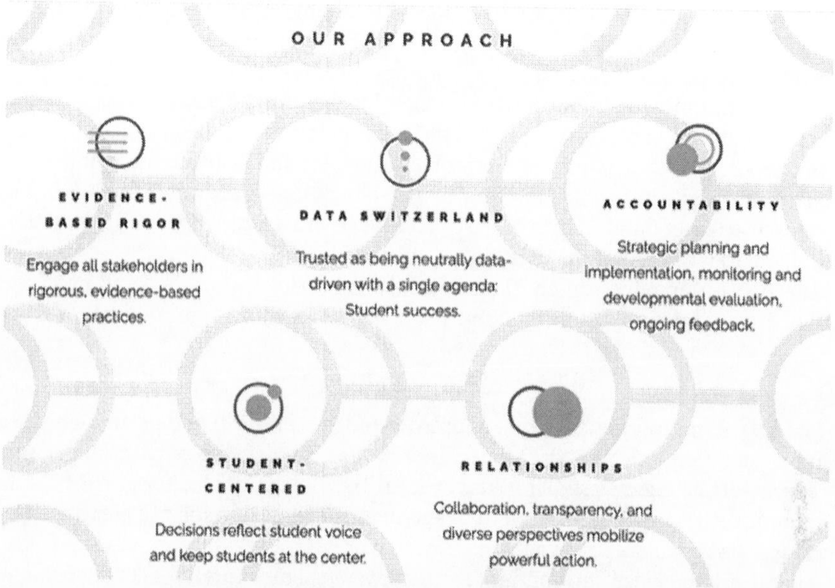

OUR APPROACH

EVIDENCE-BASED RIGOR

Engage all stakeholders in rigorous, evidence-based practices.

DATA SWITZERLAND

Trusted as being neutrally data-driven with a single agenda: Student success.

ACCOUNTABILITY

Strategic planning and implementation, monitoring and developmental evaluation, ongoing feedback.

STUDENT-CENTERED

Decisions reflect student voice and keep students at the center.

RELATIONSHIPS

Collaboration, transparency, and diverse perspectives mobilize powerful action.

Fig. 6. The Regional Learning Collaborative Approach. *Note:* This figure is reproduced, with permission, from the Regional Learning Collaborative website (www.rlcollab.com).

The Core Support Team (CST) utilizes data-driven approaches to provide independent, unbiased, evidence-based leadership that mobilizes unified, positive, collective action among a diverse set of Partners, to achieve the highest standards of equity outcomes on behalf of all the diverse students of the region. The CST ensures that all RLC strategies and actions are *student-centered*, aimed at advancing the Partners' common goal of student attainment. To realize and maintain this staunchly student-centered approach, the Core Support Team exercises a strong discipline and ethic of neutrality, remaining detached from individual agendas and operating as *Data Switzerland* in coordinating and facilitating the affairs of the RLC. Student advancement remains the central and driving agenda in all decisions. Methodologically, all RLC decisions are driven by *evidence-based rigor*, utilizing both extant research and first-hand research conducted through regular data collection and analyses with all RLC Pipeline Partners. No decision is made arbitrarily or from a top-down approach. The CST brings relevant data to the floor of Partner Convenings and facilitates a process of shared decision-making, building on the strength of its transparent and diverse Partner *relationships*. Further, the CST ensures that the data utilized for decision-making represent all key stakeholder groups across all Partner institutions, including students and their families, teachers/faculty, staff, administrators, and executive decision-makers. This *accountability* for inclusive, stakeholder-engaged practice increases rigor and relevance in data and decisions, strengthens trust and ownership among Partners, and advances the shared goals of the Collaborative. In its collegial accountability role, the CST both encourages and measures progress toward shared goals. It encourages progress through ongoing communication and monitoring of RLC Strategic Plan implementation and, as needed, removal of obstacles to progress. It utilizes developmental evaluation approaches and procedures to remain ever-adaptable to student and institutional realities and environmental and policy changes in the education landscape. The CST also holds itself accountable by regularly collecting evaluative data on its practices and on the health of the RLC as a partnership. These data are utilized for reflection on practice and continuous improvement of the systems and processes that drive Core Support efforts and Partner relations and communications.

Capacity-Building

The CST's rigorous data-driven, adaptive, student-centered, and partner-engaged approaches ensure that decisions are relevant to the life circumstances and realities of the region's students and are feasible and actionable for Partners. This commitment to true stakeholder engagement, in turn, develops further capacity among stakeholders for engagement at yet greater levels of complexity. It also generates knowledge for continuous improvement of the RLC and for broader dissemination, enabling national and international impact.

An example of the RLC's growth in capacity and complexity was the development, in 2020, of an unprecedented accomplishment – the RLC Pipeline Data Sharing and Use Agreement (DSUA). The groundbreaking DSUA, consists of agreements between the Core Support Team and each of the institutions in the RLC to support the collection of student-level Pipeline data to measure and inform the decisions, priorities, and strategies of the RLC and to generate knowledge for broader impact. The DSUA enables the CST to engage stakeholders – students, families, and staff at Partner institutions – in conversations about the realities of their circumstances, to further deepen the understanding of all Partners, sharpen the shared vision, and inform decisions. The DSUA also empowers the Core Support Team to conduct ongoing cross-segmental research, enabling longitudinal studies of RLC strategies and related outcomes, a key to success with intersegmental data partnerships (Reed et al., 2018). This development represents a significant advance in the capacity of the RLC to engage in more complex levels of collaboration and knowledge generation and dissemination.

The Core Support Team applies a similarly evidence-based rigor to its own processes and practices. The Core Support Team's framework for action derives from a robust foundation of research on collaboration. The robust research- and evidence-based framework of the RLC is largely responsible for the profound and far-reaching outcomes of the RLC (Zargarpour & Gaffaney, 2021).

The RLC's framework builds on the foundations of Collective Impact (Kania & Kramer, 2011), Research-Practice Partnerships (Henrick et al., 2017), Professional Learning Communities (DuFour et al., 2021), Network Improvement Communities (LeMahieu, 2015), and systems thinking (Senge, 2006). It is distinct, however, and best described as a Research-Practice Collaborative (RPC) in that it addresses both within-organization and cross-organization challenges with coherence and ensures that a focused set of goals drives a specific and shared strategic plan (Zargarpour & Gaffaney, 2021). The RLC, as an example of a Research-Practice Collaborative, has the single objective of advancing students across transitions in the education pipeline to degree completion.

In the above-cited collaborative frameworks, as in the Core Support approach, neutrality is a key element of practice. Within multi-segmental and cross-sectoral collaboration, there is a critical need for a neutral entity that is intellectually independent and unbiased in its decisions and practices (Klempin, 2016). This neutrality is critical in matters such as the selection of data, the engagement of all stakeholder perspectives, and facilitation of communication and decisions. This commitment to neutrality does not imply that the work of the CST is agenda-free; on the contrary, the CST is laser focused on a singular agenda – the advancement of college and career attainment for all students. Nor does neutrality imply disengagement. Rather, the CST is closely engaged with all RLC Partners in supporting the implementation of the RLC Pipeline Strategic Plan at each Partner institution. Thus, keenly in tune with and sensitive to the realities – interests, strengths, challenges, and opportunities – across the Partnership, the CST helps to bridge communication in sometimes difficult and sensitive situations and assists in removing barriers to progress.

As an example, in early conversations across institutions to discuss implementation of dual enrollment, at times misunderstandings occurred due to entrenched agendas and long-standing perceptions and patterns of practice. These interactions would interrupt the momentum and halt progress, often leading to long delays or complete suspension of progress. This pattern of fits and starts prevailed in some areas of activity. The Core Support Team's involvement as a neutral third party introduced new patterns for interaction and sustained progress. Traditional hierarchies that exist among various levels of education institutions dissolved, as RLC communication norms demanded equal respect for each member as a valued Partner in the Collaborative, operating toward a common goal. Instead of acting on assumptions based on past practices, the Partners at both the secondary and postsecondary institutions allowed for co-creation of new systems and structures for practice, facilitated by the Core Support Team. These renewed systems and structures established new patterns of communication and action that resulted in the expansion of dual enrollment and related outcomes as previously documented in this chapter.

Through its neutral engagement and data-driven approaches with each party, the Core Support Team was able to understand and document each institution's interests, perspectives, and needs, clarify a shared vision across the institutions and parties, strengthen shared understanding and mutual trust, and develop shared strategies that addressed the needs and helped advance the goals of all. Assisting with clarity of vision led to clarity of understandings.

In this Day whatsoever serveth to reduce blindness and to increase vision is worthy of consideration. This vision acteth as the agent and guide for true knowledge. Indeed in the estimation of men of wisdom keenness of understanding is due to keenness of vision. (Bahá'u'lláh, 1988, p. 35)

This win-win approach is embedded in the Core Support Team framework and is conducive to the advancement of shared understanding and progress toward a shared vision of equitable student attainment for all students.

As with all elements of the Core Support Team approach and framework, capacity building is also integrated into the internal operations of the Core Support Team. The diverse Core Support Team includes scholars, researchers, evaluators, seasoned professionals in the field of education, and a corps of dedicated and talented graduate students from Claremont Graduate University. A humble posture of learning permeates and strengthens the fabric of the team, with the professionals and graduate student researchers and evaluators on the team ever learning from one another, supporting one another's growth and advancement, and building on one another's strengths. This internal posture of collaborative learning optimizes CST performance and continuous development and generates greater outcomes for the RLC. The next-generation professionals who serve on the CST as graduate students increase their content knowledge, strengthen methodological and procedural knowledge and skills, gain research capacity and experience, develop professional relationships and know-how, and benefit from invaluable real-world experience. The professionals on the CST, likewise, continue to grow and expand their knowledge of collaborative approaches and practices, advancements in the field of education, policy implications, and latest state of the art methods and technologies.

CONCLUSION

How Do RLC Approaches, and Outcomes Inform the Responsibility of Educators Across the Globe toward Collaborative Solutions for Equity and Inclusion in Education?

We live in a world in which we need to share responsibility. It's easy to say it's not my child, not my community, not my world, not my problem. Then there are those who see the need and respond. I consider those people my heroes.

Fred Rogers (Mister Rogers). (https://inspirekindness.com/blog/mr-rogers-kindness)

The Regional Learning Collaborative incubates and scales strategies that facilitate successful transitions to and through postsecondary education and on to life-sustaining careers for over one hundred thousand students, the large majority of whom represent underserved and vulnerable populations. The RLC has been effective in this work, in large part, because its Partner members acknowledged the need that was brought to their attention and were willing to say, it may not be my child, and it may not be the problem of my institution alone or my segment of the education pipeline, but it is my responsibility, and I will respond. These Partners were willing to show up with courage and shared and collaborative responsibility. They were willing to be transparent, even when faced with difficult data and findings related to their institutional outcomes. They were willing to show up again and again, consistently over five years, with diligent, rigorous efforts on behalf of students who are not their children but are their charge.

Inspired daily by the efforts of these heroes of education, the Core Support Team continues to lead the work, with the highest professional and academic integrity, steadfast dedication to the CST's rigorous approaches and framework, and an unwavering belief and vision of equitable opportunities and desired outcomes for all students. The Core Support Team is achieving significant outcomes and impacts with its Partners, by introducing innovative strategies, co-creating systems and structures for implementation and incubation of those strategies, facilitating implementation, measuring and reflecting on outcomes and practices, and continuously expanding upon the work. Through this collective work, students and families are equipped with the agency and tools to better their own lives, their neighborhoods, and their communities. Equitable systems and structures are developed that positively impact lives for decades to come, and important knowledge is captured and disseminated to broaden impact nationally and globally. In disseminating RLC knowledge and learning about effective practices for equitable and inclusive education transitions, the Core Support Team hopes to contribute to collegial discourse and collaboration in support of student advancement across the globe.

ACKNOWLEDGMENTS

As founding Executive Director of the Regional Learning Collaborative, it has been my distinct pleasure to lead and facilitate the committed and courageous work of the Regional Learning Collaborative Partners – leaders, staff, and students from the pipeline School District and postsecondary colleges and universities, as well as, the office of the Mayor and regional education-focused organizations. I'd like to acknowledge also the dedicated and rigorous research, facilitation, and innovation of the Core Support Team of talented graduate students and professionals from Claremont Evaluation Center and Capacity To Impact, Inc. We are, all together, grateful for the powerful support of our funders and national partners, who have embraced our pioneering intersegmental work and continue to champion our innovative strategies for student success. In unity and partnership, Dr. Nazanin Zargarpour.

REFERENCES

1982 Copyright, Earth at Omega: Passage to Planetization by Donald Keys, (Epigraph of Chapter VI: The Politics of Consciousness), Quote Page 79, Published by Branden Press, Boston, MA (Google Books Preview).

Anderson, M. B. L., Bridges, B. K., Harris, B. A., & Biddle, S. (2020). *Imparting wisdom: HBCU lessons for K-12 education*. Frederick D. Patterson Research Institute, UNCF.

Asera, R., Gabriner, R., & Hemphill, D. (2017, March). *What makes a partnership work? Report commissioned by college futures foundation*. https://ies.ed.gov/ncee/edlabs/regions/west/relwest-Files/pdf/APECS_5-2-1_Literature_Compilation_clean.pdf

Bahá'u'lláh. (1983). *Gleanings from the writings of Bahá'u'lláh* (p. 260). U.S. Bahá'i Publishing Trust.

Bahá'u'lláh. (1988). *Tablets of Bahá'u'lláh revealed after the Kitáb-i-Aqdas* (p. 35). U.S. Bahá'i Publishing Trust.

Blumenstyk, G. (2020, January 22). They said, 2 out of 3 jobs would need more than a high-school diploma. Were they right? *The Edge*. The Chronicle of Higher Education. https://www. chronicle.com/newsletter/the-edge/2020-01-22?cid2=gen_login_refresh&cid=gen_sign_in

Bryson, J. M., Crosby, B. C., & Stone, M. M. (2015). Designing and implementing cross-sector collaborations: Needed and challenging. *Public Administration Review*, 75(5), 647–663.

Cahalan, M. W., Perna, L. W., Addison, M., Murray, C., Patel, P. R., & Jiang, N. (2020). *Indicators of higher education equity in the United States: 2020 historical trend report*. The Pell Institute for the Study of Opportunity in Higher Education, Council for Opportunity in Education (COE), and Alliance for Higher Education and Democracy of the University of Pennsylvania (PennAHEAD). http://pellinstitute.org/downloads/publicationsIndicators_of_Higher_Education_Equity_in_the_US_2020_Historical_Trend_Report.pdf

California Competes. (2020, July 29). A conversation about transforming an inequitable system to fuel opportunity. *Webinar*. https://register.gotowebinar.com/recording/viewRecording/50328840 42432483085/183497096613837415 6/swhalen@collegefutures.org? registrantKey=4301274503263755536&type=ATTENDEEMAILRECORDINGLINK

California Department of Education. (2021, October 28). Frequently asked questions: Dual enrollment. https://www.cde.ca.gov/fg/aa/pa/dualenrollment.asp#accordionfaq

Career Ladders Project. (2019). Dual enrollment and transitions to college. https://www.career-laddersproject.org/areas-of-focus/dualenrollment/

DuFour, R., DuFour, R., Eaker, R., Mattos, M., & Muhannad, A. (2021). *Revisiting professional learning communities at work* (2nd ed.). Solution Tree.

Freedberg, L., & Tadayon, A. (2020, February 10). High school students benefit from taking college courses, but access uneven in California. Highlighting strategies for student success. *EdSource*. https://edsource.org/2020/high-school-students-benefit-from-taking-college-courses-but-access-uneven-in-california/623558

Henig, J. R., Riehl, C. J., Houston, D. M., Rebell, M. A., & Wolff, J. R. (2016). *Collective impact and the new generation of cross-sector collaborations for education: A nationwide scan*. Teachers College, Columbia University, Department of Education Policy and Social Analysis. http://www.tc.columbia.edu/education-policy-and-social-analysis/department-news/cross-sectorcolla-boration/CI-corrected-digital-version-3-11-16.pdf

Henig, J. R., Riehl, C. J., Rebell, M. A., & Wolff, J. R. (2015). *Putting collective impact in context: A review of the literature on local cross-sector collaboration to improve education*. Teachers College, Department of Education Policy & Social Analysis. https://www.tc.columbia.edu/media/news/Putting-Collective-Impact-Into-Context.pdf

Henrick, E. C., Cobb, P., Penuel, W. R., Jackson, K., & Clark, T. (2017). *Assessing research-practice partnerships: Five dimensions of effectiveness*. William T. Grant Foundation.

Hughes, K. L., Rodriguez, O., Edwards, L., & Belfield, C. (2012). *Broadening the benefits of dual enrollment: Reaching underachieving and underrepresented students with career-focused programs*. Community College Research Center, Columbia University.

Kania, J., & Kramer, M. (2011, Winter). Collective impact. *Stanford Social Innovation Review*, 9(1), 36–41.

Klempin, S. C. (2016, February). Establishing the backbone: An underexplored facet of collective impact efforts. Community College Research Center-Research Brief, 60, Teachers College, Columbia University.

LeMahieu, P. (2015, August 18). Why a NIC? *Carnegie Foundation for the Advancement of Teaching*. https://www.carnegiefoundation.org/blog/why-a-nic/

Lile, J., Ottusch, T. M., Jones, T., & Richards, L. N. (2017, January). Understanding college-student roles: Perspectives of participants in a high school/community college dual-enrollment program. *Community College Journal of Research and Practice*, 42(3), 1–17. https://doi.org/10. 1080/10668926.2016.1264899. https://www.researchgate.net/publication/312180753_ Understanding_College_Student_Roles_Perspectives_of_Participants_in_a_High_ SchoolCommunity_College_Dual-Enrollment_Program

Reed, S., Lee, P., Kurlaender, M., & Hernandez Negrete, A. (2018, July). *Intersegmental partnerships and data sharing: Promising practices from the field*. PACE. https://edpolicyinca.org/publications/intersegmental-partnerships-and-data-sharing

Regional Education Laboratory. (2017, October). *A compilation of research on cross-sector education and career partnerships.* WestEd.

Senge, P. M. (2006). *The fifth discipline: The art & practice of the learning organization.* Doubleday.

Smith, A. A. (2019, May 23). Study finds more low-income students attending. *Pew Research Center.* https://www.insidehighered.com/news/2019/05/23/pew-study-finds-more-poor-students-attending-college

Stachowiak, S., & Gase, L. (2018, August 9). Does collective impact really make an impact? *Stanford Social Innovation Review.* https://ssir.org/articles/entry/does_collective_impact_really_make_an_impact#

Truman, H. S. (1947, December 15). *Statement by the president making public a report of the commission on higher education.* https://www.presidency.ucsb.edu/documents/statement-the-president-making-public-report-the-commission-higher-education

U.S. Census Bureau. (2019, December 19). 2014–2018 American community survey (ACS) 5-year estimates. https://www.census.gov/programs-surveys/acs/news/updates/2019.html

Vargas, J., Hooker, S., & Gerwin, C. (2017, November). Blending high school and college can sharpen the focus of each: Dual enrollment and early college experiences help students make smooth and successful transitions from high school to higher education. *Phi Delta Kappan, 99*(3), 13. https://eds.a.ebscohost.com/eds./detail/detail?vid=16&sid=723cc769-d646-477e-94d9-06d61c14 6f12%40sessionmgr4008&bdata=JkF1dGhUeXBlPXNzbyZzaXRlPWVkcy1saXZlJnNjb3Bl XNpdGU%3d#AN=edscpi.A519035530&db=conedsqd12

Yamashita, M., Franklin, K., & Cahalan, M. (2018). Travelers EDGE: 10 years of college access and success. *Pell Institute for the Study of Opportunity in Education.* http://www.pellinstitute.org/downloads/publications-Travelers_EDGE_10_Years_of_College_Access_and_Success.pdf

Zargarpour, N., Donaldson, S., Freund, M., Choi, S., Mitchell, C., Wells, L., & Briones, B. (2015a). *Pomona unified school district promise of excellence: 2015–2020 strategic plan.* Unpublished manuscript, Claremont Evaluation Center, Claremont Graduate University.

Zargarpour, N., & Gaffaney, J. M. (2021). The research-practice collaborative: A research-based framework for effective cross-segmental and cross-sectoral collaboration. Unpublished manuscript. Presented at WERA annual conference, July 9, 2021 (Virtual).

Zargarpour, N., Martin, D., & Zhang, E. J. (2015). Evaluation of the El Viento foundation program. 2nd Annual Report [Unpublished manuscript], Center for Evaluation, Claremont Graduate University.

Zargarpour, N., Wanzer, D. L., & Zhang, E. J. (2015c). *Bright prospect: A six-year longitudinal study of the relationship of psychosocial learning and academic.* Unpublished manuscript, Center for Evaluation, Claremont Graduate University.

TRANSITIONING DREAMS TO REALITY: INCLUSIVE POST-SECONDARY EDUCATION AT CONCORDIA UNIVERSITY OF EDMONTON

Barbara van Ingen, Brent Bradford, Patricia Bowman, Bruce Uditsky, Jaime Skidmore and Sarah Pereira

ABSTRACT

Inclusion Alberta and Concordia University of Edmonton share a long history of providing students with intellectual disabilities fully inclusive post-secondary education through active participation in university courses and campus life; enhancing the learning environment for all. The chapter begins with a synopsis of the partnership between Inclusion Alberta and Concordia University of Edmonton described by a senior university administrator, an overview of Inclusion Alberta and their innovative approaches to enabling children, youth, and adults with intellectual disabilities and their families to be fully included in community. Inclusion Alberta works to deeply embed individuals with disabilities in the natural pathways of life while capitalizing on community capacity, with inclusive post-secondary education as one example of how many young people normatively transition into adulthood. An Inclusion Alberta coordinator will detail her work supporting the inclusion of students at Concordia University of Edmonton. A current faculty member, and former inclusive post-secondary student, will share their experience with academics and co-curricular inclusion. The chapter provides a diversity of perspectives on inclusive post-secondary education within Alberta; this range

Transition Programs for Children and Youth with Diverse Needs
International Perspectives on Inclusive Education, Volume 18, 191–206
Copyright © 2022 Barbara van Ingen, Brent Bradford, Patricia Bowman, Bruce Uditsky,
Jaime Skidmore and Sarah Pereira
Published under exclusive licence by Emerald Publishing Limited
ISSN: 1479-3636/doi:10.1108/S1479-363620220000018014

of perspectives and deep partnership is critical for successful inclusive learning experiences.

Keywords: Inclusive education; intellectual disabilities; developmental disabilities; post-secondary education; transition from high school; collaboration

INTRODUCTION

Concordia University of Edmonton (CUE) is a small, boutique university located along Edmonton's river valley. As an institution with approximately 3,000 undergraduate and graduate students, we are a close-knit community, with strong relationships among students, faculty and staff. In January 2006, CUE started our relationship with Inclusion Alberta (then called Alberta Association for Community Living [AACL]) because of our President at that time. One of our former President's daughters has a severe developmental disability, and the family had been supported by Inclusion Alberta when their daughter was young. Inclusion Alberta was seeking to provide typical pathways into adulthood for individuals with developmental disabilities, and one of those typical pathways is post-secondary education. We started that relationship with one student, and over time that has grown to five students concurrently. Since the inception of this initiative in 2006, CUE, in partnership with Inclusion Alberta, supported 17 students. While the concurrent number of students at CUE supported by Inclusion Alberta is relatively small, Inclusion Alberta supports a significant number of students throughout Alberta's post-secondary system and this initiative is replicated nationally and globally.

Within our partnership, Inclusion Alberta provides staffing located at CUE, ensures the campus community has the support required to successfully include students with developmental disabilities, collaborates with faculty and staff, supports students in securing employment and recreational activities during the spring and summer months, and facilitates the transition of students into employment opportunities upon completion of their studies at CUE. CUE provides access to programs, facilities, activities, and resources, and formally recognizes students with developmental disabilities for their completion of a program of study with a Certificate of Completion during annual Convocation ceremonies. Inclusion Alberta staff work in partnership with CUE staff on admission and ongoing inclusion of students and are positioned within CUE's Student Life and Learning unit to work collaboratively to the benefit of students.

The objective of the partnership is to maintain an effective framework for inclusive post-secondary education and to facilitate the inclusion of students with developmental disabilities into CUE's activities and courses. Most important is the expectation that students with developmental disabilities will have a meaningful experience, the opportunity to pursue their career aspirations, and to participate and be fully included in many aspects of life at CUE. Through these opportunities, students with developmental disabilities have learned new skills, increased their self-confidence, built upon career goals and aspirations, and developed friendships. We have observed that students, faculty, and staff experienced numerous benefits and advantages from the opportunity to learn with and teach students with developmental disabilities. These benefits extend beyond CUE, as these students graduate and engage within their larger communities. Inclusive Post-Secondary Education is a direct example of how properly supported communities can develop their capacity to include people with developmental disabilities in valued ways and in valued roles. This partnership between CUE and Inclusion Alberta addresses the need for more access to inclusive post-secondary opportunities, as well as increasing the range of educational opportunities available in Alberta.

As a senior administrator, I (Barb) fully support our partnership with Inclusion Alberta, due to the many positive experiences and outcomes of the students who attended CUE. I recall our first student and the immediate impact of his presence on the campus community, and each of the students since. I have also had the privilege of participating in interviews with prospective students and their families, and seeing the hope and eagerness of the student and the family for their loved one to have the opportunity of a typical transitional experience in post-secondary education. Once students begin their experience at CUE, they engage with all aspects of our community and enrich the campus for all of us. Within this chapter, you will learn more about the inspiring work of Inclusion Alberta from its current Chief Executive Officer Patricia Bowman and CEO Emeritus Bruce Uditsky, one of its Regional Coordinators, Jaime Skidmore who works with CUE, Brent Bradford, a CUE Associate Professor, and most importantly, from one of our students, Sarah Pereira, who was included in our Bachelor of Arts program. From her first year at CUE, Sarah embraced university life, and in addition to her academics, she became involved in a number of student clubs, as a volunteer Student Ambassador, and employed as student help within our Athletics and Campus Recreation department. Following her program completion, Sarah was hired as an Assistant within Student Life and Learning. As a member of the Student Life and Learning team, Sarah supports students and provides administrative assistance for the department. To learn more about the excellent work of Inclusion Alberta, we turn now to the Inclusion Alberta CEO Emeritus and current CEO.

INCLUSION ALBERTA: INSIGHTS FROM THE CEO EMERITUS AND CURRENT CEO

The approach to fully inclusive post-secondary education for students with intellectual disabilities reflected in this chapter is based on a theory and model first developed and implemented by Uditsky with Bowman and others at the University of Alberta in 1987 (Frank & Uditsky, 1988; Uditsky & Kappel, 1988; Uditsky et al., 1988). Uditsky's approach to the development of inclusive post-secondary education was based on his theory that immersion in life's normative pathways and experiences across the lifespan, while capitalizing on community capacity, would increase the likelihood of individuals with intellectual disabilities living meaningful and inclusive lives (Uditsky & Hughson, 2008). CUE, in partnership with Inclusion Alberta, exemplifies this theory in practice.

Inclusion Alberta is a provincial family advocacy organization partnering with 14 universities, colleges, and one polytechnic in Alberta to facilitate the inclusion of students with intellectual disabilities. Inclusion Alberta facilitators are located on these post-secondary campuses to support students, faculty, and administration to enable the inclusion of students with intellectual disabilities, including those with severe disabilities. Inclusion Alberta has established an Inclusive Post-Secondary Education network that connects all the other inclusive post-secondary institutions in Alberta, plus others in Canada, to provide ongoing support for professional development and continuous quality improvement. In addition, Inclusion Alberta has developed a peer review process and tool for assuring quality (O'Brien et al., 2011), and also offers a professional development series for faculty to learn how to better accommodate students with intellectual disabilities.

Transition: A Normative Life Process

Inclusion Alberta does not support the concept of "transition programs" specific to individuals with intellectual disabilities. Normative life experiences, such as finishing high school, becoming a university student then moving on to whatever life holds, are natural progressions. It is Inclusion Alberta's experience that transition programs are far more an aspect of segregated special education and after decades of practice, and have little to show in terms of facilitating the transition to an inclusive life of meaning and belonging. Too often, transition for a student with intellectual disabilities leaving high school means placement in a segregated program for individuals with disabilities, not a true experience of transitioning into adulthood, a career or a post-secondary education. For far too many, life's normative transitions then cease as placement becomes life-defining.

It would be a fundamental error to either label or attempt to understand inclusive post-secondary education for students with intellectual disabilities as practiced at CUE or other post-secondary institutions with Inclusion Alberta through the lens of a transition program. Change and transition is inherent in the course of life, and the vast majority of us move through life's transitions naturally and inclusively, without requiring a "transition program" and often without using the term "transition" to describe our experiences. Moving through life's transitions should be no different for individuals with intellectual disabilities. When families of children with intellectual disabilities, their schools, and communities are supported to embed children with intellectual disabilities inclusively in normative life pathways, then life's transitions are not a programmatic point in time but a naturally occurring event.

Similarly, when parents and their children with intellectual disabilities are exposed to the possibility of inclusion in post-secondary institutions at an early age, their expectations grow and the commitment to an inclusive life pathway deepens with the expectation of applying to a post-secondary institution as part of a culturally normative and valued transition process. During the latter part of high school, students without intellectual disabilities, their peers, and families are engaged in figuring out what comes next through conversations over the dinner table and possibly with career guidance counsellors. Some may have presentations at their schools from post-secondary education institutions and others are given the opportunity to visit and tour post-secondary campuses to learn what they have to offer and gain a feeling for campus culture and life. Upon completing high school, those that choose to continue their education apply at the post-secondary institutions they believe provide the best path toward their goals, with hope for acceptance. Students with intellectual disabilities receiving an inclusive education are participating with the support of Inclusion Alberta in these very same processes alongside their non-disabled peers.

Foundational Desired Outcomes

From the inception of this approach of having students authentically and fully included in the totality of the post-secondary student experience, the original focus of Inclusion Alberta was on providing opportunities for students to experience five essential and desired outcomes. These remain relevant and fundamental more than 30 years later.

(1) *Relationships*: Typically, adults with intellectual disabilities have a much narrower and limited social network than individuals without disabilities. This has a significant detrimental impact on their lives, including pervasive loneliness and all its known negative impacts on social and physical well-being. Just as social networks are essential to the well-being of individuals without disabilities, this is as true, if not more so, for individuals with intellectual disabilities. From the onset, facilitating opportunities for relationships with others based on common interests and goals, not labels, was the foundation upon which all other desired outcomes rested. The knowledge that relationships hold the greatest power to make our lives rich, meaningful, fulfilled, and to keep us safe, was, and is, a driving motivation for participation and inclusion on campus.

(2) *Life Enriching Experiences*: When almost anyone is asked to recall their most memorable moments while attending post-secondary education, they share experiences and relationships; stories in contrast to a specific moment of academic progress. Some recall friendships that may only have existed during their post-secondary years while others may tell of lasting relationships. Experiences enrich our lives and inform our identities, hopes, dreams, and choices. It is the goal of Inclusion Alberta that students with intellectual disabilities experience all that post-secondary institutions have to offer; rich and memorable experiences to recall and share. Shared life experiences that contribute to their becoming more well-rounded and knowledgeable individuals, thus challenging the persistent societal stereotypes and expectations too often thrust upon them.

(3) *Learning*: Contrary to the thinking of some, Inclusion Alberta did not and does not see academic learning as the highest priority. Inclusion Alberta holds the viewpoint that learning within the educational process is best fostered by a sense of meaningful belonging, engagement, relationships, and memorable experiences. Through inclusion in every aspect of university life, such as classrooms, internships, group projects, modified assignments and exams, extra-curricular activities, and student politics, learning is ongoing and multi-dimensional. In this context of the authentic student experience, the skills of navigating life are learned, adapted, and supported in contrast to traditional life skills training individuals with intellectual disabilities are so commonly subjected to. As life skills never add up to a life, the focus of Inclusion Alberta is on enabling the best experiences post-secondary has to offer and, in that context, supporting the gaining of knowledge.

(4) *Employment*: Employment in our culture is one of the principal avenues to a life of meaning and belonging during adulthood. It is also a means of avoiding poverty and improving one's economic security. For many, meaningful employment provides an opportunity to contribute, belong, and expand relationships. However, the vast majority of individuals with intellectual disabilities experience an impoverished lifetime of marginalization and exclusion. Just as post-secondary education increases the likelihood of improved employment opportunities for students without intellectual disabilities, it should for students with intellectual disabilities as well. This means developing or enhancing the career identities of students with intellectual disabilities, inspiring high expectations for employment among families, and enlisting the support of professors, instructors, and non-disabled peers in identifying possible employment opportunities. Practica, field studies, and internships all contribute to employment outcomes as does working in inclusive competitive employment during the months when classes are not in session.

(5) *Positive Identity and Self-Confidence*: The opportunity to hold socially valued roles are frequently limited for people with intellectual disabilities. Everything described above and in practice contributes to students with intellectual disabilities expressing, through whatever means of communication they utilize, a positive sense of self and a greater degree of self-confidence as they come to see themselves as classmates, learners, and colleagues. The entirety of the process of enabling and supporting an authentic inclusive student experience contributes to this outcome.

Inclusion and Authenticity

Inclusion Alberta found it necessary to articulate the essential elements of our approach to *inclusive post-secondary education*, as the term is used to describe everything from traditional segregated special education and life skills classes being delivered on campus to partial integration or full inclusion (Hughson & Uditsky, 2019; Uditsky & Hughson, 2012). In the Inclusion Alberta model of inclusive post-secondary education, students apply to the post-secondary institution, faculty, and program of studies of their choice with the hope of being successful in their application. There are no criteria in terms of perceived ability; only an expressed interest in continuing their education after high school. Students with very limited or no formal means of communication may indicate their interest through their families, friends, or high school teachers. Inclusion Alberta facilitators assist the institutions in their interviewing and decision-making as to which applicants will be accepted into their regular programs of studies.

Students are never grouped as their identities as individuals on campus are not related to their having an intellectual disability. Their identities, as with all other students, are aligned with their faculty/program of studies, extra-curricular activities, and career interests. As the facilitators function as student and faculty support, in effect an on-campus support resource, there is no post-secondary education "program" for students to belong to or be a part of.

Students with intellectual disabilities are enrolled as auditing but participating students and are fully included in regular classes and naturally supported by their classmates. Students with multiple and severe disabilities who require personal supports have their personal support staff present to respond as needed. Students complete assignments and exams that are modified and adapted as needed by their professors, with assistance from the on-campus facilitators. During the spring and summer, most are supported to find employment, often in their field of study.

The students receive feedback from their professors on their performance and achievements. Students participate actively in study groups, group assignments, internships, field trips, and practica when and where these are part of their programs of study and courses. They are encouraged to pursue their extra-curricular interests and passions from student politics and associations, to sports and artistic endeavors, where again they are supported by their non-disabled peers to participate. They convocate with their non-disabled peers within their faculties and programs of study and receive recognition from their post-secondary institutions.

Prior to completing their studies, the majority of students have jobs and upon completion of their studies, on average 80% of students are inclusively employed at least part-time and earning an income. It is very difficult to find any transition program with a similar sustained outcome over more than 30 years of practice. In addition, individuals with intellectual disabilities demonstrate positive growth in their identity and the confidence to pursue additional dreams and possibilities, having forged relationships and been a contributing participant in post-secondary life as an equally valued student. All students develop relationships, and many continue after post-secondary studies, some for a short period of time and others for a lifetime. To learn more about the supports provided on campus, we turn now to a Regional Coordinator.

PERSPECTIVE FROM INCLUSION ALBERTA REGIONAL COORDINATOR

The Inclusive Post-Secondary Education initiative at CUE is composed of two Educational Facilitators and one part-time Regional Coordinator, who also provides support to staff teams at four other post-secondary institutions. One Facilitator provides support to three students and one alumnus working on campus, while the other Facilitator supports a single student who requires direct personal support. My role (Jaime) as Regional Coordinator is to offer leadership to the Facilitators, cultivate deep relationships within the institution, and strengthen its capacity for the meaningful inclusion of students with intellectual disabilities. The high level of collaboration between CUE and Inclusion Alberta has contributed to CUE's increased capacity for inclusion, often facilitated by the initiative's key contact, Dr. Barbara van Ingen, Vice-President, Student Life and Learning.

At first glance, it might seem that the primary role of the initiative at CUE involves supporting students with their academic engagement. When I first started as the Coordinator, this was my initial assumption as well. While academics are a critical part of the post-secondary experience, I quickly discovered that academics and coursework are only one facet of post-secondary life. As noted earlier in this chapter, students with intellectual disabilities attend for the same reasons as anyone else, including meeting new people, developing relationships, and pursuing career opportunities.

Facilitating Relationships

Understanding that people with intellectual disabilities are too often pervasively lonely, an underpinning of the work of the post-secondary team is to create opportunities for students to connect with university peers in an authentic way. At the beginning of every semester, Inclusive Post-Secondary Education Facilitators speak to each class that is including a student with intellectual disabilities. The purpose of this short presentation is to raise awareness of inclusion at CUE (and across the province) and to identify fellow students who are interested in providing voluntary support within the classroom. This may include sharing notes with the student, including and engaging each other in group work and discussions, or studying together outside of regular class time. Facilitating connections outside of the classroom is also imperative as students are looking to form connections on and off campus.

Being intentional is vital when facilitating connections between the students we support and their classmates. From past experiences, we learned that taking a more passive approach in facilitating relationships resulted in fewer connections for students. By intentionally communicating with supportive classmates, creating a space for them to ask questions, and being available to work through unexpected situations, we find students are more likely to develop deeper connections on campuses that thrive, even upon the completion of their studies. For many students, this is their first opportunity to connect with others in a meaningful way in an inclusive environment. This often expresses itself through initial anxiety in reaching out to classmates or attending a new event on campus. Facilitating relationships *behind the scenes* allows us to create positive experiences for both the students and their classmates.

An example of facilitating relationships I can share is when a student wanted to join the Visual Arts Club. The student attended the Club Fair and was eager to join this club. She was excited to connect with other students who shared a similar interest in board games and comics. Even though the student was motivated to attend, she was still hesitant about going to the first club meeting. She was nervous to attend because she did not know what to expect and did not know anyone. In response to this, I asked the student if it would be okay if I met with the president of the Visual Arts Club to learn more about what took place during the club meetings. The student agreed, and I met with the president to share about the Inclusive Post-Secondary Education Initiative and the support we provide to students. The conversation focused on the student's passion for board games and I shared strategies of how to include the student in a game if she was sitting out due to anxiety. The president offered to meet the student ahead of time so that there would be a familiar face at the first club meeting. Following the meeting with the president, I was able to provide the student with additional information about the club and arrange for her to meet the club president prior to the first meeting. This gave her the knowledge and confidence to participate fully and attend without any support.

Collaboration with Faculty

Prior to the start of each semester, the team meets directly with prospective professors to discuss the possibility of including a student in their course. Similar to the conversations we have with classmates, we provide professors who are including a student with information regarding the initiative and about the student interested in auditing their course. In this meeting, we discuss potential modifications for coursework, assignments, and exams.

Initially, professors will send us their course content as the semester progresses. Through a collaborative effort with them, the coursework is subsequently modified in a way that captures the professor's intent for the assignment and increases the accessibility of the assignment to the student. Over time, professors have become more comfortable with making their own modifications. Some standard examples of modifications include shortening exams, adding visuals to assignments, and substituting a student video for written essays. Professors provide constructive feedback to the students on their assignments.

In addition to facilitating the student's learning experience, professors and faculty members play an important role in networking to develop career opportunities in the student's field of study. Throughout a student's post-secondary journey, the Inclusive Post-Secondary Education team has intentional conversations with faculty to understand where connections can be made for potential employment. By being intentional and community-minded, the meaningful inclusion of students with intellectual disabilities in all aspects of campus life has become a natural and expected part of CUE's culture. I have seen, over and over again, how this enriches the university experience for everyone in surprising and unanticipated ways. To hear first-hand from a CUE student, we turn now to Sarah.

A STUDENT'S EXPERIENCE: SARAH'S CUE STORY

My name is Sarah Pereira. This is my CUE story! I finished high school in 2010 and took some time off from education. During this time, I volunteered at a long-term care facility. Although I enjoyed this, my dream was to attend university to become an Educational Assistant. I wanted to teach and help young children. I have a passion for working with children. I saw my older sister attend university to become a nurse, and I wanted the same experience for myself. I wanted to learn.

When I was accepted to CUE, I felt excited, but also nervous at the same time about meeting the professors and other new people. It was a challenge, but I got through it with some help and support from some wonderful people. I attended CUE for four years and audited classes in the Bachelor of Arts program. I even won the Freshman of the Year Award in 2015! I was also in many different clubs: Dance, Drama, Ping Pong, Arts, Freshman Challenge, and Wellness club. I made a lot of friends on campus. We studied together for tests and we had lunch on campus. I really liked being in classes. I enjoyed learning and experiencing them all.

I also did projects that were very interesting. My favorite professor was Dr. Bradford. I took an education class with him and he helped me understand why it was important to be a teacher for young children.

While attending university, I was employed as a Game Day staff for the soccer team catching the soccer balls that went out of play and keeping score. I also volunteered at plays, taking tickets. The most difficult thing when I was a student was finding my classes and asking for help from people I didn't know. I became more comfortable asking people for directions and became more outgoing, in time, with my friends.

Myka (pseudonym) is an amazing and wonderful friend. We met in Spanish class and became close friends. Our friendship means so much because we do fun things together like go to dinner, movies, swimming, shopping, and hanging out with our other friend Teah (pseudonym). Myka and I still attend choir together every Saturday morning and we also play Ukulele together. I am so thankful that I made such wonderful friends at CUE.

I completed my studies with my friends on May 25, 2019. It was amazing and emotional at the same time. But my CUE story was not over! On November 13, 2019, I started my employment at CUE. I am a General Assistant supporting the Academic Administration Office, the Student Life and Learning Department, the Indigenous Knowledge and Research Center, and the President's Office. I enjoy my role very much and have great support from my co-workers and my supervisor. I would like to thank everyone at CUE for their support and welcoming me. I want to thank my professors and Inclusion Alberta facilitators for their wonderful support and helping me with my studies.

Barb recalls a recent experience that illustrates Sarah's dedication and commitment to supporting students as a valued employee. Sarah planned to spend her lunch break with two colleagues, and was walking to meet them in the cafeteria when she asked a student how they were doing with preparing for a forthcoming exam. The student indicated they were stressed and not feeling ready for their exam, and Sarah offered to assist them with their studying. The student accepted the offer, and Sarah advised her colleagues she was not available to join them for lunch. This is just one example of Sarah's care for students and how she makes an impact on our community.

An important partner in the success of Inclusion Alberta is our amazing faculty members; and now we hear from one of Sarah's former professors, Dr. Brent Bradford.

PERSPECTIVE FROM A CUE ASSOCIATE PROFESSOR

In September 2017, when the Dean of Education asked if I would be willing to have a student with intellectual disabilities audit my course, PESS 293 *Introduction to the Movement Activities of Children Aged 5–12*, I stated, "Of course!" Now, please note that prior to this inquiry from the Dean, I had the absolute pleasure of meeting and getting to know the student that would be auditing my course. That said, although that information would not have swayed me in any way; I mention it solely to state that I felt, at that moment, absolutely grateful for the opportunity to get to know the student even more throughout the upcoming course.

With a wealth of teaching experiences throughout the early part of my career, including three years in a Positive Development Program (working with children who had a diverse range of learning needs), I learned first-hand about the importance of caring teachers of learners with disabilities (e.g., cognitive, physical). It was during those early teaching years (i.e., in the early 2000s) that have stayed with me as I transitioned from a school teacher to a teacher educator. The aim of this section is not to review my past school teaching experiences, but to provide information that will help readers understand a major part of what shaped me as an educator – no matter at what educational level.

When I began planning for the upcoming PESS 293 course, it was important to develop a thorough understanding of what the student requirements were for auditing a course, as it was the first time I had a student audit one of my courses. Some of the key pieces of information I learned from my conversation with Jaime Skidmore, Inclusion Alberta Regional Coordinator, was that a student with intellectual disabilities auditing a course would still be expected to participate in the course to the greatest extent possible. At that moment, I grew even more excited as I had some ideas about how to plan appropriately for Sarah to participate in both the assignments and exams – including physical activities in the gymnasium.

When considering the PESS 293 course, I believe it was set up to promote success for Sarah due to its cooperative and physical nature while comprising an emotionally-safe and positive learning environment. PESS 293, with a course description of, *Free play and organized physical activities of children 5–12 in recreational, educational, and sports environments. Involves practical physical activity and the observation of children*, was a perfect course for Sarah to participate in and collaborate with students ranging from *athletically-gifted* to *not being interested in physical activity at all*.

Moreover, the course was divided into four main sections, each with a different set of appropriate challenges for Sarah to confront and master with the support of myself, the classmates, and the CUE Community. The main sections are as follows: classroom activities/lectures; physical activities; one assignment; and two exams.

(1) Classroom Activities/Lectures
   • The classroom activities/lectures focused primarily on the theoretical pieces of information; the lesson structures were formed mainly around social constructivism
(2) Physical Activities
   • The physical activities took place in the gymnasium; focused around five dimensions of activity (i.e., alternative environment activities, dance, games, individual activities, types of gymnastics)
(3) One Assignment
   • The assignment was one which allowed Sarah to join two classmates while observing children engaged in physical activity (focused observations on fundamental movement skills); a summarized write-up of the observations was required (tying theory to practice)
(4) Exams
   • The completion of two exams (i.e., mid-term, final) was required throughout the 4-month period; the exams included questions requiring written responses

Success ... with an Asterisk

Reaching Success. In the end, Sarah's participation in PESS 293 was nothing short of highly successful. Although Sarah audited the course, from my point of view Sarah did so *with an asterisk*.

(1) Sarah fully engaged in the classroom activities/lectures.
   • Throughout the entire course, Sarah fully engaged in class discussions and activities. Moreover, Sarah consistently added to discussions willingly and was a very important part of the class (e.g., asking critical questions, working with others). For example, two such topics that Sarah inquired into further were the importance of "sleep" (ParticipACTION, 2016) and "Laban's movement framework". Specifically, in relation to "sleep" as it is described in the 24-Hour Movement Guidelines (ParticipACTION, 2016),

Sarah added to the class discussion by asking about the important role of parents/guardians for helping children to go to sleep (e.g., by asking them to put their technology away so they cannot go on social media and play video games after bedtime). This question led into a deep discussion about technology's role in sleep deprivation for children and youth, and how lack of sleep impacts children and youth during the day. In relation to "Laban's movement framework", Sarah was particularly interested in discussing more thoroughly, during a class in the gymnasium, how "relationships" have assisted in her physical literacy journey. Specifically, following a gymnastics-type activity, Sarah shared that it was her classmates that assisted her in completing a movement sentence. As Sarah explained and inquired more into the importance of "relationships" (i.e., with whom/with what the body is relating to while moving (Langton, 2007)), Sarah finished her statement by thanking her classmates for assisting with her development in the course. Sarah was thanked, profusely, right back.

(2) Sarah consistently participated in the physical activities in the gymnasium.

- Sarah, although limited in various areas (e.g., quickness of movement), participated in all activities, and was always willing to work with and learn from classmates. For example, Sarah engaged in alternative environment activities (e.g., orienteering), dance-type activities (e.g., creative movement to a musical accompaniment), games (e.g., modified handball), gymnastics-type activities (e.g., creating a movement sentence employing a variety of equipment/apparatus), and individual activities (e.g., throwing activities).

(3) Sarah completed the assignment with a group of classmates, and received feedback on the work.

- The assignment was completed and submitted. After assessing the assignment, which was done with two classmates, Sarah inquired about the graded work, and was open to the specific, positive, and constructive feedback. The feedback that was provided to Sarah was specifically focused upon her understanding of fundamental movement skill development. In a 1-on-1 discussion, I asked Sarah to explain the fundamental movement skills (i.e., locomotor, balance and stability, manipulative), and how the development of these skills can help with children's physical literacy journeys. The positive feedback centered on Sarah's understanding of the fundamental movement skills; Sarah could explain the three areas quite well. The constructive feedback focused on Sarah's understanding as to how breadth and variety is imperative for children's development of these skills. Throughout our conversation, Sarah became more knowledgeable about the importance of providing children with "lots of different learning opportunities in a variety of activities instead of just one or two" when teaching for fundamental movement skill development. To me, this was an area of growth that I observed in Sarah's learning – throughout the course – as a result of 1-on-1 conversations such as this one.

(4) Sarah wrote both the Mid-Term and Final Exams, and received feedback on her work. Sarah initiated a meeting with me following the course to review the Final Exam.

- Sarah chose to write both the Mid-Term and Final Exams. Although slightly modified to meet Sarah's learning needs, the exams were completed, assessed, and discussed. I engaged in 1-on-1 conversations with Sarah to provide specific, positive, and constructive feedback (as with the assignment). The goal of these 1-on-1 conversations was to ultimately provide learning opportunities for Sarah to gain new insights to help her to continue thriving in the course and beyond. I believe throughout the course, Sarah developed a deep level of knowledge related to physical literacy, fundamental movement skills, and the importance of breadth and variety.

All in all, Sarah went above and beyond the regular requirements for auditing a course. And, as time went on, I could really notice Sarah's enhanced levels of confidence, communication, and cooperation in the learning environment and throughout the CUE campus.

Benefits of the Experience

Throughout the semester, I witnessed several benefits unfolding in the course. Such benefits were experienced by Sarah, the classmates, the university, and by myself.

- *Sarah benefited.* It was clear that Sarah benefited due the intrinsic motivation, personal curiosity, and willingness to challenge herself as she engaged in all parts of the course, including the completion of the assignment and the two exams. Aside from the high level of participation, it was the level of Sarah's confidence and overall enjoyment I observed growing throughout the course.
- *The classmates benefited.* Unsurprisingly, due to the nature of the institution's student body, the classmates consistently worked with Sarah and helped promote an emotionally-safe and positive learning environment. For example, whenever a table activity was taking place, all classmates made sure Sarah had a table to sit at, and always invited the sharing of ideas and suggestions related to the topic area. Consistently, Sarah added much of the richness to class discussions. That said, due to Sarah's high level of interest and engagement, the classmates encouraged Sarah to take on leadership roles in the group (e.g., group reporter to the whole class), and it became evident that Sarah's classmates developed a deeper awareness and appreciation toward inclusive education. In fact, a few of Sarah's classmates willingly provided comments related to their experience of being Sarah's classmate (see Table 1).
- *The university benefited.* Whenever students with diverse learning needs can experience success in a course, the university will benefit. Since the time I had the pleasure of working with Sarah in PESS 293, I have observed Sarah working in the university carrying out a number of tasks and remaining a polite, hard-working, and caring individual. On the flip side, I consistently notice university faculty, staff, and students treating Sarah absolutely no different than everyone else – an important part of the CUE community. Now,

Table 1. Comments from Sarah's Classmates (Pseudonyms Used).

Name	Comment
Eliza	What has aided me in my practice as a pre-service teacher was learning how essential it is to work collaboratively with not only fellow educators, but students alike to assist those with differentiated needs in an academic setting. All parties benefit substantially when there is inclusion of all individuals in regards to academic learning, social interaction, and problem-solving skills.
William	Throughout the course, Sarah was very involved in all of the group activities. Sarah was an active participant and was always smiling when working with others. As an undergraduate student aiming to become a school teacher, this was one of the first experiences where I learned and acknowledged the power of an inclusive learning environment. As a student, I highly enjoyed and benefited from working and learning alongside Sarah.
Robin	Throughout the course, we covered topics of Inclusive Learning (Adaptive Physical Activity) in relation to Physical Literacy and Physical Activity. Seeing these methods and adaptive measures used first-hand in the course taught me more about the importance and value of these topics. Taking the class alongside Sarah taught me just how seamlessly inclusive education can be integrated and implemented in the learning environment; and how it can benefit at every level of learning when applied effectively.

I cannot say the university changed in its beliefs related to inclusive education as I have little to compare to since beginning my time at CUE in 2015. However, what I can say is that the university is highly enriched due to the enormity of Sarah's efforts to take part in the university community. This is evidenced by a quote from one of Sarah's colleagues: "It has been a great privilege and rewarding experience to learn and grow with Sarah. With consistency, flexibility, debriefing, as well as creating tasks that align with her existing skills and interests, Sarah has become a master of social media marketing!" As stated, when traveling throughout campus, it is evident that Sarah has continued her pursuit of being part of the CUE community (as she did so greatly in my course). And, in return, the university has embraced Sarah's presence within and beyond the university walls.

- *I benefited.* As an instructor, I benefited in so many ways. To name a few, I developed a deeper understanding of how classmates can benefit from working alongside students with diverse learning needs. I gained more awareness that through an emotionally-safe and positive learning environment, all students have opportunities to learn from both the explicit and hidden curriculum. Clearly, much can be gained from the hidden curriculum (e.g., cooperation, understanding, empathy).

Moreover, when I was initially asked if I would agree to having Sarah audit PESS 293, I did not hesitate. However, at that moment, I did not understand how this agreement would lead to such impactful and positive learning outcomes for Sarah, her classmates, the CUE community, and myself. I am grateful for this experience and wish upon every post-secondary instructor that this same opportunity is afforded. In closing, this teaching experience has helped me develop into a more effective educator—in so many ways.

CONCLUSION

Just as the experience of post-secondary education is one of our culture's normative transition processes into adulthood for youth without disabilities, so it is for students with intellectual disabilities. And just as not everyone chooses a post-secondary education or completes it if chosen, the same is true for students with intellectual disabilities.

Those who offer or create post-secondary educational opportunities make a values-based decision to either support full inclusion or something less. There is no pathway to a fully inclusive education that begins with any degree of segregation and congregation. This is as true in post-secondary institutions as it is in schools. It is only with the commitment to a fully inclusive post-secondary education that young people with intellectual disabilities will be able to participate, learn, and grow in the context of this normative and culturally valued transition to adulthood.

REFERENCES

Frank, S., & Uditsky, B. (1988). On campus: Integration at university. *Entourage, 3*, 33–40.

Hughson, E. A., & Uditsky, B. (2019). 30 years of inclusive post-secondary education: Scope, challenges and outcomes. In P. O'Brien, M. L. Bonati, F. Gadow, & R. Slee (Eds.), *People with intellectual disability experiencing university life: Theoretical underpinnings, evidence and lived experience* (pp. 51–68). Brill and Sense Publishers.

Langton, T. W. (2007). Applying Laban's movement framework in elementary physical education. *JOHPERD, 78*(1), 17–24, 39. http://users.rowan.edu/~conet/elempe/labanjoperd07.pdf

O'Brien, J., Bowman, P., Chesley, B., Hughson, E. A., & Uditsky, B. (2011). *Inclusive postsecondary education: Measuring quality and improving practice.* Government of Alberta.

ParticipACTION. (2016). *Are Canadian kids too tired to move? The 2016 ParticipACTION report card on physical activity for children and youth.* participaction/a4d484ff-8306-4461-8e3d-8600e4c2702b_participaction-2016-report-card-are-kids-too-tired-to-move-full.pdf(prismic.io)

Uditsky, B., Frank, S., Hart, L., & Jeffrey, S. (1988). On campus: Integrating the university environment. From Alternative Futures, 1988 SHAPE Conference (Conference Paper). Edmonton, AB.

Uditsky, B., & Hughson, E. A. (2008). *Inclusive post-secondary education for adults with developmental disabilities: A promising path to an inclusive life.* Alberta Association for Community Living.

Uditsky, B., & Hughson, E. A. (2012). Inclusive postsecondary education—An evidence-based moral imperative. *Journal of Policy and Practice in Intellectual Disabilities, 9*(4), 298–302. https://doi.org/10.1111/jppi.12005

Uditsky, B., & Kappel, B. (1988). Integrated post-secondary education. *Entourage, 3*(23–25), 40–41.

SECTION 4

COLLABORATIVE PROGRAMS, PARTNERSHIPS, AND RESOURCES FOR TRANSITION

CIRCLES: A THREE-TEAM INTERAGENCY COLLABORATION APPROACH TO SUPPORT SUCCESSFUL TRANSITIONS FOR STUDENTS WITH DISABILITIES

Stephen M. Kwiatek, Valerie L. Mazzotti, Jared H. Stewart-Ginsburg and Janie N. Vicchio

ABSTRACT

Interagency collaboration is an effective strategy for supporting students and families with resources and support to prepare students for life after high school. The Communicating Interagency Relationships and Collaborative Linkages for Exceptional Students (CIRCLES) is the only interagency collaboration model identified as a research-based practice, which means the CIRCLES model has the most and highest quality of evidence for its use among interagency collaboration models. Within this chapter, we overview the CIRCLES model and its history. School districts from multiple states have implemented CIRCLES, and, within this chapter, we overview stakeholder experiences with CIRCLES. When implementing any practice, evaluation and implementation fidelity are critical, so we provide suggestions for both. Finally, we discuss barriers and strategies to effective interagency collaboration, in addition to implications for policy and practice.

Keywords: Community partnerships; interagency collaboration; secondary transition; transition planning; students with disabilities; high school

Transition Programs for Children and Youth with Diverse Needs
International Perspectives on Inclusive Education, Volume 18, 209–228
ISSN: 1479-3636/doi:10.1108/S1479-363620220000018015

INTRODUCTION

Interagency collaboration is defined as "a clear, purposeful, and carefully designed process that promotes cross-agency, cross-program, and cross-disciplinary collaborative efforts leading to tangible transition outcomes for youth" (Rowe et al., 2015, p. 122). The secondary transition literature has acknowledged the importance of interagency collaboration for decades. For example, Will's (1984) Bridges from School to Working Life framework highlighted the importance of special education teacher collaboration with outside agencies (e.g., vocational rehabilitation) to prepare students for post-school employment. In 1985, Halpern built on Will's model to include support for preparing students for community adjustment, including the residential environment, employment, and social and interpersonal networks. During the 1990s, the importance of interagency collaboration was further emphasized to provide students with disabilities a seamless transition from high school to post-school life by engaging with community agencies (e.g., Halpern, 1994; Repetto & Correa, 1996). Interagency collaboration has long been considered a critical component of transition planning (e.g., Kohler, 1993; Landmark et al., 2010).

Initially identified in 2009 by Test et al. and reaffirmed by Mazzotti et al. (2021), interagency collaboration is an in-school predictor of postsecondary education and employment success for students with disabilities. While interagency collaboration has been identified as a predictor and considered a critical component of transition planning, schools and local education agencies must build collaborative partnerships with adult services providers and community partners (e.g., employers, civic organizations) to ensure transition needs of students with disabilities are met (Trainor et al., 2020). As noted by Shogren and Wittenburg (2020), interagency collaboration models are needed to address gaps in "fragmented services" (p. 18) to ensure students with disabilities experience a successful transition into adulthood.

Educators and researchers have developed multiple interagency collaboration models to promote successful interagency collaboration between schools and communities (e.g., Oregon's Youth Transition Program, Maryland Seamless Transition Collaborative, Communicating Interagency Relationships and Collaborative Linkages for Exceptional Students). Communicating Interagency Relationships and Collaborative Linkages for Exceptional Students (CIRCLES; Flowers et al., 2018; Povenmire-Kirk et al., 2015, 2018) is the only interagency collaboration model identified as a research-based practice (Rowe et al., 2021). The CIRCLES model is ideal for ensuring students with disabilities are connected with necessary resources to support a successful transition into life after high school. CIRCLES is also a model that can be easily implemented by schools, community service providers, and secondary teachers of students with disabilities to facilitate interagency collaboration.

OVERVIEW OF THE CIRCLES MODEL

Uniquely, CIRCLES includes three structured levels of interagency collaboration with teams devoted to specific tasks. This three-team approach includes the

Community-Level Team, School-Level Team, and the Individualized Education Program (IEP) Team. These teams collaborate and connect students and families with the necessary support in school to help ensure students can meet their post-school goals. Fig. 1 provides an overview of the CIRCLES process. Each team devotes time and effort to address student transition needs to support access to transition services. Education professionals benefit from more efficient use of time and more effective, efficient IEP team meetings. For the CIRCLES model to be effective, administrative and community-level support are crucial to its success.

Community-Level Team

The Community-Level Team represents individuals that can potentially address policy issues within the school, district, and community. The Community-Level Team may include school and district administrators (e.g., principals, special education directors, transition coordinators); adult agency supervisors (e.g., vocational rehabilitation, Easter Seals); employers; Chamber of Commerce representatives; community organizations (e.g., scouting troops, civic associations); and institutes of higher education representatives (e.g., disability services) to name a few. Representatives of the Community-Level Team typically meet two to four times per year to address barriers students with disabilities may face in

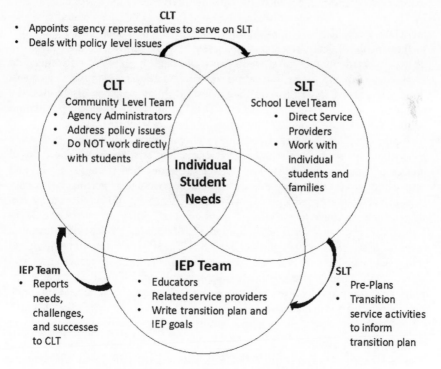

Fig. 1. The CIRCLES Cyclical Model of Interagency Collaboration.

accessing or participating in community resources, including employment and postsecondary education. The Community-Level Team works together to conduct needs assessments and identify overlapping gaps in services. They then work to solve problems, change policies, and ensure more equitable services and support for students with disabilities. To support the work of the School-Level Team, the Community-Level Team selects one representative from each organization to be a member of the School-Level Team.

School-Level Team

The School-Level Team is a defining feature of the CIRCLES model and is critical to providing effective transition services and support to students with disabilities. The School-Level Team allows students and families to meet directly with community agency representatives. Consisting of direct service providers, the School-Level Team typically includes school representatives (e.g., special education teachers, school counselors, career technical education teachers) and community agency representatives (e.g., vocational rehabilitation counselors, employers, disability service providers). Based on school context, need, and number of students participating in CIRCLES, the School-Level Team may convene one full-day meeting and/or two half-day meetings per month throughout the school year. The time commitment for meetings is based on school context and number of students being served under the CIRCLES model. For example, if a school determines they will focus CIRCLES on students with moderate disabilities, who are English learners, the school may only require two to three School-Level Team meetings across the school year because there are likely a limited number of students who are English learners with moderate disabilities receiving special education services. As another example, if a school decides to focus CIRCLES on all students with high-incidence disabilities, the school may need monthly School-Level Team meetings because this population of students is larger, meaning more meetings may be required.

At the School-Level Team meetings, the team meets with every student to learn about the student's strengths, preferences, interests, needs, and post-school goals. Each student spends 8–10 min presenting about their strengths, needs, and post-school goals. Transition assessment and interview data go into developing student presentations, which are facilitated by teachers and developed by students. The remainder of the time is spent communicating between the School-Level Team and the student and family to identify how to best provide transition services. The meeting with the School-Level Team lasts approximately 30–45 min. These meetings are beneficial because students and families meet and speak directly with agency and community service providers. The agency and community service providers benefit from the experience of the School-Level Team because it frees up time they would spend attending every student's IEP meeting.

IEP Team

The third and final level of the CIRCLES model is the IEP Team. Special education teachers serve as the liaison between the School-Level Team and IEP

Team. They are responsible for sharing information from the School-Level Team to ensure the agreed upon information about transition services and identified responsibilities are included in each student's transition component of the IEP. Based on what was agreed on by the School-Level Team, the special education teacher, in collaboration with the IEP team, writes the transition component of the IEP, including post-school goals and transition services. By holding School-Level Team meetings in advance of the IEP team meeting, the special education teacher has more time to focus on preparing students to be actively involved in the School-Level and IEP Team meetings. This provides an opportunity to help students gain self-determination skills by identifying and communicating their strengths, preferences, interests, needs, and post-school goals to adults.

Summary

By using the three-team approach, CIRCLES provides a model that allows each team to have unique roles and purposes in preparing students for adult life. CIRCLES provides a comprehensive interagency model to help ensure students are connected with the services needed post-school. Ultimately, students reap the benefits because each of the three teams can maximize their support with the focus on preparing students for adult life. To support districts, schools, and practitioners with implementing CIRCLES effectively, resources can be downloaded for free from circles.uncc.edu.

HISTORY OF CIRCLES

Although not identified as a secondary transition research-based practice until recently (Rowe et al., 2021), CIRCLES has a long and rich history of practitioner and researcher collaboration. Beginning in 1990, the first Transition Council and School-Level Team was initiated by one school in Cleveland County, North Carolina. In 1992, the first Community-Level Team was established. The School-Level Team served two schools within that same district in North Carolina. In 1994, the Teaching All Students Skills for Employment and Life (TASSEL) interagency model was developed (Aspel et al., 1999). TASSEL emphasized student-centered transition planning (Aspel et al., 1998) and was implemented as designed until 2007. In 2007, the TASSEL model was restructured due to a school system merger. TASSEL was further refined in 2011, which was the initiation of the CIRCLES model. In 2017, researchers at the University of North Carolina at Charlotte received a grant from the Institute for Education Sciences (IES), National Center for Special Education Research to explore large-scale implementation of CIRCLES in multiple school districts to examine the effects of CIRCLES on students' self-determination, IEP goals, and post-school outcomes.

RESEARCH ON CIRCLES

As mentioned previously, CIRCLES is the only interagency collaboration model identified as a secondary transition research-based practice (Rowe et al., 2021).

The CIRCLES model was initially evaluated with funding from an IES National Center for Special Education Research grant (R324A110018; Flowers et al., 2018; Povenmire-Kirk et al., 2015, 2018).

First, Povenmire-Kirk et al. (2015) conducted a study to outline the current practice for involving service providers in the transition process and introduce CIRCLES as a new delivery method to encourage interagency collaboration, while providing transition services to achieve successful post-school outcomes. This study used focus groups composed of members of the three CIRCLES teams (i.e., School-Level Team, Community-Level Team, IEP Team) to characterize perceived successes and challenges of implementing CIRCLES. These focus groups included 30 special education directors and transition coordinators in North and South Carolina who received training for and implemented CIRCLES in their high schools. Facilitators guided focus group meetings, and researchers collected qualitative perceptions on in-school achievements, in school-problem behavior, self-determination, post-school outcomes, social validity, consumer satisfaction, and interagency collaboration. Four themes arose when discussing challenges and barriers to CIRCLES implementation: (1) increasing awareness among agencies and school staff; (2) preparing students and families for School-Level Team meetings; (3) providing student information to service agencies prior to meetings; and (4) following up with service agencies after School-Level Team meetings around practical issues (e.g., transportation, meeting time constraints). Four themes arose when discussing success of CIRCLES implementation. Successes included excitement for collaboration between School- and Community-Level Teams; improvements in communication to provide student transition services; student and family empowerment for leading meetings; and focus on students' post-school schools (i.e., employment, education, independent living).

Next, Povenmire-Kirk et al. (2018) used mixed methods to measure the effectiveness of CIRCLES implementation in six school districts. First, they held 24 focus groups with 175 participants. Focus groups comprised agency personnel ($n = 62$), teachers ($n = 40$), parents ($n = 31$), and students ($n = 42$). Stakeholders communicated overall perceptions of success with the CIRCLES model. Stakeholders stated several factors that contributed to the overall success of CIRCLES implementation, such as assigning communication responsibilities to each agency and providing student profile sheets to agencies in advance. Conversely, participants experienced challenges to implementing CIRCLES, such as understanding the process and roles of each team, ensuring all required representatives were present, and following up with team members after meetings. Authors also distributed a survey to students ($n = 143$), parents ($n = 72$), and agency members ($n = 52$) who participated in the School-Level Team or Community-Level Team meetings. Overall, students and parents agreed with statements describing CIRCLES as effective. More than 90% of partners rated collaboration, role understanding, solution development, feeling trustworthy, and feeling worthwhile as *great* or *very great*. Authors identified strategies for overcoming barriers as a key finding. These strategies included (1) implementing follow-up procedures after School-Level Team meetings; (2) offering parent training on expectations for

CIRCLES; (3) bolstering communicating with agency members; and (4) providing continuous training for teachers (Povenmire-Kirk et al., 2018).

Next, Flowers et al. (2018) conducted a large-scale randomized control trial with 877 high school students with disabilities across 44 schools in the southeast United States. The authors compared levels of self-determination and IEP participation between students who received the CIRCLES intervention and students who received business-as-usual support. Results indicated students who received the CIRCLES intervention reported higher rates of self-determination and IEP participation than students who received business-as-usual support. Both students and teachers who participated in CIRCLES stated students had more opportunity to build and use self-determination skills than students who did not and participated in their more IEP meetings more often than students who did not. Authors concluded CIRCLES enabled educators to provide multiple opportunities for students to prepare and demonstrate self-determination by presenting to the School-Level Team; discussing service options with the School-Level Team; and presenting at the IEP meeting (Flowers et al., 2018). This study contributed to the evidence base; in turn, Rowe et al. (2021) identified CIRCLES as a research-based practice to teach students self-determination and IEP participation skills.

Summary

With ongoing practitioner input from the 1990s through 2018 when Flowers et al. published their results, CIRCLES has been refined to benefit students as they prepare for life after high school. Coupling practitioner input with high-quality research, CIRCLES' three-team approach to interagency collaboration is the only model identified as a research-based practice (Rowe et al., 2021).

CIRCLES IN PRACTICE

Special education teachers report having difficulty providing transition services to adequately prepare students with disabilities for adult life (Morningstar & Benitez, 2013), but interagency collaboration can help address this challenge (Test et al., 2006). Special education teachers reported needing support with preparing students for adult life (Morningstar & Benitez, 2013); therefore, a team approach to transition service delivery is an effective strategy that helps the IEP team provide tailored transition services (Morningstar & Benitez, 2013; Test et al., 2006). Stakeholders from multiple states have used CIRCLES as a three-team approach within their schools and districts. For example, Arkansas has utilized the CIRCLES model and experienced great success. The CIRCLES three-team approach has provided a variety of stakeholders' opportunities to engage with each other, families, and students to facilitate successful interagency connections for students. Arkansas is implementing CIRCLES in four local school districts. Because of CIRCLES, students have (1) not dropped out; (2) gained competitive, integrated employment; (3) connected with employers for internship opportunities; and (4) enrolled in career technical education and community college programs. The CIRCLES model has supported teacher efforts in preparing students for adult life while sharing responsibility across several agencies at several levels.

In order for team approaches to be effective, there is a need for clearly defined roles and responsibilities (Kohler & Field, 2003). Fortunately, CIRCLES provides structure for engaging multiple stakeholders to prepare students for adult life through clearly defined roles and responsibilities. These roles and responsibilities are organized by the Community-Level Team, School-Level Team, and IEP Team. We describe the roles and responsibilities of the three teams next. Table 1 includes quotes from CIRCLES team members.

Community-Level Team

As mentioned, the Community-Level Team includes representatives that can potentially affect policy within the school, district, and community. In the first video, Community-Level Team members described how community agencies collaborated with the school to provide tailored supports to meet students' unique needs Additionally, services were provided from a variety of stakeholders, including community employers and postsecondary education service providers.

School-Level Team

The School-Level Team allows students and families to meet directly with community agency representatives (e.g., vocational rehabilitation counselors, employers, disability service providers). In Rogers, Arkansas, community representatives collaborated with school members to tailor supports for a student to explore his video game interests and plan for his post-school education/training, employment, and independent living goals.

IEP Team

Multiple IEP Team members have engaged with the CIRCLES model. Teachers, students, and parents conveyed the benefits of CIRCLES.

Teachers

In Table 1, a teacher from Harrisburg High School shared her CIRCLES experience. Teachers asserted CIRCLES allowed students to learn about and present their strengths and weaknesses. Additionally, CIRCLES helped teachers learn about available resources to support their students and connect students with community agencies.

Students

Professionals were not the only people acknowledging the benefits of CIRCLES. For example, students from Harrisburg High School and Pulaski Technical Community College have highlighted how CIRCLES helped them. Students

Table 1. CIRCLES Success Stories.

	Team	Link	
1	Community-level	"[In the meeting,] we had a travel agent who worked specifically with golf dream packages. We had a student who wants to be a golfer. He got to sit down and talk with him. Not only did we have people for him that were golfers or work specifically at golf locations and play golf, but this was kind of an alternate path for him, [saying], 'I love golf, I want to be around golf, maybe I could even go into the business world of golf!' So, to be able to talk to somebody and have a one-on-one conversation with him weeks after his presentation was really huge for him."	https://bit.ly/ CIRCLESRogersCLT
2	School-level	"I consider myself a video gamer. My interest is obviously in video games, mainly in computer games, like PC. But I also, um, mri with playing with the console, such as the XBOX." – Student "I just want to call out that I love the fact that you understand the difference between the game designer and the game programmer... you not only understand that but you also know where your passions lie, and I would just say keep going after those sort of passions." – School-Level Team Member	https://bit.ly/ CIRCLESRogersSLT
3	IEP (teacher)	"[CIRCLES] helped me make those connections with those other agencies that can help my students, as well as... seeing my kids do presentations on their strengths and weaknesses has been a big...it's been a big eye-opener for us, as well as the kids."	https://bit.ly/ CIRCLESMrsParksStory
4	IEP (Students)	"When I participated at the CIRCLES at LISA Academy, I was very nervous and shy, but when I did my presentation, I did very good. I got good feedback from the other agencies. If a student wanted advice from me, I would be like, just speak up and tell the people about your goals in life, and they'll give you...CIRCLES will give you good feedback."	https://bit.ly/ CIRCLESstudentstories
5	IEP (parents)	"I'm excited for my daughter to be part of the [CIRCLES] program that will allow her to accomplish her goals after high school."	https://bit.ly/ CIRCLESparentstory

from Harrisburg High School reported CIRCLES helped them meet and communicate with peers, speak with others, articulate future goals, and make new contacts. Derrica, a student at Pulaski Tech, advised other students to speak up and share their goals. She appreciated the knowledge, skills, and support CIRCLES offered while she was in high school. Derrica indicated CIRCLES provided ideas of what she could do in the future.

Parents
Parent expectations and parent involvement are associated with positive outcomes for students with disabilities (Mazzotti et al., 2021). In Table 1, a parent of a Harrisburg High School student described how the CIRCLES process helped them increase expectations for and involvement in planning for their child's post-school goals.

CIRCLES AROUND THE GLOBE: CONSIDERATIONS FOR INTERNATIONAL IMPLEMENTATION

While school contexts vary internationally (e.g., language, policy, programs, expectations), the CIRCLES three-team approach is flexible enough to be implemented in various international settings to meet the needs of communities, schools, students, and their families. The first step to implementing CIRCLES in an international context is to identify the equivalent levels for each of the three teams. School professionals should consider available community agencies and resources that support students with and without disabilities. In other countries (e.g., Germany), students attend one of several high school options focused on post-school goals. Regardless of the particular school setting, school professionals can use the CIRCLES model to ensure relevant stakeholders are involved in providing transition supports through the CIRCLES three-team approach. While some countries (e.g., Australia) may not have IEPs for students with disabilities, school professionals can organize student-level teams to provide individualized transition supports to students. School professionals in international contexts can adapt the CIRCLES three-team approach, along with its myriad of resources (circles.uncc.edu), to support student preparation for post-school life.

Summary
The CIRCLES three-team approach provides an opportunity to build collaborative partnerships to engage students in transition planning. Table 2 includes resources available on the CIRCLES website (circles.uncc.edu) to support implementation. These resources include videos that reflect testimonials from teachers, students, and families of their perceptions of how CIRCLES impacted their experiences in the transition planning process. In addition, there are a CIRCLES Teacher's Guide, evaluation measures, and other tools to support implementation of the community-level, school-level, and IEP teams. A focus on

Table 2. CIRCLES Website Resources.

Team	Resources	Link
Community-level team resources	• Community-level team video • Team level roles and responsibilities • Community agency invitation • Student agency questionnaire • Meeting minutes template • Sample interagency agreement • Action plan • Community-level team agendas • Community-level team nomination • Pre-post interagency Collaboration Survey	https://circles.uncc.edu/circles-overview/community-level-team-clt/community-level-team-clt-resources
School-level team resources	• School level team videos • 10 Steps to planning and Conducting a Successful SLT meeting videos • Preparing Students for the School-level team meeting videos • Team roles and responsibility matrix • Resources for using technology to increase Student access • Directions for popular web-based tools • School-level team forms and documents (e.g., special education teacher tasks, meeting checklist, general agenda, student profile sheet, student dream sheet)	https://circles.uncc.edu/circles-overview/school-level-team-slt/school-level-team-resources
IEP team resources	• IEP team with CIRCLES video • IEP informational presentation • Transition assessment Surveys for parents	https://circles.uncc.edu/home-1/iep-resources

partnerships is widely reflected in international education. The CIRCLES three-team approach can be used to promote partnerships and collaboration in various international community and school contexts.

EVALUATING CIRCLES

When evaluating CIRCLES, schools and districts should collect data from multiple sources (e.g., program, stakeholders, students, families). This includes evaluating CIRCLES program implementation, measuring levels of collaboration among CIRCLES stakeholders, and student-level evaluation to determine if students are gaining knowledge, skills, and support, based on participation in CIRCLES.

CIRCLES Implementation Fidelity Evaluation

Fidelity of CIRCLES implementation is critical to ensure (1) adherence and compliance of program components; (2) exposure of amount of program content delivered; (3) participant responsiveness; and (4) program differentiation (Dane & Schneider, 1998). It is important that schools and districts interested in implementing CIRCLES include training and coaching processes that follow best practice in professional development (PD; Holzberg et al., 2018; Noonan et al., 2013). Training should include school and agency staff with follow-up coaching. There are CIRCLES training materials available for free to support fidelity of implementation at circles (e.g., CIRCLES training manual, fidelity checklists, action planning guides, training videos) at circles.uncc.edu. Tables 3 and 4 include fidelity checklists developed to support CIRCLES Community-Level and School-Level Team implementation.

Stakeholder Evaluation

Evaluating the degree of collaboration is important to ensure stakeholders are engaging in meaningful, mutually-beneficial partnerships (Plotner et al., 2018). In an interagency collaboration survey, the degree of communication was positively associated with stakeholder satisfaction (Plotner et al., 2018). The *Levels of Collaboration Scale* (Frey et al., 2006) can be used to evaluate the degree of collaboration among stakeholders. This scale encompasses a number of collaboration components to provide in-depth information about increased collaboration. The *Levels of Collaboration Scale* is a validated measure that allows stakeholders to evaluate progress across five stages of collaboration: (1) networking/building awareness of organization; (2) cooperation and providing information to each other; (3) coordination and sharing of resources; (4) coalition, which includes frequent and organized communication; and (5) building one system of collaboration.

Student-Level Evaluation

Assessing self-determination helps team members determine and track a student's choice-making and self-advocacy skills (Shogren & Wittenburg, 2020). Self-determination/self-advocacy was associated with improved student post-school education/training, employment, and independent living outcomes (Mazzotti et al., 2021). The *Self-Determination Inventory-Student Report* (SDI-SR; Shogren & Wehmeyer, 2017) can be used to collect data on student self-determination. The SDI-SR is a self-report, norm-referenced measure of self-determination (Shogren & Wehmeyer, 2017). The SDI-SR was developed to provide valid and reliable information on student self-determination to guide classroom instruction as well as to evaluate change in self-determination over time as a result of intervention. In addition to the SDI-SR, the *Student Transition Questionnaire* (STQ) can be used to evaluate students' knowledge and perspectives related to the transition planning process. The STQ is a 40-item assessment designed to elicit student perspectives on transition-related topics and perceptions of strengths and needs (Collier et al., 2016, 2017). Other free tools (e.g., the

Table 3. CIRCLES Community-Level Team Fidelity Checklist.

Item	Rating		
Procedures following 2-day CIRCLES training/Prior to 1st CLT Meeting	*Yes*	*Partial*	*No*
1. Identified potential agencies in postsecondary education, employment, and independent living	Yes	Partial	No
2. Appointed time for CLT meeting	Yes	Partial	No
3. Invited potential team members (e.g., via Doodle, email, phone call)	Yes	Partial	No
4. Reminders were sent to all participating agencies and school district personnel	Yes	Partial	No
CLT meeting	*Yes*	*Partial*	*No*
1. Agenda was developed for CLT meeting	Yes	Partial	No
2. Introduction of team members – this may include an activity to get acquainted, establish positive tone, etc.	Yes	Partial	No
3. Purpose of meeting stated	Yes	Partial	No
4. Approval of the agenda by team members	Yes	Partial	No
5. Approval and/or reading of the minutes from previous meeting (if applicable)	Yes	Partial	No
6. Selection of volunteers to facilitate meeting	Yes	Partial	No
7. Reviewed/developed mission, vision, and values statements	Yes	Partial	No
8. CIRCLES overview was provided	Yes	Partial	No
If yes, indicate who provided CIRCLES overview (circle): • District personnel • Project staff • District personnel and project staff			
9. Statement of achievements/strengths by each agency	Yes	Partial	No
10. Identification of opportunities for growth or needs by each agency (e.g., policy, practice)	Yes	Partial	No
11. Discussion of desired outcomes for individual(s) in transition and/or the service system	Yes	Partial	No
12. Listing of current known available resources	Yes	Partial	No
13. Listing of current known needs	Yes	Partial	No
14. Finalization of procedure for follow-up and confirmation assignment of responsibilities	Yes	Partial	No
15. Discussion of additional agencies to contact for future participation	Yes	Partial	No
16. Appointed school level team members (if applicable, CLT meeting #1 only)	Yes	Partial	No
17. Closure or summary	Yes	Partial	No
18. Scheduling of next CLT meeting date, place, and time (determine who will need to be present)	Yes	Partial	No
Procedures prior to CLT Meetings #2 and #3	*Yes*	*Partial*	*No*
1. Sent reminder email to CLT team members (e.g., via Doodle, email, phone call).	Yes	Partial	No
2. Invited identified agencies recommended for participation at prior CLT meeting	Yes	Partial	No

American Institutes for Research [AIR] Self-Determination Assessment, ARC Self-Determination Scale) can be downloaded from the Zarrow Center.

Summary

The importance of fidelity and evaluation cannot be overstated. For CIRCLES to be effective, there is a need to follow the prescribed process and conduct

Table 4. CIRCLES School-Level Team Fidelity Checklist.

Item	Rating		
Procedures prior to SLT meeting	*Yes*	*Partial*	*No*
1. Student (18+) informed consent received	Yes	Partial	No
2. Parent consent/student assent received (if student under 18)	Yes	Partial	No
3. Meeting times for individual students were established within timeframe allotted for full SLT meeting (district/school staff)	Yes	Partial	No
4. Parent(s)/guardian(s) of student presenting was invited (SPED teacher/case manager)	Yes	Partial	No
SLT meeting	*Yes*	*Partial*	*No*
1. Agenda was developed for SLT meeting (district/school staff)	Yes	Partial	No
2. Introduction of team members	Yes	Partial	No
3. Purpose of meeting stated	Yes	Partial	No
4. Approval of the agenda by team members	Yes	Partial	No
5. Appointed team member to record meeting minutes	Yes	Partial	No
6. Student profile sheet completed for student and given to all SLT members (SPED teacher/case manager)	Yes	Partial	No
7. Teacher introduced student and parent/guardian to SLT	Yes	Partial	No
8. Each agency member introduced to each students	Yes	Partial	No
9. Agencies shared information regarding services they can provide students before and after graduation	Yes	Partial	No
10. Agency information was given to student/parents (e.g., pamphlets, flyers, contact info)	Yes	Partial	No
11. Student used e-sharing (web 2.0) tools for presentation	Yes	Partial	No
12. Students shared strengths in presentation	Yes	Partial	No
13. Students weaknesses shared in presentation	Yes	Partial	No
14. Student's identified needs shared in presentation	Yes	Partial	No
15. Student's identified goals shared in presentation	Yes	Partial	No
16. Student presentation addressed post-school goals for employment	Yes	Partial	No
17. Student presentation addressed post-school goals for education	Yes	Partial	No
18. Student presentation addressed post-school goals for independent living	Yes	Partial	No
19. Student and parent (if applicable) completed Satisfaction Survey	Yes	Partial	No
20. Meeting minutes completed for each student	Yes	Partial	No
21. Meeting minutes provided to SPED teacher/case managers, parents, students, CIRCLES staff and agency personnel	Yes	Partial	No
22. SLT participation measure completed for student IEP meeting	Yes	Partial	No

ongoing evaluation to ensure effectiveness. Educators, students, and families benefit from using interagency collaboration. CIRCLES is an ideal and effective interagency collaboration model that, when implemented with fidelity, is associated with positive outcomes for students with disabilities and features positive perceptions from stakeholders (Flowers et al., 2018; Povenmire-Kirk et al., 2015, 2018). By measuring fidelity and making data-based decisions, CIRCLES can be implemented to effectively prepare students for life after high school.

BARRIERS FOR INTERAGENCY COLLABORATION AND STRATEGIES

Unique barriers are inherent to interagency collaboration, and these barriers fall into two broad categories: (1) structural barriers and (2) language and operational barriers. To successfully implement interagency collaboration, it is important for stakeholders to understand relevant barriers. We outline the barriers below, along with strategies to help stakeholders overcome these barriers.

Structural Barriers

Structural barriers are processes, agreements, and policies that prevent team involvement in facilitating interagency collaboration (Povenmire-Kirk et al., 2018). Structural barriers can include barriers related to a lack of memorandums of understanding to support sharing of resources and information, lack of infrastructure to support interagency collaboration, and representation of individuals critical to implement interagency collaboration activities.

Memorandums of Understanding (MOUs)

An MOU is a written and shared outline of responsibilities and responsible agencies. A lack of MOUs can create gaps in services or repetitive services being provided across multiple agencies. MOUs can maximize efficiency and ensure reduced duplication of services. To determine each partner's role and potential contributions to the team, it is critical to first get to know each other by exchanging thoughts, ideas, and information, along with collaboratively developing a shared vision and purpose of collaborative efforts (Mazzotti & Rowe, 2015). By understanding each partner's strengths and potential contributions to the partnership, MOUs should be created to maximize efficiency and ensure each party has a shared understanding of roles and expectations. To develop MOUs, it is critical to ensure clear processes in place for exchanging confidential information (Flexer et al., 2013; Test et al., 2006). These considerations should be implemented to avoid legal issues at the state and local levels (Noonan & Morningstar, 2012; Povenmire-Kirk et al., 2015).

Infrastructure

A lack of infrastructure to support interagency collaboration can affect quality of services. Administrative leadership and support have been highlighted as important aspects of interagency collaboration (Mazzotti & Rowe, 2015). For example, administrative support can include identifying community resources, addressing interagency agreements, and making data-based decisions (Mazzotti & Rowe, 2015). When implementing CIRCLES, there is a need for administrative support for implementing CIRCLES because time, resources, and flexibility are needed to organize the Community-Level, School-Level, and IEP Team meetings (Flowers et al., 2018; Noonan et al., 2008).

Ensuring Adequate Representation

Finally, it is important to ensure the correct people are represented at the table (Mazzotti & Rowe, 2015). Although each CIRCLES team has a suggested list of roles and responsibilities, additional people may need to be present as part of CIRCLES implementation. The specific individuals at the table should include a variety of individuals, representing a variety of agencies and community partners, to help support students to prepare for post-school success.

Language and Operational Barriers

In addition, language and operational barriers may prevent interagency collaboration. Different agencies may use several terms or phrases to describe similar processes across agencies (e.g., "youth development" instead of "secondary transition") or use unique organizational structures for decision making and service delivery, which can lead to confusion from personnel or families over available services (Plotner et al., 2018). Stakeholders may not be aware of community resources because agencies use differing terms to describe services; therefore, PD for agency personnel may be needed for practitioners to gain knowledge about services offered in their community or interagency collaboration processes (Morningstar & Benitez, 2013). In addition, School-Level and IEP Team members should engage students and family members as much as possible to ascertain useful community resources for students and families (Hwang et al., 2020).

IMPLICATIONS FOR POLICY AND PRACTICE

When implementing CIRCLES, it is important to consider implications for policy and practice. Considering these implications will help guide actions that stakeholders can take when implementing CIRCLES to improve transitions services for students. Next, we describe implications for both policy and practice.

Policy Implications

Legislative mandates have required the use of scientifically-based research practices and evidence-based practices and instruction for students with and without disabilities (Every Student Succeeds Act [ESSA], 2015; No Child Left Behind Act [NCLB], 2002). Furthermore, the Individuals with Disabilities Education Improvement Act (IDEA, 2004) mandates all students with disabilities are prepared for college, careers, and community engagement. Given the federal legislative focus on interagency collaboration (IDEA, 2004; Workforce Innovations and Opportunities Act [WIOA], 2015), states and districts should develop policy reaffirming the importance of interagency collaboration. Educators need support with preparing students for adult life (Morningstar & Benitez, 2013), and effective interagency collaboration seems like an ideal opportunity to provide legally mandated transition services (IDEA, 2004). To effectively prepare students for post-school success using practices supported by research, CIRCLES is the ideal model for schools and districts to use, as it is the only research-based interagency collaboration framework (Rowe et al., 2021).

As demonstrated in Arkansas, state-level policy can focus on preparing students for adult life. State-level policy focused on interagency collaboration and CIRCLES has led to student-, family-, teacher-, and professional-described improvements. The CIRCLES model provides structure and flexibility to be implemented throughout a state to prepare all students for adult life. At the school- and district-policy levels, CIRCLES can be used to maximize efforts to engage the local community within the transition processes for students and families. By engaging in community partnerships, schools, students, families, and teachers will be well supported in preparing students for adulthood.

When students have access to interagency collaboration in high school, students were more likely to experience post-school education and employment success (Mazzotti et al., 2016, 2021; Rowe et al., 2015; Test et al., 2009). Considering these implications for policy is critical for promoting post-school success. These considerations can lead to changes in practice to benefit students and families.

Practice Implications

Researchers and stakeholders who implemented CIRCLES have offered several suggestions for practice. First, local education agencies should offer school- and district-wide PD on secondary transition and interagency collaboration to explicitly instruct and train personnel to implement and sustain these services and structures. These PD opportunities should be ongoing rather than a one-time approach (Morningstar & Benitez, 2013). Resources such as the Teacher's Guide on the CIRCLES website (circles.uncc.edu) may assist practitioners.

In addition, practitioners should conduct community mapping to identify resources that can support students. In this process, practitioners pool, locate, and organize resources. Learning about services other agencies offer allows practitioners to maximize services students can access (Carter et al., 2016). The Transition community mapping guide (https://bit.ly/transitionmaps) outlines each step of the community mapping process.

CONCLUSION

When students with disabilities have access to interagency collaboration in high school, students will more likely be successful in attaining post-school outcomes (Mazzotti et al., 2016, 2021; Rowe et al., 2015; Test et al., 2009). Coupled with improved post-school outcomes, federal mandates focused on interagency collaboration (e.g., IDEA, 2004; WIOA, 2015), and the use of evidence-based practices (ESSA, 2015), interagency collaboration should be a priority focus for schools to ensure students are effectively prepared for adult life. Given its history of development beginning in the 1990s, it is logical that CIRCLES is an ideal model for facilitating interagency collaboration. Because CIRCLES is the only research-based interagency collaboration model (Rowe et al., 2021), it makes sense that CIRCLES would be an ideal, research-based model to build collaborative school and community partnerships in various international structures and contexts.

REFERENCES

Aspel, N., Bettis, G., Quinn, P., Test, D. W., & Wood, W. M. (1999). A collaborative process for planning transition services for all students with disabilities. *Career Development for Exceptional Individuals, 22*(1), 21–42. https://doi.org/10.1177/088572889902200103

Aspel, N., Bettis, G., Test, D. W., & Wood, W. M. (1998). An evaluation of a comprehensive system of transition services. *Career Development for Exceptional Individuals, 21*(2), 203–223. https://doi.org/10.1177/088572889802100208

Carter, E. W., Blustein, C. L., Bumble, J. L., Harvey, S., Henderson, L. M., & McMillan, E. D. (2016). Engaging communities in identifying local strategies for expanding integrated employment during and after high school. *American Journal on Intellectual and Developmental Disabilities, 121*(5), 398–418. https://doi.org/10.1352/1944-7558-121.5.398

Collier, M. L., Griffin, M. M., & Wei, Y. (2016). Facilitating student involvement in transition assessment: A pilot study of the student transition questionnaire. *Career Development and Transition for Exceptional Individuals, 39*(3), 175–184. https://doi.org/10.1177/2165143414556746

Collier, M., Griffin, M. M., & Wei, Y. (2017). Learning from students about transition needs: Identifying gaps in knowledge and experience. *Journal of Vocational Rehabilitation, 46*(1), 1–10. https://doi.org/10.3233/JVR-160837

Dane, A. V., & Schneider, B. H. (1998). Program integrity in primary and early secondary prevention: Are implementation effects out of control? *Clinical Psychology Review, 18*(1), 23–45. https://doi.org/10.1016/S0272-7358(97)00043-3

Every Student Succeeds Act of 2015, P.L. 114–195.

Flexer, R. W., Baer, R. M., Luft, P., & Simmons, T. J. (2013). *Transition planning for secondary students with disabilities* (4th ed.). Pearson.

Flowers, C., Test, D. W., Povenmire-Kirk, T. C., Diegelmann, K. M., Bunch-Crump, K. R., Kemp-Inman, A., & Goodnight, C. I. (2018). A demonstration model of interagency collaboration for students with disabilities: A multilevel approach. *The Journal of Special Education, 31*(4), 211–221. https://doi.org/10.1177/0022466917720764

Frey, B. B., Lohmeier, J. H., Lee, S. W., & Tollefson, N. (2006). Measuring collaboration among grant partners. *American Journal of Evaluation, 27*(3), 383–392. https://doi.org/10.1177/1098214006290356

Halpern, A. (1985). Transition: A look at the foundations. *Exceptional Children, 51*(6), 479–486. https://doi.org/10.1177/001440298505100604

Halpern, A. S. (1994). The transition of youth with disabilities to adult life: A position statement of the Division on Career Development and Transition. *Career Development for Exceptional Individuals, 17*(2), 115–124.

Holzberg, D. G., Clark, K. A., & Morningstar, M. E. (2018). Transition-focused professional development: An annotated bibliography of essential elements and features of professional development. *Career Development and Transition for Exceptional Individuals, 41*(1), 50–55. https://doi.org/10.1177/2165143417742362

Hwang, I.-T., Kramer, J. M., Cohn, E. S., & Barnes, L. L. (2020). Asian immigrant parents' role enactment while accessing and using services for their child with developmental disabilities in the United States: A meta-synthesis study. *Qualitative Health Research, 30*(11), 1632–1646. https://doi.org/10.1177/1049732320926138

Individuals with Disabilities Education Improvement Act of 2004, 20 U.S.C. § 1400 et seq.

Kohler, P. D. (1993). Best practices in transition: Substantiated or implied? *Career Development for Exceptional Individuals, 16*(2), 107–121. https://doi.org/10.1177/088572889301600201

Kohler, P. D., & Field, S. (2003). Transition-focused education: Foundation for the future. *The Journal of Special Education, 37*(3), 174–183. https://doi.org/10.1177/00224669030370030701

Landmark, L. J., Ju, S., & Zhang, D. (2010). Substantiated best practices in transition: Fifteen plus years later. *Career Development for Exceptional Individuals, 33*(3), 165–176. https://doi.org/10.1177/0885728810376410

Mazzotti, V. L., & Rowe, D. A. (2015). Meeting the transition needs of students with disabilities in the 21st century [Editorial]. *TEACHING Exceptional Children, 47*(6), 298–299. https://doi.org/10.1177/0040059915587695

Mazzotti, V. L., Rowe, D. A., Kwiatek, S., Voggt, A., Chang, W., Fowler, C. H., Poppen, M., Sinclair, J., & Test, D. W. (2021). Secondary transition predictors of post-school success: An update to the research base. *Career Development and Transition for Exceptional Individuals, 44*(1), 47–64. https://doi.org/10.1177/2165143420959793

Mazzotti, V. L., Rowe, D. A., Sinclair, J., Poppen, M., Woods, W. E., & Shearer, M. L. (2016). Predictors of post-school success: A systematic review of NLTS2 secondary analyses. *Career Development and Transition for Exceptional Individuals, 39*(4), 196–215. https://doi.org/10.1177/2165143415588047

Morningstar, M. E., & Benitez, D. T. (2013). Teacher training matters: The results of a multistate survey of secondary special educators regarding transition from school to adulthood. *Teacher Education and Special Education, 36*(1), 51–64. https://doi.org/10.1177/0888406412474022

No Child Left Behind Act of 2001, 20 U.S.C. 70 § 6301 et seq. (2002).

Noonan, P. M., Erickson, A. G., & Morningstar, M. E. (2013). Effects of community transition teams on interagency collaboration for school and adult agency staff. *Career Development and Transition for Exceptional Individuals, 36*(2), 96–104. https://doi.org/10.1177/2165143412451119

Noonan, P. M., & Morningstar, M. E. (2012). Effective strategies for interagency collaboration. In M. L. Wehmeyer & K. W. Webb (Eds.), *Handbook of adolescent transition education for youth with disabilities* (pp. 312–328). Routledge.

Noonan, P. M., Morningstar, M. E., & Gaumer Erickson, A. (2008). Improving interagency collaboration: Effective strategies used by high-performing local districts and communities. *Career Development for Exceptional Individuals, 31*(3), 132–143. https://doi.org/10.1177/0885728808327149

Plotner, A. J., Mazzotti, V. L., Rose, C. A., & Teasley, K. (2018). Perceptions of interagency collaboration: Relationships between secondary transition roles, communication, and collaboration. *Remedial and Special Education, 41*(1), 28–39. https://doi.org/10.1177/0741932518778029

Povenmire-Kirk, T., Diegelmann, K., Crump, K., Schnorr, C., Test, D., Flowers, C., & Aspel, N. (2015). Implementing CIRCLES: A new model for interagency collaboration in transition planning. *Journal of Vocational Rehabilitation, 42*(1), 51–65. https://doi.org/10.3233/JVR-140723

Povenmire-Kirk, T. C., Test, D. W., Flowers, C. P., Diegelmann, K. M., Bunch-Crump, K., Kemp-Inman, A., & Goodnight, C. I. (2018). CIRCLES: Building an interagency network for transition planning. *Journal of Vocational Rehabilitation, 49*(1), 45–57. https://doi.org/10.3233/JVR-180953

Repetto, J. B., & Correa, V. I. (1996). Expanding views on transition. *Exceptional Children, 62*(6), 551–563. https://doi.org/10.1177/001440299606200606

Rowe, D. A., Alverson, C. Y., Unruh, D. K., Fowler, C. H., Kellems, R., & Test, D. W. (2015). A Delphi study to operationalize evidence-based predictors in secondary transition. *Career Development and Transition for Exceptional Individuals, 38*(2), 113–126. https://doi.org/10.1177/2165143414526429

Rowe, D. A., Mazzotti, V. L., Fowler, C. H., Test, D. W., Mitchell, V. J., Clark, K. A., Holzberg, D., Owens, T. L., Rusher, D., Seaman-Tullis, R. L., Gushanas, C. M., Castle, H., Chang, W., Voggt, A., Kwiatek, S., & Dean, C. (2021). Updating the secondary transition research base: Evidence- and research-based practices in functional skills. *Career Development and Transition for Exceptional Individuals, 44*(1), 28–46. https://doi.org/10.1177/2165143420958674

Shogren, K. A., & Wehmeyer, M. L. (2017). *Self-determination inventory*. Kansas University Center on Developmental Disabilities

Shogren, K. A., & Wittenburg, D. (2020). Improving outcomes of transition-age youth with disabilities: A life course perspective. *Career Development and Transition for Exceptional Individuals, 43*(1), 18–28. https://doi.org/10.1177/2165143419887853

Test, D. W., Aspel, N. P., & Everson, J. M. (2006). *Transition methods for youth with disabilities.* Pearson.

Test, D. W., Mazzotti, V. L., Mustian, A. L., Fowler, C. H., Kortering, L., & Kohler, P. (2009). Evidence-based secondary transition predictors for improving postschool outcomes for students with disabilities. *Career Development for Exceptional Individuals, 32*(3), 160–181. https://doi.org/10.1177/0885728809346960

Trainor, A. A., Carter, E. W., Karpur, A., Martin, J. E., Mazzotti, V. L., Morningstar, M. E., Newman, L., & Rojewski, J. W. (2020). A framework for research in transition: Identifying important areas and intersections for future study. *Career Development and Transition for Exceptional Individuals, 43*(1), 5–17. https://doi.org/10.1177/2165143419864551

Will, M. C. (1984). Let us pause and reflect – But not too long. *Exceptional Children, 51*(1), 11–16. https://doi.org/10.1177/001440298405100102

Workforce Innovation and Opportunity Act of 2015, P. L. 113–128. 29 U.S.C. Sec. 3101, et. seq.

ADVANCING SCHOOL TO WORK TRANSITION PROGRAMS FOR STUDENTS WITH DISABILITIES IN INDONESIAN SPECIAL SCHOOLS

Nur Azizah

ABSTRACT

Transition from secondary school to adult life is a critical period in students' lives. Transition programs delivered at school play an important role in supporting students with disabilities to achieve successful post-school outcomes particularly in the case of transition to work whereby employment is acknowledged as the main target after graduating from secondary school. Post-school outcomes for students with disabilities related to employment, however, remain poor compared to students without disabilities. Using the taxonomy for transition programming and Bronfenbrenner's ecological system theory, this chapter proposes a model and action that needs to be taken in advancing school to work transition programming in Indonesia.

Keywords: School to work transition; Bronfenbrenner; taxonomy for transition programming; students with disabilities; post-school outcomes; Indonesia

INTRODUCTION TO THE TRANSITION PROGRAM

Transition from school to work can be defined as "life changes, adjustment, and cumulative experience that occur in the lives of young adults as they move from school environments to independent living and work environments" (Wehman, 2006, p. 4). Most students with disabilities experience challenges in making their transition to adult life (Crockett & Hardman, 2010a; Davies, 2014). Arguments

Transition Programs for Children and Youth with Diverse Needs
International Perspectives on Inclusive Education, Volume 18, 229–243
Copyright © 2022 Nur Azizah
Published under exclusive licence by Emerald Publishing Limited
ISSN: 1479-3636/doi:10.1108/S1479-363620220000018016

emphasizing these difficulties include: the nature of disabilities where individuals with significant disabilities are highly likely to experience more difficulty in mastering skills needed in adulthood life (Sheppard-Jones et al., 2007), changes in support systems that are often segregated and partial (Crockett & Hardman, 2010a; Winn & Hay, 2009), and lack awareness of the availability of supportive facilities (Davies & Beamish, 2009).

Post-school outcomes of students with disabilities have been a focus in special education research. Although there are developments in regard to opportunities for individuals with disabilities in participating in employment and further training and education, their post-school outcomes remain lower compared to non-disabled students (Beamish et al., 2012). Although the school is not the only party involved in assisting successful post school outcomes for students with disabilities (Winn & Hay, 2009), research signifies that transition practices delivered in schools are essential in preparing students with disabilities for life after school (Crockett & Hardman, 2010b).

Literature provides a strong recommendation that transition programs should include every aspect of life such as independent living, community participation, further education and training, and employment (Bassett & Kochhar-Bryant, 2012; Wehmeyer & Webb, 2012). However, preparing students with disabilities for job and career aspiration is a main concern that needs to be addressed in transition programs in secondary schools (Crockett & Hardman, 2010a, 2010b). Evidence indicates the benefits associated with being employed, which include promoting overall quality of life, greater independence, self-determination, and political strength (Benz et al., 2000). Therefore, improving employment outcomes for student with disabilities is critical in "building upon their social capital for effective community functioning" (Brewer et al., 2011, p. 3). Furthermore, a study conducted by Knapp et al., 2008 showed that the economic cost of unsuccessful transition programs is considerable. It not only affects students with disabilities personally, in that they cannot achieve effective employment status, but it also means missed opportunities to contribute to the economy, dependency on welfare benefits, and increased health costs and services. Furthermore, 60–90% of parent respondents wanted their children to gain employment after they graduated from secondary school (Blacher et al., 2010).

The delivery of school to work transition itself cannot be separated from a whole process of transition education as the issues across programs and services are related in regard to improving the quality of life for people with disabilities such as normalization, independent living, and self-determination (Bassett & Kochhar-Bryant, 2012). IDEA (2004) defined transition service as a coordinated set of activities for a student with a disability that

(1) Is designed to be within a result-oriented process, that is focused on improving the academic and functional achievement of the student with a disability to facilitate the student movement from school to post-school activities, including post-secondary education, vocational education,

integrated employment (including supported employment) continuing and adult education, adult services, independent living, or community participation;
(2) Is based on the individual child's needs, taking account the child's strengths, preferences, and interests; and
(3) Includes instruction, related services, community experiences, the development of employment and other post-school adult living objectives, and when appropriate, acquisition of daily living skills and functional vocational evaluation (IDEA, 2004, Section 34).

The concern to improve post-school outcomes for students with disabilities has resulted in countries such as the USA, the UK, and New Zealand authorizing legislation that requires transition services to be embedded in the student's education planning – typically, the IEP (IDEA, 2004; NZ Ministry of Education, 2011; Department for Education and Department of Health, 2015). The interest in improving post-school outcomes has resulted in the publication of empirical and theoretical studies on a best practice transition model. The taxonomy for transition programming was first developed in 1996 (Kohler, 1996) and then develop into the taxonomy for transition programming 2.0 (Kohler et al., 2016) places focus on the importance of considering five important components (student-focused planning, student development, family involvement, interagency collaboration, and program structure) in planning, delivering, and evaluating transition programs. This taxonomy is used as a framework in investigating the perspectives of students and parents in school to work transition program that will be explained in a later section and also used in the proposed model to advance the school to work transition program in special schools in the Indonesian context. The proposed model was published as part of a dissertation (Azizah, 2016).

BACKGROUND TO THE INDONESIAN CONTEXT

Indonesia is an archipelagic country consisting of 17,508 islands (Ministry of Marine & Fishery, 2020) with a population of 270.20 million people (BPS, 2020). According to BPS (2020) the distribution of Indonesia's population is still concentrated on the island of Java. Despite its geographic area of only around 7% of the entire territory of Indonesia, Java Island is inhabited by 151.59 million people or 56.10% of Indonesia's population. The second largest population distribution is on the island of Sumatra with a population of 58.56 million people, accounting for 21.68%. The Island of Sulawesi has a distribution of 7.36% and Kalimantan Island has a distribution of 6.15%. Population percentage in the Bali-Nusa Tenggara and Maluku-Papua regions are 5.54 and 3.17% respectively.

Consistency data regarding the number of people with disabilities in Indonesia is difficult to find as there are different approaches conducted by each government organization. The numbers and percentage vary between less than 1% as it is in *Podes* (Villages Potential Survey) in 2014 to more than 12% in *Sakernas* (National Labor Force Survey) in 2016 (Institute for Economic and Social

Research, 2017). This inconsistency has impacted programs and services in many ways from policy to practice.

In regards to education, many children with disabilities are left behind compared to non-disabled children. Indonesian Education Law (Sisdiknas) No 20 Year 2003 guarantees that children with disabilities have rights to education. According to Marjuki (2010), only about 40% of children with disabilities gain access to education, whereas the other 60% are not educated. Furthermore, most students with disabilities discontinue their education and only graduate from primary school level, yet Indonesian compulsory education is 9 years, that is, up to lower secondary. An analysis of education pathways for youth aged 19–21 years shows that only 46% of students with disabilities transitioned to lower secondary, as compared to 86% their non-disabled peers (UNICEF, 2019). The gap of completion rates of students with disabilities and students with non-disabilities is substantial as it is significantly broader as students' progress to higher levels of schooling.

Table 1. Completion Rate Comparison between Students with Disabilities and Non-disabilities.

School Level	Completion Rate	
	Students with Disabilities	Students with Non-disabilities
Primary school	54%	95%
Lower secondary school	37%	85%
Upper secondary school	26%	62%

Source: Susenas (2018).

Considering the data presented in the Table 1, it is not surprising that employment rates of people with disabilities are lower compared to their counterparts. In Indonesia, the employment rate of people with mild disabilities is 56.72% and 20.27% for people with moderate disabilities. These percentages are significantly lower compared to people with non-disabilities which is 70.40% (Institute for Economic and Social Research, 2017). Education plays an essential role in maintaining income and employment. According to data from the US Bureau of Labor Statistics, earnings increase and unemployment decreases as educational attainment rises (Vilario, 2016). This is also consistent in Indonesian statistics both for person with disabilities and non-disabilities (Institute for Economic and Social Research, 2017).

Improving Employment-Related Outcomes

Various measures were taken by the Indonesian government to improve employment-related outcomes for individuals with disabilities. In basic education areas, although none of the measures stated explicitly about "transition education/program/services," some of the actions are worth mentioning. This includes the revitalization of vocational schools, including secondary special schools that place emphasis on reforming the curriculum, training teachers and school staff, establishing business and industry collaboration, proposing certification and accreditation, and enhancing facilities and institution management (Direktorat Pembinaan Sekolah Menengah Kejuruan, 2017). The 2013 curriculum applied in secondary special schools also provides a curriculum structure that emphasizes specific skills by having a minimum of 60% allocated to vocational skills (Ministry of Education and Culture, 2017). Furthermore, it has also set more than 20 specific vocational skills and competencies where students can enroll in two of the 20 skills. Included in the curriculum are horticulture, agriculture, regular and fish farming, electronic, graphic design, photography, *batik* making, crafts, food and culinary, fashion, beauty, massage, and radio announcers.

Another measure is operated by the Ministry of Social Affairs. As a government organization that holds a key responsibility in disability issues at the national level, it provides vocational training in (1) institutions based in *Panti* and *Balai Besar Rehabilitasi* and (2) non-institutions based in *Loka Bina Karya*. However, this vocational training is limited and not specifically targeted to graduates from secondary special schools, but also to individual with disabilities in general. While *Panti* and *Balai Besar Rehabilitasi* provide vocational rehabilitation for individuals with disabilities, *Loka Bina Karya* provides social and vocational rehabilitation for high-risk individuals (such as sexual workers, beggars, and homeless people). There are 204 *Loka Bina Karya*, 19 *panti*, and two *Balai Besar Rehabilitasi* in Indonesia (Irwanto et al., 2010). Although program conducted in the Ministry of Social Affairs is not the main focused of this chapter, this vocational training in this institution could supplement school to work transition program applied in special schools.

PROPOSING A MODEL TO ADVANCE SCHOOL TO WORK TRANSITION PROGRAMS FOR STUDENTS WITH DISABILITIES IN INDONESIAN SPECIAL SCHOOLS

As indicated in the literature that the success of school to work transition programs requires full support from related stakeholders (Noonan et al., 2008). Actions need to be taken by everyone and for everyone. Therefore, in order to make sure the whole system functions successfully, it needs to consider the interaction of multiple contexts and fulfill the requirements of important components such as listed in the Taxonomy for transition programming (Kohler et al., 2016). Bronfenbrenner's ecological system theory (Bronfenbrenner, 1977, 1979, 1986) is a useful concept that can be adopted in delivering an integrated model of a school to work transition program in the Indonesian context. Moving from the individual through engagement with the taxonomy within the schools, to engagement with the local district/provincial level and to the national government level, it provides a framework in which to consider the influences on the transition to work programs in the school. The levels are not set, or separated, but serve only as a reminder that school transition programs do not operate in isolation. The proposed model also provides the opportunity to see the influence (or not) of external factors on the operation of a school's transition to work program.

Although the model places emphasis on collaboration between these different stakeholders concurrently, the proposed model in advancing school to work transition program also explains what these stakeholders can do individually. The model is illustrated in Fig. 1.

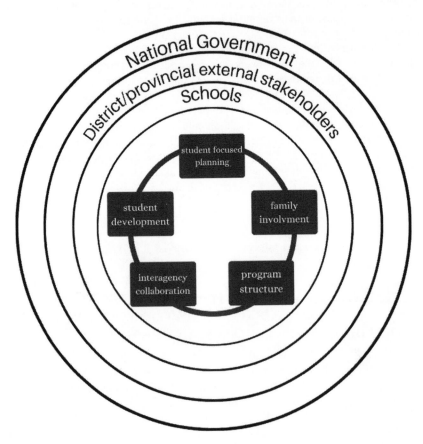

Fig. 1.   Model for School to Work Transition Program in Indonesian Setting (Azizah, 2016).

Student-Focused Planning

There are four important issues need to be address in the student focused planning category: (1) recognition of employment outcomes in curriculum planning; (2) documentation of individualized post-school employment planning; (3) consideration of student interest in planning; and (4) student involvement in program planning.

To address these issues, actions need to be taken by different stakeholders. At the school level, post-school employment outcomes should be highlighted in curriculum documents and individualized for each student according to their abilities and interests. An example of documentation that can be adopted in Indonesian special secondary schools is the Individualized Transition Program (ITP). The ITP serves two different goals: first, the identification of the student's post school outcomes, and second, the supports required to achieve the student's outcomes.

Further important issues in this category are having the student at the center of program planning, and active student involvement at all stages. Issues related to low student involvement and participation can be addressed by using person-centered planning (PCP) when planning transition services (Wehman & Targett, 2012). PCP assists students with disabilities to have greater control of their future as it is driven by the individual and their families, and it places emphasis on the student's abilities and availability of supports.

It is essential that students, teachers, and families have fundamental skills regarding PCP to genuinely place students and families at the center of program planning. Furthermore, because at the core of PCP is the active student role, the school curriculum needs to address critical skills required to ensure active involvement. These skills will be discussed under the student development category and clusters, whereas issues regarding families' and teachers' roles in PCP will be discussed in family involvement and program structure categories respectively.

At the external stakeholder level, action needs to be taken to include strict supervision from the provincial Department of Education, through their school supervisors. As a body of local education authority that has function to monitor the implementation of educational standards in schools, a school supervisor has to make sure that (1) schools documents include post school employment outcomes as part of their curriculum and (2) student individual transition planning is available and written according to a student-centered approach. Staff from Rehabilitation Centers belong to the Ministry of Social Affairs are to be consulted when developing transition programs as they hold important information regarding vocational training and job placement available for individuals with disabilities.

In the long term, action needs to be taken at the government level including formulating policy that authorizes clear, accurate, and comprehensive written statements regarding achievable post school employment outcomes for each student with a disability reflecting that student's and their family's aspirations.

Student Development

Critical elements of the model in the category of *student development* include (1) assessment; (2) career and vocational education; (3) employment skills instruction including advanced vocational skills; (4) availability of work experience; and (5) access to support services. These critical elements are discussed next.

In regards to *assessment*, practices that are age appropriate and on-target can only be achieved if the school employs proper assessment tools and competent staff to develop and conduct the assessments. Therefore, it is essential for schools to develop assessment tools that can assess student ability (pre-assessment), student progress (on-going assessment) and student achievement (summative assessment).

Furthermore, the content of assessment should cover broad areas of development, and not simply focus on basic literacy and numeracy and basic independent living skills (e.g., toilet training), which is the case currently. Most importantly, as the students move toward senior secondary school, conducting vocational pre-assessment is essential. The results of these assessment practices should be available in a well-documented, written format to provide legitimate verification for the transition support received by students. Assessment also provides clear information for developing plans with related stakeholders. As reported in the findings, most of the schools keep samples of students' work. The school should ensure that these samples are used to inform decisions for school to work transition program development.

Considering the inconsistency in implementing the vocational education ratio as required by government, schools should ensure that the ratio of 60% of vocational education is implemented correctly in their curriculum framework. In addition, the practice of career and vocational education curriculum that currently focuses on vocational skills only, should be extended. Schools should develop a clear and longitudinal career and vocational education structure that covers broad areas such as career awareness, career exploration, career preparation, and job placement according to the appropriate level of schooling. The curriculum framework should also support the connection between academic and vocational skills subjects.

The curriculum framework should also facilitate appropriate life skills and employment skills instruction. Life skills instruction, such as self-determination is an essential main component for active student involvement and future goals' direction. Moreover, schools should facilitate vocational skills that are marketable and matched with student interest, job availability, and/or further training that is available in the community. When deciding on the types of vocational skills to be offered in the schools, it is important for each school to conduct appropriate student assessments and consult with relevant stakeholders that organize further training and provide jobs for individuals with physical and intellectual disabilities in the community. In addition, considering reported accidents that occurred during vocational skills instruction and work experience, work safety skills should also be part of the curriculum. Students need to be aware of work safety and know how to react appropriately, either to avoid or act upon an emergency situation. Staff should be trained to prevent accidents, respond appropriately to incidents and teach students work safety skills.

In regards to issues in the *structured work experience* cluster, action needs to be taken by the school including providing suitable work experience regardless of the type of disabilities. This can be accomplished by establishing collaborative partnerships with local businesses. Furthermore, reflecting upon the implementation of current internship programs; there is a strong need for the schools to formulate written standard procedures of how the program is planned, implemented, and evaluated. The roles of the school and relevant stakeholders should be articulated clearly in the document with standard procedures for sharing resources and information. Furthermore, students' work experience should also be documented for monitoring and evaluation purposes.

Required school actions in the *support service* cluster include facilitated access to physiotherapy for students with physical disabilities. This physiotherapy support should occur from as young an age as possible. Schools that do not have physiotherapy facilities should establish collaborations to provide this service. In relation to accessibility, the school should consider accessibility for all facilities and infrastructure as accessibility is crucial for active student involvement. Providing information regarding further education, training and employment opportunities is important as the findings demonstrated that most students and parents were not aware of the availability of such opportunities. Schools should form partnerships with relevant stakeholders to provide this information; similar to careers guidance programs in Australian schools.

At the external stakeholder's level, the provincial Department of Education, through their school supervisors, should ensure that relevant assessment tools are available at the school, and teachers have developed the competencies to conduct assessments. Teacher competencies will be explained in detail in the *program structure* category later in this chapter. School supervisors should maintain effective procedures to ensure that the ratio of vocational education is correctly implemented and that the curriculum accommodates an appropriate balance of career and vocational education, life skills, and employment skills instruction.

External stakeholders such as the District Department of Social Affairs, NGOs, and business leaders need to be involved in the arrangement of work experience and support services. Together with the school, external stakeholders, particularly business leaders, must be included in formulating standard proced- ures for the internship program, and defining their roles in the program. These organizations hold important information on further education, training, and employment for individuals with disabilities; it is essential to develop effective collaborative practices for information sharing.

At the national government level, long-term goals include formulating policy specifically on a curriculum framework that includes transition education related skills. This policy should also obligate effective assessment practices and collaboration between related departments to facilitate quality transition pro- grams. Furthermore, to reach the transition goal in terms of employment, policies by the national government should arrange specific, adequate supports for businesses and companies to hire persons with disabilities and provide sufficient support to encourage individuals with disabilities to be involved in self- employment (if appropriate). In addition, it is recommended that government provides a support framework for special schools to operate small businesses at the school site (e.g., the bitternut cracker and *batik* production). Government policy and legislation to ensure accessibility in public spaces, transportations, and buildings are essential to the structural operations of transition programming and are necessary at the national level.

INTERAGENCY COLLABORATION

With respect to the *Interagency Collaboration* category, two main issues include (1) the current internship program in business sites and (2) collaboration with existing businesses, other government and nongovernment organizations. As mentioned earlier, there is a need for schools and related stakeholders to develop written standard procedures of how the internship program is planned, implemented, and evaluated. The roles of the school, business, and other related stakeholders such as the Provincial Department of Education, as the financier, should be clearly articulated in the document with standard procedures for sharing resources and information. In regards to collaboration with existing businesses, schools need to have clear and well-defined guidelines that provide benefits not only to business, but also to the schools and their students to avoid exploitation. This guidance should be discussed and approved by all parties in the entrepreneurial arrangement to ensure strong commitment and mutual benefit. In relation to collaboration with other related stakeholders (such as the Department of Social Affairs and nongovernment organizations), it is important to note that collaboration based on personal relationships between the school principal/ teachers with business leaders or staff in related departments, should be extended into systematic collaboration for greater sustainability. Possible collaboration includes further training and education, employment information, job placement, joint staff activities, and sharing of resources.

School supervisors are expected to ensure that the collaboration framework and practices comply with the values of mutual relationships, shared responsibility, shared resources, and jointly developed authority and accountability for success.

The action needed to be taken at the national government level is the handover/referral framework to support individuals with disability from birth until adulthood including employment, further education and training. This framework should make clear which government and non-government organizations may be involved and outline an effective scheme of interagency collaboration. In relation to some schools that have small businesses on site, the government needs to designate related ministries or departments to provide a support framework to schools in the area of staff, equipment, and marketing.

FAMILY INVOLVEMENT

Concern in the *family involvement* category includes (1) family involvement in the program planning; (2) family training in transition programs; and (3) family empowerment.

The most important issue needing to be addressed is the involvement of all parents in program planning, not only the few parents who sit on the school committee. By doing this, the unique individual family's needs and circumstances will be addressed appropriately in the planning process. Active family involvement can be achieved by employing suitable approaches such as PCP that focuses on both the student's interests and family needs. Opportunities for active family involvement can be provided by the school through parent training including (1) training to the family on effective program involvement, (2) family empowerment and advocacy, and (3) how to support their child to become a leader in program decision making. Schools can also establish collaborative partnerships with other related stakeholders to deliver training to families. In order to be able to provide considerable opportunities and effective training to parents, competent teachers are required. Schools should equip teachers with suitable knowledge and skills on how to collaborate with families effectively.

At the external stakeholder level, the school supervisor needs to create an effective scheme to ensure that families are involved in the transition program and that training is available and accessible to all families A policy framework from the national government to support greater family involvement concurrently with support for active student involvement is recommended.

PROGRAM STRUCTURE

It is suggested that the model should address important issues within the *program structure* category that include (1) employment as a post school outcome; (2) program evaluation; (3) strategic planning at district, provincial, and national levels; (4) program policy at school, provincial and national levels; (5) human resource development that includes qualified teachers, strong school leadership, ongoing staff professional development, and initial teacher education; and (6) resource arrangements that include sharing resources and improved funding.

In relation to employment as a designated post-school outcome, the school needs to acknowledge this in the curriculum through the provision of quality school to work transition programs that potentially lead to successful employment outcomes. Quality school to work transition programs cannot be accomplished unless the school seriously considers the individual needs and interests of students and families. School supervisors have the authority to ensure these provisions are performed by the school and therefore should take action accordingly. The national government is able to support this action by establishing a national framework for transition education.

As discussed earlier, improving interagency collaboration is essential in achieving quality school to work transition programs. Thus, the school needs to plan their strategies carefully to implement strong collaboration between related stakeholders at the school level, the external stakeholders at district and provincial levels, and government organizations at the national level. The most important strategies at the school level include providing school to work transition programs that are student focused, fully develop student potential, and respect family involvement. The district and provincial external stakeholder actions are discussed in the interagency collaboration section in this chapter.

The school also needs to formulate an effective scheme to evaluate school to work transition programs. This scheme should place emphasis on ongoing evaluation and use the evaluation outcomes for program improvement. This evaluation is not limited to the implementation of the transition program conducted at the school, but also places emphasis on the framework that includes related policies and procedures, and collaboration with related external stakeholders. Furthermore, the school needs to specify students' and families' roles in the evaluation, and the roles of related external stakeholders (if applicable). School supervisors should provide an effective scheme to ensure that program evaluation documentation is available at school, and that each stakeholder is actively involved in the evaluation.

Acknowledgment of the school to work transition program should be translated into school policy, and relevant actions need to be measured to ensure that the policies are implemented adequately. At the external stakeholder level, especially in government organizations, policies and practices that support school to work transition programs such as further training, work experience, and other related services should be formulated. At the national level, a policy regarding school to work transition programming is needed to ensure access to funding is equitable among provinces.

Concerning issues related to human resource development, schools need to ensure that they have competent teachers to provide adequate school to work transition programs. This could be accomplished by providing ongoing professional development. Teacher training in strategic issues such as person-centered planning, formulating an ITP from an IEP, assessment, working with family and related stakeholders, and collaboration skills are essential practices to be undertaken immediately. The Department of Education should ensure that appropriate ongoing professional development is available continuously for the teachers, whereas at the National Government level, schemes for teacher certification assessment should include assessing teaching performance and acknowledging transition competencies. The National Government should outline minimum standard competencies of initial teacher preparation programs, not only in the area of special education overall, but also in transition programs specifically. Universities that provide special education teacher preparation programs must equip their student teachers so they meet the minimum standard criteria of a beginner teacher. Furthermore, the national government should provide a framework that acknowledges ongoing professional development as a scheme to maintain teacher registration and certification. Before doing so, the national government should establish specific special education teacher standard competencies.

In order to maintain national quality education services, the Department of Education should ensure that competent teachers and funding are distributed equitably across special schools. In addition, further in-service teacher professional development opportunities should be allocated equitably among the schools, not one per school as is the current process. This will allow the development of a new, expanded cohort of competent teaching staff. Strong school leadership should be a key feature of a successful school. Therefore, school supervisors need to generate an effective scheme to ensure that quality leadership occurs in schools. This may be through a combination of professional development opportunities for principals and principal performance assessment.

Regarding resource allocation, schools need to develop a framework for sharing resources within the school and sharing resources with business. The Department of Education can outline a framework for sharing resources between special schools located in the district or provincial level, and between special schools and businesses and/or relevant stakeholders. The school should provide strategy for an effective funding scheme in school to work transition programs and school supervisors need to monitor that allocated funding is spent appropriately. The national Government can provide additional funding for school to work transition programs, not only for special schools, but also for relevant departments and businesses that support individuals with disabilities' employment.

CONCLUSION

Indonesian sustainable development goals acknowledged the agenda of improving the social and economic inequalities experienced by persons with disabilities due to the imbalance of power, influence, and voice in the development process (BAPPENAS, 2020). Therefore, effective school to work transition programs could provide broader opportunities for students with disabilities to make a meaningful economic contribution as member of society in the same basis as their non-disabled peers that eventually will improve their social status. There is no doubt that transition practices delivered in schools are essential in preparing students with disabilities for life after school (Crockett & Hardman, 2010b). However, they will only be successful if there is also an effective support system that includes the development of collaborative partnerships from relevant stakeholders.

REFERENCES

Azizah, N. (2016). *School to work transition programs for students with physical disabilities in Indonesian special schools*. Doctoral Dissertation, The Flinders University. https://flex.flinders.edu.au/file/3165517e-5f70-4c3b-94dc-1054f2d35fb0/1/ThesisAzizah2016.pdf

BAPPENAS. (2020). Pedoman teknis penyusunan rencana aksi–Edisi II Tujuan Pembangunan Berkelanjutan/sustainable development goals (TPB/SDGs). http://sdgs.bappenas.go.id/wp-content/uploads/2020/10/Buku-Pedoman-Rencana-Aksi-SDGs.pdf

Bassett, D., & Kochhar-Bryant, C. A. (2012). Adolescent transition education and school reform. In M. L. Wehmeyer & K. W. Webb (Eds.), *Handbook of adolescent transition education for youth with disabilities*. Routledge.

Beamish, W., Meadows, D., & Davies, M. (2012). Benchmarking teacher practice in Queensland transition program for youth with intellectual disability and autism. *The Journal of Special Education, 45*(4), 227–241.

Benz, M. R., Lindstrom, L., & Yovanoff, P. (2000). Improving graduation and employment outcomes of students with disabilities: Predictive factors and student perspectives. *Exceptional Children, 66*(4), 509–529. https://doi.org/10.1177/001440290006600405

Blacher, J., Kraemer, B. R., & Howell, E. J. (2010, March). Family expectations and transition experiences for young adults with severe disabilities: Does syndrome matter? *Advances in Mental Health and Learning Disabilities, 4*(1), 3–16.

BPS. (2020). www.bps.go.id. https://www.bps.go.id/indicator/12/1886/1/jumlah-penduduk-hasil-proyeksi-menurut-provinsi-dan-jenis-kelamin.html

Brewer, D., Karpur, A., Pi, S., Erickson, W., Unger, D., & Malzer, V. (2011). Evaluation of multi-site transition to adulthood program for youth with disabilities. *Journal of Rehabilitation, 7*, 3–13.

Bronfenbrenner, U. (1977). Toward an experimental ecology of human development. *American Psychologist, 32*(7), 513–531.

Bronfenbrenner, U. (1979). *The ecology of human development: Experiments by nature and design.* Harvard University Press.

Bronfenbrenner, U. (1986). Ecology of the family as a context for human development: Research perspectives. *Developmental Psychology, 22*(6), 723–742.

Crockett, M. A., & Hardman, M. L. (2010a). *Expected outcomes and emerging values successful transition programs: Pathways for students with intellectual and developmental disabilities.* Sage.

Crockett, M. A., & Hardman, M. L. (2010b). The role of secondary education in transition. In J. McDonnell & M. L. Hardman (Eds.), *Successful transition programs: Pathways for students with intellectual and developmental disabilities.* Sage.

Davies, M. (2014). Secondary school inclusion and transition to life after school. In P. Foreman & M. Arthur-Kelly (Eds.), *Inclusion in action* (4th ed., pp. 501–550). Cengage.

Davies, M., & Beamish, W. (2009). Transition from school for young adult with intellectual disability: Parental perspectives on "life as an adjustment". *Journal of Intellectual and Development Disability, 34*(3), 248–257.

Department for Education and Department of Health. (2015) *Special educational needs and disability code of practice: 0–25 years.* Department for Education.

Direktorat Pembinaan Sekolah Menengah Kejuruan. (2017). *Strategi implementasi revitalisasi SMK (10 langkah revitalisasi SMK).* Kemenrian Pendidikan dan Kebudayaan.

IDEA (Individual with Disabilities Education Improvement Act) of 2004, Pub .L. No 108-446 20 U.S.C. § 1400. (2004).

Indonesian Education Act No 3. (2003). National education system. Indonesia.

Institute for Economic and Social Research. (2017). *Mapping persons with disabilities (PWD) in Indonesia labor market–final report.* ILO.

Irwanto, Kasim, E. R., Lusli, M., & Siradj, O. (2010). *The situation of people with disability in Indonesia: A desk review.* Centre for Disability Studies, Faculty of Social and Political Science Universitas Indonesia.

Knapp, M., Perkins, M., Beecham, J., Dhanasiri, S., & Rustin, C. (2008). Transition pathways for young people with complex disabilities: Exploring the economic consequences. *Child: Care, Health and Development, 34*(4), 512–520. https://doi.org/10.1111/j.1365-2214.2008.00835.x

Kohler, P. D. (1996). *Taxonomy for transition programing.* University of Illinois.

Kohler, P. D., Gothberg, J. E., Fowler, C., & Coyle, J. (2016). *Taxonomy for transition programming 2. 0: A model for planning, organizing, and evaluating transition education, services, and programs.* Western Michigan University. www.transitionta.org

Marjuki. (2010). Penyandang cacat berdasarkan klasifikasi ICF. Kepala Badan Penelitian dan Pendidikan, Kemensos RI.

Ministry of Education and Culture. (2017). Lampiran III Peraturan Direktur Jenderal Pendidikan dasar dan menengah Nomor 10/D/KR/2017 on struktur kurikulum, kompetensi inti-kompetensi dasar, dan pedoman implementasi kurikulum 2013 pendidikan khusus.

Ministry of Marine & Fishery. (2020). Konektifitas Pulau-pulau kecil dan terluar melalui pembangunan dermaga apung. https://kkp.go.id/djprl/artikel/23283-konektifitas-pulau-pulau-kecil-dan-terluar-melalui-pembangunan-dermaga-apung

Noonan, P. M., Morningstar, M. E., & Erickson, A. G. (2008). Improving interagency collaboration: Effective strategies used by high-performing local districts and communities. *Career Development for Exceptional Individuals, 31*(3), 132–143.

NZ Ministry of Education. (2011). *National transition guidelines for specialist educators, schools and parents: Guidelines for transitioning students with special needs from school to adult life.* Ministry of Education.

Sheppard-Jones, K., Garret, B., & Huff, M. B. (2007). Community-based work experiences for students with significant disabilities: Real world work equals real-world success. *International Journal on Disability and Human Development, 6*(1), 47–52.

Susenas. (2018). Statistik Kesejahteraan Rakyat. https://www.bps.go.id/publication/2018/11/26/81ede2d56698c07d510f6983/statistik-kesejahteraan-rakyat-2018.html

Unicef. (2019). Children with disabiities and education. https://www.unicef.org/indonesia/media/2716/file/Children-with-Disabilites-and-Education-2020.pdf

Wehman, P. (2006). Transition: The bridge from youth to adulthood. In P. Wehman (Ed.), *Life beyond the classroom: Transition strategies for young people with disabilities* (4th ed., pp. 3–40). Paul H Brookes.

Wehman, P., & Targett, P. S. (2012). IEP development in adolescent transition education. In M. L. Wehmeyer & K. W. Webb (Eds.), *Handbook of adolescent transition education for youth with disabilities* (pp. 3–31). Routledge.

Wehmeyer, M. L., & Webb, K. W. (2012). An introduction to adolescent transition education. In M. L. Wehmeyer & K. W. Webb (Eds.), *Handbook of adolescent transition education for youth with disabilities* (pp. 3–31). Routledge.

Winn, S., & Hay, I. (2009). Transition from school for youths with a disability: Issues and challenges. *Disability & Society, 24*(1), 103–115.

BARRIERS TO COMMUNITY RE-ENTRY FOR INCARCERATED YOUTH: STAKEHOLDERS' PERSPECTIVES IN AUSTRALIA AND THE UNITED STATES

Iva Strnadová, Heather Griller Clark, Sue C. O'Neill, Therese M. Cumming, Sarup R. Mathur, Timothy C. Wells and Joanne Danker

ABSTRACT

This chapter examines the barriers to reentry for justice involved young people in the US and Australia from the perspectives of the 44 Australian and 14 US stakeholders who work with them. The interviews were analyzed using inductive content analysis to identify key internal and external barriers. Results suggest a need for improvement in the areas of collaboration among systems, family engagement, and student self-determination. The discussion focuses on the similarities and differences in the barriers that exist across nations and systems. Implications for future research, practice, and policy are included to improve transition services and supports for juvenile justice involved youth.

Keywords: Juvenile justice; transition reentry; community reintegration; inductive content analysis; family engagement; student self-determination

Transition Programs for Children and Youth with Diverse Needs
International Perspectives on Inclusive Education, Volume 18, 245–263
Copyright © 2022 Iva Strnadová, Heather Griller Clark, Sue C. O'Neill, Therese M. Cumming, Sarup R. Mathur, Timothy C. Wells and Joanne Danker
Published under exclusive licence by Emerald Publishing Limited
ISSN: 1479-3636/doi:10.1108/S1479-363620220000018017

INTRODUCTION

The issue of juvenile incarceration is of international concern. When young people commit crimes and are placed in residential settings like detention centers, treatment programs, or correctional facilities, they are removed from their families, schools, and communities. Most countries operate under the *United Nations Standard Minimum Rules for Administration of Juvenile Justice*, or the *Beijing Rules* (United Nations, 1985), which encourage diversion rather than punishment. Therefore, the intent of most confining agencies is to provide therapy, rehabilitation, and instruction in positive, lawful, and pro-social behavior (see Article 26.1, United Nations, 1985). However, when these young people reenter their communities, they continue to need services and supports that are equally as intense as those they received while detained or incarcerated. This chapter presents the perspectives of stakeholders who work with young people who are, or have been, incarcerated in one Australian and one US state, highlighting the similarities and differences in the barriers that exist across nations and systems.

BARRIERS TO COMMUNITY REENTRY

Youth Perspective

When young people are released from juvenile justice (JJ) facilities, they face internal and external barriers to community reentry (Unruh et al., 2009). Internal barriers refer to how young people perceive themselves – their self-concept, belief in themselves, and self-motivation to change their course of action. Studies that have explored youths' beliefs and attitudes suggest some youths could not envision a life on-the-outs (Abrams, 2012; Dawes, 2011), others voiced a lack of motivation to change their own behavior (Abrams, 2012; Unruh et al., 2009), and concerns with negative peer affiliations (Terry & Abrams, 2017), a lack of self-efficacy inhibited youths from changing their life course or resisting temptations (Todis et al., 2001; Unruh et al., 2009). Added to this were concerns about their key academic skills – i.e., math, reading, and writing – as well as not knowing details about credits and graduation requirements (Mathur & Clark, 2014; Field & Abrams, 2010). Negative perceptions of schools, and other agencies within the communities also influenced youths' views of self-worth and efficacy, leading to feelings of stigmatization and alienation (Dawes, 2011; Field & Abrams, 2010). External barriers to reentry are those that pertain to legal, situational, or procedural issues. Legal issues may include restrictions imposed due to disclosure of criminal history on education, employability and hiring decisions and housing opportunities. Procedural or situational barriers include difficulty transferring transcripts or documents from juvenile justice (JJ) facilities to schools or other educational or vocational agencies delaying or limiting access to education and employment (Unruh et al., 2009).

Youth in a number of studies have identified a lack of, or inconsistencies in mental health, substance abuse, or other treatment while in custody and during reentry as having negative impact on their success (Abram et al., 2015; Lieben-berg & Ungar, 2014). Other external barriers include dysfunctional rather than supportive social relationships with families, partners, and peers (Field & Abrams, 2010; Mendes et al., 2014; Unruh et al., 2009).

Stakeholders' Perspective

While it is important that JJ facilities document and address barriers to reentry from the point of view of the young people, it is also important to understand and identify the barriers as perceived by stakeholders who work with incarcerated and formerly incarcerated youth. Those who work to support young people reentering society are privy to the daily challenges and issues their clients experience, and the barriers that impede their ability to perform their role satisfactorily.

Research from the perspective of these stakeholders is limited. What is known is derived mostly from research conducted in the United States, with less research emanating from other countries such as Australia. The following is an overview of existing research studies regarding specific internal and systemic barriers identified by stakeholders.

Low Academic and Behavioral Expectations

Low academic and behavioral expectations, labeling, stigmatization by teachers and administrators, and bureaucracy/unsupportive policies in systems can act as barriers to youths completing their education via enrollment in their community school (Cole & Cohen, 2013; Houchins et al., 2009; Sinclair et al., 2017). In some school districts in the United States, formerly incarcerated youth do not have the choice to return to their community school and are automatically enrolled in alternate education placements, known for their poor high school graduation rates (Lopez, 2010; The Council of State Governments Justice Center, 2015). For those who are permitted to enroll, Cole and Cohen (2013) noted that some teachers refused to enroll formerly incarcerated youth under state education codes related to behavior. When one teacher refused to have a youth in their class, others often followed.

Lack of Management of Youth Behavior

Other issues included a lack of responsibility for managing issues of youth behavior (e.g., truancy). Oftentimes, probation officers are required to deal with behavioral issues that are usually handled by teachers and administrators. In one of the Australian studies by Mendes et al. (2014), the authors pointed out that these push-out practices negatively impact youths' ability to complete their secondary education and meet court-imposed parole conditions.

Lack of Access to Educational Services

A lack of systematic or flexible enrollment procedures for JJ involved youth acts as a barrier to engagement in education (Hagner et al., 2008). Efforts to re-enroll youths can be stymied by needing to un-enroll from the JJ facility school and then re-enroll in the community school, which can be heavily delayed by missing paperwork (Cole & Cohen, 2013; Mathur & Clark, 2014; Newell & Salazar, 2010).

Another barrier identified was the lack of access to the same educational services and programs that non-incarcerated youth experience in the community. JJ facility teachers have expressed concerns that state education expectations are overly demanding and unrealistic given the low literacy and numeracy capabilities of their students, high levels of under-identified special education needs, and that their classrooms are composed of students working at diverse academic levels (Houchins et al., 2009; Macomber et al., 2010). Teachers and administrators have also expressed concerns about curriculum disparities between JJ facility schools and community schools, and problems in receiving credit for courses completed while incarcerated (Houchins et al., 2009; Mathur & Clark, 2014).

For youths returning to community schools, it has been reported that some schools do not provide the mandated special education services to youth with disabilities, including strategies to manage behavior (Burke & Delmage, 2016; Newell & Salazar, 2010; Sinclair et al., 2017). Teachers in community schools have reported they are lacking the resources and training needed to support court-involved youth and find their behavior overwhelming (Crosby et al., 2015). When problems arise, many schools resort to exclusionary discipline measures such as suspension (Burke & Delmage, 2016). This can breach court-imposed conditions and cause the youth to return to the JJ facility (Cole & Cohen, 2013; Newell & Salazar, 2010).

Lack of Transition Specialists
Lack of designated personnel (e.g., transition specialists, caseworkers) to assist youths in the transition back to school can also act as a barrier (Newell & Salazar, 2010). Transition specialists can improve the communication between sending and receiving schools, which has been reported as deficient by JJ facility teachers and administrators (Macomber et al., 2010). Such specialists could also improve community engagement (Macomber et al., 2010; Mathur & Clark, 2014). This barrier impacts youths' access to state curriculum, vocational skills, meeting probation conditions, and ensuring adequate progress is made to enable transition back into local school systems, colleges, or the workforce.

Lack of Treatment and Community Services
Stakeholders also identified a lack of services and supports in the community as barriers (Mendes et al., 2014; Risler & O'Rourke, 2009; Unruh et al., 2009). A lack of economic opportunities (Hartwell et al., 2010; Risler & O'Rourke, 2009), alcohol and other drug services, mental health services (Kapp et al., 2013), services that can teach independent living skills (Mathur & Clark, 2014; Mendes

et al., 2014; Unruh et al., 2009), and leisure options leave youths without needed skills, supports, and prosocial community engagement.

A significant number of incarcerated youths have substance misuse issues (Schufelt & Cocozza, 2006). However, many youths do not engage in treatment at reentry, and continue to use (Mendes et al., 2014; Risler & O'Rourke, 2009). Wisdom et al. (2011) found that youths' and parents' denial of the problem impacted seeking out necessary treatment at reentry. Further, families had difficulties finding appropriate services and treatment facilities, and had limited knowledge about the system and how it worked. In many cases, unless services were mandated by the court, probation officers felt they could do little to get youth to attend (Newell & Salazar, 2010).

Similar issues in engaging in treatment at reentry exist for incarcerated youth with mental health issues. A 2017 Office of Juvenile Justice and Delinquency Prevention report estimated that 65–70% of young people in the JJ system in the US meet the criteria for one or more mental health disorders (Development Services Group, 2017). Unfortunately, not all youths receive treatment during confinement (Kapp et al., 2013). Further, Chung et al. (2007) found that at reentry only 35% of young people were engaged with mental health services. They suggested a lack of community services, healthcare coverage, and ability to navigate multiple systems acted as barriers.

Newell and Salazar (2010) found that of the 50–60% of youths who were involved in gangs, only 10% received aftercare programs that addressed gang membership. Further, safety issues were reported by probation staff as they traveled into communities with high gang activity to work with youths on probation.

Beyond a lack of services, barriers arose in how service systems operated. Intra- and inter-organizational barriers have been identified by stakeholders in education, employment, health, and accommodation domains (Anthony et al., 2010; Strnadová et al., 2017).

Problems in Interagency Collaboration
Poor interagency linkages have impacted service provision to youth at reentry in a number of US, Australian, and Swedish studies (Andersson Vogel et al., 2014; Marshall et al., 2012; Mendes et al., 2014; Murphy, 2018). Stakeholders in an Australian study (Mendes et al., 2014) reported that they were not always invited to contribute to case management plans. A lack of collaboration led to agencies operating in silos, causing gaps or duplication in services, and confusion as to who was responsible for what (Andersson Vogel et al., 2014; Fader & Dum, 2013; Mendes et al., 2014). Information sharing between agencies has also negatively impacted service provision, highlighting the need for privacy releases to be signed early on by families (Kapp et al., 2013). Issues have also been reported in inadequate data management and data pooling on clients between multiple agencies, which impedes aftercare planning (Newell & Salazar, 2010). Interagency agreements have been recommended by stakeholders to overcome these issues (Strnadová et al., 2017).

Large Caseloads and System Bureaucracy
Large caseloads were also problematic and impacted the time that stakeholders could spend collaborating with other agencies (Andersson Vogel et al., 2014; Fader & Dum, 2013; Kapp et al., 2013), including attending to pre-release planning (Mendes et al., 2014; Newell & Salazar, 2010), and providing services to youths (Mendes et al., 2014). This was an issue for JJ workers in Australia who had clients in rural areas (Mendes et al., 2014). High caseloads also impacted the timely delivery of reports needed for court, and the delivery services needed at reentry (Newell & Salazar, 2010). Time constraints also impacted (1) finding the right school, (2) after-school leisure activities, (3) family preparation or sustained supports, (4) medication supplied on discharge or planning for supporting its continued use, and (5) health service coordination and organization (Newell & Salazar, 2010). Large caseloads can also lead to personnel attrition, which affects the continuity of service and relationship development between youths, their families, and caseworkers.

System bureaucracy has been reported to impact the time that caseworkers can spend supporting their clients during the transition and reentry phase (Mendez et al., 2014). Excessive paperwork, one-size-fits-all programming, and inadequate remuneration create barriers to supporting youths at reentry and retaining personnel (Fader & Dum, 2013). Youth also have been reported to struggle with system bureaucracy, experiencing difficulties navigating systems, completing paperwork for financial support, and obtaining supports when transitioning to the adult service systems (Mendes et al., 2014).

Lack of Preparedness and Capacity of Stakeholders
Not knowing what support services exist in the community resulted in the absence of essential domains such as mental health services, legal services, and after-school recreational services in youth's transition plans being absent (Kapp et al., 2013). Differing philosophies between JJ and mental health agency personnel were also an issue that led to disagreements that impacted the legal decisions made for youth. Different values between stakeholders also affected youths' education. Some JJ facility teachers expressed that JJ personnel did not value the importance of education, seeing it as something that just occupied youths' days (Macomber et al., 2010). This lack of respect for the value of education led to frequent interruptions to their teaching by JJ personnel, and impacted the behavior of students adversely. It also impacted consistency in behavior management. A desire for more collaborative meetings was expressed by facility teachers.

Stakeholders' limited capacity can also create barriers to youths' successful reentry. Concerns have been raised about probation officers not meeting reentry program requirements for their clients (Newell & Salazar, 2010). Fader and Dum (2013) were concerned about the lack of person-centered planning skills of personnel developing reentry plans and programs that led to youth completing activities that did not match their needs or interests. In Australia, Trotter (2012) found that caseworkers who demonstrated more effective casework skills and good rapport with their clients had clients with lower recidivism rates, and that the converse was true. A lack of preparedness and compassion from service workers has also been reported (Mincey et al., 2008). JJ facility teachers in the Macomber et al. (2010) study also expressed a desire for more professional development, time for case management, and resources.

RATIONALE AND RESEARCH QUESTIONS

Although there have been a few studies that have explored the perspectives of stakeholders regarding the barriers that exist for youth reentering their community post-incarceration (see Mendes et al., 2014), none have taken a comparative approach, looking at stakeholders' perceptions across agencies or across two nations. In this study, stakeholders in one Australian and one US state were asked to identify barriers that adversely affect the reentry process for youth leaving JJ facilities. It is essential to ascertain the perspectives of these stakeholders across various settings so that transition services and supports can be designed to meet the needs of the youth more effectively in mitigating barriers to reentry and promoting successful engagement in school and employment.

The following research questions guided this comparative study: According to JJ stakeholders, what are the barriers that impede a youth's success when they are released and return to the community in Australia and the United States? What are the similarities and differences in barriers experienced by youth returning to their communities between the two countries?

The Australian Study

The Australian study posed the question (i.e., What are the barriers that impede a youth's success when they are released and return to the community) to stakeholders by examining the transition process, from the stance of both the education and corrections, for three or more months in six New South Wales (NSW) Australia juvenile justice facilities.

The United States (US) Study

The US study attempted to replicate the AU study in many regards in order to provide a comparative analysis of stakeholder perspectives. The US study was less exploratory in nature, as the authors have a long-standing relationship with the agency that oversees juvenile corrections and are currently working with the agency on several different projects. However, efforts were undertaken to identify a matched sample of personnel for the interviews in this study.

METHODS

Australian Participants and Setting

The Australian research study took place in six NSW rural and urban juvenile justice facilities. These facilities each have a school onsite run by the NSW

Department of Education called education and training units. These schools provide education to young people of mandatory school age serving custodial sentences. The participants ($N = 44$) in this study were the following:

- The school principals ($n = 6$), assistant principals ($n = 3$), teachers ($n = 7$), a teacher's aide ($n = 1$), a school counselor ($n = 1$), and a school transition specialist ($n = 1$).
- The juvenile justice facility managers ($n = 6$), and assistant managers ($n = 4$).
- Other juvenile justice center staff members who worked with incarcerated youth that understood transition processes; specifically, juvenile justice center psychologists ($n = 2$), unit managers ($n = 2$), assistant unit managers ($n = 2$), a justice health community integration team clinician ($n = 1$), a representative of a nongovernmental organization ($n = 1$), and youth officers ($n = 5$).
- A mainstream school principal ($n = 1$), and a mainstream school teacher ($n = 1$).

There were 22 females and 22 males participating in this study. The age of participants ranged from 30 to 64 years, with an average age of 47 years. The conducted interviews ranged in length from 9:55 minutes to 80:59 minutes, with an average length of 35:44 minutes.

Australian Study Procedures

Ethical clearance was sought and obtained from the researchers' institutional research review board, the NSW Department of Education research branch, and the NSW Department of Juvenile Justice research department. The researchers then contacted the six principals of the education and training units, and managers of the six juvenile justice centers by e-mail and invited them and their personnel to participate in the study.

The participants of this study met with the researchers at a mutually convenient time. The participants were asked a series of questions about the transition planning process for incarcerated young people of mandatory school age, with a focus on interagency collaboration during this process. The authors developed interview protocols with semi-structured interview questions, grounded in literature review conducted by the authors and following the *Taxonomy of Transition Programming 2.0* (Kohler et al., 2016).

US Participants and Setting

The US study took place at one JJ facility in the southwestern United States. This facility operates an accredited school that provides education to young people between the age of 8 and 18. The participants ($N = 14$) in this study were the following:

- The school principal ($n = 1$), assistant principal ($n = 1$), teacher ($n = 1$), school counselor ($n = 1$).

- The juvenile justice facility managers ($n = 1$), and assistant managers ($n = 1$).
- Other JJ staff members who worked with incarcerated youth that understood transition processes included psychologists ($n = 2$), unit managers ($n = 1$), assistant unit managers ($n = 2$), a justice health community integration team clinician ($n = 1$).
- Mainstream school principal ($n = 1$), and a mainstream schoolteacher ($n = 1$).

There were 6 females and 8 males participating in this study. Most participants ranged in age from 25 to 50 years.

US Study Procedures

Ethical clearance was sought and obtained from the Institutional Review Board at the university and from the agency's internal research department. The agency's research department reviewed the interview protocol developed by Australia and made changes.

The interviews were conducted in person at a mutually convenient time and location. All responses were hand written by the researchers. The participants were asked questions focusing on their role within the organization, educational background, experience working with youth with challenging behavior, and their perceptions of barriers and positive supports that impact the overall transition process.

Data Analysis

For the Australian study, the audio-recorded interviews were transcribed verbatim, and analyzed independently. As the Australian study was conducted first, Australian interview data were analyzed by the Australian authors, who then provided the findings, as well as descriptions and examples of each step of the data analysis process, to the US authors. The US authors followed the same processes to analyze their written transcripts and shared their findings with the Australian authors. This process allowed for consistency and transparency in the use of inductive content analysis across both countries (Elo & Kyngäs, 2008).

The actual data analysis process started with identifying a coding unit. Words, sentences, or paragraphs "... containing aspects related to each other through their content and context" (Graneheim & Lundman, 2004, p. 106) were considered a coding unit. In each study (i.e., Australian and US study), two interviews were independently coded by two of the authors. Another author compared the coded interviews. Any differences resulting from this process were resolved via discussion by each research team. Then, open coding (i.e., coding transcribed interviews for codes) of all of the transcribed interviews in each study was conducted by one of the authors. Another author examined the coded interviews. As a result, some of the codes were adjusted. In the next stage of coding, the researchers created categories, and resulting themes (Graneheim & Lundman, 2004). The individual research teams (i.e., Australian and US) repeatedly met, discussed, and resolved any differences. The identified internal and external

Table 1. Internal and External Barriers.

Type of Barriers	Australian Study	US Study
Internal barriers	Issues associated with youth (15/44)	Issues associated with youth (4/14)
	Stigma associated with juvenile justice (10/44)	Drugs (3/14)
External barriers	Returning to same dysfunctional community (23/44)	Returning to same dysfunctional community (10/14)
	Returning to rural/remote communities (22/44)	
	Family issues (18/44)	Family issues (9/14)
	Lack of support after discharge (13/44)	Lack of resources (7/14)
	Barriers to mainstream schooling (11/44)	Barriers to mainstream schooling (5/14)
	Short sentence (10/44)	
	Lack of collaboration among agencies (9/44)	Implementation issues (8/14) – also lack of support and lack of collaboration
	Not knowing post release accommodation circumstances (7/44)	
	Not knowing date of release (7/44)	

Note. Numbers in the brackets indicate how many participants mentioned this out of the total number of participants.

barriers in each study are shown in Table 1, in the order of frequency in which these were mentioned (from most frequently mentioned to least frequently mentioned).

Credibility and Trustworthiness of Data Analysis Process

Investigator triangulation was used in every stage of data analysis, with all authors involved to ensure credibility, validity, and trustworthiness of the process (Brantlinger et al., 2005; Whittemore et al., 2001). By discussing the results with academics from the field, the authors used a peer debriefing approach.

RESULTS

Australian Study Results

The participants identified numerous barriers to transition planning for community re-entry of incarcerated youth. These included (in the order of frequency) (1) Returning to same dysfunctional community (mentioned by 23/44 participants); (2) Returning to rural/remote communities (22/44); (3) Family issues (18/44); (4) Issues associated with youths (15/44); (5) Lack of support after discharge (13/44); (6) Barriers to mainstream schooling (11/44); (7) Stigma associated with JJ (10/44); (8) Short sentence (10/44); (9) Lack of collaboration among agencies (9/44); (10) Not knowing post release accommodation circumstances (7/44); and (11) Not knowing date of release (7/44).

Returning to same dysfunctional community. This was the most commonly identified barrier by the stakeholders in Australia. The participants reported that returning to dysfunctional communities with high levels of unemployment and poverty, negative peer influence, and high rates of crime and substance abuse interfered with successful community re-entry for a young person.

Returning to rural/remote communities. One of the major issues when returning to rural/remote communities was a lack of services across general health, mental health, education, housing, employment, etc. Another major issue was the lack of transport. The participants pointed out that it is difficult for young people re-entering the community to become successfully engaged in employment or education, when transport options are non-existent for them. This was particularly relevant to Indigenous youth, who commonly lived at missions, with no public transport available. Remote geographical locations proved to be also problematic when it comes to access to education.

Family issues. There were a number of family-related issues, which were perceived by the participants as barriers to successful community re-entry of incarcerated youth. In some instances, young people in custody were the main caretakers of their siblings, resulting in school non-attendance.

Another commonly mentioned issue was young people's experience with domestic violence, abuse and neglect, as well as their family members' issues with alcohol and drugs. Some parents had been involved with the criminal justice system themselves, and often had minimal education. Some of the participants talked about dysfunctional families, who do not provide support to incarcerated young people.

Issues associated with youths. Some of the barriers were associated with the young people themselves. These included mental health issues and disabilities (or learning difficulties), a lack of motivation to be meaningfully engaged in the community, challenging behaviors, and minimal literacy and numeracy skills. A number of participants mentioned young people's struggles with budgeting and finances in general, their problems with trusting people, and low self-esteem.

Lack of support after discharge. According to the participants, there were very limited supports available to incarcerated young people post release. The participants called for mentors, who could support the young people particularly during first three months after returning to the community. Even if some support was provided, it was not viewed as consistent and continued.

Barriers to mainstream schooling. According to the participants' experiences, young people returning back to the community had problems getting used to mainstream schooling, which is different from the education provided in juvenile justice facilities. For example, large class sizes in mainstream classrooms (compared to smaller class sizes in juvenile justice facilities) can be confronting for a young person. Sitting through approximately six hours in a classroom per day can be also difficult. The participants called for flexibility following young people's return to mainstream schools, and/or for alternative options for education.

Stigma associated with juvenile justice. Stigma was a particular barrier. The participants discussed communities' hesitance to accept back incarcerated youth. Mainstream schools were also hesitant to accept the returning young people, which meant that alternative education placements were sought after. Young people's "reputation" was also one of the reasons for difficulties with finding employment post release.

Short sentence. Some of the participants called for longer sentencing, which would allow young people to settle in, and would provide for more time to effectively work with incarcerated young people.

Lack of collaboration among agencies. Various problems related to inter-agency collaboration included a lack of communication between the sectors (e.g., juvenile justice, education), policies in place which do not match (or even contradict) each other, and a lack of clarity about roles and responsibilities of staff members. Short sentences such as 3 months were viewed as a barrier to effective transition planning. Staff members highlighted that it is particularly challenging to gather information needed (e.g., reports from previous schools), and to establish effective collaboration with all relevant stakeholders in such a short time.

Not knowing post release accommodation circumstances. Based on the participants' experience, it is particularly challenging that post-release accommodation is unknown until just prior to release. These situations can provoke anxiety in young people. Furthermore, it is almost impossible to conduct effective transition planning in such circumstances (as education placement, accommodation, etc. cannot be prearranged).

Not knowing date of release. Similarly, to the previous barrier, not knowing a release date was also a considerable obstacle to transition planning and thus to successful return to community.

US Study Results

The US participants also identified numerous re-entry barriers which both overlapped and remained distinct from the Australian participants. These barriers were coded into the following categories (in order of frequency): (1) Returning to same dysfunctional community (mentioned by 10/14 participants); (2) Family issues (9/14); (3) Implementation issues (8/14); (4) Lack of resources (7/14); (5) Barriers to mainstream schooling (5/14); (6) Issues associated with youth (4/14); and (7) Drugs (3/14). Examples of each category with explanations of decisions are provided next.

Returning to same dysfunctional community. These barriers most frequently related to the youths returning to environments (i.e., communities, peer groups) that lack positive influences that contribute to growth and development. Participants suggested that youth regularly returned to "old friends" or reestablished "gang affiliation." Additionally, responses coded in this category also referred to broader community issues, like a lack of resources to support youth upon release. For the most part, these responses indicated concern that the youth were returning to the same environments that contributed to their initial involvement with JJ.

Family issues. While similar to dysfunctional community barriers, these barriers referred directly to the family as the source of the problem. Specifically, participants identified a lack of follow-through, accountability, and involvement in transition planning and education by members of the youth's family. Additionally, some participants indicated that families not only lacked involvement but negatively influenced the youth and/or lacked the necessary skills to deal with the still troubled youth.

Implementation issues. Implementation issues referred to institutional shortcomings, service oversights and inefficiencies. While this category included the AU categories of *lack of support after discharge* and *lack of collaboration among agencies*, it also referred to services that were in place and intended to be supportive but for various reasons lacked fidelity of implementation or efficacy. Participants most frequently identified delays in service. Most often these delays related to the start times of counseling and mental health services, but also included delays in Department of Child Safety placements and parole officer assignments. Other implementation issues related to a lack of development of and follow through on success plans for the youth.

Lack of resources. Lack of resources referred to responses that directly or indirectly indicated a need for supports that were not available. Unlike implementation issues, these referred to services, programs, or supports that didn't already exist but are in fact needed. Referenced were supports both inside and outside the JJ facility. These supports ranged from mental and emotional health services (i.e. substance abuse groups and counseling support) to guidance with school enrollment upon release to supports with transportation.

Barriers to mainstream schooling. Some of the participants mentioned barriers to young people returning to mainstream schools in the community after release. One of these barriers included the length of time it takes to enroll youth in school. Participants specifically noted that there were delays in receiving school records, which causes delays in enrollment. Participants also referenced the receptiveness of mainstream schools to receiving these youth as a barrier.

Issues associated with youths. Staff also referred to youths' behavioral, mental health, or biological characteristics as barriers to success, such as youth lacking motivation and follow through, poor decision-making, and lack of compliance with facility program and rules. A number of participants mentioned that many of the young people simply lack a desire to change their criminal or substance abusive behavior. Participants also referenced disability as a barrier, this simply referred to the fact that many youth have disabilities, not that a service or accommodation was lacking, therefore we included these responses in the youth category and not the institutional or service category.

Drugs. Lastly, for some of the participants, substance abuse and drugs were identified as a leading barrier to youth reentry. Because these references were less frequent and fairly broad, we decided to keep these under a single category, separate from other categories relating to the environment or services.

DISCUSSION

This study aimed to explore the barriers that impede a youth's success when they are released and return to the community in Australia and the US. Similarities and differences in barriers experienced by youth returning to their communities between the two countries were also noted.

Similarities

The barriers to reentry, as identified by the stakeholders in this study, mirror many of those previously identified in the literature. With regard to *internal barriers*, both Australian and US participants in this study were concerned with mental health issues and disabilities, lack of motivation, poor decision making, challenging behaviors, and low self-esteem (Abram et al., 2015; Abrams, 2012). This finding further emphasizes the need for resources in treatment services, increased instruction in adaptive skills, cognitive restructuring and self-determination (McDaniel, 2015; Nelson et al., 2010).

Furthermore, Australian participants also considered the stigma related to a JJ record as a particular barrier for young people reentering the community, especially when accessing education and/or employment. US participants were also concerned about drug abuse by young people returning from JJ facilities.

With regard to external barriers, both Australian and US stakeholders reported *returning to the same dysfunctional community* as a common barrier for JJ involved youth in both countries. Both groups of participants referenced negative peers or gangs. Australian participants noted high levels of unemployment and poverty, as well as high rates of crime and substance abuse in the returning community, while US participants referenced a lack of community resources to support youth and positive influences.

Another similarity was that both groups identified *family-related issues* as a barrier to reentry. Specifically, participants referenced negative influences like domestic violence, abuse and neglect, alcohol and drugs, and parental involvement with the criminal justice system. However, both Australian and US stakeholders expressed concern that families need assistance and education, because many do not possess the necessary skills to deal with JJ involved youth.

Similar to previous research, *lack of collaboration and resources* were also barriers commonly referenced by both Australian and US stakeholders (Andersson Vogel et al., 2014; Mendes et al., 2014). Participants from both countries noted a lack of communication between juvenile justice and education, as well as a lack of clarity about roles and responsibilities of staff members. Although the US stakeholders noted that in some cases policies for services and procedures were in place, there was a lack of or delay in implementation of these services. One difference in this area was that US participants alluded to the fact some services or procedures intended to improve collaboration were in place, but for various reasons these services or procedures were not being implemented as designed, resulting in delays in counseling, mental health services, placements, and parole officer assignments.

Barriers to enrollment or re-enrollment in school were identified by stakeholders in both Australia and the US. Similar to previous research (Houchins et al., 2009; Sinclair et al., 2017) these stakeholders alluded to the fact that lack of records and receptiveness of receiving schools caused delays in enrollment.

Differences

There were also differences in perceived external barriers among the participants from the two countries. Half of the Australian participants suggested a significant barrier was the return of young people to rural and/or remote communities, where there are significantly less available services across general and mental health, education, housing, employment, etc., than in urban areas. This is not surprising, as in New South Wales, where the Australian part of the study took place, 70% of inhabitants live in regional, rural and/or remote areas (O'Neill et al., 2016).

Furthermore, the minimal to almost non-existent access to public transport, made it incredibly difficult for young people returning from JJ facilities to travel to education or employment site. In face of these adversities, the return to local rural/remote communities is almost inevitable going to result in re-engagement of a young person with juvenile justice system. Another barrier identified only by the Australian participants were short sentences. In all Australian states, incarceration is seen as a last resort, and for the shortest time deemed appropriate (Chrzanowski & Wallis, 2011). Furthermore, not knowing post release accommodation circumstances for the young people, or not knowing date of their release, made it very difficult for Australian participants to effectively plan for transition supports.

The US stakeholders were concerned with drugs as one of the internal barriers affecting the reentry success of youth in the US. They also pointed out that in some cases policies and procedures were in place for services and collaborations with mental health, education, substance abuse etc., there was a lack of resources or access causing delay in implementation of these services (Seiter, 2017).

Although the results indicate few differences pertaining to policies and implementation of services, the overall implications for future research, practice, and policy apply to both contexts.

Implications for Future Research, Practice, and Policy

The findings from this comparative study point to some important recommendations on national as well as international levels. While there are clearly differences in cultural understandings and assumptions related to reentry between the US and Australia, our findings and recommendations transcend these differences. For example, the US has federal legislation that specifically addresses reentry and youth-focused transition planning, especially for young people with disabilities, however, Australia does not. This could explain why the stigma related to having a JJ record was perceived as a barrier for Australian participants but not for US participants. Effective communication, including greater

awareness, education, and collaboration with community stakeholders is beneficial in all settings. Additionally, concern related to the provision of services and
supports for young people with mental health issues is a challenge mentioned by
both groups of participants, as was dysfunctional communities and peer groups.

The continuing lack of systematic collaboration between the involved sectors
remains a significant concern (Seiter, 2017) that needs to be addressed in both
countries. Research indicates that engagement within the first 30 days after release
is a significant predictor for positive long-term engagement (Authors, in review),
therefore JJ agencies need to collaborate with other youth serving agencies to
ensure post-release engagement. This could be facilitated by creating across-sector
professional training opportunities, so everyone serving these youth is aware of the
advantages of early engagement within the first 30 days of release. Furthermore,
allocating time and resources for team planning, with all diverse stakeholders
taking part, is yet to be achieved. A systematic response to supporting families of
the incarcerated youth is also necessary. Issues such as poverty, lack of affordable
housing, and high rates of unemployment are difficult for any family, including
those with JJ involved youth. Supports such as family counseling would make a
difference for families whose young people are in JJ facilities. Engaging families
from the time of enrollment of their young person in JJ facility, providing them
with regular updates about their children's progress, and working with them in
preparation for their child's return are essential steps to be taken by governments.
Last but not the least, a young person's cognitive restructuring and self-
determination skills need to be at the heart of any pre and post-release educational efforts to increase their ability to remain goal-directed, self-regulated, and
responsible for their actions (Griller Clark et al., 2016; McDaniel, 2015).

Strengths and Limitations of This Comparative Study

Among strengths of this study is its qualitative research design, which gave
stakeholders voice in expressing their experiences and suggestions. Another
strength of this study was the diversity of the participants from both countries
representing diverse positions from various sectors providing an in-depth
understanding about barriers facing JJ involved youth.

This study also had some limitations. First, the sample size of the US stakeholders was smaller compared to the Australian sample. In addition, the young
people in JJ facilities themselves were not interviewed, and thus their perspectives
were not captured. Future research needs to focus on capturing the views of JJ
involved youth and their caretakers.

CONCLUSION

This study contributes to the current literature on barriers to successful transition
of young people who are re-entering the community after incarceration by
providing an international comparative perspective from the viewpoints of the
stakeholders who support them. By having a comprehensive view about the

stakeholders across two countries, we have gained an in-depth understanding of the challenges faced by JJ involved youth. We have also recognized the need for specialized personnel (transition specialists, caseworkers) who work collaboratively with all stakeholders (family, school, treatment) and encourage the adoption of evidenced-based reentry practices to promote youth reentry success.

ACKNOWLEDGMENTS

The authors would like to express their sincere gratitude to the participating Australian and US stakeholders who support young people returning from juvenile justice back to the community for taking time to participate in interviews and share their experiences and perceptions. Their passion for creating a better future for incarcerated youths is truly inspirational.

The authors would like to express their gratitude to the Australian NSW Department of Education and the NSW Department of Juvenile Justice for supporting and co-funding this study. It evidences their commitment to improving the services they provide to incarcerated youth and demonstrates their intention to effectively collaborate to ensure that evidence-based transition practices are incorporated across both sectors.

FUNDING

The Australian study was supported by the Australian NSW Department of Education, the Department of Juvenile Justice, and the University of New South Wales (School of Education). The US study was made possible by a grant funded by the U. S. Department of Education, Office of Special Education Programs (H326M 120004). Opinions expressed herein do not necessarily reflect the policy of the Department of Education, and no official endorsement by the Department should be inferred.

REFERENCES

Abram, K. M., Paskar, L. D., Washburn, J. J., Teplin, L. A., Zwecker, N. A., & Azores-Gococo, N. M. (2015). *Perceived barriers to mental health services among detained youth. OJJDP Juvenile Justice Bulletin.* U.S. Department of Justice, Office of Juvenile Justice and Delinquency Prevention.

Abrams, L. S. (2012). Envisioning life "on the outs": Exit narratives of incarcerated male youth. *International Journal of Offender Therapy and Comparative Criminology, 56,* 877–896. https://doi.org/10.1177/0306624X11415042

Andersson Vogel, M., Sallnäs, M., & Lundström, T. (2014). Good idea, bad prerequisite, zero result–the meaning of context in implementing aftercare for young people in secure unit care. *Journal of Children's Services, 9,* 248–260. https://doi.org/10.1108/JCS-10-2013-0035

Anthony, E. K., Samples, M. D., de Kervor, D. N., Ituarte, S., Lee, C., & Austin, M. J. (2010). Coming back home: The reintegration of formerly incarcerated youth with service implications. *Children and Youth Services Review, 32,* 1271–1277.

Brantlinger, E., Jimenez, R., Klingner, J., Pugach, M., & Richardson, V. (2005). Qualitative studies in special education. *Exceptional Children, 71,* 195–207. https://doi.org/10.1177/001440290507100205

Burke, M. M., & Delmage, H. (2016). Special education advocacy in the juvenile justice system: Perspectives from probation officers. *Exceptionality, 24,* 151–164. https://doi.org/10.1080/09362835.2015.1064413

Chrzanowski, A., & Wallis, R. (2011). Understanding the youth justice system. In A. Stewart, T. Allard, & S. Dennison (Eds.), *Evidence based policy and practice in youth justice* (pp. 7–27). The Federation Press.

Chung, H., Schubert, C., & Mulvey, E. (2007). An empirical portrait of community reentry among serious juvenile offenders into metropolitan cities. *Criminal Justice and Behavior, 34*, 1402–1426. https://doi.org/10.1177/0093854807307170

Cole, H., & Cohen, R. (2013). Breaking down the barriers: A case study of juvenile justice personnel perspectives on school re-entry. *Journal of Correctional Education, 64*, 13–35.

Crosby, S. D., Day, A. G., Baroni, B. A., & Somers, C. L. (2015). School staff perspectives on the challenges and solutions to working with court-involved students. *Journal of School Health, 85*(6), 347–354. https://doi.org/10.1111/josh.12261

Dawes, G. D. (2011). The challenges of reintegrating indigenous youth after their release from detention. *Journal of Youth Studies, 14*(6), 693–707. https://doi.org/10.1080/13676261.2011. 580338

Development Services Group, Inc. (2017). *Intersection between mental health and the juvenile justice system: Literature review*. Office of Juvenile Justice and Delinquency Prevention. https://www. ojjdp.gov/mpg/litreviews/Intersection-Mental-Health-Juvenile-Justice.pdf

Elo, S., & Kyngäs, H. (2008). The qualitative content analysis process. *Journal of Advanced Nursing, 62*, 107–115. https://doi.org/10.1111/j.1365-2648.2007.04569.x

Fader, J. J., & Dum, C. P. (2013). Doing time, filling time: Bureaucratic ritualism as a systematic barrier to youth re-entry. *Children and Youth Services Review, 35*, 899–907. https://doi.org/10. 1016/j.childyouth.2013.03.001

Field, D., & Abrams, L. S. (2010). Gender differences in the perceived needs and barriers of youth offenders preparing for community reentry. *Child and Youth Care Forum, 39*, 253–269. https:// doi.org/10.1007/s10566-010-9102-x

Graneheim, U. H., & Lundman, B. (2004). Qualitative Content analysis in nursing research: Concepts, procedures and measures to achieve trustworthiness. *Nurse Education Today, 24*, 105–112. https://doi.org/10.1016/j.nedt.2003.10.001

Griller Clark, H., Mathur, S. R., Brock, L., O'Cummings, M., & Milligan, D. (2016). *Transition toolkit 3.0: Meeting the educational needs of youth exposed to the juvenile justice system*. National Evaluation and Technical Assistance Center for the Education of Children and Youth Who Are Neglected, Delinquent, or At Risk (NDTAC).

Hagner, D., Malloy, J. M., Mazzone, M. W., & Cormier, G. M. (2008). Youth with disabilities in the criminal justice system: Considerations for transition and rehabilitation planning. *Journal of Emotional and Behavioral Disorders, 16*, 240–247. https://doi.org/10.1177/1063426608316019

Hartwell, S., McMackin, R., Tansi, R., & Bartlett, N. (2010). "I grew up too fast for my age:" Post discharge issues and experiences of male juvenile offenders. *Journal of Offender Rehabilitation, 49*, 495–515. https://doi.org/10.1080/10509674.2010

Houchins, D. E., Puckett-Patterson, D., Crosby, S., Shippen, M. E., & Jolivette, K. (2009). Barriers and facilitators to providing incarcerated youth with a quality education. *Preventing School Failure: Alternative Education for Children and Youth, 53*(3), 159–166. https://doi.org/10.3200/ PSFL.53.3.159-166

Kapp, S. A., Petr, C. G., Robbins, M. L., & Choi, J. J. (2013). Collaboration between mental health and juvenile justice systems: Barriers and facilitators. *Child and Adolescent Social Work Journal, 30*, 505–517. https://doi.org/10.1007/s10560-013-0300-x

Kohler, P. D., Gothberg, J. E., Fowler, C., & Coyle, J. (2016). *Taxonomy for transition programming 2. 0: A model for planning, organizing, and evaluating transition education, services, and programs*. Western Michigan University. http://www.transitionta.org

Liebenberg, L., & Ungar, M. (2014). A comparison of service use among youth involved with juvenile justice and mental health. *Children and Youth Services Review, 39*, 117–122. https://doi.org/10. 1016/j.childyouth.2014.02.007

Lopez, A. R. (2010). The punishment doesn't fit the crime: The impact of juvenile adjudications on education. *Children's Legal Rights Journal, 30*, 36–47.

Macomber, D., Skiba, T., Blackmon, J., Esposito, E., Hart, L., Mambrino, E., Richie, E. T., & Grigorenko, E. L. (2010). Education in juvenile detention facilities in the state of Connecticut: A glance at the system. *Journal of Correctional Education, 61*, 223–261.

Marshall, A., Powell, N., Pierce, D., Nolan, E., & Fehringer, E. (2012). Youth and administrator perspectives on transition in Kentucky's state agency schools. *Child Welfare, 91*(2), 97–118.

Mathur, S. R., & Clark, H. G. (2014). Community engagement for reentry success of youth from juvenile justice: Challenges and opportunities. *Education and Treatment of Children, 37*(4), 713–734. https://doi.org/10.1353/etc.2014.0034

McDaniel, S. (2015). A self-determination intervention for youth placed in a short-term juvenile detention facility. *Journal of Correctional Education, 66*(3), 5–15.

Mendes, P., Baidawi, S., & Snow, P. (2014). Young people transitioning from out-of-home care in Victoria: Strengthening support services for dual clients of child protection and youth justice. *Australian Social Work, 67,* 6–23. https://doi.org/10.1080/0312407X.2013.853197

Mincey, B., Maldonado, N., Lacey, C. H., & Thompson, S. D. (2008). Perceptions of successful graduates of juvenile residential programs: Reflections and suggestions for success. *Journal of Correctional Education, 59*(1), 8–31.

Murphy, K. M. (2018). Listening to juvenile corrections school teachers: A step-by-step process for interview: Studies guided by hermeneutics. *Qualitative Report, 23*(1), 29–46.

Nelson, C. M., Jolivette, K., Leone, P. E., & Mathur, S. R. (2010). Meeting the needs of at-risk and adjudicated youth with behavioral challenges: The promise of juvenile justice. *Behavioral Disorders, 36,* 70–80.

Newell, M., & Salazar, A. (2010). *Juvenile reentry in Los Angeles County: An exploration of strengths, barriers and policy options.* https://doi.org/10.1080/1045988x.2020.1799184. www.education coordinatingcouncil.org/ECC_DOCS/.../la-county-juvenile-justice.pdf

O'Neill, S., Strnadová, I., & Cumming, T. (2016). Evidence-based transition planning practices for secondary students with disabilities: What has Australia signed up for? *Australasian Journal of Special Education, 40,* 39–58. https://doi.org/10.1017/jse.2015.15

Risler, E., & O'Rourke, T. (2009). Thinking exit and entry: Exploring outcomes of Georgia's juvenile justice education programs. *Journal of Correctional Education, 60,* 225–239.

Schufelt, J. L., & Cocozza, J. J. (2006). *Youth with mental health disorders in the juvenile justice system: Results from a multi-state prevalence study.* National Center for Mental Health and Juvenile Justice.

Seiter, L. (2017). *Mental health and juvenile justice: A review of prevalence, promising practices, and areas for improvement.* National Technical Assistance Center for the Education of Neglected or Delinquent Children and Youth.

Sinclair, J. S., Unruh, D. K., Griller Clark, H., & Waintrup, M. G. (2017). School personnel perceptions of youth with disabilities returning to high school from the juvenile justice system. *Journal of Special Education, 51*(2), 95–105. https://doi.org/10.1177/0022466916676089

Strnadová, I., Cumming, T., & O'Neill, S. (2017). Young people transitioning from juvenile justice to the community: Transition planning and interagency collaboration. *Current Issues in Criminal Justice, 29*(1), 19–38.

Terry, D., & Abrams, M. K. (2017). Dangers, diversions, and decisions: The process of criminal desistance among formerly incarcerated young men. *International Journal of Offender Therapy, 61,* 727–750. https://doi.org/10.1177/0306624X15602704

The Council of State Governments Justice Center. (2015). *Locked out: Improving educational and vocational outcomes for incarcerated youth.* The Council of State Governments Justice Center.

Todis, B., Bullis, M., Waintrup, M., Schultz, R., & D'Ambrosio, R. (2001). Overcoming the odds: Qualitative examination of resilience among formerly incarcerated adolescents. *Exceptional Children, 68,* 119–139. https://doi.org/10.1177/001440290106800107

Trotter, C. (2012). Effective community-based supervision of young offenders. *Trends & Issues in Crime and Criminal Justice, 448,* 1–7. https://aic.gov.au/publications/tandi/tandi448

United Nations. (1985). *United Nations Standard minimum rules for administration of juvenile justice (The Beijing Rules).* http://www.ohchr.org/Documents/ProfessionalInterest/beijingrules.pdf

Unruh, D., Povenmire-Kirk, T., & Yamamoto, S. (2009). Perceived barriers and protective factors of juvenile offenders on their developmental pathway to adulthood. *Journal of Correctional Education, 60*(3), 201–224.

Whittemore, R., Chase, S. K., & Mandle, C. L. (2001). Validity in qualitative research. *Qualitative Health Research, 11,* 522–537. https://doi.org/10.1177/104973201129119299

Wisdom, J. P., Cavaleri, M., Gogel, L., & Nacht, M. (2011). Barriers and facilitators to adolescent drug treatment: Youth, family, and staff reports. *Addiction Research and Theory, 19*(2), 179–188. https://doi.org/10.3109/16066359.2010.530711

LIBRARIES AS SOCIAL AGENCIES AND TRANSITION POINTS: SERVING DIVERSE POPULATIONS

Maria A. Pacino

ABSTRACT

The purpose of this chapter is to define the role of libraries as civic institutions that assist citizens in significant transition points in the lives of children and adults. Libraries play an important role in society as essential democratic spaces that help create a sense of belonging in diverse communities. They provide opportunities for inclusive services to the marginalized, a wide range of literacy development services, from early childhood to older citizens, including literacy in more than one language for immigrant families. Libraries also provide community outreach programs, such as resources for access to healthcare, housing, and food. Many of these programs are connected to life transitions, such services for veterans and a pathway for immigrants to obtain US citizenship. Most of these programs are funded by grants and use community volunteers. This chapter highlights the work of one library, referred to as City Library, in a predominantly Latinx community in Southern California, including services and resources on literacy and essential neighborhood connections and partnerships.

Keywords: Community; diversity; families; immigrants; libraries; literacy; Latinx

INTRODUCTION

Libraries have always been beacons of intellectual freedom and strong advocates in advancing the cause of literacy development, founded on the principle that literacy is a social justice issue (Crisis Point, 2020) and an empowering tool in

Transition Programs for Children and Youth with Diverse Needs
International Perspectives on Inclusive Education, Volume 18, 265–273
Copyright © 2022 Maria A. Pacino
Published under exclusive licence by Emerald Publishing Limited
ISSN: 1479-3636/doi:10.1108/S1479-363620220000018018

participatory democracies. According to Rosa and Storey (2016), "US public libraries are great democratic institutions that serve people of every age, income level, location, ethnicity or physical ability. Because libraries bring free access to all, they also bring opportunity to all" (p. 90). Klinenberg (2018) suggested that libraries also serve as examples of "social infrastructure"; that is, they provide physical spaces and places that "shape the way people act," and promote opportunities for inclusion and growth by offering a wide range of services. Many of these library services are intrinsically connected to a broad array of life transitions.

For example, although literacy development is primarily associated with schooling, public libraries routinely serve as the community agencies that often take on the responsibility of offering literacy development opportunities across all age levels. Many provide learning spaces and literacy programs for toddlers, preschoolers, and their parents, encouraging family members to employ the literacy strategies demonstrated in various library-centered programs in the home environment to promote literacy and social development, which prepares children for transition into school (Witteveen, 2017). After school activities for school aged children include homework assistance and tutoring, enabling students to transition successfully between grades in their schooling. Summer enrichment programs, such as reading challenges, storytime gatherings, and activities featuring arts and crafts, robotics, and technology, enable students to develop and expand academic knowledge, explore interests, and build on strengths in a supportive environment (Barack, 2019). Libraries also connect community members across age levels to digital literacy formats increasingly vital for accessing information and engaging in online resources for employment, education, community, and social networking (Hildreth & Sullivan, 2015; Witteveen, 2017).

Library literacy programs are situated in the cultural and linguistic diversity of the communities they serve (Witteveen, 2017). Many provide programming and resources for immigrant populations transitioning to life in the United States, including books and tutoring in an individual's first language, programs for English language learners, and resources for obtaining citizenship (Jacobson, 2016). Libraries also connect recent immigrants to others in the community who can provide information regarding community resources, and education and employment opportunities, as well as companionship and insight through shared experiences of living in a new community. Libraries affirm cultural diversity, mirroring to students both "who they are and who they might become" (Altobelli, 2018, p. 27).

Libraries serve a key role in community life, fostering inclusion and belonging. According to Zalusky (2020), libraries across the nation "… are on the front lines, playing an invaluable role in keeping communities connected" (p. 4). They are valuable civic centers for community building, especially in diverse communities, providing purposeful inclusive and equitable environments conducive to family involvement in the community and lifelong learning (Lopez et al., 2016, 2017). These services offer opportunities for families and other community members to gather together to engage in various literacy activities to promote social inclusion (Scott, 2011).

Public libraries serve a range of populations within a community, including veterans and those experiencing housing and food insecurity, homelessness, unemployment or underemployment, and psychosocial and physical health and wellness needs, many of whom view the library as a safe, sheltering, inclusive community (Rosa & Storey, 2016; Wahler et al., 2020). They can also arrange access to materials in alternate formats such as large print, audio books and materials, and uses of technology for individuals requesting accommodations. Libraries provide transitional learning opportunities for community members, including assistance to bridge the digital divide in order to locate needed services and information (Anderson, 2017; Kang, 2016; Kinney, 2010; Whitehair, 2016).

Libraries do not work in isolation; they are what Provence (2018) refers to as "service delivery hubs" (p. 1053), providing collaborative services in partnership with health and social service organizations, school districts, universities, and other community businesses and initiatives (Wahler et al., 2020; Witteveen, 2017). For example, some libraries participate in providing meals to those facing food and housing insecurity (Barack, 2019), as well as assistance in searching for employment and affordable housing (Provence, 2018). Others provide community meeting spaces, serve as voting stations, and organize forums on issues of importance to the community (Landgraf, 2019).

Through these and other programs, libraries provide essential services to individuals at a wide variety of transition points in their lives, including children transitioning to school through offering programs featuring literacy and social-emotional development, adolescents transitioning to young adulthood through tutoring, education and vocational opportunities, adults transitioning to parenthood and employment, and other populations such as military personnel, seniors, immigrants, and those seeking other services that improve life experiences and outcomes.

This chapter highlights the work of one library, referred to as City Library, in a predominantly Latinx community in Southern California where most of the community members speak Spanish and some of the families experience food and housing insecurity. The remainder of the chapter includes an overview of services offered by the library, with a focus on literacy programs for early childhood, K-12 students and adults as well as essential family neighborhood connections and partnerships.

THE CITY LIBRARY

City Library, which provides services and literacy programs to individuals from babies to senior adults, is a busy gathering place throughout the week and on Saturdays. Given the predominance of Latinx community members, many library services are in bilingual Spanish and English. There are selected story times (*cuentos bilingues*) and movie nights in Spanish and English. Some literacy programs are in Spanish only to address the majority of the community residents.

Children and families gather daily at the library after school and on the weekends. While the children attend tutoring sessions, parents and family members often engage in adult literacy opportunities, such as citizenship classes that provide the needed skills and resources for a path to citizenship. Citizenship classes have a high enrollment and interest, resulting in the majority of participants achieving their goal of becoming US citizens. English learner classes and bilingual programs, such as *Leamos* (literacy in Spanish), are also available as well as bilingual technology workshops. These specialized family programs are funded by grants, private donations, and/or volunteer services from partnerships and collaborations with area schools and other community agencies.

For a number of years the library has partnered with the school district and the neighboring private university to assist K-12 students with homework and to provide tutoring assistance in reading, writing and mathematics. Approximately 250 students from 35 local schools take advantage of these programs. Undergraduate student volunteers offer Monday–Thursday after-school tutoring services to elementary and secondary students, which also serves an opportunity for university students to fulfill their community service hours. At the end of each academic year, the city library has a reception that is attended by the library staff, the mayor and other city council members, a university representative, school district officials, K-12 students, parents/families, and other community members. Family members have stated that this tutoring service has contributed to their K-12 students' academic achievement and affirms their cultural diversity.

City Library also works with partners to provide social services to the community. Since many local children and families experience food insecurity, they rely on school lunches throughout the school year. During the summer months, the Library offers literacy programs at a local park where the school district provides lunch for children up to 18 years of age. The Library's Bookmobile is quite popular and provides outreach throughout the community making stops at schools, local parks, and senior centers where students and families gather to check out reading materials.

The library offers a range of programs geared to individuals across age ranges and at specific life transition points. A number of these are listed here.

PROGRAMS AND SERVICES THAT ADDRESS TRANSITION NEEDS

- Career Online High School (COHS) offers a high school diploma, workforce development, and certification (child care and education, commercial driving, food and hospitality, homeland security, office management, protection officers, and retail customer service)
- I CAN program for adults with cognitive and developmental disabilities, exploring interests, work, and careers
- Citizenship preparation as a path to US naturalization

- Classes on health and well-being, nutrition, and fitness taught by the local university nursing students and staff from local community service organizations
- Grassroots ESL, a collaborative of community organizations, including schools, committed to meeting the English language needs of the community
- Mental Health Services
- Services and Resources for Veterans
- Neighborhood Connections. Funded by grants, this initiative provides access to essential resources to families and children in the community, including food and temporary housing for those in need. Created and developed by a graduate student from the Social Work department from the local university, the program now serves as a model for other public libraries in California.

PROGRAMS FOR CHILDREN AND YOUNG ADULTS

- Tutoring services for K-12 school children by local university students
- Summer Lunch program with literacy activities in the Library and in the park
- *Cuentos Bilingues*, story time with crafts (in Spanish)
- Discovery Club which includes science experiments for children from 5 years of age and beyond; this program focuses on conservation and environmental issues
- Family Place (parents/families with babies and toddlers; English language)
- Movie Nights in English and Spanish
- NASA Space Themed Programs
- STEM Program (science, technology, engineering, and mathematics) kits
- Summer Reading Program (serving babies through older kids) and Teen book Club

PROGRAMS FOR ADULTS

- Arts and crafts
- Cultural events
- *Leamos* (Spanish literacy; Let's Read)
- Voting by Mail (to facilitate citizen engagement)
- Technology instruction in computer, Internet use, and other digital technologies, including access to laptops that can be checked out

The following are descriptions of three selected programs and services funded either by partnerships with local schools, and community agencies, and/or grants from businesses and organizations to foster literacy development and other services for individuals from infancy through adulthood; the Adult Literacy Programs, Family Place, and Neighborhood Connections.

FAMILY PLACE

Family Place is a program for public libraries funded by a grant from Family Place Libraries within the California State Library. This program is especially designed to encourage families in the literacy development of infants and toddlers. The goal of the Family Place Libraries program, established in 1996, is to enable public libraries to become the literacy centers of communities by expanding the role of children's services in promoting healthy child and family development from birth, parent and community involvement, and lifelong learning. Core components of Family Place Libraries include a collection of appropriate materials for babies, toddlers, parents, and service providers; parent-child workshops; coalition building with community organizations and agencies; developmentally appropriate programming; library staff trained in family support; and outreach to new and nontraditional library users.

Family Place Libraries incorporate toys, books, music, multimedia, and other resources for child development and parenting workshops. Library spaces are redesigned to accommodate age-appropriate furniture and materials to provide library services to infants, connect families with community resources and service agencies, and reach out to nontraditional library users. These family community connections nurture children and prepare them for school readiness. Family Place Libraries, part of a network of public librarians who oversee these children and family services, provide a wide range of resources on parenting and child care; early childhood development, literacy, and education; health, safety, and nutrition; books and toys and other materials for young children (Family Place Libraries https://www.familyplacelibraries.org/).

ADULT LITERACY PROGRAMS

The purpose of the Adult Literacy Services (ALS) program, funded by California Library Literacy Services (CLLS), is to provide critical literacy services to English-speaking adults who lack the literacy proficiency and skills needed to participate fully in society. Volunteer tutors are English-speaking adults who are trained by a literacy specialist and given teaching and learning materials. Instruction in the Adult Literacy Program is delivered as a one-on-one to establish a relationship between instructor and learner. It is important that volunteers understand their role in dealing with adult learners. Adult learners are defined as those at least 16 years old; seeking literacy services for themselves; completing the process to qualify for services; establishing literacy goals; and attending the tutoring sessions.

Most learners seek literacy services for job improvement, to become active in their children's school, or to participate fully in the community and society. Tutors and learners meet regularly, a minimum of once a week for at least 90 minutes. Adult learners are also introduced to community resources and services that may benefit them or their families. Participants in the Adult Literacy Program report a very positive experience for both learners and volunteer tutors. The

Adult Literacy Services website of the California State Library (http://librar-yliteracy.org/about/als/index.html) shares videos depicting many rewarding stories of program participants in different libraries.

Neighborhood Connections

This particular outreach program has become vital to the community because it offers temporary housing, food, and other basic services to individuals and families who are facing difficult, challenging times. The goal of the program is to assist individuals of any age group and families with basic living needs like housing, food, healthcare, education, including citizenship classes, and employ-ment. The social work director identifies needy families and helps connect them with local agencies and organizations, including churches, foodbanks, and health clinics. This library program has become so successful that it has become a model of community library services for other public libraries in surrounding cities and neighborhoods. The program has been presented at library conferences to encourage other city and public libraries to replicate these services in their own communities (www.ci.azusa.ca.us/1495/Neighborhood-Connections).

FUNDING

City Library programs demonstrate that even in times of severe budget cuts, public libraries can continue to collaborate with partners to make a difference in diverse communities, expanding literacy services to their constituents of all ages from babies, children, teens, and adults to those nearing retirement and older citizens. These programs are successful because of grant funds from the Cali-fornia State Library, local organizations like the Canyon City Foundation, Friends of the Library, and other community agencies and partnerships, including businesses that provide ongoing funding, as well as volunteer services from community members.

The Transformative Experience of Volunteering

Many of the programs offered by City Library depend on the willingness of volunteers to serve their communities. As a volunteer tutor in the Adult Literacy Program, I would like to close the chapter by sharing an experience I had that, for me, was a truly a transformative life moment when I recognized that my rela-tionship with a woman I was tutoring allowed me the privilege of getting to know her as a person – a community member like myself, who desired to become a more engaged parent in her children's education. The following is an excerpt from a personal reflection regarding my volunteer experience.

> I recall my own experience as a volunteer literacy tutor several years ago. It was humbling going through the training process, especially when the trainer used examples from the Arabic language. For the first time in my life, I experienced being illiterate; I could empathize with the adults with whom I would be working. The first person assigned to me was a mother who wanted to be able to advocate for her children in school but felt uncomfortable and intimidated

facing school personnel. After months of working together, she came in one day and announced, "I spoke up and asked questions about my kids' education; I was not afraid, and I know I can do it from now on." (Tutoring session Pacino. Personal reflection, 2000)

As we celebrated her growth and increased confidence toward achieving this goal, what I realized was that the opportunity to partner in a transformative point in this mother's life also served as a transition point in my own. Volunteering allows one the opportunity to enable others to achieve self-determined outcomes benefitting life for many.

City Library is a catalyst in transition. And as the world endures COVID-19, the United States faces yet another "pandemic" – the recognition of pernicious racism against Black Americans. Racism also extends to Brown, Indigenous and immigrant populations and reveals serious social and educational disparities. When local schools closed due to the virus, teaching and learning shifted from face-to-face to remote settings, thus exacerbating a racial and digital divide, especially in minoritized neighborhoods where many families face housing and food insecurity, lack adequate medical care, and often cannot afford computers or internet access. During these difficult times, libraries, beacons of light and literacy, continue their mission, as democratizing institutions across communities and as safe havens for diverse families and children by providing internet access, studying spaces, educational resources, and links to social services as children and families await transition back into the classroom.

CONCLUSION

City Library is an effective model of a public library serving a diverse, Latinx community and providing meaningful literacy programs across generations, from babies to older adults. Funding is always a challenge; however, City Library relies on a variety of grants from local businesses and organizations, such as Friends of the Library, Rotary Clubs, as well as the California State Library. It is essential, therefore, that one or more librarians should be experts in grant writing to support these community programs, including offering transition points, such as a path for citizenship for immigrant families. Librarians and staff should also be able to speak the language of the citizens they serve; this is the case in City Library. Recruiting and hiring skilled library staff is important as well as providing ongoing professional training, including social justice advocacy (Jaeger et al., 2016). Collaborating with local schools, universities, and agencies taps the expertise of volunteers to help sustain library programs.

Librarians are the voice for community libraries. According to Neal (2017),

Libraries are about education, employment, entrepreneurship, empowerment, and engagement. But [they] are also about the imperatives of individual rights and freedoms and about helping and supporting people in [their] communities. (p. 5)

As places where all are welcome and served, libraries shape communities, offering personnel and spaces to network and gain information. Community libraries, such as City Library, also promote social justice and inclusion through resources and services that promote growth toward self-determined outcomes and support individuals through many of the defining, transformative transition points in their lives.

REFERENCES

Altobelli, R. (2018, January/February). Creating space for agency: Including LGBT and intersectional perspectives makes students future-ready. *American Libraries*, 27.

Anderson, M. (2017). Digital divide persists even as lower income Americans make gains in tech adoption. *Pew Research Center*. http://www.pewresearch.org/fact-tank/2017/03/22/digital-divide-persists-even-as-lower-income-americans-make-gains-in-tech-adoption/

Barack, L. (2019, June). Public library summer programming is vital to communities. *School Library Journal*, 65(5), 30–33.

Crisis point: The state of literacy in America. (2020). https://resilienteducator.com/news/illiteracy-in-america/

Family Place Libraries. (n.d). http://www.familyplacelibraries.org

Hildreth, S., & Sullivan, M. (2015). Rising to the challenge: Re-envisioning public libraries. *Journal of Library Administration*, 55, 647–657. https://doi.org/10.1080/01930826.2015.1085247

Jacobson, L. (2016, November). A path forward: How libraries support refugee children adjusting to life in the U.S. *School Library Journal*, 62(11), 26–29.

Jaeger, P. T., Shilton, K., & Koepfler, J. (2016). The rise of social justice as a guiding principle in library and information science research. *The Library Quarterly: Information, Community, Policy*, 86(1), 1–9.

Kang, C. (2016, May 22). Unemployed Detroit residents are trapped by a digital divide. *New York Times*. https://www.nytimes.com/2016/05/23/technology/unemployed-detroit-residents-are-trapped-by-a-digital-divide.html?_r=0

Kinney, B. (2010). The internet, public libraries, and the digital divide. *Public Library Quarterly*, 29(2), 104–161.

Klinenberg, E. (2018, September 8). To restore civil society, start with the library. *New York Times*. https://www.nytimes.com/2018/09/08/opinion/sunday/civil-society-library.html

Landgraf, G. (2019). Discourse for democracy: Promoting civic literacy with forums. *American Libraries Magazine*, 50(11/12), 30–32.

Lopez, M. E., Caspe, M., & McWilliams, L. (2016). *Public libraries: A vital space for family engagement*. Harvard Family Research Project/Public Library Association.

Lopez, M. E., Caspe, M., & Simpson, C. (2017). Engaging families in public libraries. *Public Library Quarterly*, 36(4), 318–333.

Neal, J. (2017). Our shared responsibility: Working together for advocacy. *American Libraries Magazine*, 48(9/10), 5.

Provence, M. A. (2018). From nuisances to neighbors: Inclusion of patrons experiencing homelessness through library and social work partnerships. *Advances in Social Work*, 18(4), 1053–1067.

Rosa, K., & Storey, T. (2016). American libraries in 2016: Creating their future by connecting, collaborating and building community. *IFLA Journal*, 42(2), 85–101.

Scott, R. (2011). The role of public libraries in community building. *Public Library Quarterly*, 30(3), 191–227.

Wahler, E. A., Provence, M. A., Helling, J., & Williams, M. A. (2020). The changing role of libraries: How social workers can help. *Families in Society: The Journal of Contemporary Social Work*, 101(1), 34–43.

Whitehair, K. (2016, July 5). Reaching across the digital divide. *Public Libraries Online*. http://publiclibrariesonline.org/2016/07/reaching-across-the-digital-divide/

Witteveen, A. (2017, July 7). Lifelong literacy: A core concentration on literacy from the top of the org chart yields next-level outcomes. *Library Journal*, 20–23.

Zalusky, S. (Ed.). (2020). *The state of America's libraries*. American Library Association. http://www.ala.org/news/state-americas-libraries-report-2020

COLLABORATIVE PARTNERSHIPS AND STRATEGIES TO PROMOTE EFFECTIVE TRANSITIONS AND SUPPORT FOR STUDENTS WITH DISABILITY: THE ROLE OF PARENT GROUPS IN MALAWI

Msenga Anyelwisye Mulungu

ABSTRACT

Inclusive practices are supported and increasingly being implemented in Malawi. Transition to inclusion requires partnerships in which parents, educators, policymakers, and community leaders come together to build an understanding of disability which values inclusion and promotes the use of innovative, contextualized strategies to facilitate inclusive perspectives and practices. The purpose of this chapter is to highlight how one agency, the Parents of Disabled Children Association of Malawi (PODCAM), is working with parents, educators, and community members to build more inclusive schools and communities for students with disability.

Keywords: Parent support groups; home-school collaboration; inclusive education; community support for inclusion; teacher practices for inclusion; transition from home to

INTRODUCTION

In Malawi, like in other developing countries, children with disability face many challenges in order to fulfill their right to education. A baseline survey, which was

Transition Programs for Children and Youth with Diverse Needs
International Perspectives on Inclusive Education, Volume 18, 275–289
Copyright © 2022 Msenga Anyelwisye Mulungu
Published under exclusive licence by Emerald Publishing Limited
ISSN: 1479-3636/doi:10.1108/S1479-363620220000018019

conducted in 2013 by the Federation of Disabled Organization in Malawi (FEDOMA), indicated that 80 % of children with disability were out of school and that of those who were in school only 20% completed primary education. Traditionally, there have been very few children with disability in Malawi that enroll for Integrated Early Childhood Development Education (IECDE). This is a comprehensive approach to policies, programs, strategies, and services for children from conception to age eight for their survival, growth, development, and participation to ensure thriving in all dimensions (National Policy on Childhood Development, Republic of Malawi). The IECD includes both pre-school and primary school (Grades 1 and 2).

There are a number of possible reasons for non-enrolment of children in schooling. One commonly held reason is connected to the beliefs and mis-conceptions attached to the causes of disability. For instance, disability is often considered as a punishment from God on parents for offending other people. As a result, some parents are reluctant to accept the possibility of disability in their children and thus engage in overprotection to avoid experiencing shame (Mariga et al., 2014). Others may be reluctant to disclose that their children have learning or other types of challenges, due to concern that their children might also experience shame and humiliation.

Some parents do not enroll their children with disability in pre-schools or in primary schools because of late identification of their child's disability. Parents lack the knowledge and skills for identifying problems and difficulties, and there are few therapists to provide diagnoses, and scarce rehabilitation services available to address them. By the time a child acquires some basic life skills, their age is already advanced. As children are placed in classes according to academic ability and not age, this poses a further problem for schooling. Depending on the type of disability, a child might not feel comfortable to play or learn with younger children, or a parent may feel the discomfort on behalf of her or his child.

Parents, teachers, disabled persons' organizations (DPOs), nongovernmental organizations, and other education stakeholders, have realized that a child with disability might drop out of school or enroll late or not be enrolled at all due to the following factors:

- *Eligibility*: Depending on the nature of the disability, especially if severe, parents may feel the child would not be eligible for school education (Mariga et al., 2014). This is not a government policy but rather an attitude held by parents and the society at large.
- *Concern for teachers*: Some parents are worried that inclusion of their child with severe disability might overburden school teachers and caregivers (Mariga et al., 2014). They feel concern that teachers or caregivers might concentrate on such a child at the expense of other learners.
- *Mobility challenges*: Long distances to schools have demotivated parents to enroll children with disability for education. When a child has mobility challenges, parents may not be able to carry their child every day to an educational center, especially when a wheelchair or other means of transport is not available.

- *Perceptions regarding the value of education for persons with disability*: Perceptions by members of the community, parents, or others that devalue education for children with disability have negatively impacted opportunities to access education. For example, knowledge of persons with disability who have attained education but who have not been able to secure employment results based on the assumption that education has little value for children with disabilities.
- *Physical and psycho-social wellbeing*: Parents of children with disability are concerned about the safety of their children. For instance, Malawi and some neighboring countries have been experiencing abductions and killings of children and persons with albinism for ritual benefits (Essa & Furcoi, 2019). Other children with disability experience bullying on their way to and from school, or other types of abuses (World Bank/FEDOMA report 2016). Hence, parents choose to keep them indoors for their safety.

Parents of Disabled Children Association of Malawi (PODCAM)'s Viewpoint on Teacher or Caregiver Perspectives toward School Inclusion

- Some teachers or caregivers may feel that there are already too many children in their classes. Hence, a child with disability may be viewed as an extra burden.
- Teachers or caregivers might feel concerned because they do not have sufficient knowledge about a child's disability and, therefore, might not be able to meet the child's needs; especially teachers who have not been able to access special needs educational teacher training.
- Many teachers or caregivers feel pity for the child and, therefore, end up being overprotective. As a result, they may do everything for the child, even when included, minimizing the child's opportunity to acquire new skills.

The education system in Malawi comprises five subsectors. These are: Basic education, which includes early child development, complementary basic education, adult literacy, primary education; secondary education; teacher education; tertiary education (universities, technical and vocational education); and cross cutting services. One of the challenges in Malawi affecting both teachers and students is the large student population in classes. For instance, according to the 2017–2018 Education Sector Performance Report (Ministry of Education: Government of Malawi), there are about 5.4 million learners in the primary education sector with 76,781 teachers, which translates to an average ratio of 1: 67 (teacher: learner).

Despite some of these barriers in Malawi, there have been recent strides in education policy that aim at promoting inclusion of learners with diverse needs. In recent years, the National Inclusive Education Strategy (Ministry of Education, Government of Malawi, 2017–2021) has been put in place, which utilizes a twin track approach to service delivery and stresses the need for education for all learners in an inclusive setting. This strategy, which emanates from the National Education Policy statement, recognizes the importance of promoting inclusive education. Malawi has now embarked on the development of a National Inclusive Education Policy as an independent document.

According to Mariga et al. (2014), it is asserted that the objective of achieving inclusive education for all requires a collaborative approach involving families, communities, policymakers, and the educational system. The purpose of this chapter, therefore, is to highlight how one agency, the PODCAM is assisting parents, families, and children to transition to school and other educational formats.

SUPPORTING SCHOOL ENTRY FOR STUDENTS WITH DISABILITY

Parents often feel that a problem shared is half way solved. Hence, the formation of an association called Parents of Disabled Children Association of Malawi (PODCAM). PODCAM is a nonprofit organization registered under the Malawi Government's Trustees Incorporation Act and is also an affiliate of the Federation of Disability Organization in Malawi (FEDOMA), which is the member of the Malawian Council for nongovernmental organization. PODCAM provides education and support to parents, families, communities, and children with disability to access community and educational programs and services.

The main objectives of the Association are the following:

(1) To represent and support the interests of children with disabilities at all levels of social, economic, political, and cultural activities.
(2) To mobilize parents of children with disabilities toward the uplifting of their living conditions.
(3) To lobby the government and the private on the aspirations of children with disabilities:
(4) To create awareness on the plight of children with disabilities through provision of information on the development, protection, and survival of children; and
(5) To facilitate provision of conducive learning environment for children with disabilities.

Strategies for inclusion were designed by PODCAM following the implementation of the Inclusive Education Project with input from Lilian Mariga, who served as an advisor to parent support groups in Southern Africa and East Africa. A number of the strategies used by PODCAM have been adapted from the resource manual by Mariga et al. (2014).

The organization consists of a Board of Trustees that is elected by parent members. In addition, there is a Parents Executive Committee, which is the planning unit for programs and activities that involve both parents and their children. The Association also has full time staff and volunteers who work as support staff at district level.

PODCAM seeks to assist children with disabilities regardless of age and their parents/guardians status, to maximize their potential as individuals and enjoy maximum opportunity to determine every aspect of their lives be it physically, emotionally, socially, or economically. This is achieved through the support branches the Association has established in districts. PODCAM support groups are found in 23 of the 28 districts of Malawi and are run by district committees. Currently, it has a membership of about 20,000 country-wide (PODCAM General Assembly reports, 2019) and as of data collected in 2018, there are 16,243 children with disabilities registered with PODCAM.

The following case study illustrates the role of a parent's group in supporting a family to obtain schooling for their son who was born blind and living in a rural community. Challenges faced by this family are not uncommon in Malawi and point to the need for parent support for inclusion. [*Note*: The scenarios contained in the chapter are based on observations made by the author or accounts shared at meetings. All names of people, schools, and places described within the chapter are fictitious.]

Case Study 1: Tayamika Parents Support Group

Moffat is a boy who was born totally blind, and at the age of 12 years his parents thought of enrolling him in a primary school. His parents lived in a rural outskirts of Lilongwe district where they earned their living through peasant farming. Both parents had little education so when Moffat reached the age of six, they were uncertain of where to enroll him. In 2012, they tried to enroll him at Muchinga Primary School but the request was denied because there was no teacher who was qualified to assist learners with visual impairment.

However, with the establishment of an Inclusive Education Project in 2013, Moffat's parents joined the local parents support group. That same year, the support group arranged with the Special Needs Directorate to consider the boy for entry to a special school. The support group had to contribute transport money, the purchasing of a school uniform, and upkeep for Moffat. When the time came at the age of 12, the father took his son to a residential Special School for the visually impaired. He explained that the boy had never been in school and had never been away from the home. Mr. Medson said that while at this Special School, the matron told him that the Special Needs Teachers (SNET) had gone out for other duties and she advised that the boy should remain at the school for admission when responsible teachers were available. When the father was bidding farewell, Moffat started crying uncontrollably. In order to stop Moffat from crying, the matron placed him in an empty dust bin and he stopped crying. However, this did not please the father who was watching the drama at a distant. He later returned and decided to take Moffat back home.

The family was fortunate in that year to witness the opening of an Early Child Development Centre (ECDC) in their village where they enrolled Moffat at 13 years of age. Mr. Medison described his son as intelligent since he was able to explain what he learned each day at school. When Moffat turned 14, his father went to plead again with the teachers at the nearest primary school to enroll him for the first grade (Standard 1). Unfortunately, the boy was sent back as the Specialist Teacher still claimed she had no capacity to accommodate a learner with total blindness. The term ended and Moffat was still idling at home while his friends and peers attended school. The parent support group then negotiated with Mtendere Boarding School for the Visually Impaired administration for readmission. He was enrolled and continues to acclimatize with the school environment. Mtendere has proved to be an ideal school for Moffat and he is excelling socially and academically due to continued counseling.

Note: All the names used for people, schools and places are fictitious.

PARENT GROUPS PROVIDE CHILDREN AND FAMILIES WITH OPPORTUNITIES AND SKILLS REQUIRED FOR TRANSITION TO SCHOOL ENVIRONMENTS

From the case study, it is clear that parent groups, such as the ones affiliated with PODCAM, are important in transition because they equip parents as they enable their children with disability to acquire needed knowledge, skills, and competencies before they enroll for kindergartens or primary schools. Parent group involvement can also serve to influence parent attitudes, since children with disability have asserted that "changes in their parents' attitudes and understanding would be the most effective means of ending their social exclusion" (Lansdown, 2009, p. 53).

Parent groups, therefore, can provide a range of opportunities for growth and development for both parents and children.

- *Opportunities to experience new environments and develop relationships*: PODCAM encourages parents to bring their children with disability with them as they attend support group meetings. This enables the children to experience new environments away from the home and provides an opportunity for a child who is in the home most of the time to interact with other children. One outcome is that this involvement reduces feelings of fear and anxiety in the children when entering unfamiliar environments or meeting people they may not know.
- *Acquiring understanding of disability*: Due to the role parents can play in advocating for their children, it is important that parents recognize and counter any common beliefs or misconceptions regarding disability. It is

equally important that they find ways to explain to their children that they have a physical or learning problem, which may cause them to look or learn differently from their peers. This information can help to build the child's self-understanding and self-acceptance, and prepare the child psychologically, emotionally and socially for various situations that they may experience in school and in society due to their disability.

- *Becoming familiar with and within the community*: Families are also encouraged to introduce their children with disability to community activities and events building connection to the communities in which they live. For example, children with disabilities might accompany their parents to religious cere-monies, local entertainments, or other activities. This promotes social devel-opment as children learn informally about their communities, as well as allows them to participate in various activities, such as singing in a church setting.
- *Designing activities for physical and psychosocial development*: Parent groups enable parents to organize activities and games for their children, both with and without disability, that promote developmental skills such as running, role playing, crafts, or making play materials. School games can also be initiated by school children at parent support group meetings, which provide psychosocial, cognitive, and physical development to those who are about to enroll for school.
- *Building skills for academic and personal functioning*: In preparing children for schoolwork, parents can share strategies for teaching their children with disability various skills such as how to hold pencils, write in and use note-books, sit and attend to others, and toileting procedures, while still in the home. Parents of children who are already in pre-school or in primary school and who are more familiar with the education system and school work can assist other parents with knowledge about what is expected in the school or classroom.
- *Sharing experiences and documenting growth and development*: Support group meetings also provide parents with an opportunity to learn from each other's experiences and share information regarding where their children could be referred for further evaluation and support. Being able to document the rehabilitative progresses that their children have made, as well as observing the development achieved by other children with disabilities in areas such as mobility, communication, and personal care can instill confidence and promote mutual encouragement.
- *Connecting with professionals*: Creation of a parent support group or local association enables health workers, social workers, specialist teachers, and others to meet parents and their children with disabilities at a cluster. This allows parents to access certain services and information within their com-munity. In addition, with professional guidance parents can learn how to acquire and teach their children to use assistive devices like wheelchairs, hearing aids, and magnifying glasses. They are also provided with information regarding where they can access service providers and service centers, including special schools.

ASSISTING PARENTS DURING TRANSITION OF A CHILD WITH DISABILITY FROM HOME TO SCHOOL OR EARLY CHILDHOOD DEVELOPMENT CENTRE (ECDC)

In Malawi, parents or caregivers have key responsibilities for ensuring the realization of the rights to education for children with disabilities. The United Nations Convention on the Rights of Persons with Disabilities (UNCRPD) Article 24, explains that parents should be vigilant regarding the way in which teaching and learning processes address the needs of their children. Parents assert that while they are experts on their children, teachers are experts in the classroom. This highlights the need for collaboration between parents and teachers if children with disabilities are to be effectively assisted to develop to their full potential.

Case study #2 illustrates the need for collaborative communication between the parents and the school.

Case Study 2: The Importance of Communicating About the Diverse Needs of Children

John was born with hearing problems. His parents enrolled him at Lusoko Primary School based on the information that the school had a learning resource center. However, they did not inform the teachers that their son, John, had hearing problems. The resource center at the Lusoko school, though, was for children with visual impairments. John spent two terms in the school without his teachers realizing that he had hearing problems. As a result, during the time of his stay in the school, he could not actively participate in classroom activities and his performance was below expectation. Later in the following school term, the class teacher discovered that John had hearing impairment, and he facilitated John's transfer to another school that focused on learners with hearing difficulties. John is now happy and can participate in class and other school activities. PODCAM staff assisted by building awareness among parents and teachers about disabilities and about screening learners at the school. They also provided information to the family about the importance of informing teachers of John's condition during the time of enrollment in school.

Note: All the names used for people, schools and places are fictitious.

Given the importance of communication between parents and teachers, PODCAM staff encourage and support parents to engage in the following activities and strategies during the period of transition from home to school.

Connect with and visit schools prior to enrollment: Parents are advised to visit the school before their child enrolls to determine how the school might meet their child's educational needs and provide suitably qualified staff and appropriate specialist facilities and supports required to promote an inclusive environment.

Indicators of inclusion also incorporate having a staff with a caring attitude toward learners with diverse needs, and a welcoming atmosphere where all children are treated as individuals with talents and gifts to share – where there is a balance between academic and citizenship components, and an emphasis on community spirit.

Acknowledge each child's strengths and needs at enrollment: One of PODCAM's intentions is to help its members promote a more positive understanding of disability, with focus on each child's strengths and possible outcomes when appropriate services are provided. Because teachers may not have the time or expertise to identify the needs of all learners at the outset of the school term, PODCAM advises parents to accompany their children with disability to school during enrollment, register any problems that their wards have, and share information regarding effective learning strategies that have been utilized in the past.

Promote relationships with and support of teachers: In Malawi, as well as in other developing countries, parents may have little or no choice over the school their child attends. For this reason, PODCAM counsels parents to build trust with and in the teachers at the local school. Making an effort to meet a child's teacher early in the year enables parents to establish a positive relationship with the teacher, which will provide opportunity for continued discussions of their child's progress throughout the year. This collaborative relationship allows the teacher or caregiver opportunity to advise the parents regarding what supports to provide in the home, as well as parents to provide information regarding their perspectives on schooling.

Be present in the classroom: When parents visit their child's class and observe the teaching methods used, they are more likely to also utilize the same strategies when supporting their child with schoolwork at home, which can provide instructional continuity. In addition, parents can help their child pay attention when the teacher is providing instruction, and assist the child with various needs, such as toileting, until the child is able to be independent or has befriended peers for support.

Share materials and resources: Parents can also provide the school or the center with play and teaching materials that the child was using in the home. This ensures continuity through using familiar materials for learning. In the same way, assistive devices used at home could be taken for use in schools or ECD centers. For example, a parent might bring a Cerebral Palsy (CP) chair or other devices for the child to use in school.

Participate in the development of the School Improvement Plan (SIP): Parents' active involvement in the SIP will ensure that important components, such as the literacy and social needs of children with disability, are included in the plan. This can also be reflected in the School Improvement Grant (SIG) so that parents can be assured that resources are available to meet the unique needs of their children. The SIG is funding provided by the government to support school development strategies which can differ from school to school depending on varying needs. For example, one school can use the funds for renovations, another for continuous professional development, while another may use the grant to purchase text books.

Assist children with school homework and provide continued opportunities for learning: Parents are encouraged to assist children with their school homework where acquisition of skills can take place in an informal and familiar setting. One way to communicate learning responsibilities between home and school is to use a notebook that is signed by both parties and passed back and forth. PODCAM enables children from families whose parents do not have academic skills to benefit from the shared support from others. For example, parents with some formal education, or those who have received training to assist others, can assist learners with diverse needs with schoolwork, such as reading and numerical skills.

Because learning disparities among children with disability often begin in early childhood and persist through all levels of education, many learners with diverse needs drop out before they can complete junior primary grades. Parents who are able to support their children at home can reduce the knowledge gap resulting from time away from school, which facilitates school reentry.

ENGAGING THE COMMUNITY IN SUPPORTING THE TRANSITION OF CHILDREN WITH DISABILITIES

The school community creates a vital environment for all children. It determines the culture that is manifested in its learners. Mariga et al. (2014) claim that "schools thrive best when they are fully part of their local community" (p. 62). Typically, the school community is comprised of parents, teachers, school governing committees, local chiefs, religious leaders, politicians, and others. Community members and leaders are the gatekeepers and custodians of customs and cultural beliefs. PODCAM works directly with these community structures because its branches are community based and some of the local leaders are PODCAM members. The following are ways in which PODCAM suggests community members and leaders can promote inclusive practices.

Creating and staffing pre-school centers: In Malawi, most pre-school centers are established or constructed by communities to ensure that children succeed at school by enabling them to acquire essential foundation skills. Community leaders take a leading role in identifying capable members who have acquired qualifications, like the Malawi Junior Certificate (JCE) or the Malawi Schools Certificate of Education (MSCE), and, with the help of the government, local, or other stakeholders, enrolling them in orientations or training workshops to acquire basic skills in teaching, including equipping them with principles and practices for inclusion. One difficulty experienced in Malawi, however, is that many of the young men and women who meet the criteria are not available in rural communities, due to relocating to urban centers to seek other opportunities.

Mobilizing resources and equipment for inclusion: Members of the community are in a position to mobilize resources for the school to either purchase the materials for making structural adjustments, such as constructing ramps for access, or resourcing the school with teaching materials like books and other assistive materials such as braille paper, machines, and magnifying glasses. The community can also ensure that the roads and paths to schools are safe and disability accessible, especially for wheelchair users or those with visual problems.

Constructing in-school resource centers: The community can also mobilize its members to construct resource centers in their regular schools so that learners with disability can have elementary lessons before they are integrated into the mainstream. Learners with diverse needs can be taught how to use assistive devices like vision and hearing aids, while other learners who are identified as having problems in the mainstream could also be referred to the resource center for remedial support. The community through school governing structures such as School Management Committees (SMCs), Parent Teacher Associations (PTAs), and Mother Groups can also secure needed learning devices and accommodations from well-wishers, nongovernmental organizations, and the government through SIG.

Promoting safety and protection for children with disabilities: Community leaders can initiate the establishment of child protection committees to assure the safety of learners with diverse needs on their way to and from school. Community child protection members can also help fight abuses that children with and without disabilities experience in home or at school. Parent Associations can also help in mobilization and sensitization by carrying out door-to-door campaigns supporting the benefits of education for all children.

Establishing legal mandates for education and inclusion: Local leaders (chiefs, religious leaders, councilors, school governing bodies, teachers, and parents) can make by-laws in favor of children/learners with diverse needs. For example, some chiefs have required villagers to send their children with disabilities to school. Parents that do not oblige may be reprimanded or asked to relocate to other villages where inclusion may not be practiced. In addition, teachers who are unwilling to accept learners with diverse needs in their classes may also be transferred.

Addressing cultural barriers and promoting inclusive practices: PODCAM engages local chiefs through meetings to identify harmful cultural practices and work to remove the cultural barriers that have been used to hinder children with disability from accessing education and community participation. For example, local leaders can conduct awareness meetings to dispute and condemn traditional thoughts about the causes of disabilities or actions such as ridiculing or discriminating against persons with disability. It is suggested that school administrators also provide opportunity during assemblies in the morning, break time or after classes, for community leaders to address all the learners in the school on disability issues.

Community leaders have a significant role to play in the perception of persons with disability within their communities. The following example illustrates the role of a community leader in addressing misconceptions through promoting respect for a child with disability.

Comments of a Chief made at an Inclusive Education Stakeholders meeting (Traditional Authority).

During one of the Inclusive Education Stakeholders meetings, a chief told a story to the audience, "One day I was sitting at the veranda of my house in the palace. There came a boy of about three or 4 years of age to play with my grand-child. I pretended not to watch them but, I keenly listened to what they were conversing. As they were playing another child of their age, who had no cloth on his body joined them, and immediately one of the two pointed at the new comer while laughing loudly. My grand-child asked his friend, 'Why are you laughing?' His friend answered, 'Look at this undressed friend of ours!' My grand-child retorted, 'In our family, when my sister is not dressed, we do not laugh. And when my elder brother is not dressed we do not laugh too.' The chief then said, 'The child who was laughing at the undressed friend was doing that because that was how he was raised by his parents. In the same way, children whose parents have taught them not to laugh at persons with disabilities, can never do so wherever they go, be it in the village or at school. Therefore, if I hear any complaints about any child or any person laughing at a learner or any other person with disabilities, I will address the guardian for failure to teach their wards good manners."

PROMOTING SCHOOL AND TEACHER PRACTICES FOR INCLUSION

Inclusive education involves the process of reforming education systems, policies and practices to address and respond to the needs of all learners, including those with disability. Central to this process are teachers who are equipped with the knowledge and pedagogical skills to support all learners to achieve their full potential. Schools can assist teachers to prepare for inclusion of learners with diverse needs through regular professional development workshops. In addition, teachers can support one another by identifying and sharing creative ways to adapt the curriculum according to different ability levels of learners. This can be accomplished through modifying, changing, extending, and varying strategies for learning and assessment, and adjusting curriculum content.

In school communities where PODCAM support groups are well established, the schools allow the parents to sit in classes with their children with severe disabilities so as to act as assistants. Some resource centers employ these parents as teacher assistants for effective teaching and learning processes. These parents also aid in instilling discipline to allow the teacher to concentrate on teaching. Some members of PODCAM have been coopted into school governing structures such that they attend some workshops that concern children with disabilities together with class teachers. This has also enhanced the academic support that parents provide in class and at home to their children.

The following are practices PODCAM supports for schools and teachers to build collaboration with parents to develop and encourage an inclusive classroom environment.

Inquire about any needs during registration: Teachers should ask parents or caregivers if their wards have any physical or learning problems during registration. If a child has recently graduated from a pre-school, the teacher can initiate contact with pre-school teachers for advice on behavior and learning needs and strategies. The teacher can also request progress records to determine ability levels.

Initiate home visits: The teacher can also take the initiative to build knowledge about the home environment of a learner with diverse needs. During home visits teachers can learn about a child's strengths, interests and activities, as well as social involvement and friendships in the community. Teachers are also able to inform parents when children do not report to school or address other issues.

Encourage parent involvement in IEP and other planning meetings: Teachers should invite parents to planning meetings to discuss their child's Individualized Education Plan (IEP) and progress in school. Through collaboration, teachers and parents can identify aspects of the curriculum that they feel are important for each child, and discuss ways to generalize learning and behavioral strategies to achieve consistency between home and school.

Invite participation in school governance and advocacy: Teachers, especially the Special Needs Education Teacher (SNET), should strive to co-opt parents of learners with diverse needs to participate on school governing committees so that they can speak on behalf of children with disabilities. Teachers can also train parents to advocate and lobby for the rights of their children, and advise parents regarding additional service providers or rehabilitation facilities that might offer additional training or services for their children.

Promote mutual understanding of and respect for all students as learners: At the beginning of the school term, teachers should explain to the whole class that students learn differently and therefore some may experience different approaches to learning or behavior in the classroom. Teachers can also instill a spirit of helping, both within and outside the classroom, in which students assist their peers with diverse needs, highlighting benefits that are mutually experienced.

Encourage class bonding and participation to promote unity: Teachers can incorporate strategies to encourage participation of all members of a class. One way to do this is through use of cooperative learning group assignments and activities. Group tasks allow students to learn to share responsibilities and by so doing, support one another to achieve a successful outcome. Within groups students can be given roles that match their strengths allowing each to contribute to the activity. Students are then able to recognize and validate the abilities of each participant, fostering respect.

Provide information to reduce social stigma and ridicule: Teachers can also provide information about disability that builds understanding to promote acceptance and reduce experiences of stigma and ridicule. The following example provides information that a teacher might utilize to address bullying and ensure the safety of all students.

Case Study 3: Sensitization of Learners on Disabilities

Mary, a Standard 3 girl, has physical disability. In class, Mary is often ridiculed by her peers. Her classmates did not understand why Mary's hand was different from theirs. One day during break time, the other learners decided to help her out by stretching her hand. Little did they know that they were inflicting a lot of pain on her. Out of anger, Mary started beating up the other learners. The other learners decided to revenge on their way back home by throwing stones at her. Mary arrived home crying and bleeding with a lot of bruises. Her parents were very angry and informed the school that they had decided to withdraw their child from the school. The school officials convinced the parents that they would ensure that their child was safe. They called for a parent – teacher meeting and together with community leaders held community awareness meetings on disability. Mary was then able to return to school.

Note: All the names used for people, schools and places are fictitious.

Proper transition of learners with diverse needs is necessary if all children are to excel in school. Therefore, a concerted effort is needed to remove all barriers, both educational and social, that hinder children with disability from attaining their educational rights, and to invite them into classrooms where they are welcomed and respected.

CONCLUSION

Inclusive practices are supported and are increasingly being implemented in Malawi. But, as can be seen, transition to inclusion requires partnerships in which parents, educators, policy makers and community leaders come together to build an understanding of disability which values inclusion and promotes the use of innovative, contextualized strategies to facilitate inclusive perspectives and practices. Parent groups are an important component of this process.

To support inclusion, PODCAM promotes engagement between parents, educators, and community members and supports strategies for creating effective parent–teacher–community partnerships with the objective providing education regarding disability and access to services and resources to educators, family members, and community members; and securing understanding and respect for all. Effective transition occurs at the policy making level. But it also occurs at the community level. PODCAM's objective is to help equip families and communities in securing inclusion for all members.

REFERENCES

Essa, A., & Furcoi, S. (2019). *Out of the shadows: Exposing the killings and attacks of persons with albinism in Malawi*. Amnesty International.

Lansdown, G. (2009). *See me, hear me: A guide to using the UN convention on the rights of persons with disabilities to promote the rights of children*. Save the Children.

Mariga, L., McConkey, R., & Myezwa, H. (2014). *Inclusive education in low-income countries: A resource for teacher educators, parent trainers and community development workers*. Atlas and Alliance and Disability Innovations Africa.

Ministry of Education, Science and Technology. (2017). *National strategy on inclusive education 2017–2021*. Lilongwe.

INDEX